David Dalrymple

Annals of Scotland

David Dalrymple

Annals of Scotland

ISBN/EAN: 9783741171949

Manufactured in Europe, USA, Canada, Australia, Japa

Cover: Foto ©Andreas Hilbeck / pixelio.de

Manufactured and distributed by brebook publishing software (www.brebook.com)

David Dalrymple

Annals of Scotland

ANNALS

OF

SCOTLAND.

FROM

The Accession of ROBERT I. Surnamed BRUCE,
To the Accession of the HOUSE of STEWART.

By Sir DAVID DALRYMPLE.

EDINBURGH:
Printed by BALFOUR & SMELLIE,
FOR
J. MURRAY, No 32. Fleetstreet, LONDON.

M.DCC.LXXIX.

ANNALS

OF

SCOTLAND,

From the ACCESSION of

ROBERT I.

1306.

ROBERT BRUCE had many and formidable obstacles to surmount in his progress to sovereign power; the solemn oaths, and even the general inclinations of the nobility; the revenge of the potent house of Comyn; the whole force of England; and the guilt of what was commonly held to be a *sacrilegious murder*.

Without any resources but in his own valour, and in the untried fidelity of a few partisans [*], Bruce ascended the throne of his ancestors, [at Scone, 27th March 1306.] *Fordun,* xii. 9.

The Earls of Fyfe, descendants of the celebrated M'Duff, had the privilege of crowning the Kings of Scotland. At this time Duncan Earl *Triv.* 340. *M.West.* 454.

---

[*] ' Manum erexit contra omnes et singulos de regno Scotiae, *exceptis paucissimis* ' sibi benevolis,' *Fordun,* L. xii. c. 9.

Vol. II. A

ROBERT I.
1306.

Earl of Fyfe favoured the English interest; but his sister Isabella, wife of the Earl of Buchan, secretly withdrawing from her husband, repaired to Scone, asserted the pretensions of her ancestors, and again placed the crown on the head of ROBERT I. * [29th March.]

M. West. 453.
Barbour, ib.

Posterity ought to remember the chief associates of Bruce in his arduous attempt to restore the liberties of Scotland.

They were, William of Lambyrton Bishop of St Andrews; Robert Wistheart Bishop of Glasgow; the Abbot of Scone; the four brothers of Bruce, Edward, Nigel, Thomas, and Alexander; his nephew Thomas Randolph of Strathdon; his brother-in-law, Christopher Seaton of Seaton; Malcolm [5th] Earl of Lennox; John of Strathbogie [10th] Earl of Athole; Sir James Douglas; Gilbert de la Haye of Errol, and his brother Hugh de la Haye; David Barclay of Cairns in Fife; Alexander Fraser, brother of Simon Fraser of Oliver Castle; Walter de Somerville of Linton and Carnwath; David of Inchmartin; Robert Boyd; and Robert Fleming †.

Edward

---

* In *Scalae Chron.* ap. Leland. Collectanea, vol. 1. p. 542. this bold action is ascribed to her mother-in-law, Elizabeth de Quinci, daughter of Roger de Quinci, Earl of Winchester, Constable of Scotland, and widow of Alexander Comyn, Earl of Buchan. ' The Countess of Boughan, *becaufe her fanne was abfent,* lying at his manor of Witnick, [r. *Whitwick*] by Leicestre, *take upon her to crowne Robert Bruce at* ' Scone, in Scotland.' This authority is very express; yet I incline to follow the writers of that age, *Trivett,* p: 341. and *M. Weftm.* p. 454. M. Weftm. accuses this intrepid lady of a criminal partiality for the new King; ' transgresso maritali thoro, ' exarferat in speciem et concupiscentiam fatui coronati.' The Monk who calls Robert Bruce *a fool,* may be permitted to call the Countess of Buchan *an adulteress;* such idle stories are always circulated by malice and credulity in times of public disorder.

† *Randolph,* afterwards Earl of Moray; *Seaton,* ancestor of the Duke of Gordon, Earl of Winton, Earl of Dunfermline, and Viscount Kingston; *De la Haye,* of Earl of Errol; *Frafer,* of Lord Lovat and Lord Salton; *Somerville,* of Lord Somerville; *Inchmartin,* of Earl of Findlater, Earl of Airlie, and Lord Bamf; *Boyd,* of Earl of Kilmarnock; *Fleming,* of Earl of Wigton. *Math. Weftm.* p. 452. adds, Alan Earl of Menteth.

ROBERT I.

1306.

Edward I. was at Winchester when tidings of the revolution in Scotland arrived; he immediately appointed Aymer de Vallence, Earl of Pembroke, to be guardian of that kingdom [*], and despatched a messenger to the Pope, informing him of the violation of the sanctuary, and of the slaughter of Comyn. With equal diligence the Pope issued an

Trivet, 343. Fœdera, ii. 988. 997.

Menteth. Nigel Campbel, the predecessor of the Duke of Argyle, &c. and Fraser of Oliver Castle, were also engaged in the cause; but it does not appear that they assisted at the coronation of Robert I.

To this list, David Moray Bishop of Moray, might be added. The English asserted, that he preached to the people of his diocese, 'that it was no less meritorious to 'rise in arms for supporting the cause of Bruce, than to engage in a crusade against 'the Saracens.—*Quia dedit eis intelligere, prædicando, periculo animæ suæ, quod non 'minus possent mereri, qui cum Domino Roberto in ipsius auxilium contra Regem 'Angliæ et suos insurgerent, et partem ipsius Roberti juravernt, quam si in Terram Sanc- 'tam contra Paganos et Saracenos proficiscerent.'* [Sic MS.] *Records, London.* This Bishop was the founder of the Scots College at Paris. *Keith, Catalogue, p 82.*

As there will be frequent occasion for quoting the metrical life of Robert Bruce, by John Barbour, it may be proper to premise some particulars concerning the author. He was bred to the church, and obtained the office of Archdeacon of Aberdeen: While he enjoyed that office, he had leave to study at Oxford, 3 tmo Edw. III. *Calendars of Antient Charters, p. 219.* He finished his history in 1375, and he died an aged man in 1396. This circumstance is to be learned from *The Chartulary of Aberdeen*, fol. 115. where, 10th August 1398, mention is made of *'quondam Joh. Barber Archi- 'diaconus Aberd.'* and where it is said that he died two years and a half before; therefore, in 1396. Barbour, when he describes the person of Thomas Randolph, Earl of Moray, seems to speak as from his own observation. Randolph died in 1331. Supposing Barbour to have been 80 at his death, he was 15 at the death of Randolph. Fordun, L. xii. c. 9. says, ' Magister Johannes Barbarii, Archidiaconus Aberdonensis, 'in lingua nostra materna diserte et luculenter satis ipsa ejus particularia gesta, nec non 'moltum eleganter peroravit.' There is reason to believe that the language of Barbour, obsolete as it may now seem, has been modernized by some officious transcriber.

[*] The letters patent to Pembroke are drawn up in an enraged and vindictive style. In them Edward says, That Bruce was a person in whom he reposed entire confidence; [*de quo plenam fiduciam habebamus.*] *Fœdera, T. ii. p. 988.* The Pope's bull is dated from Bourdeaux, 18th May 1306. *Fœdera, T. ii. p. 997.*

A 2

4   ROBERT L

1306.

an order, authorising the Archbishop of Yorke, and the Bishop of
Carlisle, to excommunicate Bruce and his adherents.

Trivet, 341.
Hemming-
ford, l. 211.
Langtoft, li.
331.

Edward, now become infirm, and having lost the use of his limbs,
proceeded to London by slow journeys *. At his arrival *there*, he conferred the honour of Knighthood on his son the Prince of Wales,
on the Earls of Warenne and Arundel, and on near 300 more. At a
feast given on occasion of this solemnity, the King, although aged
and debilitated, made a vow †, that he would take vengeance on Robert
Bruce for his insult offered to God and the church; and this duty having been performed, that he would not, for the future, unsheath his
sword against Christians, but would haste to Palestine, wage war with
the Saracens, and never return from that holy enterprise.

The

---

* Movit se Rex versus Londonias currizando, quia, *ob infirmitatem quam habuit
in tibiis*, non potuit equitare; *Trivet,* p. 342.

† The circumstances attending this vow, as related by *M. Westm.* p. 454. are singular. 'Tunc allati sunt in pompatica gloria duo cygni vel olores ante Regem, pha-
' leratis retibus aureis vel fistulis deauratis, desiderabile spectaculum intuentibus. Qui-
' bus visis, Rex votum vovit Deo coeli et cygnis,' &c. This is a most extraordinary
passage, for the interpretation of which I have consulted antiquaries, but all in vain.
The same ceremony is mentioned in *La Livre des trois fils de Rois,* f. 91. ' Apres
' paroles on fist apporter *ung paon* par deux damoiselles, et *jura le Roy premier de
' deffendre tout son dit royaume à son pouvoir,'* &c.

Sir Henry Spelman, *Aspilogia,* p. 132. observes, that the antient heralds gave a swan
as an *imprese* to confidents and fugitive men. He adds, ' sed gloriae studium ex eodem
' hoc symbolo indicari multi asserunt.' He then quotes the passage from *M. Westm.*
but he neither remarks its singularity, nor attempts to explain it.

Ashmole, *History of the Garter,* c. 5. sect. 2 p 185. observes, that Edward III. had
these words wrought upon ' his surcoat and shield, provided to be used at a tourna-
' ment,

   ' Hay, Hay, the *wythe swan,*
   ' By G——s soul, I am thy man.'

This shews that a *white swan* was the *imprese* of Edward III. and perhaps it was also
used by his grandfather, Edward I. How far this circumstance may serve to illustrate
the passage in *M. Westm.* I will not pretend to determine.

ROBERT I.   5
                1306.

The Prince of Wales vowed, in aid of his father's vow, that he *Trivet, 343.*
would not remain two nights in the same place until he reached Scotland *.

The Earl of Pembroke, Robert de Clifford, and Henry de Percey,
hasted to Scotland to oppose the progress of Bruce, and the Prince
of Wales followed with his companions. Edward appointed his army
to rendezvous at Carlisle: He himself moved slowly towards the north,
being conveyed in a litter. He was seized with a dysentery, halted in
the neighbourhood of Carlisle, and remained in those parts during the
winter †.

The first enterprise of the King of Scots was against Perth, where *Trivet, 343.*
Pembroke, the English guardian, had fixed his head-quarters. The *Barbour, 29—*
Scots, in the popular strain of chivalry, challenged the English com- *34. M. West.*
mander to the open field; he answered, ' that he would fight them on *953. Fordun,*
' the morrow.' The Scots betook themselves to the neighbouring *lib. 2.*
wood of Methven. Towards the close of the day, Pembroke sallied
forth and attacked them. Sir Philip de Moubray unhorsed the King;
                                                                Seaton

* It is probable that that age did not discover the strange nature of the vow which
the heir apparent made for enabling the King to go into perpetual exile.

† The English historians, antient as well as modern, assert, that Edward I. marched
into Scotland in 1306, and, in the manner of a savage conqueror, over-ran the country.
It is certain, however, from the dates of various instruments in the second volume of
Fœdera Angliae, that Edward did not march into Scotland in 1306. On the 22d July
1306, he was at Beverley; *Fœdera*, T. 2. p. 1005. 28th July, at Thirsk; *ib.* p. 1009.
14th August, at Corbridge; *ib.* p. 1017. 18th and 31st August, at Newburgh in Tindale; *ib.* p. 1018. 1020. 6th and 7th September, at Thirlewall; *ib.* p. 1025. 7th October, at Lanercost; *ib.* p. 1027 He speaks at that time of his having been recovered
from a dangerous illness by the care of Nicolas de Tynchewyk his physician. He appears to have remained at Lanercost during the months of October, November, December, January, and February: *ib.* p. 1042.—1057 He was at Lynstock on the 6th
of March; *ib.* p. 1045; and at Carlisle, or in that neighbourhood, from 10th March,
to the beginning of July 1307; *ib.* p. 1046.—1058.

1306.

Leland, i. 142.
Barbour, 36.

Seaton refcued him [*]. It is said that John de Haliburton, who served in the English army, made the King prisoner; but, discovering who he was, set him at liberty. Hugh de la Haye [†], Barclay, Fraser, Inchmartin, Somerville, and Randulph, were taken, and the Scottish army was dispersed. [19th June.]

Barbour, 37.

Robert retired with the broken and dispirited remains of his party into the fastnesses of Athole [‡]. After having lurked for some time among the mountains, and endured much hardship, they came down into the low country of Aberdeenshire. At Aberdeen the King met his wife, and many other ladies, whom his brother Nigel had conducted thither, all determined to share the worst of fortunes with their fathers and husbands.

Barbour, 39. 40.

Bruce and his followers, at the approach of the English, again sought refuge among the mountains; and, accompanied with their faithful women, retreated into Breadalbine.

Barbour, 40. 41.
Fordun, xii. 3.

The King was now on the borders of Argyle. Alexander of Argyle, Lord of Lorn, had married the aunt of Comyn. Eager to revenge the death of his nephew, he attacked the King. A fierce combat ensued: Douglas and de la Haye were wounded, and the royalists were overpower-

---

[*] Barbour ascribes this honour to Seaton, and minutely relates the circumstances of the story. p. 34. Seaton's office of Esquire to the King adds probability to Barbour's relation. M. *Westminster* says, that the King was thrice unhorsed, and that Simon Fraser *thrice* rescued him. ' Ter a desperatis profligatus est, et per Simonem de ' Freysel, bellatorem egregium, ter levatus;' p. 455.

[†] This is probably the same person whom M. *Westm.* p. 455. calls *Hutting Marescallus et vexillifer pseudo-Regis*. He also mentions *Hugh*, the King's chaplain, as among the prisoners.

[‡] Of that army, with which, a few weeks before, he had asserted his title to the crown, he could hardly collect 500 men. Barbour relates, that his brother Edward Bruce, the Earl of Athole, Douglas, Gilbert de la Haye, and Nigel Campbel, remained with him. Barbour also mentions a *Sir William the Barondrum*, as one of the band, p. 36. 37. Who this person was, I know not.

1306.

overpowered. Bruce placed himself in the rear of his small disordered band, and, by persevering valour, checked the pursuit of the enemy *.
[11th August.]

Hitherto the King and his associates had earned a hardy sustenance by the chace of wild animals, and by fishing; but winter now approached, and there was no hope of subsisting at that season in the open fields.

Barbour, 39, 40.

Bruce sent his Queen, and the other ladies, to the strong castle of Kildrummie in Marre, under the escort of his brother Nigel, and all his horsemen; himself, with two hundred men, resolved to force a passage into Kintyre, and from thence to cross over into the northern parts of Ireland.

Barbour, 51.

At the banks of Lochlomond their progress was interrupted. Douglas, after long search, discovered a small leaky boat, in which he passed over with the King. The rest followed, some by the conveyance of the boat, and others by swimming. They were now reduced to the extremities of famine. While they roved in quest of food through the adjacent forests, they met Lennox, ignorant till then of the fate of his sovereign: They all wept.

Barbour, 53.

Barbour, 55.

Angus of the isles, Lord of Kintyre, hospitably received the King into his castle of Dunavarty. From thence the King, with a few faithful companions, passed over to Rachrin, an island on the northern coast of Ireland †, and there eluded the search of his enemies.

Barbour, 61.

A

* According to Barbour, p. 43. two brothers named *Makrendorfer*, which he interprets *the sons of Durward*, and another person, had vowed, if they encountered Bruce, either to slay him, or perish in the attempt. They overtook him at a narrow pass, and were all slain by his single prowess. This story, related with many minute circumstances, may be true; I could not, however, venture to place it in my narrative. The place where Bruce was defeated by the Lord of Lorn, is called *Dalry*, i. e. the *King's field*, probably from that event. See *Fordun*, L. xii. c. 11. It is in the neighbourhood of a village which now bears the name of *Clifton*.

† This island is described by Mr Donald Monro, Dean of the isles, 1549, in the following

1306.

A miserable destiny awaited his friends and partisans whom he had left in Scotland.

Ryley, 510. An ordinance was issued by Edward in council, commanding the guardian of Scotland 'to make proclamation, that all the people of 'the country do search for, and pursue, all who have been in arms 'against the English government, and have not delivered themselves 'up; and also, all who have been guilty of other crimes; and that 'they apprehend them dead or alive.' And declaring, 'That they who 'are negligent in the discharge of this duty, shall forfeit their castles, 'and be imprisoned during the King's pleasure.'

The guardian was also commanded to punish, at his discretion, all who harboured the offenders described in the proclamation.

Farther, it was ordered, that all who were at the slaughter of Comyn, or were abettors of that deed, or voluntarily and knowingly harboured the guilty persons, or their accomplices, should be drawn and hanged.

And that all who were already taken, or might hereafter be taken, in arms, and all who harboured them, should be hanged or beheaded.

As for those, who, having been in arms, had surrendered themselves, it was ordered, that the most distinguished and dangerous offenders among them should be imprisoned during the King's pleasure.

And that all, whether of the ecclesiastical order, or laymen, who had willingly espoused the party of Bruce, or who had procured †, or exhorted,

---

following words: 'On the south-west frae the promontory of Kintyre, upon the 'coast of Irland, be four myle to land, layes an iyle, callit *Raeblaine*, pertaining to 'Irland, and possesst thir mony yeires by Clan Donald of Kynayre, four mykes long, 'and twa myle braide, guid land, inhabit and manurit;' *Description of the Western isles.* p. 6.

† 'Preschantz le poeple d'Escose de lever contre le ley;' *Ryley,* p. 510. *Tyrrel,* Vol. lii. B. 9. p. 174. has committed several errors in his translation of this ordinance.

ROBERT I.
1306.

exhorted the people of Scotland to rise in rebellion, should, upon conviction, be imprisoned during the King's pleasure.

With regard to the commons, who might have been constrained to take up arms, a discretionary power of fining or ransoming them was committed to the guardian.

This ordinance was rigorously enforced.

The wife of Bruce, and Marjory his daughter by a former marriage, dreading to be besieged in Kildrummie, fled to the sanctuary of St Duthac, at Tain in Rosshire. The Earl of Ross violated the sanctuary, and delivered them to the English [*].

Barbour, 65. Fordun, xii. 11.

The Countess of Buchan, who had crowned Bruce, was committed to close confinement in the castle of Berwick [†].

M.West. 455.

William

---

[*] *M. West.* relates, p. 454. that Bruce, returning from his coronation, said to his wife, ' Yesterday we were Earl and Countess, now we are King and Queen;' and that she answered, ' You may be a summer King, but, I suppose, you will not be a winter ' King;' that Bruce, enraged at this contemptuous speech, would have killed her, had not the bystanders prevented him: That, however, he banished her to Ireland; and that the Earl of Ulster, her father, transmitted her to the English King. These circumstances may be considered as fabulous.—The directions given for the entertainment of Elizabeth, the wife of Bruce, are preserved in *Fœdera*, T. ii. p. 1013. She was to be conveyed to the manor of Brustewick: To have a waiting-woman, and a maid servant, advanced in life, sedate, and of good conversation: A butler, two men-servants, and a foot-boy, for her chamber, sober, and not riotous, to make her bed, [" Eit ele un ' garzon a pée, por demorer en sa chambre, tiel qi soit sobre et ne un riotous, por son ' lit faire"]: Three greyhounds when she inclines to hunt: Venison, fish, and the fairest house in the manor. This unfortunate lady was removed to another prison in 1308. *Fœdera*, T. iii. p. 94. In 1111, she was removed to Windsor castle, twenty shillings weekly being allowed for her maintenance; *ib.* p. 302. 306. She was committed to the castle of Rochester in 1314; *ib.* p. 475. She was not set at liberty till towards the close of 1314; *ib.* p. 489. 496—Marjory, the daughter of Bruce, was given in charge to Henry Percey; *Fœdera*, T. ii p 1014.

[†] *M. West.* p. 455. says, ' Capitur etiam et illa impiissima conjuratrix de Buchan, ' de qua confultus Rex, ait, quia gladio non percussit, gladio non peribit; verum, propter ' illicitam

VOL. II. B

1306.

Trivet. 345.
M.W'ost. 455.

William of Lambyrton, Bishop of St Andrews, owed his preservation to the dignity of his ecclesiastical character. Edward would have inflicted

' illicitam confervationem quam fecit, in domicilio lapideo et ferreo, in modum coronae
' fabricato, firmissimè obstruatus, et apud Bervicum sub dio forinsecus suspendatur, ut
' sit dam, in vita et post mortem, speculum viatoribus, et opprobrium sempiternum.'
Other English historians, copying *M. Westminster*, have said the same thing. We cannot, therefore, blame Abercrombie for saying, ' She was put in a wooden cage, shaped
' like a crown, and in that tormenting posture hung out from high walls, or turrets,
' to be gazed upon and reproached by the meanest of the multitude;' vol. i. p. 579.
Hemingford, vol. i. p. 221. relates the story in a manner somewhat different. He says,
that the Earl of Buchan, her husband, fought to kill her for her treason; but that Edward restrained him, and ordered her to be confined in a wooden cage.

The intentions of Edward I. touching the durance of the Countess of Buchan, will
be more certainly learned from his own orders, than from the report of *M. Westminster*.
His orders run thus: ' By letters under the privy seal, be it commanded, that the
' chamberlain of Scotland, or his deputy at Berwick upon Tweed, do, in one of the
' turrets of the said castle, and in the place which he shall find most convenient, cause
' construct a cage strongly latticed with wood, [*de suist*, i. e beams of timber or palisades], cross-barred, and secured with iron, in which he shall put the Countess of
' Buchan.

' And that he take care that she be so well and safely guarded therein, that in no
' sort she may issue therefrom.

' And that he appoint one or more women of Berwick, of English extraction, and
' liable to no suspicion, *who shall minister to the said Countess in eating and drinking, and
' in all things else convenient, in her said lodging-place.*

' And that he do cause her to be so well and strictly guarded in the cage, that she
' may not speak with any one, man or woman, of the Scottish nation, or with any one
' else, saving with the women who shall be appointed to attend her, or with the guard
' who shall have the custody of her person.

' And that the cage be so constructed *that the Countess may have therein the conveni-
' ence of a decent chamber*, [*esement de chambre courtoise*]; nevertheless, that all things
' be so well and surely ordered, that no peril arise touching the right custody of the said
' Countess.

' And that he to whom the charge of her is committed shall be responsible, body
' for body, and that he be allowed his charges;' *Foedera*, T. ii. p. 1014.

Such

1306.

inflicted a capital punishment on him, had he been a layman; and, indeed, the duplicity of his conduct merited the severest vengeance.

The Stewart of Scotland had given his eldest son, Andrew, as an *Records, Lon.* hostage to Edward. Edward placed him with the Bishop of St Andrews. On hearing of the slaughter of Comyn, Edward demanded back the youth, probably with a view of securing the fidelity of his father. The bishop, instead of restoring his charge, put him into the hands of Bruce [*].

It appears, also, that the Bishop had been accused to Pembroke the guardian, of having had some share in the slaughter of Comyn; the Bishop not only asserted his innocence of the charge, but also disclaimed

Such were the orders of Edward I. and he surely was not a man who would suffer his orders to be disobeyed. Here, indeed, there is a detail concerning the custody of a female prisoner, which may seem ridiculously minute, but which is inconsistent with the story related by *M. Westminster*, and other historians.

To those who have no notion of any cage but one for a parrot or a squirrel, hung out at a window. I despair of rendering this mandate intelligible.

[*] This singular incident is to be found in the answers made by the Bishop of St Andrews, when he was examined before commissioners appointed by Edward, at Newcastle, 9th August 1306. ' Objectum fuit adhuc praefato Domino Episcopo, per prae-
' dictum Dominum Robertum de Cotingham, quod eum Dominus Rex Angliae eidem
' Episcopo, tanquam illi de quo prae caeteris terrae suae Scotiae, tam nobilibus quam
' praelatis, confidebat, personam Andreae filii et haeredis Domini Jacobi Seneschalli
' Scotiae tradiderit custodiendam, auditoque demum, tam de modo [l. mundio] et in-
' terfectione quondam Domini Johannis Comyn Domini de Badenaugh, quam infi-
' delitate, rebellione, et excogitata nequitia Roberti de Brus, et eidem adhaerentium, ei-
' dem Episcopo per suas literas mandaverat, quod statim visis suis literis dictum Andre-
' am eidem Domino Regi remandaret; quare idem Episcopus regio mandato praedicto
' recepto et intellecto non paruit, sed ipsum Andream dicto Roberto de Brus, ejusdem
' Domini Regis Angliae inimico notorio et proditori, liberavit. Palam et expresse
' cognovit organo vocis suae Episcopus prelibatus, quod negare non potuit bono modo
' quin ipse eundem Andream dicto Roberto de Brus, etiam postquam dictum manda-
' tum regium receperat, ut praemittitur, liberaverat, et non potuit inde [*sic MS*] ut
' dicebat.' *MS. Records.* London.

12   ROBERT I.
                         1306.

ed any concern in the infurrection, and offered to make every fort of
fubmiffion to the King of England *.

Records, Lon.   Immediately after this, he renewed his oath of fealty to Edward,
in prefence of the guardian. Under pretence of urgent bufinefs,
he obtained leave to return home. He then affembled a confiderable
                                                                  body

* This also is to be learned from the fame records. The bifhop of St Andrews
thus writes to the Earl of Pembroke: ' A noble bourne e fage Monſieur Aymar de
' Valence, Seigneur de Montignak, lieutenant noſtre Seygneur le Roi en les parties
' d'Eſcoce, William par la grace de Dieu Evefque de St Andrew, ſalut en Dieu.
' Sachez nous par noſter volonté eſtre obligé a noſter Seygneur le Roi d'Engleterre,
' que nous enoſterons en toutes les manieres que nous deverons ſelom ceo que noſtre
' Seygneur le Roi e foun counſeil ordonera que faire devoms, que vous ny avons nule
' manere de coupe de la morte Mooſire John Comyn, ne mon Sire Robert foun uncle,
' ne de la commencement de ceſte guerre, e a ce nous nous enobligoms de nous oſter
' auſſi bien devers le linage cum devers la peez noſtre Seygneur le Roi. E ſi ceo faire
' ne povins, demorryoms a la volonté noſtre Seygneur le Roi com ataint. E de toutes
' autres choſes que noſtre Seygneur le Roi favera dire vers nous, nous nous menoms
' a ſa volonté de hatu e de bas, e a ceſtes choſes faire e performer al avaunt dit Mon-
' ſieur Aymar avoms doné nos lettres overtes enſealés de noſtre ſeal. Doné a la Foun-
' taine d'Eſcoce le 9 jour de Juyn, l'an du regne le Roi Edward 34.' This is, in fub-
ſtance, as follows: ' Be it known, that we have voluntarily agreed to clear ourſelves,
' in whatever manner our Lord the King and his counſil ſhall appoint, of any acceſ-
' ſion to the death of John Comyn Lord of Badenoch, and Robert his uncle, or of
' having had any ſhare in the riſe of the preſent war, and we will clear ourſelves
' thereof, both with reſpect to the kindred of the deceaſed, and to public juſtice; and
' if we fail herein, we conſent to be at the will of the King as a perſon convicted.
' And as to whatever elſe our Lord the King may have to alledge concerning us, we
' ſubmit ourſelves wholly to his pleaſure. And, in teſtimony of our willingneſs to
' perform all theſe things to Aymer de Vallence, Lord of Montignae, the King's
' lieutenant in Scotland, we have granted theſe our letters patent, ſealed with our
' ſeal. Given at Scotland well, this 9th June, and of King Edward the 34th year.'
The Biſhop of St Andrews was, at firſt, confined in the caſtle of Nottingham, but
was afterwards removed to the tower of the caſtle of Wincheſter; *Fœdera*, T. ii. p.
1015-16. There will be occaſion hereafter to relate the other incidents of the life of
this ſingular perſon.

ROBERT I.   13

1306.

body of his vassals and dependents, and sent them to the aid of Bruce*.

Robert Wisheart, Bishop of Glasgow, held the castle of Coupar in Fife against the English. He was made prisoner there†, arrayed in armour; and, in that uncanonical garb, was conducted to the castle of Nottingham ‡. *M. West.* 455. *Records*, Lon.

The castle of Kildrummie was besieged by the Earls of Lancaster and Hereford. One Osburn treacherously burnt the magazine. The garrison, deprived of provisions, surrendered at discretion. Nigel, the brother of Bruce, a youth of singular comeliness, was among the captives. *Barbour,* 6 f. *Leland,* li. 543.

---

* In a memorandum for drawing up a charge against the Bishop of St Andrews to be presented to the Pope, are these words: ' Idem Episcopus Sancti Andreae, per mo-
' dicum tempus ante diem Dominicum, quo Robertus de Brus, cum toto posse suo,
' cum Domino Adomaro de Valencia, et suis secum ibidem ex parte Domini nostri
' Regis existentibus, praeliabat, ad praefatum Dominum Adomarum venit, et ad fidem
' et pacem Domini Regis rediens, ipsius gratiae et voluntati se submisit, et admissus
' fuit ab eodem, et juramentum praestitit corporale dicto Domino Adomaro, nomine
' Domini Regis, de fideliter se tenendo ; et subsequenter causam fingens, per tres vel
' quatuor dies proximo praecedentes diem belli ad disponendum super quibusdam suis
' agendis, petiit ab eodem Domino Adomaro licentia et obtenta, sub manucaptione
' tum competente recessit, et per illos dies quotquot potuit de suis adunare equitum
' armatorum, et aliorum dicto Roberto de Brus, ad juvandum eum dicto die belli con-
' tra dictum Dominum Adomarum et suos, destinavit, sicut evidentia facti ipso die
' evidenter apparebat, tam per eorum aliquos ibidem captos, quam ipsorum alios quo-
' rum cadavera testimonium perhibent veritati ;' *Records*, London.

† ' Le chastel de Coupre en Fiff en Escoce, lequel meisme l'Evesque, come hom de
' guerre, tynt puis contre les gents nostre Seigneur le Roi, jusques à tant qu'aucuns
' de gents nostre Seigneur le Roi, qui feurent de la compagne Monsieur Aymer de
' Vallence vindrent au dit chastel e le prisirent par force, sur le dit Evesque et illoques
' feust mesme l'Evesque pris ;' *Records*, London.

‡ ' Exercitus tamen regius discurrens per totum regnum Scotorum, corpia persequi
' fugitivos, et plures perimerunt, et aliquos vivos comprehenderunt, utpote Episcopos
' et Abbatem praedictos [the Bishops of St Andrews and Glasgow, and the Abbot of
' Scone], loricatos et armatos subtus exterius tegumentum ;' *M. Westm.* p. 455.

1306.

tives. He was tried by a special commission at Berwick, condemned, hanged, and afterwards beheaded [a].

Barbour, 65. *Trivet*, 345.
A like sentence was executed against Christopher Seaton at Dumfries [†]. He had married the sister of Bruce, and had assisted at the slaughter of Comyn. His brother Alexander suffered a similar death at Newcastle.

M. West. 456.
The Earl of Athole, attempting to escape by sea, was discovered, and conducted to London. He there underwent the complicated punishment which, in *those* times, the law of England inflicted on traitors [‡]. [7th November].

Simon

---

[a] *Trivet*, p. 344. and *M. West.* p. 455. relate, that he was taken at a castle in Kintyre, which the English besieged, in hope of finding Bruce there; but I follow *Barbour*, p. 65. *M. West.* calls him *miles pulcherrimæ juventutis*. The only time that that historian seems to feel compassion in describing the varied punishments inflicted on the partisans of Bruce, is, when he speaks of this young man; indeed, his only offence appears to have been, that he followed the fortunes of his brother.

[†] Barbour says, that he was betrayed by his confident and familiar friend, one M'Nab, p. 63. *Trivet*, p. 365. says, that he was taken at the castle of Lochore [in Fife]; he adds, ' quem, cum non Scotus sed Anglicus esset, jussit Rex deduci usque ' Dumfries, ubi quondam militem de parte Regis occiderat, ibique judicium subire ' conflictu, tractus suspensusque est, ac ultimò decollatus.' I suppose the meaning of this to be, that, as Seaton was an English baron, Edward honoured him with a trial by jury, while he inflicted capital punishment on the others, without any such formalities

[‡] ' In equuleo 30 pedum suspensus est: Postea *semivivus demissus*, ut majores ' cruciatus sentiret, crudelissimè decollatur. Truncus verò Illius, *præcortenso* in com- ' *spectu ejus urbementi igne*, unà cum carne et ossibus, in favillas et cineres funditus ' conflagratitur.' *M. West.* p. 456. *Langtoft*, vol. ii. p. 335. says, That the Earl ' was ' not drawn, *that poynt was forgyvyn*.' He was in some sort allied to the royal family of England, his mother being a daughter of Richard the natural son of King John. *Scot's Chron.* ap Leland, vol. ii. p. 543. says, ' The Earl of Atholes, by cause ' he was cosin to the King of England, and sonne to Maude of Dour *his aunte*, was ' sent to London, and there was hanged upon a pair of galows 30 foote hyer then ' others.' *Taute*, here translated *aunt*, means the father's cousin-german. *M. West.* p. 456.

1306.

Simon Fraser, a renowned warrior, was executed at London, and his head was placed on the point of a lance, near the head of Wallace*. With him Herbert de Norham suffered. Both had repeatedly sworn fealty to Edward.

M. West. 455. Langtoft, ii. 335.

Many other Scotsmen of inferior degree were punished capitally †. *M. West. 455.*

Edward bestowed the lordship of Annandale, the paternal estate of Bruce, on the Earl of Hereford; the earldom of Carrick, his maternal estate, on Henry Percey; and the earldom of Athole on Ralph de Monthermer, commonly styled Earl of Gloucester ‡; but he soon after repurchased the grant of Athole, at the price of 5000 merks.

Hem. l. 224. Ford. lii. 7.

Thus

---

p. 456. relates, That Edward, at that time, was grievously sick; but hearing that the Earl of Athole was taken, he endured the pains of his disease with more patience: 'Quo audito, Rex Angliae, etsi gravissimo morbo tunc langueret, levius tamen tulit 'dolorem.'

* 'What pity,' cries Langtoft, 'that a person of such prowess, and endued with so 'many virtues, should have incurred the guilt and the punishment of treason!' vol. ii. p. 335.

 'Allas, it was to mene, his vertus and his prueffe
 'So feke in him were sene, that perisht for falsneffe.'

† There is a strange witticism to be found in *M. Westm.* p. 455. 'Hugo Capellanus 'patibulo ante caeteros primitus est affixus, quasi diceret, Ego presbyter vobis praebeo 'iter.' The author, himself an ecclesiastic, might have recollected, that, to hang a churchman by evil authority, was no jesting matter. *Barbour* relates, p. 74. That, when the pleasure of Edward was demanded concerning those who had been made captive in the Scottish war, he answered, after his abrupt manner, 'Hang them all.' This anecdote is, perhaps, not true; yet it is characteristical.

‡ Joan the daughter of Edward I. and widow of Gilbert de Clare Earl of Gloucester, married Ralph de Monthermer, a person neither distinguished for his rank nor his military prowess. *Hemingford* calls him *miles simplex et segnis*; T. i. p. 224. *E. Dicie, not. in N. Upton de studio militari*, says, That he had the title of Earl of Gloucester, untill his stepson became of age, and that he then divested himself of it: 'Dum ... eseret privignus ejus Gilbertus de Clare, *Comitis Glocestriae* titulo est or-' natus, et ... ue Gilbertus annum aetatis 21 explesset, cum exuit, et inter barones 'acceer.

1306.

Thus did Edward chastise the Scots for their breach of faith. It is remarkable, that, in the preceding year, he himself procured a papal bull, absolving him from the oath which he had taken for maintaining the privileges of his people *. But the Scots, without papal authority, violated their oaths, and were punished as perjured men. It is a truth not to be disguised, that, in those times, the common notions of right and wrong were, in some sort, obliterated. Conscience, intoxicated with indulgences, or stupified by frequent absolution, was no longer a faithful monitor amidst the temptations of interest, ambition, and national animosities.

Many Scotsmen of considerable distinction submitted themselves to the conqueror, and were either received into his favour, or slightly punished †.

Randolph,

‘ accensebatur.’ Bisse has given an engraving of the seal of Ralph de Monthermer, with this inscription, ‘ S. Radulfi de Monte Hermerii. Com. Gloverniae et Hertford.’ Yet it seems, that, in public instruments, he was constantly styled *Ralph de Monthermer*, without any addition.

* The title of this memorable instrument in *Fœdera*, T. II. p. 978. is, ‘ *Bulla de Rege absolvendo et juramentis et excommunicationibus super observatione Magnæ Chartæ et Forestæ adimplendis.*'

† As Allan Earl of Menteth, Sir Patrick de Graham, Sir William de Moray de Sandford, Sir Walter de Moray, Sir Hugh Lovel and his brother William ; *Fœdera*, T. II. p. 1012.—1014. At that place there is a singular memorandum inserted, ‘ Falt a remembrer les terres Monsieur Gilbert de la Haye pour Monsieur Huge le Despencer;’ *Fœdera*, T. II. p. 1013. These lands, it would seem, were a ministerial morsel. Malise, Earl of Strathern, accused as an accomplice in the Scottish insurrection, successfully pleaded, that he had been compelled, through fear of death, to acknowledge the sovereignty of Bruce. There is extant a long narrative drawn up by the Earl of Strathern: In it he says, ‘ That, when he refused to do homage, Robert Boyd said to Bruce, *Give me the lands, and put him to death, and cut off his head, and the heads of all who refuse homage to you.* [Sir Robert Bold dist a son Roy, que il donnast les terres, et ly meist au mort, et ly coupa la teste, et tut les autres quy grueerent a ler homage].' *Records*, London.

1306.

Randolph, the nephew of Bruce, obtained mercy, through the intercession of Adam de Gordon, and was admitted to swear fealty to Edward. *Lel.* ii. 542. *Barbour*, 36.

The young Earl of Marre, nephew of the first wife of Bruce, was imprisoned, ' but not chained, in respect of his tender years *.' This special favour vouchsafed to a child shows how closely state-prisoners were guarded at that time. *Fœd.* II. 1013.

It does not appear that James the Stewart of Scotland had joined in the revolt against Edward; nevertheless, a new oath of fealty was exacted from him †. He did homage in person to the English King, [at Lanercost near Carlisle, 23d October 1306.] *Fœd.* II. 1022.

To conclude all, Bruce and his adherents were solemnly excommunicated. This ceremony was performed by the Cardinal Legate ‡, [at Carlisle, about February 1306-7.] *Hem.* I. 226.

During the winter, Bruce had remained in Rachrin, a retreat unknown to his enemies. At the approach of spring § he secretly passed over into the island of Arran. From thence he despatched a person *Bark.* II. &c.

---

* ' Q'il soit hors de fers, tant come il est de si tendre age ;' *Fœdera*, T. ii. p. 1013.

† He swore fealty on the two crosses of Scotland most esteemed for their sanctity, [called *la Croix Neyts et la Blacke Rode*], on the consecrated host, on the holy gospels, and on the relics of the saints, and he submitted himself to instant excommunication in the event of his violating this complicated oath ; *Fœdera*, T. ii. p. 1022.

‡ ' Cardinalis Hispaniæ—revestivit se et ceteri Episcopi qui aderant, accensisque ' candelis et pulsis campanis, terribiliter excommunicaverunt Dominum Robertum de ' Bruce, cum fautoribus suis, tanquam hominem perjurum et perturbatorem injustum ' communis pacis et quietis ;' *W. Hemingford*, T. I. p. 226. The person here called the *Cardinal* of Spain was Peter, a cardinal priest under the title of S. Sabinus ; *Fœdera*, T. ii. p. 1031.

§ Fordun says, that he had received aid from a powerful lady, Christina of the isles; L. xii. c. 12. According to the English historians, Bruce appeared in arms about Michaelmas 1306. This circumstance, in itself improbable, is inconsistent with the narrative of Barbour.

Vol. II. C

ROBERT I.

1306.

son of confidence * into Carrick, to learn how his vassals in that territory stood affected to the cause of their antient Lord. He injoined the messenger, if he saw that the dispositions of the people were favourable, to make a signal at a day appointed, by lighting a fire on an eminence above the castle of Turnberry.

The messenger found the English in possession of Carrick; Percey, with a numerous garrison, at Turnberry; the country dispirited, and in thraldom; none to espouse the party of Bruce, and many whose inclinations were hostile.

From the first dawn of the day appointed for the signal, Bruce stood with his eyes fixed on the coast of Carrick. Noon had already passed, when he perceived a fire on the eminence above Turnberry. He flew to his boat, and hasted over. Night surprised him and his associates while they were yet on the sea. Conducting themselves by the fire, they reached the shore. The messenger met them, and reported, that there was no hope of aid. 'Traitor,' cried Bruce, 'why did you 'make the signal?' 'I made no signal,' replied he; 'but observing 'a fire on the eminence, I feared that it might deceive you, and I 'hasted hither to warn you from the coast.'

Bruce hesitated amidst the dangers which encompassed him, what to avoid, or what to encounter. At length, obeying the dictates of valour and despair, he resolved to persevere in his enterprise †.

He

---

* Barbour says, that the name of the messenger entrusted with this commission was *Cuthbert*, p. 82.

† *Barbour*, p. 91. ascribes this bold resolution to the counsels of his brother, Edward Bruce, whom he represents as thus speaking:

———' I say you sickerly,
' There shall no peril that may be
' Drive me eftsoons unto the sea;
' Mine aventure here take will I,
' Whether it be easeful or angry.'

1306.

He attacked the English, carelesly cantoned in the neighbourhood of Turnberry, put them to the sword, and pillaged their quarters. Percey, from the castle, heard the uproar, yet durst not issue forth against an unknown enemy. Bruce, with his followers, not exceeding three hundred in number, remained, for some days, near Turnberry; but succours having arrived from the neighbouring garrisons, he was obliged to seek shelter in the mountainous parts of Carrick.

He looked for aid from his brothers Thomas and Alexander, who had assembled a band of adventurers in Ireland and the adjacent isles. With seven hundred men they landed at Lochrian in Galloway. Duncan M'Dowal, a powerful chieftain of that country, attacked them at their landing, and totally routed their little army *, [9th February, 1306-7.] The two brothers, and Sir Reginald Crawfurd, were grievously wounded, and made prisoners. M'Dowal presented his bleeding prisoners

---

* *Langtoft*, vol. ii. p. 337. says, that *M'Ikdrwal*, *a sergeant of Galwaie*, surprised them on Ash-Wednesday, as they were returning from divine worship. But *M. Westm.* p. 458. relates the event in the following manner: ' Hoc itaque anno, nono die Februarii, quidam Scotus de Galvedia, Duncanus M'Doil nomine, occurrit navigio magno, ' repleto septingentis bellatoribus, applicantibus super terram suam, cum decentiis non ' multis to amplius viris, et peremit sere omnem exercitum, hos in acie, hos in salto, ' hos in fuga, et plures submersi sunt in mari; sed hos praecipuos de interfectis In prae- ' lio obtulit Domino Regi, videlicet Malcolmi M'Kail, Domini de Kentir caput, et du- ' orum Regulorum Hiberneusium capita, Reginaldum de Crawfurd, et Thomam Brus ' milites, et Alexandrum de Brus, germanos pseudo-regis, sauciatos et semineces prae- ' sentavit.' Lest there might be any doubt of Edward's severity, *M. Westm.* adds, after having given an account of the execution of the prisoners, That to this their heads bare witness, being placed on the castle and gates of Carlisle; ' testimonium huis per- ' bibent eorum capita super castellum et super portas urbis confixa;' *Barbour*, p. 65. says, that Sir Brice Blair was executed in company with Sir Reginald Crawfurd; but he erroneously supposes this to have happened in Scotland. *Langtoft*, vol. ii. p. 336. observes, that Alexander Bruce had been educated at Cambridge, where he made very extraordinary proficiency in literature; and adds, that he was Dean of Glasgow.

C 2

1306.

prisoners to the English King at Carlisle. The King ordered them to instant execution.

Barbour, 96. —102.

While Bruce endeavoured to strengthen his party in Carrick, Douglas passed secretly into Douglasdale, and discovered himself to some of his vassals in whom he could confide. They concerted a plan for surprising the English at Douglas castle, on Palm Sunday. The whole garrison went in solemn procession to a neighbouring chapel. Douglas and his vassals suddenly rushed in, and put them all to the sword. They then plundered and burnt the castle *, [19th March, 1306-7.]

1307.

Trivet, 346. M. West, 458. Barbour, 157.

The Earl of Pembroke advanced into the west of Scotland to encounter Bruce. Barbour relates, that, according to the mode of those times, the English commander and Bruce appointed a day for the combat: That Bruce entrenched himself at Lowdoun-hill: That Pembroke attacked him and was defeated. But the English historians relate, that Bruce attacked Pembroke. It is certain that Bruce obtained the victory. Three days after this action, Bruce routed Ralph de Monthermer with great slaughter, and obliged him to fly to the castle of Air. For some time Bruce blockaded that castle; but, at the approach of succours from England, he retired.

Barbour, 104. —156.

It was at this period, according to the English historians, that the partisans of Bruce were dispersed, while he himself wandered among woods and morasses, destitute of aid, and beset with enemies on every side. Barbour, however, asserts, that this happened before the combat

---

* *Barbour*, p. 98. says, That the person in whom Douglas placed his chief confidence was called *Thomas Dickson*. He adds, That about ten persons were made prisoners in the chapel, that Douglas put them all to death, and, placing their bodies in the magazine of the castle, set fire to the whole. This was termed *Douglas's larder*, in the savage pleasantry of that age. In 1306-7, Palm Sunday, the sixth Sunday of Lent, fell on the 19th of March.

1307.

bat at Lowdoun-hill *; and he minutely describes the dangers that Bruce underwent, and his many perilous escapes. It must be acknowledged, that, in the narrative of Barbour, some adventures are recorded which have a romantic, and others which have a fabulous appearance. To separate what may be true, or probable, from what is exaggerated, incredible, or false, would be a laborious task, and might lead into a longer inquiry than the nature of this work will admit.

In this year the English burned the monastery of Paisley. *Ford. xiii. 14.*

The tedious indisposition of the English King had retarded his preparations for quelling the insurrection in Scotland. Edward now flattered himself that the violence of his malady was abated. As a proof of his recovery, he offered up his horse-litter in the cathedral church of Carlisle. Impatient to chastise the Scots, he mounted on horseback, and proceeded towards Solway. He was so weak that he could advance no farther than six miles in the space of four days. On the 6th of July 1307, he reached Burg on Sande, and next day expired, in sight of that country which he had devoted to destruction. *Trivet, 347. Langtoft, ii. 339.*

By will, he appointed his heart to be conveyed to the Holy-land; *Trivet, 347.* and he settled a stipend for the maintenance of a hundred knights, who, during one year, were to perform military service in honour of the cross.

With

---

* *Barbour* is positive that the battle of Lowdoun-hill was fought on the 10th May 1307. The English historians, as *Trivet*, p. 346. and *M. West.* p. 458. say, That it was fought *post pascha*; this naturally implies *soon after Easter*; as, in 1307, Easter fell on the 26th of March, it would seem, that the English historians supposed the battle to have been fought long before the 10th of May. *W. Hemingford*, contradicting all other writers, says, That Bruce lurked amidst moors and morasses with about 10,000 men, '*quasi cum decem millibus virorum pedestrium*,' T. ii. p. 237. as if 10,000 men could have found subsistence in the deserts which are on the frontiers of Airshire and Galloway!

ROBERT I.

1307.

M. West. 458.
Froissart, l. 27.

With his dying breath, he gave orders that his corps should accompany the army into Scotland, and remain without burial until that country was totally subdued *.

Tyrrel. iii.
179.

The dying injunctions of Kings are seldom regarded. The body of Edward was deposited in the Royal sepulchre of Westminster, by his son Edward II. †

Foed. iii. 1.

The young King marched into Scotland. His first act of royalty was the making a grant of the earldom of Cornwall to his favourite Piers de Gaveston, whom Edward I. had lately banished ‡.

Foed. iii. 7.

The Earl of Pembroke was continued in the office of guardian of Scotland, and impowered to receive to mercy all the Scots, excepting those who had had a share in the slaughter of Comyn, or who had been originally engaged in the insurrection §, [28th August].

Foed. iii. 7.

Edward II. advanced to Cumnock, on the frontiers of Airshire, and then returned to England. By this inglorious retreat, after such mighty preparations for a decisive campaign, he rendered Bruce and his partisans more bold, and he disheartened all in Scotland who favoured the English cause.

Foed. iii. 10.

He had declared Pembroke guardian of Scotland; yet, within a fortnight

---

* *Froissart*, T. l. c. 27. relates this circumstance in the following manner: 'Quand il mourut, il fit appeler son aisné fils, par devant ses Barons, et lui fit jurer sur les saints, qu'aussi tost qu'il seroit trepassé, il le feroit bouillir en une chaudiere, tant que la chair se departiroit des os, et apres seroit mettre la chair en terre et garderoit les os, et toutes les fois que les Escoçois se rebelleroient contre lui il semordroit ses gens et porteroit avecques lui les os de son pere.'

† On his tomb there was this inscription: 'Edvardus primus Scotorum malleus hic est. Pactum serva.' See *Tyrrel*, vol. iii. B. p. p. 179.

‡ This grant, soon followed by others no less extravagant, impolitic and odious, is dated at Dumfries 6th August 1307.

§ 'Qu'il ne fuesrat mie conseillants ne assistants au compassement de celle darreine guerre en Escosse.' [at Cumnock 28th August 1307]; *Foedera*, T. iii. p. 7.

ROBERT I.   23

1307.

night after, he conferred that office on John de Bretagne, Earl of Richmond *, [13th September].

As soon as the English King had retreated, Bruce invaded Galloway. He commanded the inhabitants to repair to his standard; and, on their refusal, wasted the country with fire and sword †. Edward ordered the guardian to march against him. Bruce was put to flight ‡.

Bruce retired into the north of Scotland, and, without opposition, over-ran the country. Returning southwards, he was encountered by John Comyn, Earl of Buchan, with a tumultuary body of English, and of Scots who adhered to the English interest. At the first approach of the enemy, the troops of Buchan fled, [25th December].

About this time, a grievous distemper began to consume the strength of Bruce, and gradually to enfeeble his active spirit, so that there remained no hope of his recovery §.

Fœd. iii. 14.

Fordun, xii. 13.

Fordun, xii. 16.

The

---

* He was taken bound to maintain 60 men at arms in his houshold, and for this he was to have an allowance of ten merks daily; *Fœdera,* T. iii. p. 10.

† John de St John appears at this time to have commanded the English troops in Galloway. Mention is also made of ' *Douegal,* &c. et tota communitas majorum et ' hominum Galewydiae,' as being faithful to England; *Fœdera,* T. iii. p. 14. I suppose that *Douegal* or *Danegan,* is the same with the *M'Doil* or *M'Dowal,* who had lately defeated the brothers of the Scottish King. Edward II. thus describes the invasion of Galloway by Bruce : ' Robertus de Brus, et complices sui, inimici et rebelles ' nostri, ad easdem partes Galewydiae jam venerunt, ibidem roborias, homicidia, de- ' praedationes, incendia, et alia damna quamplurima perpetrantes, necnon et *homines* ' *partium illarum et partium adjacentium contra nos insurgere procurantes et compellen-* ' *tes.*' Ib.

‡ The evidence of this fact rests on the authority of the *Chronicle of Lanercost,* quoted by *Tyrrell,* vol. iii. p. 225. *Abercrombie,* vol i. p. 583. seems to question the truth of it; and yet, unless it is supposed to be true, it will be difficult to account for the march of Bruce into the north.

§ ' Rex fame, frigore, et infirmitate depressus;' *Fordun,* L. xii. c. 16. It is probable that his disease was of a scorbutic nature. Ever since the unfortunate action at Methven, in summer 1306, he had been exposed to the vicissitudes of the seasons, and had endured all kinds of hardships.

1308.

Fordun, xii. 17. The Earl of Buchan, with Moubray, an English commander, assembled a numerous body of troops, eager to efface the dishonour of the former year. Not far from Inverury, in Aberdeenshire, the armies met. Bruce requested that he might be lifted from his couch, and placed on horseback. Too feeble to support himself, he was held up on each side. He led on his companions, charged and discomfited the enemy, and pursued them for many miles with great slaughter *, *Barbour, 177.* [22d May]. It is a traditional report, that, by the agitation of his spirits on that day, he was restored to health. ' The insults of those ' men,' said he, ' have wrought my cure †.'

Fordun, xii. 17. After the manner of that fierce age, Bruce took revenge on the Earl of Buchan, by wasting his territory ‡.

At this dawn of prosperous fortune, many Scots, who had hitherto adhered to the English interest, ranged themselves under the standard of Bruce. Among them Sir David de Brechin is mentioned §.

Fordun, xii. 18. Meanwhile, Edward Bruce, the King's brother, invaded Galloway. He defeated the inhabitants of that country near the river of Dee, [29th June].

John

---

* On the feast of the Ascension, which fell that year on the 22d of May.

† *Barbour*, p. 177. thus relates the expression which the King used-

' Yes, said the King, withoutten weer
' Thair boast has maid me haill and feer,
' For should no medicine so soon
' Have cured me, as they have done.'

‡ *Barbour* speaks feelingly of the ravages committed in Buchan.

' After that well fifty year
' Men menned the birthship of Buchan '

It is probable that Barbour here described what fell under his own observation.

§ From a circular letter addressed by Edward II. to the Scottish Barons, it appears, that, on the 10th May 1308, the following persons were understood to be faithful to the English interest, David Earl of Athole, William Earl of Ross, and Hugh his son, Patrick Earl of Dunbar, and Patrick his son, *David de Brechin*, David de Graham, Reginald de Cheyne, Robert de Keith, Henry de St Clair, John de Kingston, Adam de Swinburn, and Henry de Haliburton; *Foedera*, T. iii. p. 81.

1308.

John de St John, with 1500 horsemen, had advanced to oppose the *Barbour*, 188. inroad of the Scots. By a forced march he endeavoured to surprise them; but intelligence of his motions was timeously received. The courage of Edward Bruce, approaching to temerity, frequently enabled him to atchieve what men of more judicious valour would never have attempted. He ordered the infantry, and the meaner sort of his army, to entrench themselves in strong narrow ground. He himself, with fifty horsemen, well harnassed, issued forth under cover of a thick mist, surprised the English on their march, attacked and dispersed them *.

Having thus overthrown his enemies, Edward Bruce assailed the *Barbour*, 191. various fastnesses of Galloway, expelled the English garrisons, and at *Fordun*, xii 17. length subdued the whole country †.

It was probably about this time that Douglas, while roving about *Barbour*, 191. the mountainous parts of Tweedale, surprized and made prisoners &c. Alexander Stewart of Bonkill, and Thomas Randolph the King's nephew ‡.

Douglas conducted Randolph to the King of Scots. 'Nephew,' *Barbour*, 193. said the King, 'you have been an apostate for a season; you must now
'be

---

* Sir Alan de Cathcart, the companion of Edward Bruce, related the particulars of this expedition to Barbour: 'He was a knight,' says Barbour, ' worthy, brave, and ' courteous.' It is pleasing to trace a family likeness in an ancient portrait.

† In an old monkish rhyme preserved by *Fordun*, L. xii. c. 17, it is said,
 ' *Insula combusta, semper scotis inimica.*'
By *Insula* I understand interior Galloway, or that part of the country which is adjacent to Ireland.

‡ Barbour says ' at the water of *Line.*' This I understand to be the stream which, passing near Kirkurd, falls into the Tweed above Peebles Douglas approaching a house in the moor-lands, heard some one say, ' The D —— !' hence be concluded that there were strangers in that house: He found in it Stewart, Randolph, and Adam de Gordon: The last made his escape, the others were made prisoners; *Barbour*, p. 192. 193.

Vol. II.   D

1308.

' be reconciled.' Randolph fiercely answered, ' *You* require penance ' of *me*, yourself rather ought to do penance. Since you challenged the ' King of England to war, you ought to have asserted your title in ' the open field, and not have betaken yourself to cowardly ambus- ' cades.' The King calmly replied, ' *That* may be hereafter, and ' perchance e'er long : Meanwhile, it is fitting that your proud words ' receive due chastisement; and that you be taught to know my right ' and your own duty.' Having thus spoken, he ordered his nephew into close confinement.

Barbour, 194. &c.

The King was now able to take vengeance on the Lord of Lorn, who, after the discomfiture at Methven, had reduced him to such extremity of danger. He invaded Lorn, and arrived at a narrow pass, having a high mountain on the one side, and a precipice washed by the sea on the other *. *There* the troops of Lorn lay in ambush. Bruce ordered Douglas to make a circuit, and gain the summit of the mountain. He himself, with the rest of his army, entered the pass: They were instantly assaulted. Douglas, from the superior ground, discharged a shower of arrows, rushed down sword in hand, and overthrew the enemy. John, the son of Alexander de Argyle, Lord of Lorn, who had conducted this unsuccessful ambush, from his galley was spectator of the discomfiture of his people †, [about 23d August].

Robert

---

* *Barbour*, p. 195. calls the mountain *Cretchinben*.

† At this place, Barbour has introduced a generous sentiment :
' To John of Lorn it should displease
' I trow, when he his men might see
' Be slain and chased in the hill
' That he might set no help theretill.
' But it angers as greatumly
' To good hearts that are worthy,
' To see their foes fulfill their will
' As to themselves to tholl the ill.'

1308.

Robert fpoiled the country, and took the caftle of Dunftaffnage, *Barbour*, 198. the chief refidence of this too independent Lord. Lorn and his fon *Ford. xii. 18.* were permitted to depart with their fhips *.

While Bruce and his affociates thus exerted themfelves in wrefting Scotland from the Englifh, every thing was feeble and fluctuating in the counfels of their enemies.

Edward II. fondly imagined that he might reconcile the Scots to *Ford. iii. 81.* the Englifh government by the mediation of William de Lambyrton, Bifhop of St Andrews. This turbulent, though timid ecclefiaftic, after having been conveyed from prifon to prifon, at length made fubmiffions which procured his enlargement, then his full liberty, and prefently the confidence of Edward.

William de Lambyrton took a moft folemn oath to be the faithful *Ford. iii. 98.* liege-man of England; and, with the zeal of a new convert, engaged to publifh the fentence of excommunication againft Bruce and all his adherents †, [11th Auguft.]

The

---

* *Barbour*, p. 48. fays, That Alexander of Argyle, Lord of Lorn, fubmitted himfelf to Bruce; but that his fon John retreated to his fhips. I follow the narrative of *Fordun*, L. xii. c. 18. who fays, That Alexander of Argyle retired into England, where he foon after died.

† Edward made an allowance to him of L. 100 yearly out of the revenues of the fee of St Andrews, [20th May 1308], *Fædera*. T. iii. p. 80. John de Moubray, Alexander de Abernethy, Robert de Keith, Adam de Gordon, and Henry de Haliburton, became furaties for his good behaviour. Edward permitted him to be a prifoner at large, within the county of Northampton; *Fædera*, T. iii. p. 82. He informed the Pope, That he had fet the Bifhop of St Andrews at liberty. 'He has been well advifed,' faid Edward, 'to make his fubmiffions in the moft ample manner, and I no longer apprehend any bad offices from him;' [23d July 1308], *Fædera*, T. iii. p. 98. The Bifhop took the oath of fidelity to Edward ' fuper corpus Domini facratum et crucem ' Gnaith;' (11th Auguft 1308]. *Fædera*, T. iii. p. 98. He was one of the Englifh commiffioners for negotiating a treaty with Scotland; [10th February 1309-10] *Fædera*, T. iii. p. 201. Edward informed the Pope, That he expected much aid from the exhortations

1308.

Fœd. iii. 94. 160. 161. 175. 195. 203.

The measures of Edward varied from day to day. This is visible from the frequent changes which he made in the government of Scotland. The Earl of Richmond was removed from the office of guardian, and Robert de Umfraville, Earl of Angus, and William de Ros de Hamelake, were appointed joint guardians. To them Henry de Beaumont was added: But, within four days, a commission was issued, appointing Robert de Clifford sole guardian, and another appointing Robert de Umfraville sole guardian, because the King knew not which of the two would accept of the office. It appears that Clifford accepted, and was constituted sole guardian. After an interval of about three weeks, Gilbert de Clare, Earl of Gloucester, was named captain-general in Scotland; Clifford was again named guardian, and soon after was succeeded by John de Segrave *.

Fœd. iii. 117.

Philip King of France endeavoured to promote a reconciliation between Edward II. and Bruce. With the permission of Edward, he sent a special messenger, Oliver des Roches, to treat with Bruce and the Bishop of St Andrews. The situation of that prelate was singular: After having renewed his fealty to Edward, he appears to have returned to Scotland, and to have had confidential intercourse with Bruce, [4th March 1308-9.]

Through

hortations of the Bishop of St Andrews, in whom the Scots had especial confidence; [24th July 1311] *Fœdera*, T. iii. p. 274. To the same purpose he wrote 7th March 1311-12. and 11th July 1313; *Fœdera*, T. iii. p. 308 331.

* Robert de Umfraville Earl of Angus, and William de Ros de Hamelake, were appointed joint guardians, 21st June 1308; *Fœdera*, T. iii. p. 94. Henry de Beaumont was added to the commission, 16th August 1309; *Fœdera*, T. iii. p. 160. Robert de Umfraville Earl of Angus, and Robert de Clifford, had each of them a commission to be sole guardian, 10th August 1309; *Fœdera*, T. iii. p. 161. because the King knew not ' quis eorum custodiam illam admittere deberet.' Gilbert de Clare Earl of Gloucester was appointed Captain General in Scotland, 14th September 1309; *Fœdera*, T. iii. p. 175. Robert de Clifford was again appointed guardian, 15th December 1309; *Fœdera*, T. iii. p. 195. John de Segrave succeeded him, 10th March 1309-10; *Fœdera*, T. iii. p. 203.

1309.

Through the mediation of the King of France, Edward consented [Fœd. iii. 147.] to a truce with the Scots.—Edward charged the Scots as guilty of a violation of the truce *, and summoned his barons to meet him in arms at Newcastle, on the 29th of September, in order to march against the enemy.

Still, however, inclining to pacific measures, he authorised Richard [Ford. iii. 150.] de Burgh, Earl of Ulster, to treat with Bruce, [2d and 21st August.] [163.] The commissioners appointed by Bruce for conducting this treaty, were Sir John de Menteth, and Sir Nigel Campbell.

The Sieur de Varennes, the French ambassador at the English court, [Fœd. III. 150.] acted a treacherous part. He openly sent a letter to Bruce, under the title of *Earl of Carrick*; but, in secret, he entrusted the bearer with other despatches, addressed to *the King of Scots*. Edward having intercepted the letters, transmitted them to Philip King of France; for he either believed, or affected to believe, that Philip had not authorised the duplicity of his ambassador, [2d August.]

Philip sent his brother Lewis, Count de Evreux, and Peter Guy, [Ford. iii. 192.] Bishop of Soissons, ambassadors to the English King, and again solicited a truce with Scotland. Edward impowered Robert de Umfraville, and three others, to negotiate and conclude the truce; but, at the same time, he declared that he did this ' at the request of Philip, ' as his dearest father and friend, but who was in no sort to be con-
' sidered as the ally of the people of Scotland †, [29th November.]

This

---

* Edward, however, in an Instrument 29th November 1309, *Fœdera*, T. iii. p. 192. candidly acknowledged that the infringement of the truce was reciprocal; but it was not judged expedient to acknowledge this in a deed of a public nature.

† ' Come de nostre tres chere pere [father-in-law] et ami, et cume a celui que de
' riens ne se tient d'estre alyer as gentz d'Escoffe.'—The other commissioners for concluding the truce were, John de Crombewell, [Cromwell,] John Wogan, and John de Benstede. It was specially provided that nothing done should be valid, unless consented to by Wogan and Benstede; *Fœdera*, T. iii. p. 192.

1309.

Fœd. III. 193. This negotiation was soon interrupted. Bruce laid siege to the castle of Rutherglen in Clydsdale: Edward sent his nephew, the young Earl of Gloucester, to raise the siege *, [3d December.]

Fœd. iii. 201. The treaty was renewed. Edward appointed commissioners for that purpose. The Bishop of St Andrews was one of the number, [16th February 1309-10.] It appears that the truce was concluded, but that the Scots disregarded it.

Fœd. xii. 18. In this year, James, the Stewart of Scotland, died, [16th July.]

1310.

Fœd. iii. 20. The progress of Bruce now became alarming. Perth, where John Fitz Marmaduke commanded, was threatened by the Scots. Edward made preparations to secure that important post, and he appointed a fleet to sail to the Tay †.

Fœd. iii. 213. He named the Earl of Ulster to the command of a body of troops which was to assemble at Dublin, and from thence to invade Scotland.

Fœd. iii. 203.
Fœd. iii. 38. He commanded his barons to meet him in arms at Berwick; but the English nobility, disgusted at the government of Edward, and of his favourite Gaveston, repaired unwillingly and slowly to the royal standard.

The

---

* Historians are silent as to this event; but, it is probable, that the siege was raised; for, according to our writers, Edward II. in the following year, penetrated to Renfrew. Had Rutherglen been in the possession of the Scots, it is not to be supposed that Renfrew would have remained under the English dominion, or that Edward would have directed his march thither. Rutherglen appears to have been won from the English in 1313. See *Barbour*, p. 120.

† At this time Alexander de Abernethy was appointed warden of the country between Forth and the mountains of Scotland, 15th June; *Fœdera*, T. iii. p. 211. John de Cauton was appointed Admiral of the fleet for the succour of Perth, 15th June; *Fœdera*, T. iii. p. 211. but his command was soon after conferred on Simon de Montague, 6th August; *Fœdera*, T. iii. p. 223. John de Argyle, or Lorn, was at this time in the service of England, and had his station on the west seas; *Fœdera*, T. iii. p. 223.

1310.

The season was now far advanced. Edward countermanded the troops which were to have invaded Scotland under the Earl of Ulster: But, although he relinquished one part of his plan, he resolved to execute the other. Towards the end of September he invaded Scotland. Quitting the common track, he marched his army by a route which would have proved exceedingly hazardous, had there been any enemies to oppose him. He passed from Rokesburgh, through the forest of Selkirk, to Biggar; from thence, it is said, that he penetrated to Renfrew. Without making any abode in those parts, he turned back by the way of Linlithgow, and retreated to Berwick. After this ill-concerted and fruitless expedition, he remained inactive at Berwick for eight months [*].

During this invasion Bruce avoided encountering the English [†]. He recollected the disasters at Dunbar and Falkirk, where the Scots, instead of protracting the war, hazarded the fate of the nation on a single battle. He also knew that an invasion undertaken in autumn would ruin the heavy armed cavalry, on which the English placed their chief confidence. At that time there was a famine in Scotland incredibly grievous [‡]. This national calamity may be said to have fought for

---

[*] Edward was at Rokesburgh 20th September 1310; Foedera, T. iii. p. 225. at Biggar, 1st and 6th October, ib. p. 226. 227. Fordun, L. xii. c. 18. says, that Edward proceeded as far as Renfrew. But he certainly did not halt there: For he was at Linlithgow on the 13th October. There he remained till the 25th; Foedera, T. iii. p. 228. He appears to have returned to Berwick before the 10th November, ib. p. 230. He remained at Berwick until 24th July 1311. ib. p. 274.

[†] Of this Edward made a boast to the Pope. 'R. de Brus et sui complices, dum ' prius in partibus Scotiae ad eorum rebellionem reprimendam suimus, in abditis la-' titabant, ad instar vulpium;' Foedera, T. iii. p. 283.

[‡] 'Propter guerrarum discrimina tanta erat panis inopia, et victualium charistia in ' Scotia, quod in plerisque locis, impellente famis necessitate, multi carnibus equorum ' et aliorum pecorum immundorum vescebantur;' Fordun, L. xii. c. 18. The English historians mention a great dearth in England at that period; Trivet. continuatio, p. 8.

1310.

for Bruce. It must have embarrassed and retarded the motions of an army in that age, when magazines and the other resources of modern war were unknown.

Neither is it improbable that Bruce might have had secret wellwishers in the camp of the enemy, and have received intelligence from them of the discontents which prevailed among the English nobility, more eager to destroy Gaveston, than to recover Scotland.

Ford. iii. 233. Certain it is, that, on his arrival at Berwick, Edward learned that many of his English subjects had supplied the Scots with provisions, arms, and horses. By proclamation, under the pains of forfeiture, he prohibited this abuse. As England was not at that time a commercial nation, it may be conjectured, that the persons who supplied their enemies with military stores, and exposed their countrymen to the miseries of war, were not so much actuated with the desire of gain, as with the spirit of thwarting an odious administration.

Ford. iii. 238. The King of Scots projected a winter invasion of the isle of Man*. He had partisans in that quarter who infested the coasts of England. Edward, however, took measures for repressing those piratical incursions, and secured the island from invasion.

1311.

Barbour, 199. About this time the castle of Linlithgow was surprised by the stratagem of a poor peasant, one William Binnock. The English garrison dreading

---

* During the disputed succession, Sir William Montacute, said to be descended from the antient Kings of Man, expelled the Scots. He mortgaged the island to Anthony Beck Bishop of Durham. Edward I. granted it to the Bishop for his life. On the death of that Bishop, Edward II. bestowed the island on his favourite Gaveston, and, after his demise, on Henry de Beaumont, ' with all the demesn and royal jurisdic- ' tion thereto belonging;' *Camden,* Britannia, p. 1060. At this time [1310], the Bishop of Durham had possession and governed the island by his Stewart (Seneschallus), Gilbert M'Askil; *Fordera,* T. lii. p. 238.

1311.

dreading no enemy, kept a flight guard. Binnock engaged eight resolute men in his enterprise. He concealed them in a load of hay, which he had been employed to drive into the castle. As soon as the gate was opened to let in the carriage, the conspirators sprung from their concealment, mastered the guard, and possessed themselves of the place.

Robert dismantled the castle of Linlithgow, and the other castles which he won in the course of the war. This was one of the favourite maxims of his policy *. He saw that the English, by means of castles judiciously placed, had maintained themselves in Scotland, with little aid from their sovereign. And, perhaps, he apprehended, that, when the country came to be settled in peace, the possession of castles might render his own barons no less formidable to the crown, than the English garrisons had been to the nation.

Edward,

---

* The maxims [or political testament] of Robert Bruce are preserved in old Scottish metre. See *Fordun*, L. xii. c. 10. They are curious, and not difficult to be understood.

'On fut fald be all Scottis weire
'Be hyll and mosse thaimself to weire,
'Let wed for wallis be bow and spere
'That innymeis do thaim na dreire;
'In strait placis gar keip all stoire,
'And byrn the planen land thaim befoire;
'Thanen sall they pass away in haist
'Quhen that they find nalthing bot waist,
'With wyllie and waikenen of the nicht
'And mekill noyes maid on hycht,
'Thanen sall they turnen with gret affrai,
'As they were chasit with swerd away.
'This is the counsall and intent
'Of gud King Robert's testament.'

ROBERT I.

1310.

Ford. iii. 171. Edward, projecting a second expedition into Scotland, ordered his army to rendezvous at Rokesburgh. This rendezvous, however, did not take place.

Ford. III. 184. Ford. xii. 18. Bruce had so well established his authority throughout his own dominions, that he now resolved to invade England. He led his army into the bishoprick of Durham, and ravaged the country with that cruelty and licentiousness which disgrace the character of a brave man [*]. Yet it was not strange, that, in a fierce age, one who had seen the ruin of his private fortunes, the captivity of his wife and only child, and the tortures and execution of his dearest relations and tried friends, should have thus satiated his revenge. He led back his army into Scotland, loaded with spoil.

Barbour, 180. Ford. xii. 18. At his return Bruce laid siege to Perth. The conditions which he offered to the garrison were scornfully rejected. After having lain before the town for six weeks, he raised the siege; but, in a few days, he provided scaling ladders, and, with a chosen body of infantry, approached the works. The night was dark, and favoured his enterprise. The King himself carried a ladder, and was the foremost to enter the ditch [†]. There chanced to be present a French gentleman, who,

---

[*] Edward II. in a letter to the Pope, 17th October 1311, *Fœdera*, T. iii. p. 284. thus describes the inroad of Bruce: ' Robertus et sui complices—Regnum nostrum ' Angliæ hostiliter ingressi, in diversis partibus Marchiæ ejusdem regni, et praecipué in ' Episcopatu Dunelmensi, rapinas, depraedationes, incendia, et homicidia perpetrârunt, ' aetati vel sexui innocenti, aut immunitati ecclesiasticae libertatis, pro dolor! non ' parcentes.' *Fordun*, L. xii. c. 18. relates the same event, although in another style : ' Angliam intravit, ipsam devastando, praedas innumeras abducendo, et ingentem ' stragem igne et ferro inferendo. Sicque Dei virtute gens Anglorum perfida, quae mul- ' tos injuriâ spoliaverat et cruciaverat, jam justo Dei judicio diris subjicitur flagellis.'

[†] *Barbour* says, p. 182. that when the King passed the ditch at Perth, in order to scale the walls, *the water stood to his throat*. This shews that Bruce was not of a stature

ROBERT I.   35
                   1310.

who, when he saw the King pass on, exclaimed, 'What shall we
'say of our French Lords, who spend their days in good cheer and
'jollity, while so worthy a knight hazards his life to win a miserable
'hamlet *?' Saying this, with the gay valour which has always distinguished the French nobility, he threw himself into the water, followed
the King, and shared his danger and his glory. The Scots, animated
by the example of their Prince, scaled the walls †. The town was ta-
                                                                 ken,

ture beyond that of other men. If he had been much taller than his soldiers, the water which flood to his throat must have drowned them.

* The words of *Barbour*, p. 182. are these:
    ' That time was in his company
    ' A knight of France, wight and hardy,
    ' And when he in the water saw
    ' The King pass so, and with him ta
    ' His ladder unabasedly,
    ' He sained him for the ferly,
    ' And said, O Lord! what shall we say
    ' Of our Lordis of France, that ay
    ' With good morsels farces their paunch,
    ' And will but eat and drink and daunce,
    ' When sik a knight, and so worthy
    ' As this, through his great chevalry,
    ' Into sik peril has him set
    ' To win a wretched hamilet!'

† *Barbour* says, That the King was *the second man that took the wall*. This little
circumstance adds much to the credibility of Barbour's narrative. A writer of romance would have represented the King as the *first*. From the manner in which Barbour relates the story, it seems probable, that the gallant Frenchman first entered the
town. I could not, however, venture to affirm this, though it would have adorned
the narrative. One William Oliphant commanded in Perth at this time; *Fordun*,
L. xii. c. 18. It is not certain whether he was the same person who so resolutely defended Stirling castle against Edward I. This much is certain, that Oliphant, the gover-
                                                                 nor

                          E 2

1311.

ken, plundered, and burnt, and the works levelled, [8th January 1311-12.]

Ford. iii. 300. — Edward again attempted to make a truce with the Scots. For this purpose he gave ample powers to David Earl of Athole, and five others, [at Berwick 26th January 1311-12.]

Ford. iii. 303. — At this time, his mode of policy was to attach to his interest those among the Scots nobility who had hitherto favoured the cause of England. With this view he granted two manors to the Earl of Athole, [8th February 1311-12].

Ford. iii, 303. — William Sinclair, Bishop-elect of Dunkeld, had been the enemy of England, and on that account Edward had opposed his election. Edward now solicited the Pope in his favour. This he did at the request of Henry de St Clair, the Bishop's brother, who had continued faithful to the English interest, [8th February 1311-12].

1312.

Ford. iii. 313. *Ford.* xii. 19. — The King of Scots invaded England, burnt great part of the city of Durham, and threatened to besiege Berwick. Edward fixed his residence *there*, to repress the incursions of the Scots, as he pretended; but, in truth, because he dreaded the machinations of his own barons, and judged himself insecure in the south.

Ford. xii. 19. — In the course of this year, the King of Scots assaulted and took the castles of Butel [*], Dumfries, and Dalswinton, with many other fortresses.

The

---

nour of Stirling castle was set at liberty by Edward II. on finding sureties for his fidelity to England; [14th May 1308] *Fœdera*, T. lii. p. 82. At the same time, and on like conditions, the Earl of Strathern was set at liberty; *Ibid.* Barbour mentions the Earl of Strathern as being with the English garrison at Perth when the town was stormed. He adds, that the Earl's son fought under the banners of the King of Scots, and made his father a prisoner, p. 183.

[*] *Fordus*, L. xii. c. 19. calls it 'castrum de Botho,' or ' de Bothe.' I imagine that same

1312.

The castle of Rokesburgh, a post of the utmost importance, had been committed by Edward to the charge of Gillemin de Fiennes, a knight of Burgundy. While the English garrison was revelling on the eve of Lent [*], Douglas scaled the castle. Simon of Leadhouse, who had constructed the scaling-ladders, was the first to mount the wall. The garrison retreated into the inner tower. De Fiennes received a mortal wound, and his soldiers capitulated, [6th and 7th March 1312-13.]

*Ford ill. 19.
Barbour, 205.
&c.
Lelan. II. 546.*

Randolph having been received into favour by his uncle the King of Scots, eminently distinguished himself in the common cause. Barbour, who probably had seen Randolph, thus describes him: 'He was of comely stature, broad visaged, and of a countenance fair and pleasant; the friend of brave men, loyal, just, and munificent.' Barbour adds, ' That he was jovial and amorous, and altogether made up of virtue [†].'

Barbour, 204.

The castle of Edinburgh had for governor, Piers Leland, a knight of Gascony. Randolph blockaded it so closely, that all communication with the adjacent country was cut off. The garrison, suspecting the fidelity

*Lelan. II. 546.
Barbour, 205.*

---

[*] some castle in Galloway is here meant, rather than Rothsay in the island of Bute; probably the castle of Butel in Galloway, belonging to the Balliol family.

[*] Boece's description of the revels of Shrove Tuesday is lively and judicious; ' quum omnes homines, metu abstinentiae instantis, vino libidinibusque indulgent;' L. xiv. fol. 301 a.

[†] The words of Barbour, p. 204, are these:
  ' In company solacious
  ' And therewith blyth and amorous—
  ' And if that I the sooth sall say,
  ' He was fulfilled of bountie
  ' Als of virtues all made was he.'

This portrait, drawn by a grave ecclesiastic, is of a singular style, yet it has great appearance of truth.

1312.

fidelity of Leland, thruſt him into a dungeon, and choſe another commander in his ſtead.

Barbour, 111.
—119.
Ford. xii. 19.

Matters were in this ſtate, when one William Frank preſented himſelf to Randolph, and offered to ſhew him how the walls of the caſtle might be ſcaled. This man, while young, had reſided in the caſtle, and having an amorous intrigue in the neighbourhood, had been wont to deſcend the wall during the night, by means of a ladder of ropes, and through a ſteep and intricate path to arrive at the foot of the rock. The road, although amidſt perilous precipices, had become familiar to him, and he ſtill retained a perfect remembrance of it. Randolph, with thirty men, undertook the enterpriſe of ſcaling the caſtle at midnight. Frank was their guide, and the firſt who aſcended the ſcaling ladder [*]. Before the whole party could reach the ſummit of the wall, an alarm was given, the garriſon ran to arms, and a deſperate combat enſued; but their governor having been ſlain, the Engliſh yielded, [14th March, 1312-13.]

Barbour, 119.
Lelan. il 546.

Leland [†], the former governor, being releaſed from his impriſonment, entered into the ſervice of the Scottiſh nation.

1313.

Ford. iii. 404.

The number of Bruce's partiſans increaſed with his ſucceſſes. The Earl of Athole, who had lately obtained a grant of lands from the King of England, revolted to the Scots.

Through

---

[*] Sir Andrew Gray followed him: Randolph himſelf was the third that mounted the ladder, *Barbour*, p. 215.

[†] Barbour calls him *Piers Lombard*. But Leland, the antiquary, has preſerved his name, *Collectanea*, vol. ii. p. 546. On the margin he gives him the appellation of *Petrus Lelandius, Vicecomes of Edinburgh*, and adds, that ' Drus, after, ſurmiſed treaſon
' upon hym, becauſe he thought that he had an Engliſh hart, and made him to be
' bangit and drawen.'

1313.

Through the mediation of France, the conferences for a truce with the Scots were renewed, [17th May, 1313.] *Foed. lil. 411.*

This, however, did not retard the military enterprises of the Scots. They invaded Cumberland, and wasted the country. The people of Cumberland demanded succour from Edward. He being just about to depart into France, extoll'd their fidelity, and desired them to defend themselves until his return, [23d May.] *Ford. lii. 416.*

The invasion of Cumberland appears to have been only a feint to conceal the designs of Bruce against the isle of Man. He landed there, overcame the governor *, took the castle of Russin, and subdued the country, [11th June.] *Chr. Man, ap. Camden, Bri. tannia, 1057. Ford. iii. 19.*

Edward, on his return to England, found that many of his nobles had refused to give their attendance in a parliament summoned to meet at London. In order to raise troops for resisting the Scots, who still threatened the English borders, Edward endeavoured to borrow money from the clergy, and he again summoned his parliament to meet. The Earl of Lancaster, and other discontented lords, appointed a muster of their forces under the less offensive appellation of *a tournament*. The King, by repeated proclamations, prohibited that assembly. Nevertheless, Lancaster and his associates, in contempt of the royal authority, repaired to the tournament, and refused to concert measures for opposing the common enemy. An inquiry into the causes of this obstinate disregard of the national interest would be a matter of long investigation, and is foreign to the subject of these annals. *Foed. lll. 411. 418. 433.*

Such of the Scots as still remained faithful to England, deputed *Ford. III. 458.*
Patrick

---

* In the Chronicle of Man subjoined to *Camden*, Britannia, p. 1057. this person is called *Dingowy Dowill*. In the Annals of Ireland, *ib.* ad an. 1313, he is called *the Lord Donegan O-hwill*. If he was a Galwegian, I imagine him to have been that *Duncan M'Dowal* who defeated and made prisoners the two brothers of the King of Scots, near Lochryan, in 1306.

ROBERT I.

1313.

Patrick Earl of March, and Adam de Gordon, to lay their miserable state before Edward, both from the increasing power of Bruce, and from the oppression which they suffered under the government of the English ministers. Edward bestowed high encomiums on their faithfulness and constancy; required them to persevere in their duty; promised to lead an army to their relief; and assured them that he would redress all their grievances, [28th November.]

Barbour, 220. Meanwhile the Scottish arms prospered. Edward Bruce made himself master of the castles of Rutherglen and Dundee, and laid siege to the castle of Stirling. Philip de Moubray, the governor, offered to surrender, if he was not relieved on the feast of St John the Baptist,
Barbour, 221. Ford. iii. 20. Ford. iii. 482. [24th June.] in the following year: To this offer, Edward Bruce, without consulting his brother, agreed.
Barbour, 212. The King of Scots was highly displeased at this rash treaty. By it the military operations were interrupted, and a long interval allowed to the English for assembling their utmost force; while, at the same time, the Scots were reduced to the necessity either of raising the siege with dishonour, or of hazarding the kingdom on the event of a single battle. Robert, however, consented to the treaty, and resolved to meet the English by the appointed day.

1314.

Immense were the preparations made by Edward for relieving the castle of Stirling. They were suitable to the power and resources of a mighty people on an occasion so important.

Ford. iii. 463. 478. Edward ordered ships to be assembled for invading Scotland; invited to his aid Fth O'Connor, chief of the Irish of Connaught, and twenty-six other Irish chiefs; summoned his English subjects in Ireland to attend his standard, and put both them and the Irish auxiliaries under the command of the Earl of Ulster. [26th March.]

Ford. iii. 463. 481. 482. After having summoned his barons to meet him in arms at Berwick on the 11th of June, he issued a proclamation, requiring about
22,000

ROBERT I.

1314.

22000 foot soldiers from different counties in England and Wales, to rendezvous at Werk [*].

The

[*] The writ addressed to the sheriff of Yorkshire may serve as a specimen of the style used at that time. ' Rex vicecomiti Eborum, salutem : Cum pro expeditione guerrae
' nostrae Scotiae, quatuor millia hominum in comitatu tuo eligi, et ad nos ad partes
' Scotiae duci mandaverimus, iis quod effent ad nos ibidem ad diem jam transactos ;
' ac jam intellexumus, quod Scoti inimici et rebelles nostri nituntur, quantum possunt,
' se in magna multitudine peditum, in locis forubus et morosis, ubi equitibus difficilis
' patebit accessus, ad invicem congregare inter nos et castrum nostrum de Struyvelin,
' ut sic refcussum ejusdem castri, quem citra festum nativitatis Beati Johannis Baptistae
' proximum futurum, juxta conditionem, cum dictis inimicis nostris per constabularium
' dicti castri initam, sub paena amissionis ejusdem, facere aportebit, et quem, divina opi-
' tulante clementia, citra festum dictum facere proponimus, pro viribus impedirent ,'
Foedera, T. iii. p. 481. An eminent historian says, ' That the army of Edward, which,
' according to the Scots writers, amounted to an hundred thousand men, was pro-
' bably much inferior to that number,' Hume, History of England, vol. ii. p. 115.
In proof of this, he observes, that ' we find in Rymer, T. iii. p. 481. a list of all the
' infantry assembled from all parts of England and Wales, and they are only 21,540.'
It is strange that the author should have so widely mistaken the sense of the record. In
Rymer there is not a list of all the infantry assembled from all parts of England and
Wales, but merely an order to the sheriffs of twelve counties, to two Earls, and to six
or seven Barons, requiring them to furnish certain quotas of infantry. The counties
mentioned are Cheshire, Derbyshire, Durham, Lancashire, Leicestershire, Lincoln-
shire, Northumberland, Nottinghamshire, Shropshire, Staffordshire, Warwickshire,
and Yorkshire.

A writ, indeed, was directed to the Earl of Gloucester and Hertford, and another
to the Earl of Hereford and Essex ; but those writs respected the particular estates belonging to the two Earls, and not the counties under their administration.

The writs published by Rymer relate not to the southern or western counties of
England. It is not probable that Edward would have invited the aid of 17 Irish chiefs,
and yet have neglected to require the assistance of the most populous parts of his own
dominions. If we take into the account the Irish, and the English subjects residing in
France, and if we suppose that all the counties and all the barons in England furnished
their quotas in equal proportion, we shall have no difficulty in pronouncing, that the
numbers of the English army, as related by our historians, are within the limits of
probability.

Vol. II.   F

1314.

Barbour, 119. The King of Scots appointed a general rendezvous of his forces at the Torwood, between Falkirk and Stirling. Their number somewhat exceeded thirty thousand. There were also upwards of fifteen thousand, an unarmed and undisciplined rabble, who followed the camp, according to the mode of those times.

Barbour, 131. To J-la More, ap. Camden, 594. The King determined to wait the English in a field which had Stirling on the left, and the brook of Bannock on the right *. What he must dread was the strength and multitude of the English cavalry. The banks of the brook were steep in many places, and the ground between it and Stirling was partly covered with wood. The place, therefore, was well adapted for opposing and embarrassing the operations of horsemen. The King commanded many pits to be dug in every quarter where cavalry could have access. These pits were of a foot in breadth, and between two and three feet deep. Some slight brushwood was laid over them, and they were carefully covered with sod, so as not to be perceptible by a rash and impetuous enemy. Barbour describes their construction in a lively manner: ' They might be ' likened,' says he, ' to a honeycomb.' This implies that there were many rows of them with narrow intervals †.

By probability, Edward himself says, and it is a circumstance which merits attention, that he had summoned to the rendezvous all who owed military service ; [totum servitium nostrum,] *Fœdera*, T. iii. p 478.

* The author of *the history of Stirlingshire* is positively certain that the King of Scots drew up his army, having its front to the south, and with Stirling on the rear. After having examined the ground, I am as positively certain, that Barbour, whom I follow, has justly described the position of the Scots in that memorable day. Their front appears to have extended from the brook called *Bannockburn* to the neighbourhood of St Ninians, pretty nearly upon the line of the present turnpike road from Stirling towards Kilsyth. The stone in which Bruce is reported to have fixed his standard is still to be seen.—The partisans of the other hypothesis will do well to point out what was Randolph's post, and how he came to be engaged with Clifford.

† The description given by Barbour shews, that Buchanan had a very imperfect notion

1314.

By this disposition the King exposed his left flank to the garrison of Stirling; but the inconsiderable number of soldiers in that garrison could not have greatly annoyed the Scots. Besides, Moubray the governor had consented to a truce, and, if he had assailed the Scots before the fate of the castle was determined by battle, he would have been deemed *a false knight.* In those days, the point of honour was the only tie which bound men; for dispensations and absolutions had effaced the reverence of oaths.

Edward proceeded triumphantly on his march for the relief of Stirling castle [*]. Barbour, 227.

On the 23d June, the alarm came to the Scottish camp, that Edward was approaching. Barbour, 233.

The King of Scots resolved that his troops should fight on foot. Barbour, ib. He drew them up after this manner. He gave the command of the center to Douglas, and to Walter the young Stewart of Scotland; of the right wing to Edward Bruce, and of the left to Randolph; he himself took charge of the reserve, composed of the men of Argyle, the islanders, and his own vassals of Carrick. In a valley to the rear [†], he

---

tion of the artifice employed by Bruce. His words are: " Bruffeos—in locis aequiori-" bus foff s praeshaas duxit, in quibus palos acutos ita infixit, ut superne integumen-" tum e levi cespite fraudem celaret: Murices autem ferreos, ubi commodum videba-" tur, spargi jussit." L. viii. p. 145. Barbour speaks not of the *caltrops*, which Buchanan mentions; but it is possible that they also may have been used.

[*] *Barbour,* p. 227. describes this march with an elegance not unworthy of Chaucer.

  'Then sol was bright, and shining clear,
  'And armours that bright burnished were
  'Sa blonyt with the sun its beam
  'That all the land seemed in a lem,
  'Banners right fairly flawinand
  'And pensels to the wind wavand.'

[†] According to the report of the country to the west of a rising ground, called *Gilles hill*; and, indeed, there appears not any other place in that neighbourhood which corresponds with the account given by Barbour.

1314.

he placed the baggage of the army, and all the numerous and useless attendants on the camp.

He enjoined Randolph to be vigilant in preventing any advanced parties of the English from throwing succours into the castle of Stirling.

Barbour, 138. &c.

Eight hundred horsemen, commanded by Sir Robert Clifford, were detached from the English army; they made a circuit by the low grounds to the east, and approached the castle. The King perceived their motions, and coming up to Randolph, angrily exclaimed, 'Thoughtless man *I you have suffered the enemy to pass.' Randolph hasted to repair his fault, or perish. As he advanced, the English cavalry wheeled to attack him. Randolph drew up his troops in a circular form, with their spears resting on the ground, and pretended on every side †. At the first onset Sir William Daynecourt, an English commander

Barbour, 240. Trivet contin. 14.

---

* The words of *Barbour*, p. 239. are:

    'For the King had said him rudely,
    'That a rose of his chaplet
    'Was fallen, for where he was set
    'To keep the way, these men were past.'

The phrase, 'a rose has fallen from your chaplet,' is obscure. I imagine that *rose* implies the large bead in a rosary or chaplet, for distinguishing a *Pater noster* from an *ave Maria* in the enumeration of prayers. Hence, to say, 'that a rose has fallen from 'a person's chaplet,' means, literally, that he has been careless in his devotions, and has omitted part of the prayers which he ought to have repeated; and, by metonymy, that he has neglected any charge committed to him. 'He was set to keep the way,' means, 'he had the charge of guarding that passage:' Hence we may learn, that Randolph commanded the left wing. That circumstance is not clearly expressed by Barbour.

† So I understand the words of *Barbour*, p. 240.

    'Set your spears you before;
    'And back to back set all your rout,
    'And all the spears their points out;
    'So gate us best defend may we,
    'Environed with them if we be.'

1314.

commander of diftinguifhed valour, was flain. The enemy, far fuperior in numbers to Randolph, environed him, and preffed hard on his little band. Douglas faw his jeopardy, and requefted the King's permiffion to go and fuccour him. 'You fhall not move from your 'ground,' cried the King; 'let Randolph extricate himfelf as he beft 'may. I will not alter my order of battle, and lofe the advantage of 'my pofition.' 'In truth,' replied Douglas, 'I cannot ftand by and fee 'Randolph perifh; and therefore, with your leave, I *muſt* aid him.' The King, unwillingly, confented; and Douglas flew to the affiftance of his friend. While approaching, he perceived that the Englifh were falling into diforder, and that the perfeverance of Randolph had prevailed over their impetuous courage. 'Halt,' cried Douglas, ' thofe brave 'men have repulfed the enemy; let us not diminifh their glory, by 'fharing it.'

Meanwhile the vanguard of the Englifh army appeared. The King of Scots was then in the front of the line, meanly mounted, having a battle-ax in his hand, and a crown above his helmet, as was the manner in thofe times. Henry de Bohun, an Englifh knight, armed at all points, rode forward to encounter him. The King met him in fingle combat; and, with his battle-ax, cleft the fcull of Bohun, and laid him dead at his feet [*]. The Englifh vanguard retreated in confufion.

Monday the 24th of June 1314, at break of day [†], the Englifh army moved on to the attack.

The

[*] In *Scala Chron.* ap. *Leland,* Collectanea, T. il. p. 546. it is faid, ' Bruſe, with 'his owne hands, killed *Piers Monfort,* an Englifh knight, in the wooder by Strivelin.' I obferve that *Piers Monfort* is not mentioned in the lift of the flain; *Trivet,* contin. p. 14. but that *Henry de Bohun* is. *Barbour* relates, that the Scottifh leaders blamed the King for his temerity in encountering Bohun. The King, confcious of his error, changed the difcourfe, and faid, ' I have broke my good battle-ax;' p. 246.

[†] Thomas de la More fays, edit. *Camden,* p. 594. That the Englifh fpent the night

before

1314.

<small>Lelan II 546.
Walsing. 105.</small> The van, consisting of the archers and lancemen, was commanded by Gilbert de Clare Earl of Gloucester, nephew of the English King, and Humphry de Bohun, Earl of Hereford, constable of England [*].

<small>Barbour, 257.</small> "The ground was so narrow, that the rest of the English army had not space sufficient to extend itself. It appeared to the Scots as composing one great compact body [†].

<small>Barbour, 257.</small> Edward, in person, brought up the main body. Aymer de Vallence, Earl of Pembroke, and Sir Giles d'Argentine, two experienced commanders, attended him [‡].

Maurice

before the battle in drunkenness and riot:' ' Vidisses primâ nocte Anglos haud Anglicè
' more vino madentes, crapulam eructantes, Wassails et drinkhails plus solito intonan-
' tes.'

[*] The Earls of Lancaster, Warenne, Warwick, and Arundel, were absent from the English army. They pretended that Edward had failed in performing certain conditions promised to them. *Walsingham*, p. 104.

[†] *Barbour*, p. 257. says,

'———In a shiltrum,
' It seemed they were all and some,
' Outtane the vaward allenarly,
' That right with a great company
' By themselves arrayed were.'

In another passage, p. 260. he says, that the English had nine *battles*, or large bodies. *Walsingham*, p. 105. says, ' Duces Anglorum pedites cum arcubus atque lan-
' cels, in prima componunt acie, equites *diversis aliis retro constituunt*.' It would seem that the intervals between the different bodies of infantry were small.

[‡] ' His own battle ordained be,
' And who should at his bridle be?
' Sir Giles de Argentine be set
' Upon a half his reinzie to get,
' And of Vallange Sir Aymer
' On the other half, that was worthy,
' For in their sovereign bountie
' Out o'er the lave assed he.' *Barbour*, p. 217.

Thomas

ROBERT I.

1314.

Maurice Abbot of Inchaffray, placing himself on an eminence, celebrated mass in fight of the Scottish army. He then passed along the front, barefooted, and bearing a crucifix in his hands, and exhorted the Scots in few and forcible words, to combat for their rights and their liberty. The Scots kneeled down. 'They yield,' cried Edward; 'See, they implore mercy.' 'They do,' answered Ingelram de Umfraville, 'but not ours. On that field they will be victorious, or die.'

The two armies, exasperated by mutual animosities, engaged. The conflict was long and bloody. The King of Scots, perceiving that his troops were grievously annoyed by the English archers, ordered Sir Robert Keith, the Marshall, with a few armed horsemen, to make a circuit by the right, and attack the archers in flank. The archers having no weapons, were instantly overthrown, and falling back, spread disorder throughout the army *. The King of Scots advanced with the reserve †. The young and gallant Earl of Gloucester attempted

---

Thomas de la More admits that Edward was in the third body; but, he adds, that he was accompanied by Bishops, and other ecclesiastics, and by that cowardly bird of prey, H. le Despencer, 'vecors ille milvus,' p. 594.

* It is generally supposed that the English horsemen were entangled in the snare which Bruce had laid for them. But Barbour makes no mention of that circumstance, although he minutely describes the nature of Bruce's stratagem. If I mistake not, the movement executed by Sir Robert Keith was decisive of the battle. The English had crowded their whole infantry into the van, or first line, and, confiding in their unwieldy numbers, had not foreseen the danger of being taken in flank by a few men at arms.

† It would seem, from some expressions in Barbour, p. 287, that the King of Scots brought up the reserve to the right of his army. This shows that there had been a great slaughter of the Scots, by which, in that circumscribed ground, there was place left for the reserve to fall into the line. The words of Barbour are,

'When this was said, they held their way,
'And on *one field* assembled they,—

' All

48   ROBERT I.

1314.

tempted to rally the fugitives, but was unhorsed, and hewen to pieces *—the confusion became universal. At that moment the numerous attendants on the Scottish camp, prompted by curiosity, or eager for plunder, issued from their retirement in the rear. It seemed as if fresh troops had arrived in aid of the Scots. The English fled with precipitation on every side. Many crowded to seek relief among the rocks in the neighbourhood of Stirling castle; and many rushed into the river and were drowned.

Barbour, 372. Pembroke and Sir Giles d'Argentine had attended on Edward during the action. When Pembroke saw that the battle was irretrievably lost, he constrained Edward to quit the field. 'It is not my wont to 'fly,' said d'Argentine, renowned for his prowess in the Saracen wars; then spurring on his horse, and crying out, ' *An Argentine,*' he rushed into the battle and met death †.

Douglas,

'*All their four battles, with their weir*
'*Fightand in a front haillily.*'
a in this place, as in others, is, in modern language, not *a* but *one*.

* *Th. de la Moor,* ap. Camden, p. 594. says, That the Scots would have saved the Earl of Gloucester, had they known him, but that, on that day, he had neglected to put on ' *togam proprias armaturas,*' that is, the upper garment on which his arms were depicted, or his *coat armorial.*

† I know little of this singular personage. In Scotland his renown was great. According to the vulgar opinion, the three most eminent worthies of that age were, the Emperor Henry of Luxemburg, Robert Bruce, and *Sir Giles d'Argentine; Fordun,* L. xiii. c. 16 in *Scala Chron.* ap. Leland. T. ii. p. 547. it is said, ' Giles de Argentine, 'a stoute warrior, and late come from the werres of Henry Lufenburg Emperor, said, 'that he was not wont to fly, and so returnt to the Englifche host, and was flayne.' It is reported, that, in the wars of Palestine, he thrice encountered the Saracens, and in each encounter slew two of their warriors: ' It was no mighty feat,' said he, ' for ' one Christian knight to overcome and slay two Pagan dogs,' *Fordun,* L. xii. c. 16. Ballon the Carmelite, ap. *Fordun,* L. xii. c. 22, thus speaks:

' *Nobilis*

1314.

Douglas, with sixty horsemen, pursued the English King on the *Barbour, ibid.*
spur. At the Torwood he met Sir Laurence Abernethy, who was
hasting with twenty horsemen to the English rendezvous. Abernethy
abandoned the cause of the vanquished, and joined with Douglas in
the pursuit. Edward rode on without halting to Linlithgow. Scarcely had he refreshed himself there, when the alarm came that the Scots
were approaching. Edward again fled. Douglas and Abernethy pressed hard upon him, and allowed him not a moment of respite [*]. Edward at length reached Dunbar, a place distant more than sixty miles
from the field of battle. The Earl of March opened the gates of that *Leland. ii. 547.*
castle to Edward, protected him from his pursuers, and conveyed him
by sea into England [†].

Such

'*Nobilis Argenteo, pugil inclyte, dukis Egidi,*
'*Via seieram mentem, cum te succumbere vidi.*'

The first line mentions the three chief requisites of a true knight, noble birth, valour, and courteousness. Few Leonin couplets can be produced that have so much
sentiment. I wish that I could have collected more ample memorials concerning a
character altogether different from modern manners. Sir Giles d'Argentine was a
hero of romance in real life.

[*] *Barbour* describes the constancy of the chace in a lively manner, but which I chuse
to express in Latin, '*Scoti pertinacius inslabant, ita quidem ut ne vel mingendi locus
' hostibus concederetur;*' p. 282.

[†] '*Counte Patrik of Marche ful gentely receivid King Edward into his castell of
' Dunbar, and thens the King cam by water to Berwick;*' *Scala Chron.* ap. Leland, T.
ii. p. 547. *Th. de la More,* p. 594. relates a circumstance which is characteristical:
'*Hic non equi velocitas, non hominum industria Regem ab inimicis liberavit, sed Ma-
' ter Dei quam Rex invocavit. Cui Rex et filio suo vovit, si salvus evasisset, se erec-
' turum pauperibus ejus Carmelitis mansionem, in Matris Dei titulo insignitam, pro
' 24 fratribus Theologiæ studio deputatis, quod et postea fecit Oxonii et expensis di-
' tavit, dissuadente Spensero.*' To this vow of Edward II. Oriel college in Oxford,
where Sir Walter Rawleigh was educated, owes its establishment; *Antiq. Oxon,* T. ii.
p. 103.

ROBERT I.

1314.

Barbour, 278. Such was the event of the battle of Bannockburn [*]; an action glorious in its circumstances, and of decisive moment.

On the side of the Scots, no persons of note were slain, except Sir William Vipont, and the favourite of Edward Bruce, Sir Walter Ross. When Edward Bruce heard of his death, he passionately exclaimed, ' Oh that this day's work were undone, so Ross had not died [†].'

Triv. contin. 14. Walsing. 105. But the loss of the English was exceedingly great. Of barons and bannerets, there were slain twenty-seven, and twenty-two made prisoners.

---

[*] The English call it the battle of Bannokmoor; *Walsingham*, p. 105. or, of Stirling; *Murimuth*, p. 46. *Leland*, T. ii. p. 546.

[†] *Barbour*, p. 278. Thus relates the incident.

  ' That he said, making evil cheir
  ' That him were levir that journey were
  ' Undone, than he so dead had bene.
  ' Outtaken him, men has not sene
  ' Where he for any man made meaning,
  ' And the cause was of his loving
  ' That he to his sister per amours
  ' Loved,' &c.

Barbour, ib. relates a singular incident, which, according to his account, is connected with the friendship of Edward Bruce and Sir Walter Ross. Bruce had married Isabella the sister of David de Strathbogie Earl of Athole; he slighted her, and engaged in an unlawful intercourse with the sister of Sir Walter Ross. Athole brooked not this affront, and resolved to revenge his private wrongs, although at the hazard of the state. While the two armies were about to engage, he assaulted the King's head quarters at the abbey of Cambuskenneth, and slew the guard, with Sir William Keith his commander. Barbour adds, That for this base deed he forfeited. I know not what judgment to form of this story. It is certain that the Earl of Athole returned to the service of England,· *Fœdera*, T. iii. p. 644 [an. 1312.] And it is equally certain, that sentence of forfeiture was pronounced against him in parliament, 1323. ' Per judicium in par-
' liamento nostro tento apud Cambuskynet, de consensu totius cleri et populi editam, in
' festo Sancti Jacobi apostoli, anno 1323,' *Chart. Dunferm.* T. ii. fol. 24. It is strange that punishment should have been delayed, until 1323, of an offence so atrocious, said to have been committed in 1314.

1314.

soners. Of knights there were slain forty-two, and sixty made prisoners [a]. The English historians mention as the most distinguished among the slain, the Earl of Gloucester, Sir Giles d'Argentine, Robert Clifford, Payen Tybetot, William le Mareshal, and the Seneshal of England Edmund de Mauley. Of esquires there fell seven hundred [b]; the number of common men killed or made prisoners is not related with any certainty.

The Welshmen who served in the English army were scattered over the country, and miserably butchered by the Scottish peasants. *Barbour, 276.*

The English who had sought refuge among the rocks in the neighbourhood of Stirling castle, surrendered at discretion. Moubray the governor performed the conditions of his capitulation, yielded up the castle, and entered into the service of the King of Scots. *Barbour, 276. 280.*

The privy-seal of the English King fell into the hands of the enemy [c]. *Triv. contin. 15. Fæd. II. 483.*

The

[a] In *Trivet*, Contin. p. 14. there is a list of some of them. From the specimen there given, it may be presumed, that, if the list were complete, most of the antient English families would find the names of their predecessors among the slain, or among the prisoners, at Bannockburn.

[b] 'Scutiferorum septingentorum;' *Walsingham*, p. 105. As to the meaning of the word *Esquire*, it is said by *Spelman* Gloss. p. 508. 'Scutifer, nobilitatis, (ci). appellatio apud Anglos penultima, hoc est, Inter equitem et generosum;' *i. e.* 'A *squire* is that rank which is below that of a *knight*, and above that of a *gentleman*.' This description is not satisfactory; it has a modern look.

[c] 'Dominus Rogerus de Northburgh, custos Domini Regis *targiæ*, ab eo ibidem ablatæ, una cum Dominis Rogero de Wikenselde et Thoma de Switnne, dicti Domini Rogeri clericis, pariter detinebantur ibidem, ob quod Dominus Rex cito postea fieri fecit sigillum, volens illud *privatum sigillum* appellari ad differentiam *targiæ* sic, ut præmittitur, ablatæ;' *Trivet*. contin. p. 15. Spelman understood not the meaning of the word *targia*: He says, *Glossar.* p. 532. '*Targia* pro scuto, a Gall. *Target*. Walf. in Edw. II. A. D. 1314. p. 105. *Rogerus de Northburgh, custos* Targiæ Domini Regis.' The continuator of Trivet seems to distinguish this *targia* from *the privy-seal*.

G 2

ROBERT I.

1314.

Barbour, 277. The Scots were enriched by the spoils of the English camp, and the ransoms of many noble prisoners.

In the treatment of the prisoners who were allotted to him, the King of Scots displayed much generosity. He set at liberty Ralph de Monthermer, and Sir Marmaduke Twenge *, without ransom. By humane and courteous offices, he alleviated the misfortune of the captives, won their affections †, and shewed the English how *they* ought to have improved *their* victories.

Trev. contin. Walsingham, 106. The King of Scots sent the dead bodies of the Earl of Gloucester ‡ and Lord Clifford to be interred in England with the honours due to their birth and valour.

Fœd. xii. 20. There was one Baston, a Carmelite friar, whom Edward had brought with him in his train to be spectator, as was popularly reported, of his atchievements, and to record his triumphs. Baston was made prisoner, and

---

seal. This is a matter of small importance; it may, however, be observed that is is fully explained by an instrument in *Fœdera*, T. iii. p. 483. ' Rex, &c. quia privatum ' sigillum nostrum a nobis est elongatum, tibi præcipimus, &c. ne quis pro aliquo manda- ' to sibi, sub dicto sigillo ex tunc porrigendo, seu etiam liberando, quæquam facias, nisi ' aliud a nobis habuerit mandatum, de priore mandato sub dicto *privato sigillo* con- ' tento, specialem faciens mentionem,' &c. ap Berwick 27th June 1314. Bruce, to shew that he meant nothing dishonourable by holding the seal in his possession, restored it to Edward, under the condition, however, that Edward should not use it; *Trivet,* contin. p. 16.

* He yielded himself up to the King in person, on the day after the battle; during that interval he had lurked in the field undiscovered; *Barbour,* p. 279.

† ' Captivos quos ceperat tam civiliter tractari fecit, tam honorificè custodiri, quod ' corda multorum in amorem sui indivisibiliter commutavit;' *Walsingham,* p. 106.

‡ *Walsingham,* p. 106. Relates a singular incident concerning the succession of the Earl of Gloucester. He left no issue, and the pregnancy of his widow was waited for *during two years* [per biennale tempus]. This is improbable. A learned friend ingeniously conjectures, that *brumale* ought to be read for *biennale,* which makes the sense to be, that her pregnancy was waited for until the end of winter.

1314.

and paid a poet's ransom in a poem on *the Scottish victory at Bannockburn* [*].

The Earl of Hereford had retreated after the battle to the castle of Bothwell. He was besieged there by Edward Bruce, and soon capitulated. He was exchanged for the wife, sister, and daughter of Bruce, for the Bishop of Glasgow, and the young Earl of Marre [†].

Edward Bruce and Douglas entered England by the eastern marches, wasted Northumberland, and laid the bishoprick of Durham under contribution. After having penetrated to Richmond, they proceeded westward, burnt Appleby and other towns, and returned home loaded with plunder. Walsingham avers, that many Englishmen, at that time,

---

[*] 'They are excellent rhymes,' says the continuator of Fordun, 'and ought not to be hid under a bushel, but to be set in a candlestick;' L. xii. c. 22. This poem is well known; and although the rhymes may not be so excellent as the historian imagined, they are curious. The poet begins with lamenting the subject of his work.

' De planctu cudo metrum cum carmine nudo,
' Risum retardo, dum tali themate ludo.'

He prudently disclaims any knowledge of the merits of the quarrel between the two nations.

' Sub quo Rege reo, nescio, teste Deo.'

The intemperance of the English soldiery, mentioned by Th. de la More, affords matter for two lines.

' Dum se sic jactant cum Baccho nocte jocando,
' Scotia, te mactant, verbis vanis reprobando.'

His own singular fate is aptly enough described thus:

' Nescio quid dicam, quum non sevi meto spicam.'

I suspect that this unhappy poet had great part of the description of the battle ready made when he was taken prisoner. His poem is a most extraordinary performance, and must have cost him infinite labour.

† *Barbour* says, p. 285. That Wishart Bishop of Glasgow was now become blind. John de Segrave had been made prisoner at the battle of Bannockburn; he was now exchanged for David de Lindesay, Andrew Murray, Reginald de Lindesay, and Alexander his brother; [10th November 1314,] *Fœdera*, iii. p. 502.

54 ROBERT I.
1314.

time, revolted to the Scots, and aided them in their depredations. 'The English,' adds he, 'were so bereaved of their wonted intrepi-'dity, that a hundred of that nation would have fled from two or 'three Scotsmen *.'

Ford. iii. 491.
—493.

The English King summoned a parliament at Yorke, in order to concert measures for the public security. To repress the incursions of the Scots, he appointed the Earl of Pembroke, formerly Guardian of Scotland, to be Guardian of the country between the Trent and Tweed.

Foed. iii. 495.
—497.

At this season of dejection, the King of Scots made overtures of peace. He wrote to Edward, that a lasting concord between the two nations was his chief wish, and he desired a passport for commissioners to treat on his part †: Edward granted the passport, and appointed commissioners to treat with the Scots, [18th Sept. and 7th October.] But the conclusion of this ruinous war still remained at a distance. The Scots were too prosperous to make any concessions, and the English were not yet sufficiently abased by ill fortune, or enfeebled by faction, to yield every thing.

Chr. Lanercost.
ap. Tyrrel,
iii. 262.
Foed. iii. 498.
506.

The Scots again invaded England; and, without meeting resistance, levied contributions in different places. During the winter, they continued to infest, or to threaten, the English borders ‡.

About

---

* 'Nempe tunc Anglis confusis ademptu suit audacia, ut a facie duorum aut trium 'Scotorum fugerent Angli centum;' *Walsingham*, p. 106. Never were the consequences of a national panic more severely felt.

† Ralph Chilton a friar was the messenger sent by Bruce. The Scottish commissioners were four knights, Nigel Campbell, Roger de Kirkpatrick, Robert de Keith, and Gilbert de la Haye; *Foedera*, T. iii. p. 495. Edward granted the passport, 18th September 1314, and consented to the negotiating a peace, 7th October 1314, [at Yorke] *Foedera*, T. iii. p. 495. 497.

‡ *Tyrrel*, vol. iii. p. 262. says, from the MS. Chronicle of Lanercost, 'The Scots a-'gain entered England by Redesdale and Tindale, driving away the cattle, burning 'the

ROBERT I.

1314.

About this time the unfortunate John Balliol died. He left a son, Edward, the heir of his pretensions to the crown of Scotland.

Ford. lib. 566.

1315.

While the English King vainly endeavoured to assemble an army [*], the Scots again invaded England, penetrated into the bishoprick of Durham, and plundered Hartlepool.

Ford. lib. 511. Chr. Lanercost. ap. Tyrrel lib. 264.

The King of Scots besieged Carlisle, but was repulsed by the valour of the inhabitants, [July 1315.] About the same time, the Scots endeavoured to surprise Berwick, but failed in their enterprise.

Chr. Lanercost. ap. Tyrrel lib. 164.

This year was remarkable for the act settling the succession to the crown of Scotland.

Anderson, Independency of Scotland, app. No. 24.

A parliament was held at Air on Sunday 26th April 1315 [†]. The persons who met were, ' the Bishops, Abbots, Priors, Deans, Archdeacons, and the other prelates of churches. The Earls, Barons, ' Knights,

---

' the towns, and destroying the inhabitants; none being able to resist them. Then ' they went and reduced all Gillesland, (in Cumberland,) so that the people in all ' those parts swore allegiance to the King of Scots, and paid him tribute. In the space ' of six months, the county of Cumberland alone paid no less than six hundred merks ' for its share.' Tyrrel observes, that this happened *even whilst the English parliament was sitting*; as if that assembly could have been formidable to the Scots while dissensions and party animosities prevailed in it.

[*] *Walsingham*, p. 107. well describes the state of England at that time : ' In quindena Paschae Rex per brevia citari fecit ad parliamentum Londoniis praelatos et proceres regnique communes. Sed quia multi de magnatibus impedimentorum causas praetenderunt, per quas merito excusati poterat eorum absentia, dictum parliamentum tunc temporis nullum sortiebatur effectum. Sed unusquisque sunt Londoniis congregatorum quo sibi placuit divertebat, et qui terram defendere tenebantur,' vacabant ' otio et jocis.' Edward had just before caused the body of Gaveston to be raised and re-interred with great funeral pomp; *Walsingham*, p. 106. This injudicious measure served, no doubt, to exasperate the malecontent Lords who had murdered Gaveston.

[†] ' Domini 1 proximâ ante festum Apostolorum Philippi et Jacobi.' Mr Ruddiman, *not. ad Buchanan*, mistakes the feast of St Philip and St James for the feast of the other St James; and hence he places this event in July 1315. The mistake is not trivial, for it throws that part of our history into inextricable confusion.

ROBERT I.

1315.

'Knights, and others of the community of the Kingdom of Scotland,
'as well clergy as laity.' Their resolutions were unanimous, and in
substance as follows *.

I. They all and each became bound to be faithful, and bear true
allegiance to Robert King of Scots, and the heirs-male to be lawfully
procreated of his body, and *that against all men*.

II. With the consent of the King, and of Marjory his daughter,
and heir *apparent* †, they ordained that, in case the King should die
without leaving heirs-male of his body, then his brother, Edward
Bruce, as a man of valour, and one much tried in war for the defence
of the rights and liberty of Scotland ‡, should succeed to the kingdom; and, failing him, the heirs-male lawfully to be procreated of his
body.

III.

---

* This act of settlement is in *Anderson*, Independency of Scotland, *appendix*, No 24.
It is also to be found in *Fordun*, L. xii. c. 24. There are some variations between the
two transcripts; but they are too minute to deserve notice.

† 'De consensu—Marjorae filiae.' Marjory, at that time, was the only child of Robert I. She is said to be *haeres apparens* of the King. It is hardly necessary to remark,
that *apparens* is here incorrectly used for *praesumptivus*.

‡ 'Tanquam vir strenuus, et in actibus bellicis, pro defensione juris et libertatis reg-
'ni Scotiae, quamplurimum expertus.' *Abercrombie*, vol. i. p 632. says, that 'Ed-
'ward Bruce, since the lawful son of his father, had, but for his being the second bro-
'ther, as much right to the crown as King Robert himself; nay, had he [Robert] been
'a woman, would have been preferred to him; but King Robert was a man, and the
'eldest brother, and reigned accordingly.' Here there is the appearance of a solemn
argument, which implies, if I misunderstand not the author, 'That Edward, if he had
'been the eldest son, as well as Robert, would have had as good a right to the crown
'as Robert; nay, more, that he would have had a better right than Robert, if Robert
'had been a woman, for then Edward the son would have been preferred to Robert
'the daughter; but Robert was a man, and not a woman, was the eldest son, and not
'the second, and therefore was preferred.' q. e. d. !

Abercrombie

ROBERT. I.

1315.

III. With the consent of the King, and of Edward Bruce [*], it was provided, that, failing Edward, and the heirs-male of his body, Marjory, and failing her, the nearest heir lineally descended of the body of Robert, King of Scots, should succeed to the crown; but under this condition,

Abercrombie adds, 'upon the decease of Robert, *Who* ought, by *the then constitu-tion*, to succeed? No doubt the children of the eldest brother, if males, if not, the second brother, Edward, *because a male, and, as such, preferable to any woman what-ever in the same degree and relation to his father*. For this reason 'twas, that Robert Bruce, the competitor, was, by King Alexander's determination, and the peoples judgment, preferred to Dervergild: And for that same reason did King Robert, and the parliament he held at Air in the year 1315, declare, with express consent of *Marjory his only daughter*, that if he should have no heirs-male of his own body, the Lord Edward Bruce his brother-german, and the heirs-male of his body, should suc-ceed him in the throne. It is true, that the act itself enlarges upon the great worth and noble atchievements performed in defence of the nation by the Lord Edward. And why should not the parliament put all the just value they could upon the suc-cessor of their King? Indeed, *'twas at that time highly necessary*, that a man capable to perfect the great work begun by King Robert, should, in case of his death, be made to supply his deficiency. Upon that account, most authors think, that, con-trary to the rights of hereditary monarchy, this settlement was made; and that, for that reason, the express and willing resignation of Princess Marjory was required. It may be so; for it cannot be doubted but a sovereign may resign, if not for his heirs, at least for himself.' From all this crude and perplexed reasoning, it is im-possible to discover whether Abercrombie was of opinion that the King's brother did, of right, exclude, or did not exclude, the King's daughter. Indeed, he seems to have blended together the three several hypothesis, that *the heir-male* was preferred, 1*st*, of right; 2*d*, by reason of the present exigencies of the state; and, 3*d*, by express cove-nant with *the heir-female*. After all, he says, 'To me it seems probable, that, in those days, the uncle was thought preferable to the niece.' It will be remarked, that this seems adverse to the record, which mentions Marjory as the *heir* of Robert I. and as a consenter to the limitations.

[*] 'De consensu—dicti Domini Edwardi.' Edward Bruce, if once in possession, might have pretended, that the right of governing ought to devolve on his issue at large, and, therefore, his consent to this limitation was required.

1315.

condition, that Marjory should marry with the consent of her father, or, after his death, with the consent of the majority of the community or states of Scotland *.

IV. Should the King, or his brother, die during the minority of the heir-male of their bodies, it was ordained that Thomas Randolph, Earl of Moray, should be the Guardian of the heir, and of the kingdom, until the major part of the states should hold the heir fit to administer the government in his own person †.

V. Should Marjory die in widowhood, leaving an heir under age, and succeeding to the crown, the Earl of Moray shall be Guardian of the heir, and of the kingdom, if he chuses to accept the office ‡.

VI. Should Marjory die, and there remain no heir of the body of Robert King of Scots, the Earl of Moray shall be Guardian of the Kingdom, if he chuses to accept that office, until the Prelates, Earls, Barons,

---

* ' Dum tamen de consensu dicti Domini Regis, vel, ipso deficiente, quod absit, ' de consensu majoris partis communitatis regni, dicta Marjoria matrimonialiter fuerit ' copulata.' Whether the King and parliament did in this exceed their powers, I inquire not. Certain, however, it is, *that the succession of Marjory was, by the act of settlement, made to depend upon her marrying with the consent of her father, or, after his death, with the consent of the majority of the community or states of Scotland.*

† ' Quousque communitati regni, vel majori parti, visum fuerit, ipsum haeredem ad ' sui regni regimen posse sufficere.' It is impossible to suppose that a power was referred to the states of protracting the minority of the Sovereign beyond his *perfect age*. A power to *abridge* the minority of the Sovereign is the only thing here implied.

‡ ' Si idem comes ad hoc suum praebuerit consensum.' It would seem that the Earl of Moray had consented to accept the office of Guardian to the issue-male of Robert I. and Edward Bruce, but that he had reserved to himself liberty of declining the office, in case the succession should devolve on females.—Supposing Marjory to have predeceased her husband, and to have left issue, this statute has not said who should be Guardian of her children, and of the kingdom. The possibility of this event must have been foreseen; perhaps it appeared too delicate to be a matter of discussion; and yet the neglect in providing for it might have excited a fatal controversy between the states and the surviving husband of Marjory.

1315.

Barons, and others of the community of Scotland, may be conveniently assembled to consider and determine as to the rightful succession to the crown of Scotland *.

VII. *Lastly*, The parties submitted themselves, and their successors, to the jurisdiction of the Bishops and Prelates of Scotland, whereby they might be compelled, by all spiritual censures, to observe and fulfil the premisses †.

The

* It is remarkable that the states of Scotland declined to come under any obligations to the issue-female of Edward Bruce.

† ' Se in jurisdictionem Episcoporum et Praelatorum regni Scotiae submiserunt.' I understand this to imply, that the provincial council, or general assembly of the Scottish clergy, might enforce the observance of the act of settlement, by the terror of ecclesiastical censures. To have invested every dignified churchman with such authority, would have been elusory or absurd.

Anciently, provisions of this nature were frequent in deeds executed by private persons. Thus, Reginald de Chene, in a grant to the chapter of Moray, says, ' Et si con-
' tingat, quod absit, me vel haeredes meos, vel aliquem haeredum meorum, contra
' praemissa in toto vel in parte, de facto vel de jure venire, volo et concedo, pro me et
' haeredibus meis, quod Episcopi Aberdonensis et Sancti Andreae, et eorum officiales,
' qui pro tempore fuerint, vel eorundem Episcoporum vel officialium alter possint vel
' possit me et haeredes meos ad observationem omnium et singulorum praemisforum,
' per censuram ecclesiasticam, sine strepitu judiciali, compellere et coercere;' *Chart.*
Morav. vol. I. fol. 2.—A grant of the lands of Drumeleisinene bears these words:
' Horum omnium testes et fidejussores Episcopum Glasconensem et Comitem Dune-
' canum et haeredes ejus [elegi], ut si aliquando ego vel haeredes mei a tenore hujus
' cartae deviaverimus, ipsa ecclesia et ejus pontifices per censuram ecclesiasticam ad
' correctionem nos revocent. Haec autem omnia propria manu affidavi in manu Domini
' Jocelini Glasguen. Episcopi;' *Chart. Melros* fol. 46.—Resignation was made upon oath of the lands of Ardoch, by *Robertus dictus* Frank *de Lambenister*, in the presence of Alexander [III.] King of Scots, *et Regni magnatum ap. Rokesburgh*, 13. Kal. Jul. 1266. with this proviso, that if he ever made any claim to the lands, ' concedo quod
' ab agendo unquam perjurii repellamur, et quod omnis actus judicialis nobis tan-
' quam perjuris omni modo interdicatur.' He subjects himself to the jurisdiction of

the

1315.

The King of Scots gave his daughter Marjory in marriage to Walter the Stewart of Scotland [*].

Ford. xii. 15.
An. Hibern.
ap. Camden.
Britannia.

The Irish of Ulster, oppressed by the English government, implored the aid of the King of Scots, and offered to acknowledge his brother Edward for their sovereign.

The wisdom of the King of Scots must have foreseen, that, to expel the English from Ireland, unite the discordant factions of the Irish, and reconcile them to the dominion of a stranger, was an enterprise attended with mighty, if not insuperable difficulties. Yet there were motives which engaged him in an undertaking seemingly beyond his strength. The offer of a crown, however visionary, inflamed the ambition of Edward Bruce, whose intrepid spirit never saw obstacles in the path to fame. It might have appeared ungenerous, and, perhaps it would not have been politic or safe, to have rejected the proposals of the Irish for the advancement of a brother, to whom the King of Scots owed more than he could recompense. Besides, the invasion of Ireland seemed to afford a fit expedient for dividing the forces, and multiplying the perplexities of the English.

An. Hibern.
ut sup.
Barbour, 288.

Edward Bruce landed with six thousand men at Carrickfergus, in the north of Ireland [†], [25th May 1315.] The principal persons who accom-

the Bishop of Glasgow, and consents to be *excommunicated*, and *also* to pay a penalty of L. 200 Sterling, ' ut quos divinus amor a malo non amoveat, poenalis saltem ti-' mor coerceat;' *Chart. Melros,* fol. 73.

In this parliament, Randolph appears under the title of Earl of Moray. The grant of the earldom of Moray to Randolph is printed, *Essays concerning British Antiquities,* § 103.—109. I have never been able to discover its precise date. Sir James Balfour, Lion King at arms, in his MS. collections, supposes the grant to have been made in the 7th year of Robert I.

[*] The grant which the King made to the Stewart, in consequence of this marriage, is to be found in *Crawfurd, History of the house of Stewart,* p. 14.

[†] Edward Bruce embarked at Air, where the parliament had been lately held; *Barbour,*

1315.

accompanied him in this expedition were, Thomas Randolph Earl of Moray, Sir Philip Moubray, Sir John Soulis, Sir John Stewart, Sir Fergus of Ardrossan, and Ramsay of Ochterhouse *.

The Irish Lords of Ulster repaired to the standard of Edward Bruce, solemnly engaged themselves in his service, and gave hostages for performance of their engagements: Aided by his new subjects, he ravaged, with merciless barbarity, the possessions of the English settlers in the north †.

Lib. Clonmacnois. MS. ap. T. Leland. l. 266. 267.

The Scottish army stormed and plundered Dundalk, [29th June.] They burnt that town, together with Atherdee, and other places of less note.

Annal. Hiber. ut sup.

To repel this invasion, Richard de Burgh, Earl of Ulster, assembled his vassals, and having been joined by some Irish chiefs of Connaught, marched through the county of Meath, and entered the northern province, spreading desolation around him.

Lib. Clonmac. MS. ut sup.

Edmond

hour, p. 288. It is probable that the expedition was undertaken with the approbation of the parliament.

* The Annals of Ireland, subjoined to Camden's *Britannia*, add the following persons, John Menteith, John de Bosco, John Bisset, and John Campbell, the son, as it would seem, of Sir Niel Campbell of Lochow, and nephew of the King of Scots.

† The history of this invasion is imperfectly known. Several circumstances concerning it are related in the annals of Ireland, subjoined to Camden's Britannia; but they are related in a perplexed manner, as might well be expected in a work which is an injudicious compilation of different chronicles. Barbour has given a long account of the events of that war. It would seem that he gathered his intelligence from the stragglers who survived the Irish campaigns. He often mistakes the names of places and persons. He figured to himself that Richard d'Clare was the English deputy in Ireland; and, from an error natural enough, he supposed that the deputy always commanded the armies opposed to Edward Bruce. He omits some events altogether, and is too apt to magnify skirmishes into battles; yet his narrative contains circumstances curious and characteristical.

1315.

An. Hibern.
ut sup.

Edmond Butler, the justiciary of Ireland *, collected the forces of Leinster, [about 22d July,] and offered to assist the Earl of Ulster in repelling the invaders: 'You may return home,' said the haughty Earl, 'I and my vassals will overcome the Scots.' Butler withdrew his troops, and left the conduct of the war to the Earl of Ulster.

Barbur, 306.
An. Hibern.
ut sup.

The Scots precipitantly retreated, and were pursued by Ulster: They halted near Coyners. The English, ignorant of the motions of an enemy whom they despised, advanced to the attack; the Scots, by the counsel of Sir Philip Moubray, left their banners flying in the camp †, and having made a circuit, suddenly assaulted the flank of the English army. The English fell into confusion, and were routed, [10th September.] Lord William Burk, and many other persons of distinction, were made prisoners. Some of the fugitives, under the command of Lord Poer of Dunville, retired into the castle of Carrickfergus, where their valour and perseverance checked the progress of the Scots.

An Hibern.
ut sup.

Soon after this battle, Randolph repaired to Scotland in order to procure reinforcements ‡, [15th September.] Meanwhile Edward Bruce pressed the siege of the castle of Carrickfergus. His efforts were vain, and he at length abandoned the enterprise, [6th December.]

---

* In those days, the English deputy, or Lord Lieutenant, was termed the *Justiciary*, or *Justice*. The vestiges of that appellation are still to be discerned in the phrase, Lords *Justices*.

† If I mistake not, this simple stratagem has been successfully employed in later wars. It can never succeed, unless against a commander equally opinionative and remiss.

‡ Randolph took with him Lord William Burk [or de Burgh], who had been made prisoner in the late affray. By a mistake of the transcriber, it is said in *Annal. Hibern.* ap. Camden. that Randolph had with him ' Lord William *Brus*,' (instead of *Burk*.) From the name *Bruce*, Cox concluded that this person must have been the *brother* of Edward Bruce; and hence he has confidently said, that ' Edward sent his *brother William Bruce* into Scotland for a supply;' *Hist. of Ireland*, vol. I. p. 93. It is well known that no such person existed.

1315.

ber.] Randolph joined him with 500 men. They marched southwards by Dundalk, and penetrated through Meath into Kildare.
Near Aricull in Kildare, the Scots encountered Edmond Butler the justiciary. The English, although far superior in numbers to the Scots, were enfeebled by difcord, and became an easy prey to their enemies. Unmindful of their duty, and of their reputation in arms, they fled. In this action two Scottish commanders, Fergus of Ardroffan, and Walter Moray, were slain, [26th January.]

An. Hibern. ut sup.

At this time, a famine, grievous beyond example, prevailed in Ireland. Many of the Scots perished through want, in a country which their favage and inconsiderate fury had desolated. Edward Bruce, unable to procure subsistance for his army, again retreated towards the province of Ulster, [14th February.]

An. Hibern. ut sup.

Roger, Lord Mortimer, endeavoured to cut off the retreat of the Scots. His numerous troops were dispersed by the Scots at Kenlis in Meath*. Mortimer, with a few attendants, took refuge in Dublin.

An. Hibern. ut sup.

The

---

* I have placed the rout at Kenlis, after the engagement where the justiciary was defeated. In this point of chronology the Annals of Ireland, published by Camden, contradict themselves. I must acknowledge that I perused, with no small surprise, the account of this war, as given by Dr Leland, Hist. of Ireland. vol. 1. B. 2. c. 3. although he quotes Camden in every page, he may be said to have overlooked, or to have placed in a doubting parenthesis, every battle in which the Irish Annals, published by C. mden, represent Bruce as victorious. Thus, of the battle where the Earl of Ulster was defeated, he says, p 268. ' We are told, that after some inconsiderable actions, a ge-
' neral battle was fought, which ended in the difconfiture of Richard. However this
' may be, the advantage could not be effectually secured,' &c. Of the action in Kildare, where the justiciary was defeated, Dr Leland says not a word. How are we to reconcile this with the generous sentiment in his preface, ' Even at this day, the
' Historian of Irish affairs must be armed against censure, only by an integrity which
' confines him to truth, and a literary courage which despises every charge but that of
' wilful and careless misrepresentation?' What he says concerning the difaster of Mortimer is remarkable: After having related the assembling of an army at Kilkenny in 1317.

64 ROBERT I.

1315.

This difaster was afcribed, but I know not with what truth, to the treachery of the Lacies who ferved under the banners of Mortimer.

An. Hibern. ut fup. Edward Bruce now affumed the office of chief magiftrate in Ulfter, tried caufes, and inflicted capital punifhments on offenders. Randolph again departed into Scotland to procure additional fuccours [*], [about the beginning of March.]

Barbour, 314. Throughout the year 1315, Scotland enjoyed a tranquillity to which fhe had been long ftranger. The King of Scots made an expedition into the weftern ifles, and without meeting any refiftance, reduced them under his government [†].

Marjory

1317, he adds, 'Intelligence arrived, that Roger Mortimer of Wigmore, a nobleman 'who is faid, by fome hiftorians, to have already taken a part in the prefent war, and to 'have been defeated by Bruce, had arrived at Youghall with a train of forty knights and 'their attendants, to take upon him the adminiftration of government, and was on his 'march to join the main body.' Here, while fpeaking of what happened in 1317, Dr Leland hints at what is faid to have happened in 1315-16; and he feems to queftion the truth of the event, as related by hiftorians. I cannot account for his fcepticifm as to the defeat of the Earl of Ulfter, or for his omitting altogether the defeat of Butler the Jufticiary; but I think that one may trace the origin of his hefitation in treating of the difafter which befel Mortimer. He faw that Mortimer, invefted with the fupreme command, arrived at Youghall about the beginning of the year 1317; hence he too haftily concluded, that Mortimer was a ftranger in Ireland until 1317, and confequently could not have commanded an army at Kenlis in 1315-16. But the truth is, that although Mortimer was not appointed jufticiary till 23d November 1316, *Fædera*, T. lii. p. 580. 581. yet he had refided much in Ireland before that time, as appears from the Annals publifhed by Camden; neither will it efcape obfervation, that when the Annals fpeak of his ill fortune in the war with Bruce, they call him *Lord Mortimer*, and not *Jufticiary*, and that the fame Annals mention his arrival as jufticiary in 1317.

[*] The Irifh Annals fay, 'In the firft week of Lent.' In 1316, Eafter day fell on the 11th of April.

[†] It feems that John of Lorn, who had been driven from Scotland in 1308, ftill maintained himfelf in the weftern iflands *Barbour*, p. 314. relates, that the King of Scots drew his veffels acrofs *the Tarbet*, or neck of Land which joins Knapdale to

Cantire;

ROBERT I.

1315.

Marjory the King's daughter, and wife of the Stewart of Scotland, died *, leaving an only child *Robert* (born 2d March 1315-16.)

Ford. lib. 15.
Excerpta e
Chron. MS.
Adv. Lib.

1316.

Edward Bruce now refumed the fiege of the caftle of Carrickfergus. Thomas Lord Mandeville, with a confiderable body of troops, haftened to its relief, and found means to enter the caftle. The Scots were over fecure in their quarters; fixty men, commanded by Neil Fleming, were their only guard. Early in the morning after his arrival, Mandeville made a defperate fally. Fleming perceived that the Scots were furprifed, and that, unlefs they had time to array themfelves, all was irretrievably loft. He refolved to devote himfelf and his companions for the prefervation of the army. 'Now, of a truth,' cried he, 'fhall men fee how we can die for our Lord.' He defpatched a meffenger to fpread the alarm, and advanced, and checked the firft impetuofity of Mandeville. Fleming received a mortal wound, and, of all his companions, not one was left alive. Mandeville fent part of his troops to environ the quarters of the Scots, that none might efcape. Himfelf, with a chofen body, proceeded through the principal ftreet. He was encountered by Edward Bruce and his houfehold. Among them was one Gilbert Harper, renowned in the Scottifh army for ftrength and intrepidity. Harper, the firft in the affray, knew Mandeville by his armour, and, with one blow of his battle-ax, felled him

Barbour, 3 cft.
An. Hibern.
ut fup.

Cantire: That the inhabitants of the neighbouring iflands had a prophecy among them, importing, that they were never to be fubdued, unlefs by him who fhould fail acrofs the Tarbat: That they confidered the prophecy as now fulfilled, and fubmitted themfelves. That Bruce might have drawn his flight veffel acrofs the ifthmus, is not impoffible; but it is not probable that he, who was acquainted with thofe feas, fhould have beftowed fo much labour, merely to avoid doubling the Mull of Cantire.

* Concerning the manner of her death, fee a differtation in the Appendix.

1316.

him to the ground. The English were daunted at the loss of their commander, while the Scots, increasing in numbers, pressed on, and were gallantly seconded by two hundred Irish spearmen [*]. The English sought refuge in the castle; but the garrison, fearing lest the enemy should rush in, drew up the bridge, shut the gates, and abandoned their companions to the fury of the conquerors [†], [11th April.]

When the carnage had ceased, Bruce surveyed the field. He found Fleming in the agonies of death, and all his soldiers stretched around him. He bitterly lamented their fate: 'Howbeit,' says Barbour, ' he 'was not wont to bewail himself; neither could he endure to hear men 'make lamentation.'

Barbour, 313.

The garrison of the castle of Carrickfergus consented to surrender, unless relief arrived within a limited space.

Barbour, 315. An. Hibern. ut sup.

Edward Bruce was solemnly crowned King of Ireland [‡], [2d May.] He

An. Hibern. ut sup.

---

[*] *Barbour*, p. 312. says, That the spearmen were commanded by M'Nahil; not knowing any such name in Scotland, I presume that he was some Irish commander.

[†] *Barbour*, p. 308. says, That a truce had been concluded, to endure until Tuesday after Easter, i. e. until the 13th of April, but that Mandeville brought the succours to the castle on Easter-eve, and, in violation of the truce, attacked the Scots on the morning of Easter-day, [11th April.] The Irish Annals in Camden give a different account. They say, that Mandeville having brought succours to the castle, skirmished successfully with the Scots on the 8th and 10th days of April, and that, in another encounter with them, he was slain, about the kalends; whether this means the 16th April or the 1st May, is not certain; it more probably means the 16th April; for Edward Bruce was crowned on the 2d May, and it is not to be presumed that that ceremony was performed on the very day after the action. Barbour's account is exceedingly distinct; he speaks so forcibly of the guilt of violating the truce, and disregarding the sanctity of Easter, that it is plain he did not invent the story. The truth seems to have been this: The garrison had agreed to a truce; but Mandeville, by a kind of military casuistry, did not consider himself, and the succours which he brought, as bound by the agreement which the garrison had made.

[‡] ' Post &c. Quum S. Philippi et Jacobi Apostolorum ;' *Annal. Hibern.* The translation, in Gibson's edition of *Britannia*, says, ' *After* the feast of St Philip and St James.'

Nothing

1316.

He required the garrison of the castle of Carrickfergus to surrender according to treaty, [31st May.] To this the English agreed, and desired that a detachment from the Scottish army might be sent in to take possession of the place. Thirty men were sent; but the English treacherously seized them, and declared that they would defend the castle to the uttermost *.

Meanwhile, the King of Scots had formed the magnanimous resolution of conducting in person a reinforcement to his brother. He intrusted the kingdom, in his absence, to the Stewart and Douglas, embarked at Lochrian in Galloway, and landed at Carrickfergus.

The garrison of the castle of Carrickfergus, after having endured the extremities of famine, capitulated. They had subsisted for some time on the hides of beasts, and it is even said, that hunger constrained them to feed on the Scots whom they had basely made prisoners. Nevertheless their savage obstinacy was in vain. The great English Lords of Ireland professed much zeal for the interest of the public, and formed loyal associations; yet they suffered Carrickfergus to be reduced by famine.

At length, after the fortress was lost, the English appeared in Ulster. John Logan † and Hugh Lord Bisset encountered and defeated

An. Hibern. ut sup.
Ford. lii. 25. Barbour, 314.
An. Hibern. ut sup.
An. Hibern. ut sup.

---

a Nothing can be more ridiculous than that English version. Thus we have, 'after the 'feast of *Carnis Privium*,' for 'the day following *Shrove Tuesday*,' and 'the Lord 'Piacern,' for 'Lord Butler.'

* I should have hesitated to relate this incident, had its authenticity depended on the testimony of the enemies of the English; but it is mentioned in the annals of Ireland, a work by no means unfavourable to the English. I do not observe any mention made of it by the Scottish historians.

† I should conjecture that the name of this person was *Cogan*, not *Logan*. But I dare not depart from the printed authorities.

68   ROBERT I.

1316.

a part of the Scottish army *, [25th October.] In this action, Allan Stewart was made prisoner †.

An. Hibern. ut sup.

The King of Scots, and his brother, by forced marches, passed through the county of Lowth, and advanced to Slane, [10th February]. The annals of Ireland report, that the Scottish army, consisting of 20,000 men, eluded the English who were posted to prevent their entrance into the province of Leinster. Barbour, however, asserts, that the King of Scots fought and defeated the English. It is probable that some slight action may have been magnified by partial relaters into a general battle.

Barbour, 307.

Some circumstances reported by Barbour to have happened previous to this battle, are lively and characteristical. The Scottish army, while passing through a wood, marched in two divisions. The first was led by Edward Bruce, and the other by the King. The English lay concealed in the wood, purposing to attack the rear, as soon as the first division had passed. Edward Bruce, with his wonted impetuosity, hurried on, regardless of his brother, who advanced slowly, and with circumspection. The English archers, in small parties, began to annoy the rear of the Scottish army. The King concluded, that stragglers advancing so far were powerfully supported; and, therefore, enjoined his soldiers to move on in order of battle, and on no pretence whatever to leave their ranks. It happened that two English yeomen

---

* The Irish annals seem to mention the principal loss as having been of the cavalry. It is said, that 300 of them were slain, and 300 made prisoners. Hence I am induced to believe, that it was part of the army brought over by the King of Scots, which Logan and Bisset overthrew. It is not probable that Edward Bruce would have had such a body of cavalry left, after having remained so long in an impoverished country. The place where this engagement happened is unknown.

† He appears to have been a chief commander; for the annals of Ireland mention his being brought to Dublin as a remarkable event, [5th December 1316.] He was, if I mistake not, the eldest son of Robert Stewart of Darnley and Crookstoun; *Crawfurd*, History of the house of Stewart, p. 72.

1316.

yeomen discharged their arrows at Sir Colin Campbell, the King's nephew. The youth rod off at full speed to revenge the insult. The King followed, and struck him so violently with his truncheon, that he was well nigh unhorsed. 'Return,' cried the King, 'your diso-
'bedience might have brought us all into jeopardy.' After the English were dispersed, Edward Bruce regretted his having been absent. 'It was owing to your own folly,' replied the King; 'you ought to
'have remembered that the van must always protect the rear *.'

The Scottish army advanced towards Dublin: On its fate the existence of the English government in Ireland depended. The public spirit, and intrepidity of the citizens of Dublin, at that critical season, ought to be held in perpetual remembrance. They burnt their suburbs, which might have facilitated the approach of the enemy; demolished a church, repaired and strengthened their walls with its materials, and resolved to defend their city, or perish amidst its ruins. *An. Hibern. ut sup.*

Hardly can the patriotic zeal of the populace be ever restrained within the bounds of reason and law. The Earl of Ulster, suspected of favouring the Scottish invaders, was seized, and committed to prison, by the Mayor of Dublin. This commitment appears to have been equally illegal and extravagant, and without a colourable plea of necessity. The sister of the Earl of Ulster, it is true, had married the King of Scots; but that alliance with Scotland ought not to have excited

---

* This is related by *Barbour*, p. 331. 332. in the following words:

'And when Sir Edward Bruce the bold
'Wist that the King had foughten so,
'With so feil folk, and he therefro,
'Might no man see a waer man.
'But the good King said to him than,
'That it was in his own folly,
'For he rade so unwittingly
'So far before, and *his vanguard*
'*Made to them of the rereward*, &c.

ROBERT I.

1316.

cited fufpicions of *his* fidelity, who from intereft, no lefs than honour, was the implacable enemy of Edward Bruce.

An. Hibern. ut fup.

The King of Scotland, and his brother, took poffeffion of Caftle Cnoc [*], [23d February]. Defpairing, however, of fuccefs againft Dublin, they turned afide, and encamped at Leixflip [†], on the banks of Liffy, [25th February]. Having remained there during four days, they marched to Naas, and arrived at Callen, in the county of Kilkenny, [12th March]. Their rapacious and unruly foldiers ravaged the country, plundered and burnt religious houfes and churches, and even violated the fepulchres of the dead in queft of treafures.

An. Hibern. ut fup. Barbour, 331.

It is certain, however ftrange, that the Scots carried their arms as far as Limerick [‡]. We cannot determine what were the motives which induced the two brothers to undertake a march fo long and hazardous, efpecially at that feafon of the year. That they led their troops from Carrickfergus to Limerick, by the way of Dublin, merely to brave the power of the Englifh government, or to expofe its weaknefs, would be an extravagant fuppofition. Perhaps, by placing themfelves at Limerick, in the center, as it were, of Connaught and Mounfter, they hoped to excite the Irifh chiefs of thofe provinces to repair to their ftandard. It is, however, a more probable conjecture,

---

[*] Near Dublin, beyond Phoenix Park. This caftle belonged to the Tyrrels. *Camden*, p. 994.

[†] Called, in the annals of Ireland, *Salmon leap*. I cannot omit the account of this campaign by *Tyrrel*, vol. iii. p. 268. It is concife. 'The Scots durft not befiege Dublin, but approaching near it, turned back to Leiflip, which they burnt, and then marched to the Naas, and plundering it, went back into the north ; fo that I do not find that King Robert performed any great matter in Ireland this fummer.' It muft appear fingular that Tyrrel fhould have told this ftory, and yet have quoted *Annal. Hibern.* as his voucher.

[‡] In *Barbour*, p. 331. it is called *Kinrile*. The errors committed by tranfcribers, in that once popular book, are very numerous.

1316.

jecture, that famine constrained the Scots to roam for sustenance into the remote parts of the island, while by their licence and ravages they carried with them and diffused that calamity which they sought to avoid.

1317.

Meantime the English assembled all their forces in the neighbourhood of Kilkenny, [31st March.] It might have been expected that the commanders of an army far superior in numbers to the Scots [*], would have concurred in some plan, either for advancing to attack the enemy, or for preventing their return into the east parts of Ireland; yet, instead of acting, they deliberated, and they held councils of war during a whole week, without forming any final resolution. *An. Hibern. ut sup.*

At this juncture the celebrated Roger Mortimer, invested with the character of deputy, landed from England, [7th April.] He despatched orders to Butler, his predecessor in office, and to the other English commanders, not to attempt any thing against the Scots before his arrival at the army. On his arrival he learned that the Scots, by forced marches, had extricated themselves from the embarrassment of their position, and while the English were deliberating as to the mode of carrying on the war in Mounster, had secured their own retreat to Kildare. Mortimer dismissed to their respective abodes the tumultuary troops assembled at Kilkenny. The Scots, after having halted for some *An. Hibern. ut sup.*

---

[*] The annals of Ireland make the army to amount to 30,000 men. It is probable that this is greatly exaggerated. As, however, the same annals make the Scots to have been 20,000 strong at the beginning of this winter campaign, we may conclude, that the exaggeration, as to the force of each army, is proportional; and, consequently, that the English, assembled at Kilkenny, were more numerous than the Scots. The chief commanders of the English were, Edmond Butler the deputy, Thomas Fitz-John, Earl of Kildare, Richard Clare, Arnold Poer, Maurice Rochfort, and Thomas Fitz-Maurice.

1317.

some days near Trim, returned into Ulster, (about the beginning of May 1317)

Ford. xii. 25. In the course of this fruitless expedition, the Scots were reduced to the necessity of feeding on horse flesh, and multitudes of them perished through hunger *. The King repaired soon after to his own dominions, with the glory of having over-run Ireland, at the expence of the lives of many of his most faithful subjects.

Barbour, 334. —340. Leland. i. 547. During his absence, the English had made various attempts to disturb the tranquility of Scotland. The Earl of Arundel, with a numerous body, invaded the forest of Jedburgh. Douglas drew the English into an ambush, forced them to fight at disadvantage, and defeated them. In this action Thomas de Richemont was slain †. Ed-
Barbour, 316. Leland. i. 547 mond de Cailaud ‡, a knight of Gascony, and governor of Berwick, made

---

* ' In eadem expeditione multi fame perierunt; reliqui vero carnibus equorum us
' sunt;' *Fordun,* L. xii. c. 25. The annals of Ireland say, ' That the Irish who were
' with the Scottish army, eat flesh in Lent without any necessity; and that, next year,
' they were punished for their sin, being constrained, through famine, to eat one
' another.' The same annals add, ' That it was reported, that some wretches had dug
' dead bodies out of the graves, *boiled the flesh in their skulls,* and fed on it;' as if the
famine had consumed the spits and the kettles! But the aim of the annalist was to
display the enormity of the sin of eating flesh in the season of Lent. It is probable
that the poor Irish violated Lent by eating horse-flesh; this, surely, was a venial transgression.

† *Barbour,* p. 337. supposes, that Thomas de Richemont commanded the English;
but *Scal. Chron.* ap. Leland, T. i. p. 547. says, ' King Edwarde sent the Erle of Arun-
' del as capitayne yn to the marches of Scotlande, where he sofered reprouche by James
' Duglas at Lincelby, yn the forest of Jedworth, and ther was Thomas of Richemont
' slayne.' Barbour says, that Thomas de Richemont fell by the hand of Douglas, and
that Douglas took the furred hat which he wore above his helmet. In *Histoire de Bretagne par Lobineau,* T. i p 665. there is a portrait of Arthur de Richemont, Duke of
Britany, with *a furred hat,* such as is described by Barbour.

‡ Such I conjecture his name to have been. *Barbour,* p. 316. calls him *de Cailow.*
In *Fordun,* L. xii. c. 25. he is called *Aylow.* Both these words are evidently corrupted.

1317.

made an inroad into Teviotdale, and wasted the country. While he was returning loaded with spoil, Douglas set on him, and killed him, and many Gascons under his command. Intelligence was conveyed to Douglas that Robert Neville had boasted that he would encounter him whenever he saw his banner displayed. Douglas advanced to the neighbourhood of Berwick, displayed his banner, burnt some villages, and provoked Neville to take the field. Neville fell, and his forces were discomfited *.

The English invaded Scotland by sea, and anchored off Inverkeithing in the frith of Forth †. Five hundred men, under the command of the Earl of Fyfe and the sheriff of that county, attempted to oppose their landing; but, intimidated by the numbers of the English, they made a precipitate retreat. William Sinclair, Bishop of Dunkeld, happened to meet the fugitives ‡; 'Whither are you flying?' said he to the commanders, 'You deserve to have your gilt spurs hacked off.' Then throwing aside his ecclesiastical vestment, he seized a spear, and cried, 'Who loves Scotland, follow me.' He led the Scots again to the charge, and impetuously attacked the enemy, who had not compleated their landing. The English gave way, and were driven to their ships,

* In Scot. Chron. ap. Leland, T. i. p. 547. It is said, 'the same James Douglas, by ' treason of the marchers, discomfited the band of Englishmen at Berwike, where Ro' bert Neville was slain.' It is not explained wherein the treason of the marchers consisted.

† Barbour, p. 341. says, that the English landed to the west of Inverkeithing; but Fordun, L. xii. c. 25. says, that they landed at Dooibriffel, which lies to the east of that place. The variation is of little consequence: It serves, however, to show, that Fordun did not implicitly transcribe from Barbour.

‡ He had a country-seat at Ouchtertool, in that neighbourhood; Fordun, L. xii. c. 25. Barbour, p. 344. says, that the Bishop was 'right hardy, mcikle, and stark.' This courageous prelate was the brother of Henry Sinclair of Roslin. See Keith, catalogue of Bishops, p. 51.

Vol. II.   K

74   ROBERT I.

1317.

ships, with considerable loss. When the King heard of the intrepidity of this prelate, he said, 'Sinclair shall be my bishop, under the appellation of *the King's Bishop*.' Sinclair was long remembered by his countrymen.

Ford. lib. iii. 594. After the return of the King of Scots from his expedition into Ireland, Pope John XXII. issued a bull commanding a truce for two years between England and Scotland, under pain of excommunication. He despatched two Cardinals into Britain to make known his commands, and he privately impowered them to inflict the highest *Ford. lib. iii. 614.* spiritual censures on Robert Bruce, and on *whomever else* they thought fit *.

There is extant an authentic account of the negotiations of the cardinals: It may be said to exhibit the best original portrait of Robert Bruce which has been preserved to our times.

Ford. lib. 657. 661,—665. About the beginning of September 1317, the Cardinals sent two messengers to the King of Scots. The King graciously received the messengers, and heard them with patient attention. After having consulted with his barons †, he made answer, 'That he mightily desired to procure a good and perpetual peace, either by the mediation, 'of the Cardinals, or by any other means.' He allowed the *open* letters from the Pope, which recommended peace, to be read in his presence, and he listened to them with all due respect; but he would not receive the *sealed* letters addressed to *Robert Bruce governing in Scotland* ‡.

'Among

* ' Quosvis alios;' *Fœdera*, T. iii. p. 614. The cardinals, entrusted with such liberal powers of damnation, were Gaucelin Johannis, i. e. Fitz Jean, a cardinal priest under the title SS. *Marcellini et Petri*, and Lucas de Flisco, a cardinal deacon, under the title *Sanctae Mariae in via lata*.

† ' Like a judicious person,' *tanquam prudens*, says the despatch from the cardinals to the Pope; *Fœdera*, T. iii. p. 662.

‡ ' Gubernator Scotiae;' it would be read in French *Regent d'Escosse*, or *en Escosse*. I have endeavoured to retain this ambiguity of which Bruce took advantage.

1317.

'Among my Barons,' said he, 'there are many of the name of *Robert* *Bruce*, who share in the government of Scotland; these letters may possibly be addressed to some one of them, but they are not addressed to *me*, who am *King of Scotland*; I can receive no letters which are not addressed under that title, unless with the advice and approbation of my parliament. I will forthwith assemble my parliament, and with their advice return my answer.'

The messengers attempted to apologize for the omission of the title of *King*: They said, 'That the holy church was not wont, during the dependence of a controversy, to write or say ought which might be interpreted as prejudicial to the claims of either of the contending parties.' 'Since, then,' answered the King, 'my spiritual father and my holy mother would not *prejudice* the cause of my adversary, by bestowing on me the appellation of *King* during the dependence of the controversy, they ought not to have *prejudiced* my cause by withdrawing that appellation from me. I am in *possession* of the kingdom of Scotland; all my people call me *King*; and foreign Princes address me under that title; but it seems that my parents are partial to their English son.—Had you presumed to present letters with such an address to any other sovereign Prince, you might, perhaps, have been answered in a harsher style; but I reverence you as the messengers of the holy see.' He delivered this sarcastical and resolute answer with a mild and pleasant countenance [*].

The messenger next requested the King to command a temporary cessation of hostilities. 'To that,' replied the King, 'I can never consent, without the approbation of my parliament, especially while the English daily invade and spoil my people.'

The

---

[*] ' Laeth facie et amicabili vultu, semper ad patrem et matrem reverentiam ostendendo;' *Fœdera*, T. lii p. 661.

1317.

The King's counsellors told the messengers, that if the letters had been addressed to *the King of Scots*, the negotiations for peace would have instantly commenced. They imputed the flighting omission of the title of King to the intrigues of the English at the papal court, and they unguardedly hinted, that they had this intelligence from Avignon.

'While the title of King is with-held,' said the messengers to their constituents, 'there can be no hopes of a treaty.'

Fœd. iii. 683. 684. On receiving this intelligence, the Cardinals resolved to proclaim the papal truce in Scotland. In this hazardous office they employed Adam Newton, guardian of the monastery of Minorites at Berwick: He was charged with letters to the Scottish clergy, and particularly to the Bishop of St Andrews. He found the King of Scots with his army in a wood near Old Cambus *, making preparations for the assault of Berwick. Although personal access to the King was denied, the obedient monk proclaimed the truce by authority of the Pope. When the King of Scots was informed that the papal instruments still denied him his titles, he returned them back, saying, 'I will listen to 'no Bulls, until I am treated as King of Scotland, and have made my-'self master of Berwick.'

The monk, terrified at this answer, requested either a safe conduct to Berwick, or permission to pass into Scotland, and deliver letters to some of the Scottish clergy. But both his requests were denied, and he was commanded forthwith to leave the country. In his return to Berwick he was way-laid, stripped, and robbed of all his parchments, together

---

* ' Ad quendam villam vral, quae vocatur *Haldecambebus*, dictamem a Derewico
' per duodecim milliaria: Juxta quam villam, in quodam nemore, Dominus Robertus
' de Bros, cum suis complicibus, latebat, cum diversis machinamentis suis, ad obsi-
' dendam et destruendam villam Bervvici, et circa hujusmodi insidiationes die soole-
' que laborat sine requie;' *Fœdera*, T. iii. p. 683. The mention of a wood near Old Cambus, will induce some of my readers to remark what mighty alterations have happened in that country since the beginning of the 14th century.

1317.

together with his letters and instructions *. The robbers, it is said, tore the Pope's Bull †.

Fœd. iii. 708.

In the whole transaction concerning the truce, the Pope appears to have been the servile tool of England. Edward submitted to an ordinance which, probably, he himself had projected, and which he saw to be necessary in the present exigencies of his affairs; but Bruce despised and derided it.

Fœd. iii. 707. —709.

1318.

We have seen that the messengers from the Cardinals found the King of Scots occupied in military preparations for the siege of Berwick. The King, however, laid aside his purpose of employing force alone in the reduction of that place.

One Spalding, a citizen of Berwick, having been harshly treated by the governor ‡, resolved to revenge himself. He wrote to a Scottish Lord ‖, whose relation he had married, and offered, on a certain night,

Barbour. 347. —350. *Leland.* i. 547. *Walsing.* 111.

* ' In itinere men obviam habui quatuor vespiliones armatos obsidiose et insidiose ' destinatos, qui spoliaverunt me omnibus literis et vestimentis usque ad carnem, et ' ut conjicio dictus Dominus Robertus, et complices sui qui talia procurarunt, nolunt ' literas; quid de eis fecerunt penitus ignoro,' *Fœdera*, T. iii. p. 684. This letter from the Minorite, is dated *in vigilia S. Thomas Apostoli*. (i. e. 20th Dec.) 1317. By *Vespiliones*, the writer means *Night-walkers*. It is probable that the robbers sought to discover any secret correspondence that might have been carried on with the Scottish clergy to the prejudice of the state.

† This circumstance, though not related by the messengers, is mentioned in a Bull issued June 1318; *Fœdera*, T. iii. p. 707. If the Bull was indeed torn, it must have been owing to accident; there could be no reason for doing it intentionally.

‡ Barbour does not mention his name. It is probable, however, that Roger Horsely was governor or captain of Berwick at that time. See *Leland*, I`` i. p. 547.

‖ Although this person is called by Barbour *the Mareschall*, yet I suspect this to be a corruption of *the Marche Earl*, or *Patrick Earl of March*, who had now abandoned the

78   ROBERT I.
1318.

night, to betray the post where he kept guard. The Scottish Lord durst
not of himself engage in an enterprise so perilous and important; he
therefore communicated this intelligence to the King. 'You did well,'
said the King, ' in making me your confident; for if you had told this
' either to Randolph or to Douglas, you would have offended the one
' whom you did not trust. Both of them, however, shall aid you in
' the execution of the enterprise.' The King commanded him to assemble a body of troops, and to repair to a certain place. He gave
separate orders to Randolph and Douglas, for rendezvousing at the
same place and hour. The troops, thus cautiously assembled, marched
to Berwick, and, assisted by Spalding*, scaled the walls, and, in a
few hours, were masters of the town, [28th March 1318.] The English historians acknowledge that the Scots gave quarter to all who
demanded it †. The garrison of the castle, and the men who had fled
into it from the town, perceived that the number of the Scots was
small,

A. Murimuth.
13. Th. de la
Mart. 394.

the English interest, and espoused the party of Bruce. My reasons are, 1*st*, When Barbour has occasion to mention the Marshall of Scotland, as in describing the battle of
Bannockborn, he calls him *Sir Robert Keith.* 2*d*, The Earl of March often resided in
the neighbourhood of Berwick, and, consequently, could hold intercourse with Spalding more easily than Sir Robert Keith could, who had no residence in those parts.
3*d*, Barbour says, that the person whom he terms *the Marefhall* was, at that time,
Sheriff of Lothian. This office seems better fitted for the Earl of March than for the
Marshall of Scotland. 4*th*, In *Scal. Chron.* ap. Leland, T. i. p 547. it is expressly
said, ' James Douglas, by help of *Patrike Counte of March,* and *Peter Spalding of*
' *Berwike,* got Berwike owt of the Englishmennen handes.'

* From some expressions in *Walfingham,* Hist. p. 111. and *Ypod Neustr.* p. 503. Tyrrel
has concluded, vol. III. p. 272. that Spalding was governor of the castle, while another
person commanded in the town; and that, after the castle was betrayed, the town su-
stained a siege. When the fact is explained, as I have done from Barbour, there will
be no occasion for this aukward hypothesis.

† ' Neminem occidendo qui voluit obedire,' *A. Murimuth,* p. 53.

ROBERT I. 79

1318.

small, and made a desperate sally; but they were repulsed, chiefly by the extraordinary valour of a young knight, Sir William Keith of Galston.

When the King of Scots heard of the prosperous result of the enterprise against the town of Berwick, he collected what forces he could, hasted to the siege of the castle, and obliged the English to capitulate. He committed the charge of this important acquisition to Walter the Stewart of Scotland. The Stewart not doubting that the English would endeavour to recover Berwick, made preparations for sustaining a siege, and assembled his own kindred and vassals to aid him in the discharge of his trust. *Barbour*, 315.

Immediately after the reduction of Berwick [a], the Scots entered Northumberland, took the castles of Werk and Harbottle by siege, and Mitford by surprise. *Chr. Lanercost, ap. Tyrrell. ii. 272.*

In May they again invaded England, penetrated into Yorkshire, burnt Northallerton, Burroughbridge, Scarborough, and Skipton in Craven, and forced the inhabitants of Rippon to redeem themselves by payment of one thousand merks. They then returned to Scotland with much booty, and, as an English historian expresses it, ' driving ' their prisoners before them like flocks of sheep.' So helpless and contemptible was England become through civil dissensions. *Chr. Lanercost, ap. Tyrrel. ii. 272.*

The

---

[a] It is strange that historians should have so grossly mistaken the time of the reduction of Berwick. *Buchanan*, L. viii. p. 146. places that event in 1316. *A. Murimuth*, p 52. in 1317. and *Walsingham*, p. 111. in 1319. There is a considerable variation between our authors and the English, as to the endurance of the siege of the castle. Barbour says, that it surrendered on the sixth day after the surprise of the town, i. e. on the 2d of April 1318. But *Scala Chron.* ap. *Leland.* T. i. p. 547 says, 'The castle 'kept a xi weekes after, and then for lak of vitaile and refcue, was gyven up. Ther 'Roger Horseley, the capitayn of the castel for the Englishmen, lost one of his eyen.' The invasion of England by the Scots in May, renders this account of the long endurance of the siege altogether incredible.

1318.

Fœd. iii. 707. 711.

The interposition of the Pope was now obtained, with the view of intimidating the Scottish nation. The Pope ordered the two Cardinals in England to excommunicate Robert Bruce and his adherents. The reasons which he assigned for this were the treatment of the messengers of the holy see, and the assault of Berwick, in violation of the truce which had been proclaimed by papal authority [*].

Fœd. iii. 713.

Edward had summoned a parliament to meet at Lincoln; but he was obliged to prorogue it, on account of the Scottish invasion [†], and to assemble an army at Yorke for the defence of the country. [8th and 10th June 1318.]

Walsing. 111.

In a parliament held at London [about Michaelmas,] it was agreed, that every city and town in England should furnish a certain proportion of soldiers compleatly armed [‡]. Thus a considerable body of troops

---

[*] In the Bull addressed to the Cardinals, the Pope says, That there were other reasons for this excommunication, which he chose at present to pass over in silence; *Fœdera*, T. iii. p. 708. In the Bull addressed to Edward, he says, That they had been communicated to him by the two Cardinals; *Fœdera*, T. iii. p. 712. It is impossible to determine what were the reasons for excommunication thus referred in *petto*.

[†] *Tyrrel*, vol. iii. p. 272. gravely says, 'That the incursions of the Scots should have 'rather produced the quite contrary effect; for, what fitter provision could be made 'against this invasion of the Scots, than the unanimous advice and assistance of the clergy 'and great men of the kingdom.' This author has composed many volumes concerning the constitution and history of England, and yet he seems to have forgotten that the military tenants of the crown, who composed the greatest part of the parliament, did also compose the army, and that the same persons could not at once deliberate in parliament, and oppose the enemy in the field.

[‡] *Walsingham*, p. 111. says, That London furnished 200 men compleatly armed [ducenti viri armati ad unguem.] Canterbury 40, St Albans 10, and the other cities and towns in proportion. It were to be wished that Walsingham had recorded more of the quotas; the small proportion furnished by London is remarkable. Walsingham well describes the fate of this army, 'qui congregati magnam conflaverunt exercitum 'et

ROBERT I.

1318.

troops was collected; but when they came to the rendezvous at Yorke, their party-animosities and mutual distrust rose to such a height, that it was found necessary to disband and send them back to their habitations.

Edward Bruce, contrary to the judgment of all his officers *, engaged in battle with the English at Fagher near Dundalk, [5th October 1319.] The English, commanded by John Lord Bermingham, obtained a compleat victory. John Maupas slew Edward Bruce, and was found, after the battle, stretched dead on the body of his enemy. The Lord Soulis, and John the brother of the Stewart of Scotland, were among the slain. Philip de Moubray was mortally wounded †. After the defeat, John Thompson ‡, leader of the men of Carrick, collected

Barbour, 377. —383. *Chron. Hibern.* ap. *Camden.*

‘ ex hostibus melius formidandum; sed cum pervenissent ad Eboracum, *suborto tumultu*
‘ *pariter et* *sonuitate* cum aliis impedimentis, infecto negocio licentiati ad propria re-
‘ dierunt.’

* It is a prevailing notion among our historians, that Edward Bruce rashly fought, while powerful succours, under the command of the King his brother, were approaching. This, however confidently and repeatedly asserted, appears to be altogether a popular fiction. The King of Scots was too much engaged at home, and too intent on the preservation of his important conquest of Berwick, to risk his forces in a new invasion of Ireland.

† *Barbour* says, that Moubray, after having been stunned by a blow, and made prisoner, extricated himself out of the hands of the enemy; but he does not say that Moubray recovered of his wounds. The Irish Chronicle, subjoined to Camden's *Britannia*, computes the number of the Scottish army at 3000. *Barbour* says, that they were about 2000, not including the Irish; so that there is no contrariety in the two accounts. *Walsingham*, p. 111 says, that there fell of the Scots 29 barons and knights, and 5800 common men. In *Cox's history of Ireland*, vol. i. p. 99. it is said, that ‘ there ‘ were under Lord Bermingham 1324 good soldiers.’ I presume, that men compleatly ‘ armed are here meant; for it is not probable that there were no archers in the English army.

‡ It is probable, that Barbour learned his intelligence of the Irish war from this *John Thompson*. The account is curious, although, in some particulars, exaggerated.

1318

collected a few ftragglers, and, through many difficulties, led them into the north of Ireland. From thence they returned home, with the intelligence, that the ambitious project of eftablishing a new kingdom on the ruins of the Englifh power, was annihilated.

Chron. Hiver. ut fup.

The corps of Edward Bruce was not treated with honours like thofe which the King of Scots beftowed on the brave Englifh who fell at Bannockburn. His body was quartered, and diftributed for a public fpectacle over Ireland. Bermingham prefented the head of Edward Bruce to the Englifh King, and obtained the dignity of *Earl of Lowth*, as a reward of his fervices *.

The death of Edward Bruce, and of Marjory the King's daughter, made fome new regulations neceffary with refpect to the royal fucceffion.

Anderfon, Independency of Scotland, App. No. 15 Fard. xiii. 15.

In December 1318, a parliament was affembled at Scone. The whole clergy and laity renewed their engagements of obedience to the King, and folemnly promifed to affift him in the defence of the rights and liberties of Scotland, againft all mortals, *however eminent they may be in power, authority, and dignity* By this memorable expreffion they, no doubt, intended to defcribe the Pope, as well as the Englifh King.

They declared, that whoever violated this engagement, fhould be held in very deed as a betrayer of the kingdom, and guilty of high treafon without remiffion †.

It

---

* The grant was made in a parliament at Yorke, 12th May 1319. *Fœdera*, T. III. p. 767. It fhews the manner in which Earls were created at that time. It confers twenty pounds *per annum* on him for his fervices in the battle of Dundalk, under the name of *Earl of Lowth*, [Lowth,] and gives that Earldom to him, and the heirs-male of his body, by the fervice of one fourth of a knight's fee.

† Such appears to be the import of the expreffion ' criminis laefae Majeftatis reus ' in perpetuum habeatur.'

1318.

It was enacted, That if Robert King of Scots died without issue-male, Robert Stewart, the son of Marjory the King's daughter, should, as his nearest and lawful heir, succeed to the crown of Scotland.

In the event of the succession devolving on Robert Stewart, or on any other heir of the King's body, while under age, the King, with the unanimous consent of the parliament, granted the offices of tutor or curator of the heir, and of guardian of the kingdom, to Thomas Randolph Earl of Moray, and, failing him, to James Lord Douglas.

But, it was declared, that this appointment should cease, whenever it appeared to the major part of the community †, that such successor was capable of administrating the government in person.

Randolph and Douglas declared their willingness to accept the offices provisionally conferred on them; and they made oath faithfully to discharge their duty, and to observe, and cause to be observed, the laws and customs of Scotland.

' And for that, in certain times past, doubts had arisen, although
' without sufficient cause, by what rule the right of succession to the
' kingdom of Scotland ought to be judged, it was now declared and
' defined, That it ought not to have been regulated according to the
' practice in cases of inferior fees or inheritances, since no such prac-
' tice had been hitherto introduced in the succession of the crown, but
' that the male nearest to the King, at the time of his death, in the
' direct line of descent, should succeed to the crown; and, failing such
' male, the nearest female in the same line; and, failing the whole di-
' rect line, the nearest male in the collateral line, respect being had to
                                                                      ' the

† ' Quousque communicari regni vel majori et saniori parti visum fuerit,' &c. The words *sanior pars*, or *the most judicious part*, are certainly exegetical, and mean nothing else than *the majority*. Were they understood in any other sense, the provisions of the statute would appear inextricable.

1318.

'the right of blood by which the last King reigned *. And this,' says the statute, 'appears agreeable to the imperial law.'

Many salutary laws were enacted in this parliament †. The liberties of the Scottish church were asserted, and provision made for the security of the persons and property of ecclesiastics. All men were required to array themselves for war; and, according to their different conditions, the armour and weapons of each order of men were defined. Every person, on his road to the King's host, was required to live at his own charges, without oppressing the country; and the manner of punishing transgressors, while on their road, was accurately laid down.

margin: 1. Stat. Rob. I. c. 1. 2.
id. c. 27.
id. c. 4. 5.

The

---

* 'Praeterea, cum aliquibus praeteritis temporibus a quibusdam, licet minus sufficienter, in dubium fuisset revocatum, quo jure successio in regno Scotiae, si clara forsitan non exiterit, decidi deberet ac terminari: In eodem parliamento per clerum et populum declaratum extitit ac diffinitum, quòd per consuetudinem in inferioribus feudis seu haereditatibus in regno observatam, cùm in successione regni aliqua talis consuetudo non fuit introducta, minimè debuit, seu in futurum debeat, dicta successio terminari; sed quòd proximior masculus tempore mortis regis, ex linea recta descendente, vel, masculo deficiente, proximior femella ex eadem linea, vel illâ lineâ penitus deficiente, proximior masculus ex linea collaterali, attento jure sanguinis quo ipsi Regi defuncto jus regnandi competebat, Regi de cujus successione agi forsan contigerit, sine contradictione aut impedimento quocunque in regno debeat succedere, quod juri imperiali satis consonum censetur;' See *Anderson,* Independency of Scotland, App. No. 25. *Fordun,* L. xiii. c. 13. I have rendered the words of this act of settlement as justly as I could; at the same time, I acknowledge, that I do not understand their precise import, nor the consequences which might have arisen from them in certain supposable cases. I have not translated the expression, 'si successio clara forsitan non exiterit,' because it seems redundant.

† The statutes of Robert I. have been published by Skene. After having collated various MS. copies of those statutes, I can venture to assert, that Skene's edition is most incorrect. As for his Scottish version of the statutes of Robert I. it strangely perverts, or mistakes, the sense of the original; yet we have been so long habituated to the errors of Skene, that I know not whether a more accurate edition of the statutes which he has disfigured would be acceptable to the public.

1318.

The parliament declared those to be guilty of a capital offence, who supplied the enemy with weapons of any kind, or with any assistance whatever*.

By another statute, ecclesiastics were disabled from remitting money to the papal court for the purchase of bulls. The measure was violent; but the partiality of the Pope to the interests of England might serve to justify it.

The statute also prohibits the English absentees from drawing money out of Scotland †.

There

---

* This is a singular statute. In the MSS. it is C. 6. but I quote it according to Skene, C. 35. ' Quam per leges sit denegata facultas fidelibus barbaros victualibus seu armo-' rum generibus confortare, sub poena capitalis sententiae, omnibus et singulis incolis ' nostris cujuscunque conditionis existant firmiter et stricte inhibemus, ne quis arcus, ' sagittas, aut aliquid genus armorum, seu equos aut alia ayslamenta, Anglicis, hostibus ' nostris et nostri regni publicis, donent vel vendant, vel apud eos transferant, per quae ' nobis seu confederatis nostris et benevolis inferri valeat nocumentum, sub poena vi-' tae et membrorum, ac omnium quae erga nos amitti potuerint quoquo modo.' The expression per leges, alludes to l. 2. Cod. Quae res exportari non debent. This is one of the most express references to the Roman law that occurs in any of our authentic statutes. The constitution of the Emperor Marcian was adopted as an apology for the severity of this ordinance. The Scottish legislature, however, improved upon the model of the Emperor, by adding the clause of alia ayslamenta. Every kind of exportation to England, in time of war, was declared to be punishable with death and forfeiture.

The parallel between alienigenae Barbari and Angli, exhibits a lively portraiture of the national animosities which then prevailed.

Had Skene remarked the allusion to the Roman law, he would never have translated the passage thus; ' For sa meikill as be the lawes, liberty or licence is denied to all ' faithfull subjects to help or confort the enemies with any kind of armour, under the ' paine of death.'

† It is probable that the person principally aimed at by this clause of the statute, was David de Strathbolgie, Earl of Athole. At this time he stood high in the confidence of Edward II. yet the merits of his father continued to screen him from a severer punishment than that which this statute provides.

1318.

There were also various laws enacted in this parliament respecting the polity of the kingdom: To explain them all would require a much longer detail than is consistent with the nature of this work. There are two, however, which shall be briefly illustrated. The one relates to *theft-bute*. He who paid the *bute*, composition, or ransom, was to be held as a thief convicted; and he who received it was to be severely fined; and, if unable to pay the fine, was to be imprisoned during the King's pleasure *.

ib. c. 9.

The other statute enacted, that no one should invent rumours by which there might arise matter of discord between the Sovereign and his people: And it was provided, that the offender should be imprisoned until the King's pleasure was known.

ib. c. 11.

The offence, which makes the subject of this statute, is but too well known by the general name of *leasing-making*. The statute neither defines the crime nor the punishment. It is borrowed from a statute of Edward I. Robert I. introduced some English laws into Scotland. An antipathy at Edward I. was not inconsistent with favour for his laws, as being politic engines in the hands of an able prince.

Sta. 1. Westm. c. 34. 1tio. Edw. I. an. 1275.

It appears, that, about this time, the two cardinals who resided in England, pronounced the sentence of excommunication against the King

Ford. lib. 75 2.

---

* The 4th section of this statute is remarkable; '*salvis tamen libertatibus illorum dominorum, qui per Reges Scotiae ante Dominum Regem qui nunc est in talibus habent libertates sibi concessas.*' How are we to understand this singular reservation? It appears to imply that a permission to compound with thieves was indulged to some landholders, by special grant. There may be many such grants in antient deeds, although they have not occurred to me. Indeed, the sovereign might be justified for permitting what he could not effectually prohibit. There is a proviso in c. 137. James I. which may possibly serve to illustrate this obscure passage: ' Saifand that this ' statute sall not strike to bordourers, dwelling on the marches, but for theift to be ' done after the making of this statute.' Hence there is a probability that if *theft-bute* was ever authorised at all, it must have been upon *the marches*.

1318.

King of Scots and his adherents *. Meſſengers were ſent to the Pope, from the Scots, to ſolicit a reverſal of the ſentence; but Edward deſpatched the Biſhop of Hereford, and Hugh d'Eſpencer the elder, to counteract this negotiation. Edward alſo informed the Pope of certain intercepted letters which had been written from Avignon to the Scots.

The Pope ordered the Scots at Avignon, and the perſons who had corresponded with Scotland, to be taken into cuſtody. *Fœd.* iii. 761.

1319.

Robert Count of Flanders was not ſo obſequious in granting the requeſts of the Engliſh King. The Scots were wont to trade with Flanders, and had received from thence arms and military ſtores. Edward requeſted the Count of Flanders to prohibit the Scots from entering his country; but the Count made this memorable anſwer: 'Flanders is the common country of all men; I cannot prohibit any 'merchants from trafficking there, as they have been wont; for ſuch 'prohibition would tend to the ruin of my people †.' *Fœd.* iii. 761. 770.

At this critical period, there were ſome perſons of authority in Scotland who ſecretly expreſſed their wiſhes of deſerting the national cauſe, and of being received into favour by the Engliſh government. Edward obtained permiſſion from the Pope to treat with the traitors; *Fœd.* iii. 758. 764.

he

---

* In an inſtrument dated 14th January 1318-19, Edward ſpeaks of the ſentence as lately pronounced. I know not what occaſion there was for renewing a ſentence againſt Bruce, who ſtood already under the papal curſe.

† 'Terra noſtra Flandriae univerſis cujuſcunque regionis eſt communis, et cuique 'liber in eadem patet ingreſſus, nec poſſumus mercatoribus ſuas exercentibus mer- 'caturas ingreſſum, prout hactenus conſueverunt, denegare, quia illa cederent in de- 'ſolationem noſtrae terrae et ruinam;' *Fœdera,* T. iii. p. 770.

1319.

he having assured the Pope that he expected by this negotiation to divide and weaken the Scots *.

Triver. cont. 27.
Ford. iii. 777.

Edward was now, to all appearance, in amity with the Earl of Lancaster, and the other malecontent Lords. He determined to regain Berwick; and, with a view to that enterprise, ordered his army to assemble † [at Newcastle upon Tyne, 24th July 1319]

Ford. iii. 774. 784.

He requested the prayers of the clergy for the success of his expedition, and he demanded a great loan of money from them, [20th July.]

Ford. iii. 786. 787.

To prevent the approach of succours, the English drew lines of countervallation round Berwick. Confiding in their numbers, they made a general assault. The Stewart and his garrison, after a long and obstinate contest, repulsed the enemy, [7th September.]

Walfing. 111. Barbour. 355. &c. Ford. iii. 37.

Barbour. 359.

The next attempt of the besiegers was on the side towards the river. At that time the walls of Berwick were of inconsiderable height, and it was proposed to bring a vessel close to them, and by means of a draw-bridge, let down from the mast, to enter the town. But the Scots so annoyed the assailants, that the vessel could not be brought within the proper distance. At the ebb of the tide it grounded, and was burnt by the besieged.

Another

---

* The expressions of Edward are remarkable: 'Ut nobis est relatum in secreto, 'quamplures de Scotis inimicis et rebellibus nostris, super pace sua et benevolentia 'nostra procurandis, tractare desiderant, afferentes praeter ipsorum quietem nostra 'commoda et honores in eisdem procurari.—Speramus etiam quod redeuntibus ad pa-
' cem nostram aliquibus de dictis inimicis perfouit gravibus, alii in se diuidentur, et gra-
' vius turbabuntur, sicque ad ecclesiae sanctae et nostram obedientiam facilius reverten-
' tur.' Fœdera, iii. 764.

† 3300 foot soldiers from Wales were summoned to his army; Fœdera, T. iii. p. 774. And of the vassals and tenants of the Earl of Lancaster 1000 foot soldiers completely armed, and 1000 archers; Fœdera, T. iii. p. 784.

1319.

Another engine employed by the English is called a *sow*.[*] It *Barbour, 365.* appears to have been a large fabric, compoſed of timber, and well roofed, having ſtages within it, and in height ſurpaſſing the wall of the town. It moved upon wheels, and was calculated for the double purpoſe of conducting miners to the foot of the wall, and armed men to the ſtorm.

There was in the ſervice of the Scots one John Crab, a Fleming, eſteemed a moſt expert engineer. He conſtructed a moveable crane, whereby ſtones of great weight might be raiſed on high, and then let fall upon the enemy.

The Engliſh made a general aſſault on the quarter towards the ſea, as well as on the land-ſide. The garriſon, exhauſted by continual duty, could ſcarcely maintain the numerous poſts. The great engine moved on to the walls; ſtones were diſcharged againſt it from the crane, but without effect; and all hopes of preſerving Berwick were loſt. At once the beams of the engine gave way, by the force of a huge

---

[*] In many particulars it reſembled the *teſtudo ariſtaria* of the antients. ' Sus, ma-
' china bellica, quae et *ſcropha*, Gallis *truie*,' *Du Cange*. ' Unum fuit machinamen-
' tum, quod noſtri *ſuem*, veteres *vineam* vocant, quod machina levibus tignis colligata,
' tecto tabulis crauibuſque contexto, lateribus crudis coriis communitis, protegit in ſe
' ſubſidentes, qui quaſi more *ſuis* ad murorum ſuffodienda penetrant fondamenta;'
W. Malmſb. L. iv. *Hiſt.* ' Dum quidam nobiles, ligneis obumbrati machinis, quae
' quia *verrere* videbantur in antris, *ſues* appellari non videtur incongruum;' *Elmham,*
Hen. v. c. 50. This note is tranſcribed from that very curious and inſtructive work
The Antiquities of England, by Mr *Groſe.* See *Preface,* p. 13. 4. In Scotland a long
hay-ſtack is termed a *ſow*; probably from a traditionary remembrance of the warlike
engine which went under that name; hence we may have a diſtinct notion of the
figure of this engine. We muſt always remember, that in 1319, the walls of Berwick were ſo low, that, according to Barbour's expreſſion, ' one man with a ſpear
' might, from the outſide, ſtrike in the face another who ſtood on them.'

Vol. II. M

1319.

huge stone, happily directed [*]. The Scots poured down combustibles and burnt it.

Nevertheless, the English, eager to regain their antient reputation in arms, continued the assault with unremitting ardor. The Stewart, with a reserve of a hundred men, went from post to post, and relieved those who were wounded and unfit for combat. One soldier alone remained with him of the reserve, when the alarm came that the English had burnt a barrier at the port called *St Mary's*, possessed themselves of the draw-bridge, and fired the gate. The Stewart hasted thither, called down the guard from the rampart, ordered the gate to be set open, and rushed through the flames upon the enemy. A desperate combat ensued, and continued until the close of day, when the English commanders withdrew their troops on every quarter from the assault, [13th September].

The King of Scots could not, with any probability of success, attack the fortified camp of the English, and he saw that the Stewart and his garrison, if not relieved, would, at last, be reduced to the necessity of capitulating; he, therefore, resolved to make a powerful diversion in England, by which he hoped to constrain Edward to abandon his enterprise.

Walsingh. 111.
112.
Barbour, 363.
Leland, l. 462.

Fifteen thousand men, under the command of Randolph and Douglas, entered England by the west marches. They had concerted a plan for carrying off the wife of Edward from her residence near Yorke [†]; and, in exchange for a captive so valuable, they expected to

---

[*] *Barbour*, p. 369. relates, that when the engine gave way, the Scots cried out from the walls, 'See your sow has farrowed.' Barbour's account of the siege of Berwick is valuable for the many characteristical circumstances which it contains.

[†] *Walsingham*, p. 111. asserts, that some persons about the Queen had been bribed to betray her into the hands of the Scots.

1319.

to purchase the safety of Berwick. Having been difappointed in the execution of this plan, they wafted Yorkefhire. The Archbifhop of Yorke haftily collected a numerous rabble of commons and ecclefiaftics, and encountered the Scots at Mitton, near Burrough-bridge, in the North-riding of Yorkfhire. The Englifh were inftantly routed. Three thoufand were left dead on the field, and great part of the fugitives drowned in the Swale *. In this action there fell three hundred ecclefiaftics, [20th September.] According to the favage pleafantry of thofe times, this rout was termed by the Scots, the *Chapter of Mitton*. Barbur, 365.

When the news of the inroad and fucceffes of the Scots reached Berwick, a diverfity of opinions arofe among the Englifh commanders. The Barons whofe eftates lay in the fouth, remote from the Scottifh depredations, were eager to continue the fiege; but the northern barons were no lefs determined in their refolution of abandoning a doubtful and hazardous enterprife, and of returning to protect their own country. With them the Earl of Lancafter concurred; his favourite manour of Pontefract was now expofed to the ravages of the Scots; and therefore he departed from Berwick with his numerous adherents †. Edward, upon this, drew off the remains of his army, and attempted to intercept Randolph and Douglas. But they eluded him, and returned with fafety and honour into Scotland. Barbur, 375.

Walfingh. 112.

And

* The words of *Walfingham*, p. 112. are, ' Sed quia jam penè totus eorum exerci' tus in armis fuerat, mox contra noftros inexercitatos et inexpertos, et fine duce vel
' ordine venientes, ordinatiffimè occurrerunt, et levi negotio noftros fuderunt, et ad tria
' millia hominum in ore gladii perimerunt, et magna pars eorum qui fugerunt in flu-
' vio de Swale rapaci gurgite fuffocata.'

† *Walfingham*, p. 112. relates this event in a different manner. He fays, that Edward, with his wonted foolifhnefs [confuetâ folitiâ,] thus expreffed himfelf: " As foon
" as

1319.

Fœd. iii. 791. 797. 803— 805. 809.   And now Edward began to entertain serious thoughts of peace with Scotland. Commissioners for negotiating the treaty were appointed by both nations *.

Fœd. iii. 797. &c.   It may seem strange that Pope John XXII. the obsequious tool of England, should have chosen this season for enforcing spiritual censures against Bruce and his adherents; yet certain it is, that he ordered his delegates to publish the general sentence of excommunication, at whatever times and places they might judge expedient, [17th November.] Not satisfied even with this, he commanded the antient sentence to be published, which his predecessor Clement V. had passed on Bruce for the slaughter of Comyn [8th January 1319-20.] Whether this unseasonable exertion of authority ought to be ascribed to the zeal of the Pope, or to some visionary policy of Edward II. it is impossible to determine.

Fœd. iii. 816.   A truce was concluded between the two nations [21st December 1319.] to endure until Christmas 1321 †.

The

* as Berwick is won, I will give the command of the town to Hugh le d'Espenser, and of the castle to Roger Tamari [r. Dammory,] and that the Earl of Lancaster, disgusted at this resolution, marched off with his adherents. But the account which Barbour gives is more probable: Although le d'Espenser was the enemy, yet Roger Dammory was one of the confidents of Lancaster. Walsingham himself observes this. p. 116. And, indeed, we have evidence of it under the Earl's own hand, *Fœdera,* T. iii. p 927. The retreat from Berwick appears to have been a judicious measure. Randolph and Douglas had advanced far into England, at the head of a well-disciplined and victorious army. Had Edward remained before Berwick, they might have committed such devastations in a few days, as it would have required a century to repair.

* The Scottish commissioners were William de Soulis, Robert de Keith, Roger de Kirkpatrick, Alexander de Seton, and William de Montfichet, all knights ; to them four ecclesiastics were joined ; *Fœdera,* T. iii. p. 809.

† *Tyrrel* vol. iii. p. 278. says, that the Scots immediately violated this truce, invaded England, burnt the suburbs of Yorke, and made prisoner John de Bretagne Earl

of

1320.

The Scots having obtained this interval of tranquillity, resolved to justify their cause, in a manifesto addressed to the Pope.

Anderson, Diplomata, No. 51. 52. Ford. xiii. 27.

In a parliament assembled at Aberbrothock, [6th April 1320,] a letter to the Pope was drawn up by the Barons, freeholders, and whole community of Scotland.

They began with mentioning the fabulous origin of the nation from Scythia and Spain, their boasted line of one hundred and thirteen native Kings, the establishment of the Christian religion in Scotland, by the ministry of Andrew the apostle, and the favour which the Roman pontiffs had shewn to their forefathers, as being under the special patronage of the brother of St Peter.

After this puerile preamble, full of the prejudices of an ignorant and superstitious age, they proceeded in a more elevated and manly stile.

' We continued to enjoy peace and liberty with the protection of
' the papal see, until Edward, the late King of England, in the guise
' of a friend and ally, invaded and oppressed our nation, at that time
' without a head, unpractised in war, and suspecting no evil. The
' wrongs which we suffered under the tyranny of Edward, are beyond
' description, and, indeed, they would appear incredible to all but those
' who actually felt them. He wasted our country, imprisoned our
' prelates, burnt our religious places, spoiled our ecclesiastics, and slew
' our people, without discrimination of age, sex, or rank. Through
' the favour of Him *who woundeth and maketh whole*, we have been
' freed from so great and innumerable calamities by the valour of our
' Lord and Sovereign *Robert*. He, like another Josuah, or a Judas
' Maccabeus,

of Richemont. This is a mistake copied from *Walsingham*, p. 213. Walsingham himself says, p. 117. that the Earl of Richemont was made prisoner long after this time. The account of that event will be related in its proper place.

1320.

' Maccabeus, gladly endured toils, diſtreſſes, the extremities of want,
' and every peril, to reſcue his people and inheritance out of the hands
' of the enemy. The Divine Providence, that legal ſucceſſion, which
' we will conſtantly maintain, and our due and unanimous conſent,
' have made him our chief and King. To him, in defence of our
' liberty, we are bound to adhere, as well of right, as by reaſon of his
' deſerts, and to him we will, in all things, adhere; for through him
' ſalvation has been wrought unto our people. Should he abandon
' our cauſe, or aim at reducing us and our kingdom under the domi-
' nion of the Engliſh, we will inſtantly ſtrive to expel him as a public
' enemy and the ſubverter of our rights and his own, and we will
' chuſe another King to rule and protect us; for, while there exiſt an
' hundred of us, we will never ſubmit to England. We fight not for
' glory, wealth, or honour, but for that liberty which no virtuous man
' will ſurvive.

' Wherefor, we moſt earneſtly requeſt your Holineſs, as the Vice-
' gerent of *Him* who giveth equal meaſure unto all, and with whom
' there is no diſtinction either of perſons or nations, that you would
' behold, with a fatherly eye, the tribulation and diſtreſſes brought
' upon us by the Engliſh, and that you would admoniſh Edward to
' content himſelf with his own dominions, eſteemed in former times
' ſufficient for ſeven kings, and allow us Scotſmen, who dwell in a
' poor and remote corner, and who ſeek for nought but our own, to
' remain in peace. In order to procure that peace, we are willing to
' do whatever is conſiſtent with our national intereſts.

' Herein it behoves you, Holy Father, to interpoſe. You behold
' with what cruelty the Heathen rages againſt the Chriſtians, for the
' chaſtiſement of their ſins, and that the boundaries of Chriſtendom
' are daily contracted. How muſt your memory ſuffer in after ages,
' ſhould the Church be diminiſhed in glory, or receive reproach under
' your adminiſtration?

' Rouſe,

1320.

'Rouse, therefore, the Christian Princes, and call them to the rescue
' of Palestine: They pretend that wars with their neighbours hinder
' that enterprise; but the true cause of hinderance is, that, in subduing
' their weaker neighbours, they look for less opposition, and profit
' more immediate. Every one knows, and we now declare it to you,
' and to all Christendom, that our King and we are willing to under-
' take the holy expedition, if Edward will permit us to depart in
' peace.

' Should you, however, give a too credulous ear to the reports of
' our enemies, distrust the sincerity of our professions, and persist in
' favouring the English, to our destruction, we hold you guilty, in the
' fight of the Most High, of the loss of lives, the perdition of souls,
' and all the other miserable consequences which may ensue from war
' between the two contending nations.

' Ever ready, like dutiful children, to yield all fit obedience to you,
' as God's Vicegerent, we commit our cause to the protection of
' the supreme King and Judge: We cast our cares on him, and we
' steadily trust that he will inspire us with valour, and bring our ene-
' mies to nought.'

It will be remarked, that, in this manifesto, no mention is made of
the clergy of Scotland. We must not however, suppose that they
were less zealous than the laity in the national cause. But the stile of
the letter was such, that it could not, with propriety, be avowed by
ecclesiastics, especially in an address to the head of their church.

Although the Scottish Barons appeared unanimous in their resolu- *Ford.* xiii. 1.
tion to maintain the government of Robert, yet there were concealed *Barbour*, 395.
traitors among the patriots. William de Soulis, and some other per- —398.
sons of quality, conspired against the King. The plot was revealed

by

1320.

by the Countess of Strathern [*]. Soulis having been apprehended, made a full confession.

The conspirators were tried in parliament, [at Scone, August 1320.] Soulis and the Countess of Strathern were condemned to perpetual imprisonment.

Gilbert de Malerb and John de Logie, both Knights, and Richard Brown an Esquire, were found guilty of treason, and suffered the punishment of traitors.

Roger de Moubray died before sentence. Yet a like sentence was pronounced upon his dead body. The King, however, mitigated this rigour, and allowed him all the honours of sepulture.

The fate of David de Brechin was much deplored. That brave young man, the nephew of the King, had served with reputation against the Saracens. To him the conspirators, after having exacted an oath of secrecy, had revealed their plot. He condemned their undertaking, and refused to share in it; yet, entangled by his fatal oath, he concealed the treason. Notwithstanding his relation to the Royal Family, his personal merits, and the favourable circumstances of his case, he was made an example of rigorous, although impartial justice.

Sir Eustace de Maxwell, Sir Walter de Berclay Sheriff of Aberdeen, Sir Patrick de Graham, Hamel de Troupe, and Eustace de Rattray, were tried and acquitted.

Ford. xiii. 1.
Barbour, 396.

It is impossible to discover the nature of this conspiracy. Fordun says in general, that the Lord Brechin and the rest were convicted of high treason. Barbour asserts that the plot was formed against the life

---

[*] *Fordun*, L. xiii. c. 1. says, That the Countess of Strathern confessed her offence, and was punished with perpetual imprisonment. *Barbour*, p. 396. says, That the conspirators were discovered *through a lady*, whose name he does not mention. From comparing the two narratives, there is reason to conclude, that the Countess of Strathern revealed the plot.

1320.

life of the King, and he seems to insinuate, that the conspirators meant to place the crown on the head of Soulis *.

Boece relates the circumstances of this event with as much confidence as if he had assisted at the condemnation of the criminals. According to him, the King of Scots had in parliament required his barons to produce the titles by which they held their lands: But the barons at once drew their swords, intimating, that by arms they would maintain their estates against all legal encroachments. The King desisted from his requisition; nevertheless, he entertained secret thoughts of revenge. The barons, dreading his resentment, conspired to betray their country to England †.

This parliament, in which so much noble blood was shed, continued long to be remembered by the vulgar, under the appellation of *the black parliament*.

It appears that the Pope was alarmed at the language which the Scottish barons had used in their manifesto; for he addressed a Bull to Edward, earnestly recommending peace with Scotland. Neither ought it to escape observation, that, in this Bull, the Pope sometimes employs the very expressions of the Scottish manifesto ‡, and that he bestows

---

* This William de Soulis seems to have been the grandson of Nicolas de Soulis, one of the competitors at the time of the disputed succession. Nicolas claimed in right of his grandmother, the daughter of Alexander II. and he would have excluded the other competitors, had her legitimacy been ascertained.

† This is a tale ill connected and improbable. It cannot be supposed that all the barons should have been so much offended at the King's requisition; for some of them had received renewed charters, and others, original grants from him; neither could the barons be alarmed at what was indeed conformant to the law and practice of that age. See *Reg. attachiamenta*, c. 25.

‡ Thus the Scottish barons said to the Pope, ' *corporum exitia, animarum exitia, et caetera, quae sequuntur incommoda.*—Vobis ab Altissimo credimus imputanda.'

Vol. II. N

ROBERT I.

1320.

bestows on Bruce the ambiguous title of *Regent of the kingdom of Scotland* *.

Fœd. iii. 848. The King of Scots sent ambassadors † to the Pope, and solicited a repeal of the sentence of excommunication. The Pope pretended that the instructions of the ambassadors were not sufficiently ample; he, however, allowed the King of Scots to renew his solicitations at any time before the 1st of May 1321.

Fœd. iii. 855. 853. 854. 860. The English King appointed commissioners for treating of peace with Scotland, [15th September]. *Philip le Long*, King of France, under pretence of consulting the honour and advantage of Edward, desired that some persons on his part might be present at the congress. Edward thanked the King of France for his *good will*, yet he thanked him, as if suspecting his sincerity. The Pope also made a like request. Edward consented to it; but desired that Rigand, Bishop elect of Winchester, might be one of the persons present at the treaty on the part of the Pope. In all this there is an air of reserve, which seems to intimate that Edward distrusted both the King of France and the Pope.

Fœd. iii. 861. Edward still entertained hopes of exciting dissension among the Scots. With this view, he appointed commissioners for receiving into favour all the Scots who might be desirous of reconciliation with England, [17th November]. He even granted an indemnity to all the inhabitants of Scotland, excepting only the rebels who were of English

---

* 'lands.' The Pope in his Bull speaks thus of war, 'quot animarum exitia, excidia corporum, et alia non facile enumeranda incommoda secum trahat;' *Fœdera*, T. iii. p. 847.

* 'Inter te et Regentem regni Scotiae,' *ibid*.

† The ambassadors were Edward de Maunbuisson and Adam de Gordon, knights; *Fœdera*, T. iii. p. 848. The Pope made excuses to Edward II. for his lenity in permitting Bruce to be still heard against the sentence of excommunication.

ROBERT I. 99

1320.

lish birth, or who claimed right to estates in that kingdom *, [11th December].

1321.

The Pope had sent the Bishop of Winchester, and one William, a friar, to the King of Scots with letters. Edward would not suffer the letters to be delivered; and he made this apology to the Pope, 'that 'there were certain expressions in them which it was not held safe to 'communicate to Bruce †. [14th May].

Edward had lately endeavoured to excite dissensions among the Scots; but the dissensions in his own kingdom now required all his solicitude. The violence of the Earl of Lancaster, and his associates, against the two D'Espensers, made an irreparable breach between the King and many of his most powerful barons.

The Earl of Lancaster was one of those politicians who estimate the lawfulness of actions by their probable success. This person, a Prince of the blood, and, in the opinion of the people, an eminent patriot, entertained a treasonable correspondence with the Scots.

A passport granted by Douglas to Richard de Topclif, an emissary of Lancaster, is the first proof that we have of this correspondence ‡,

[7th

---

* This is a singular instrument. David Earl of Athole is one of the commissioners for granting the indemnity. The only exceptions from the indemnity are thus expressed: 'Illis de regno nostro Angliae, qui contra nos hostiliter extiterant, et aliis qui 'terras infra dictum regnum nostrum clamium habere, omnino exceptus;' *Foedera*, T. iii. p. 865. Hence some of the persons who assisted at the slaughter of Comyn, might have taken the benefit of the indemnity, and thus one great object of the Seventh war would have been overlooked.

† 'Propter aliqua verba, in dictis literis insertis, sanum videbatur eas non esse dicto 'Roberto porrigendas;' *Foedera*, T. iii. p. 884.

‡ Le beau 'escript a Etbbredulphi de dimaigne en la feste Seint Nicolas, l'an de 'grace 1321.' The feast of St Nicolas is celebrated on the 6th December. I wish to know

1321.

[7th December 1321]. This passport was ratified by Randolph, as acting for the King of Scots, who appears at that time to have been indisposed.

Fœd. III. 927. The Scots, encouraged by the prospect of an alliance with the malecontents, invaded Northumberland, and the bishoprick of Durham, as soon as the truce expired [*]. It is probable that they were conducted by Douglas in this invasion [†].

H. Knyghton, 2539. While the Earl of Lancaster, and his associates, were endeavouring to collect their forces, Edward took the field, and disconcerted the whole plan of their ambition. Lancaster marched to Burton upon Trent with what troops he could assemble; but he was dislodged from thence, and obliged to retreat to his castle of Pontefract.

Fœd. III. 927. He wrote a letter to Douglas in his own name [‡], and in the name of the Earl of Hereford, and other barons of that party, requesting an interview, 'that we may,' said he, 'adjust all points of our alliance, ' and agree to live and die together.' At the same time, he desired a passport for messengers to be sent into Scotland.

The bearer of this letter was to have delivered it on the 7th of February; but Douglas had removed his quarters, and by that accident there was some time lost. More time still was lost, because Douglas judged it necessary to procure the passport from Randolph, who then lay in Scotland, near the borders. And thus it happened that Douglas

know what place is meant by *Etkbretbelys*. This is of moment for ascertaining a certain material circumstance in our history.

[*] 'Finish trough, inter nos et ipsos super iniri, regnum nostrum in magna mahitu- ' dine ingressi,' *Fœdera*, T. iii. p. 927.

[†] This is collected from the letters which passed between Douglas and the English malcontents; *Fœdera*, T. iii. p. 926, 927. and from this other circumstance, that at that time Randolph was at Cavers in Scotland; *Fœdera*, T. iii. p. 926.

[‡] The letter is in *Fœdera*, T. iii. p. 930. Although not signed, it must have been addressed to Douglas from the Earl of Lancaster.

1321.

glas could not return any anſwer before the 17th February. His anſwer was general, referring to the meſſenger for particulars. It was addreſſed to *King Arthur*, which ſeems to have been a ſort of cypher denoting the Earl of Lancaſter [*]. It does not appear that the unhappy man had ſo much as concerted the terms of his treaty with the enemies of England. After ſo many days had been loſt at this critical conjuncture, Lancaſter continued his retreat towards the north. Sir Andrew Hartcla met him near Borrough-bridge, and defeated his army, [16th March 1321-2]. The Earl of Hereford was ſlain in the action. Lancaſter fled, and next day ſurrendered himſelf. Having been tried in preſence of the King and barons, he was found guilty and beheaded [†], [22d March 1321-2.]

H. Knyghton, 1540.—41. Tho. de More, 596 Ford. Tn. 936, &c. Walſ. 116.

The ſervices of Sir Andrew Hartcla were rewarded with the dignity of *Earl of Carliſle*, conferred on him and his iſſue-male. To this an annual penſion of 1000 marks was added.

Ford. iii. 943.

1322.

In a high ſtrain of exultation, Edward informed the Pope, that he had cruſhed his rebellious ſubjects, and was preparing to invade Scotland. ' Give yourſelf no farther ſolicitude,' ſaid he, ' about a truce
' with

Ford. iii. 944.

---

[*] This is more probable than that *Thomas Earl of Lancaſter* ſhould have aſſumed to himſelf the title of King, under the fantaſtic appellation of *Arthur*. 1. In the propoſal for an alliance with Scotland, which was found upon the Earl of Hereford, he is called *Earl of Lancaſter*. 2. In his trial no mention is made of his having aſſumed or received the appellation of King; yet the circumſtance of the letter addreſſed to *King Arthur* was known at that time; for *Walſingham*, p. 116. ſays ' cum Thomas Comes ' introductus fuiſſet in villam [Pontefract] a tota gente deriſus eſt, et acclamatus *Rex* ' *Arthurus*, et ubique ſubſannatus.'

[†] The people of England imagined that many miracles were wrought through the interceſſion of the Earl of Lancaſter; and, which is more extraordinary, Edward III. ſolicited the Pope to canoniſe this perſon, who was undoubtedly a traitor to his country; *Fœdera*, T. iv. p. 268.

1322.

'with the Scots; the exigencies of my affairs inclined me formerly to
'liften to fuch propofals; but now I am refolved to eftablifh peace by
'force of arms,' [25th March.]

H. Knyghton,
2542.
Ford. xiii. 4.
While Edward was making his preparations for fubduing Scotland,
the Scots penetrated by the weftern marches into Lancafhire, fpoiled
the country at pleafure, and returned home loaded with extraordinary
booty *.

Ford. iii. 958.
959. 967.
Walfing. 116.
Edward, after having requefted the Pope to inforce the fentence of
excommunication againft the Scots, invaded Scotland with a formidable army, [Auguft.]

The King of Scots had been obliged, at Bannockburn, to rifk the
fate of his kingdom on the event of one battle; but now there was no
fuch neceffity; and therefore he avoided a general engagement, where
every thing might have been loft, and where nought but glory could
Barbour, 385. have been won. Having ordered the whole cattle and flocks to be
driven off, and all effects of value to be removed from the Merfe and
Lothian, he fixed his camp at Culrofs, on the north fide of the frith of
Forth.

Barbour, 386.
His orders were fo exactly obeyed, that, as tradition reports, the
only prey that fell into the hands of the Englifh was a lame bull at
Tranent in Faft-Lothian. 'Is that all that ye have got,' faid Earl
Warenne, when the fpoilers returned to the camp, 'I never faw fo
'dear a beaft †.'

Edward

---

* This inroad is well defcribed by *Knyghton*, p. 2542. 'Anno gratiae 1322, circa
'tranflationem Sancti Thomae, intraverunt Scoti in Angliam per medium Foroefiae,
'et comitatum Lancaftriae devaftaverunt undique, abique aliquo damno fuorum, col-
'ligentes immenfam praedam auri et argenti, animalium, ornamentorum ecclefiaftico-
'rum, lectualium, mentalium, abducentes muftas carrectas de omnibus horis patriae ad
'fuum placitum.'

† This farcaftical and ill-timed reflection is related as in *Barbour*, p. 386. *Ferdun,*
L. xiii. c. 4. gives it in ftill fewer words: 'Quod illius tauri caro erat nimis cara;'
that

1321.

Edward advanced to the neighbourhood of Edinburgh, without opposition, indeed, but also without hope of mastering the kingdom. His provisions were soon consumed, and there was no possibility of obtaining any supplies. Famine began to prevail in the English camp, and many of the soldiers perished for want of food. Edward, after all his mighty preparations for subduing Scotland, was obliged to retire without having ever seen an enemy. His soldiers, in their retreat, plundered the abbeys of Holyrood and Melros, burnt the abbey of Dryburgh, and other hallowed places, slew many monks, and violated whatever was most sacred in their religion *. Returning to commodious and plentiful quarters in England, they indulged themselves in excesses productive of mortal diseases, in so much that, according to an English historian, almost one half of the great army which Edward had led into Scotland, was destroyed either by hunger or intemperance †.

Edward,

that is, 'This beef is very dear.' Had Warenne spoken thus to the King, it might have been considered as a gallant freedom of speech, suiting a baron of those times; but the words addressed to the soldiers, would have been petulance and mutiny in any age.

* 'Spoliatis tamen in reditu Anglorum, ex praedatis monasteriis Sanctae Crucis de
' Edinburgh et de Melros, atque ad magnam desolationem perductis; in ipso namque
' monasterio de Melros Dominus Willelmus de Peblis, ejusdem monasterii prior, unus
' etiam monachus tunc infirmus et duo conversi caeci effecti, in dormitorio eorundem
' ab eisdem Anglis sunt interfecti, et plures monachi lethaliter vulnerati, corpus Do-
' minicum super magnum altare fuit projectum, ablata pixide argentea in qua erat re-
' positum. Monasterium de Driburgh igne penitus consumptum est, et in pulverem
' redactum, ac alia pia loca quamplurima per praedicti Regis violentiam ignis flamma
' consumpsit;' Ford. L. xiii. c. 4.

† 'Cumque multi de Regis exercitu pervenissent ad propria, et gustassent cibos avi-
' dius, mox vel dirupta visceribus moriebantur, aut consumpta natura semper imbecil-
' les et debiles permanserunt, vires praehabitas recuperare non valentes;' Walsingham.

1322.

Fæd. iii. 973. Edward, on his return to England, appointed Andrew Hartcla guardian of the west marches, and David de Strathbolgie Earl of Athole, guardian of the east, [15th September.]

Fæd. iii. 973. Edward had scarcely taken these precautions for the security of his kingdom, when the Scots appeared with a numerous army before the castle of Norham. Edward lay at the abbey of Biland in Yorkshire; a body of his troops was advantageously posted in the neighbourhood. The Scots, by a forced march, endeavoured to surprise him; to this, it is said, they were incited by some traitors who were about *Walsing. 117.* his person [a]. Edward escaped to Yorke, with the utmost difficul- *Murimuth. 59.* ty, abandoning all his baggage and treasure to the enemy. The En- *Barbour, 342.* glish camp was supposed to be accessible only by one narrow pass. —394. Douglas undertook to force it. Randolph, leaving that part of the army which he commanded, presented himself as a volunteer under Douglas his friend. The attack was resisted by the English with undaunted courage. The King of Scots ordered the Highlanders and the men of the Isles to climb the precipice in which the English con- *Fæd. iii 978.* fided. They obeyed, and the English fled. John de Bretagne Earl *982. T3. de la* of Richemont, Henry de Sully, a Frenchman of quality, and many *Mort, 596.* other persons of note, were made prisoners. The Stewart with five hundred

---

[b] *Idem*, p. 117. ' Ubi pene perdidit mediam gentem suam pudibundè maximè;' *ibid.* Knyghton, p. 2542. says, that near 16000 men perished. Knyghton erroneously supposes, that, in the following year, Edward again marched into Scotland, and returned after having proceeded no farther than to Melros.

[a] Edward himself seems to have ascribed this to the negligence of Lewis de Beaumont Bishop of Durham. Henry de Beaumont had said, that if his brother Lewis, or any other person of noble birth, was appointed to the see of Durham, he would so well defend the frontier, as to be like a *stone wall* against the invasions of the Scots. ' I 'named you Bishop, said the King to Lewis de Beaumont, and yet your negligence has ' been so great, that your territory and the adjacent parts have suffered more from the ' Scots under your administration than in the days of any of your predecessors;' *Fædera*, T. iii. p. 994.

ROBERT I. 105

1322.

hundred men, purſued the Engliſh to Yorke, and, in the ſpirit of chivalry, remained at the gates until evening, waiting for the enemy to come forth and renew the combat [*].

The King of Scots had formerly received ſome diſcourteſies from the Earl of Richemont. In the firſt exultation of victory, he ſo far forgot his own character and dignity, as to reproach his priſoner [†]; but to Sully and his companions, he expreſſed every kindneſs. 'I 'know,' ſaid he, 'that ye fought to prove yourſelves valiant knights 'in a ſtrange land, and not from enmity to me.' *Barbour, 393. 394.*

The Scots committed great outrages in Yorkeſhire; at Rippon, as if they had meant to uſe repriſals, they murdered many eccleſiaſtics. They had ſo little apprehenſions of any enemy, that they continued their *Murimut. 59. Tb. de la Mor. 596.*

---

[*] 'Walter Stewart that great bountie
'Set ay upon by chevalry,
'With five hondred in company,
'Unto York's gates the chace can ma
'And there ſome of their men can ſla,
'And there abade while near the night,
'To ſee if any would iſh and fight.'
Barbour, p. 393.

[†] 'And when he ſaw John of Britain
'He had at him right great engraigne,
'For he was wont to ſpeak highly
'At home, and o'er deſpitouſly,
'And bad him have him away on hy
'And look he keeped were ſtraitly;
'And ſaid, were it not that he were
'Sik a cative, he ſhould buy ſore
'His words that were ſo angry.'
Barbour, p. 393. 394.

The ſentiment, as expreſſed by Barbour, ſeems obſcure; the meaning may be, that the Earl of Richemont would have been worſe uſed, had it not been on account of his eminent rank.

VOL. II. O

1323.

their incursions to Beverley in the East-riding *; but the clergy and citizens, by paying a large ransom, purchased immunity from pillage †. After having wasted England, and braved the power of their late invader, the Scots returned home unmolested.

Andrew Hartcla Earl of Carlisle, had received the highest honours and the most distinguished trust from Edward; he now betrayed his King and his benefactor.

Much has been related by historians concerning the nature of his treason. I propose to make mention of those circumstances alone which appear from authentic instruments.

Fœd. iii. 983.   About the beginning of January 1322-3, Edward received intimation that the barons of the north of England had entered into a treaty for a truce with the Scots. He prohibited any further proceedings in this treaty, and commanded Hartcla instantly to inform himself of its nature and conditions, to provide for the security of Carlisle, and to repair to court; ' that I may be directed,' said the King, ' by your ' advice, and the advice of my other faithful counsellors.'

Either the English King had at that time no suspicions of the fidelity of Hartcla, or he acted with the most profound dissimulation.

Fœd. iii. 988.   But Hartcla having avoided the presence of his injured Sovereign, Edward ordered him to be arrested as a traitor, [1st February 1322-3.]

Ibid.   Edward appointed his brother, Edmund Earl of Kent, to be sole guardian of the marches, [5th February 1322-3]; and thus deprived both Hartcla, and the Earl of Athole, of their offices.

Commissioners

---

* It is evident, that, after the rout near Biland abbay, Edward was not able to oppose the Scots in the field. We learn from *Fœdera*, that he remained at Yorke, while the Scots extended their arms to Beverley, in a remote corner of the East riding of Yorkeshire, and almost to the banks of the Humber.

† ' In villa de Beverlaco neminem occiderunt, quia pro CCCC libris se burgenses ' et canonici redemerunt, et sic Scoti, propter instantem hiemem, redierunt;' *A. Murimuth, p. 39.*

ROBERT I.

1322.

Commissioners were appointed to try the offences of Hartcla, [27th February 1322-3]. *Fœd. iii. 999.*

It was found at his trial that he had had an interview with Bruce, and had become bound, as well by writing as by oath, to maintain him and his heirs in the right and possession of Scotland *: That Bruce had agreed to name six persons, and Hartcla as many, who, by common consent, were to regulate the weighty affairs of both kingdoms: That Hartcla had promised to resist all those who might endeavour to obstruct this treaty; and that he had induced the people of the country to swear to the observance of it. *Ibid.*

Edward also charged Hartcla with having pretended to act under the royal authority in the negotiations for a truce with Scotland; but this charge, however probable, appears not to have been proved to the court. *Fœd. iii. 994.*

The court condemned Hartcla to be degraded, and to suffer the punishment of a traitor †. This sentence was immediately executed, [at Carlisle, 2d March 1322-3]. *Fœd. iii. 999. & Murim. 60.*

Dishonoured

---

* ' Pur maintenir le dit Robert d'estre Roi d'Escosse proprement, et pur maintenir
' au dit Robert et ses heirs le royaume d'Escosse entirement;' *Fœdera*, t. iii. p. 999.

† ' That you shall be degraded, and lose the title of Earl for yourself and your heirs
' in all time to come: That you shall be ungirded of your sword, and have your gilt
' spurs cut off from your heels;' *Fœdera*, T. iii. p. 999. The sentence also bears,
' That his heart, bowels, and intrails, should be plucked out, burnt to ashes, and the
' ashes scattered in the air.' It assigns what, it seems, is the moral of this savage mode
of punishment: ' Because from them your traiterous devices proceeded,' [dount les
 treiterouses penses vindrent], *Fœdera*, T. iii. p. 1000. His quarters were to be exposed on the towers of Carlisle and Newcastle, on the bridge of York, and at Shrewsbury,
and his head was to be fixed upon London bridge. The English historians relate some
other particulars concerning Hartcla, which are more dubious; as, that the King of
Scots had agreed to give him his sister in marriage; *A. Murimuth*, p. 60. *Walsingham*,
p. 118. I doubt much whether the King of Scots had any unmarried sister at that
time.

108   ROBERT I.

1322.

Ford. III.
1003.

Dishonoured by his flight from Biland, impoverished and weakened by the repeated calamities of war, and betrayed by those in whom he placed confidence, Edward now agreed to a cessation of arms ' with
' the men of Scotland who were engaged in war against him.' But the King of Scots would not consent to the truce in that form. He thus wrote to Henry de Sully, who acted as a mediator between the two nations: ' I see from the copy of the letters of the King of Eng-
' land which you have transmitted to me, that he says *he has granted*
' *a cessation of arms to the men of Scotland who are engaged in war*
' *against him.* This language is very strange. In our former truces,
' I was always named as a principal party, although he did not vouch-
' safe to give me the title of King; but now he makes no more men-
' tion of me than of the least person in Scotland; so that, if the treaty
' were to be violated by him, I should have no better title than the
' very meanest of my subjects to demand redress. I cannot consent
' to a truce granted in such terms; but I am willing to consent, if the
' wonted form is employed. I send you a copy of the King's letter;
' for I imagine that you have either not perused it, or not adverted
' to its tenor,' [21st March 1322-3. Dated at Berwick].

It

time. Walsingham says, That Hartcla became a traitor from his enmity to Hugh le D'Espenser, whom he perceived to increase daily in the favour of the King; *ibid.* Murimuth says, That he was arrested by Anthony de Lucy, his special confident, p. 60. But it appears from *Fædera*, T. iii. 988.—1000. that Henry Fitz-Hugh was the person appointed to arrest Hartcla, and that de Lucy was at that time sheriff of Carlisle; so that, if de Lucy took Hartcla into custody, he did no more than what the duty of his office, superior to the rights of private friendship, indispensibly required. The Chronicle of Lanercost, quoted by *Tyrrel*, vol. iii. B. 10. p. 301. says, 'That by Hartcla's treaty with Scotland, the King of Scots was to pay 80,000 merks to Edward, in annual payments of 8000 merks, and that Edward was to have the disposal of *the marriage* of the eldest son of the King of Scots. All this, however, is improbable; the sum of money, as matters then stood, exceeds credibility; and the clause as to *the marriage of the eldest son* of the King of Scots, must seem strange, when we recollect that, at that time, he had no son at all.

1322.

It is probable that the omission which gave rise to this animated *Fædera*, III. letter, was accidental. For, in Edward's consent to the cessation of 1001. arms, [dated 14th March], Bruce is treated as a principal party.

1323.

Edward demanded the opinion of his counsellors as to the expedi- *Fædera*, III. ency of this truce. Henry de Beaumont, one of the counsellors, re- 1021. fused to give his opinion. Edward then commanded him to depart from the council-board. 'I had rather go than stay,' answered Beaumont. He saw, but he was too proud to acknowledge, the necessity of the truce. His behaviour admits of no apology. In questions as to what is constitutional, and what is illegal, a counsellor, from diffidence of his own knowledge, or from ignorance, may hesitate: But, when the question is as to expediency, a counsellor ought to deliver his opinion with that dignity which suits his rank, and with the spirit of a free man, [30th March 1323].

On the same day, the treaty of truce, to endure until the 12th *Fædera*, III. June 1336, was concluded, [at Thorpe in the neighbourhood of 1022. Yorke].

It was agreed that, during the truce, no new fortresses should be erected in Cumberland, to the north of the Tine, or in the counties of Berwick, Rokesburgh, and Dumfries.

By a very singular article it was provided, 'that Bruce, and the 'people of Scotland, might procure absolution from the Pope; but, 'in case there was no peace concluded before the expiration of the 'truce, that the sentence of excommunication should revive.' It does not appear how laics, by their own authority, could limit or qualify the operations of a spiritual sentence; and, therefore, it may be presumed, that this provision was made with the consent of the Pope, implied, if not expressed.

Bruce,

1323.

Fœdera, III. 1031.

Bruce, under the style of *King of Scotland*, ratified the treaty, [at Berwick, 7th June 1323], with the consent of his Bishops, Earls, and Barons [*].

Ford. iv. 32. 34.

Edward, while he was negotiating this truce, employed his ambassadors at the Papal court to widen the breach between Scotland and the Pope. He requested the Pope to ratify and publish, in due form [†], the sentence of excommunication against Bruce and his adherents. He said that the Scots, by their contempt of the censures of the church, had incurred the suspicion of heresy, and that they had proceeded to the criminal excess of inflicting tortures, and even capital punishments, on ecclesiastics, without regard to their sacred character [‡]. He farther requested the Pope not to give his sanction for electing Scotsmen to the episcopal office in their native country; 'because,' said Edward, ' the Scottish prelates are they who cherish the nation in its ' rebellion and contumacy.'

Before the Pope had made answer to this request, accounts of the truce between the two nations arrived. This afforded to the Pope an opportunity of denying the request of Edward. He said, that it was his duty to promote, and still more to enforce, a truce; and that, as the King of England had consented that the Scots might obtain a temporary absolution at least, it would be improper to ratify and publish the sentence of excommunication. As to the demand concerning

---

[*] The persons who, together with the King, made oath for the observance of this truce, are thus described in the instrument. All the Earls of Scotland; but their names are not specified. The Stewart, James Douglas, John Menteth, Robert Keith, Henry St Clair, Gilbert de la Haye, David Lindesay, David Graham, Alexander Fraser [or Frisel,] Hugh Rose, Robert Boyd, and Robert Lauder the elder; *Fœdera*, T. iii. 1015.

[†] ' Per crucis fignationem et alia juris remedia ;' *Fœdera*, T. iv. p. 31.

[‡] ' Hiis diebus, in contemptum ecclefiae, indifferenter personas ecclefiafticas tormentis et occidunt ;' *Fœdera*, T. iv. p. 32.

1323.

cerning Scottish Bishops, the Pope made answer, that to grant it, would be to deprive the flock of pastors altogether, seeing no Englishman could receive admittance into Scotland.

The King of Scots, on his side, resolved to send ambassadors for soliciting a reconciliation with the church. Previous, however, to this embassy, he judged it expedient that his nephew Randolph should endeavour to sound the dispositions of the Papal court.

The Pope sent a narrative to the King of England of the conversation which passed between him and Randolph. The narrative is exceedingly curious and characteristical.

Randolph having been admitted to an audience, informed the Pope, that he had made a vow to repair to the Holy-land, but that he could not accomplish it without the permission of the Papal see; and that the main purpose of his journey to Avignon was to seek the indulgences usually bestowed on those who undertook that religious expedition.

The Pope made answer, that it was not fit to grant such permission and indulgences to one who, as a simple individual, could not perform any effectual services; and, as an excommunicated person, could not further his own salvation in Palestine: But, he added, that he would hereafter lend a favourable ear to this petition, if Randolph did his utmost endeavours for procuring the establishment of peace between the two nations.

Randolph then said, that ambassadors were speedily to be sent from Scotland, to solicite a reconciliation with the church, and he requested the Pope to grant them his *own passport* in ample form.

The Pope, although he could not grant this, offered to issue letters requisitorial for their *safe conduct*, addressed to all the Princes through whose territories they might have occasion to journey.

Randolph next produced a commission from his uncle of the following tenor: ' The King of Scots makes offer to the Pope, that he
' will accompany the French King in his intended expedition to the
' Holy-

1323.

'Holy Land; and, if that expedition should not take place, that he
'himself will repair in person to the Holy Land, or send his nephew,
'Thomas Randolph, Earl of Moray, in his stead.'

To this proposal the Pope made answer, 'that, until Bruce con-
'cluded a peace with England, and was reconciled to the church, it
'would not be decent to receive him as a crusader, either in society
'with the French King, or by himself.'

Then the shrewd ambassador observed, that his own wishes were
most ardent for peace with England, and for a perfect reconciliation
with the catholic church: That to this end he would sincerely labour,
were he assisted by the good offices of his Holiness; but that, for rendering such interposition effectual, it would be expedient, and indeed
absolutely necessary, that a Bull should be addressed to Bruce, under
the appellation of *King*. He was confident that a Bull, with that
conciliating title, would be reverently received; but he greatly feared,
that if the name of *King* was with-held, that which had happened formerly would again happen, and the Bull would remain unopened.

The Pope hastily consented to a proposal made with so much appearance of candour; but, recollecting the consequences of what he
had done, he endeavoured to apologize for it to the King of England.
'I remember to have told you,' said he, 'that my bestowing the
'title of *King* on Robert Bruce, would neither strengthen *his* claim,
'nor impair *yours*. My earnest desires are for reconciliation and
'peace; and you well know, that my Bull, issued for attaining those
'salutary purposes, will never be received in Scotland, if I address it to
'Bruce under any other appellation but that of *King*. I therefore
'exhort you, *in your royal wisdom, that you would be pleased, pa-
'tiently to suffer me* to give him that appellation [*]. I hear that re-
'ports

[*] 'Providentiam Regiam exhortamur quatenus—*Velit Regia circumspectis aequani-
'miter tolerare*, quod nos scribamus eidem Roberto sub titulo Regiae dignitatis;' *Fœdera*, T. iv. p. 19. This singular language is preserved in the translation.

1323.

'ports have reached you, as if Randolph had made other proposals,
'prejudicial to you, and your kingdom; but you may assure your-
'self, that I would not have permitted any proposals of that nature to
'have been so much as mentioned in the absence of those to whom
'you have committed the superintendency of your affairs *. Besides,
'Henry de Sully, a person of known zeal for your honour and in-
'terest †, was present at the audience which I gave to Randolph; he
'heard all that passed, and he would not have suffered me, even if I
'had been so inclined, to receive any proposals prejudicial to you, or
'your kingdom,' [13th January 1323-4].

This narrative displays Randolph in the character of a consummate politician.

His first request to the Pope was merely personal, expressing his own zeal in the service of the church, and the estimation in which he held her indulgences; this he represented as the chief business of his journey to Avignon. Although the Pope could not grant the *first and principal request* of Randolph, yet he declared himself willing to listen to it whenever a proper opportunity should offer; and he made his future favour to depend on Randolph's sincerity in promoting the establishment of peace.

Randolph then talked of a reconciliation with the church, an essential preliminary of peace; he mentioned an embassy from Scotland, having that object in view; and he demanded a passport for the ambassadors in a form which would have persuaded the world that the Pope

---

* ' Negotiorum regiorum promotoribus non vocatis;' *Foedera*, T. iv. p. 29. It is uncertain whether the Cardinals pensioned by England, or the Bishop of Winchester and the Dean of Lincoln, the English ambassadors, are here meant.

† He was a pensioner of England, as the Pope well knew; for the Pope, in a letter to Edward, of the same date, requested him to continue his favours to Henry de Sully; *Foedera*, T. iv. p. 28. Sully was probably the bearer of the letter giving an account of what passed at the audience of Randolph.

1323.

Pope himself had invited a reconciliation. The Pope perceived the tendency of the request, and eluded it.

Randolph next produced his commission from the King of Scots, offering to perform a service meritorious in itself, and connected with the glory of the French King, which could not fail of being interesting to a Pope born a Frenchman, and residing at Avignon. The Pope eluded this offer also, but without shewing any marks of displeasure at the extraordinary proposal, that a person lying under the curse of the church, should engage in a crusade by authority of the Pope.

After Randolph had soothed the passions, and conciliated the favour of the Pontiff, he opened the true business of his embassy; and *that*, not as from the King of Scots, but merely as the amicable suggestion of his own zeal for peace, and the honour of the church; and he so judiciously enforced the topics of persuasion, that the Pope consented to give the title of *King* to *one excommunicated person*, by the advice of *another*.

Ford. iv. 46. Edward, however, was not convinced by that casuistry which held, 'that, to bestow the title of *King* on his antagonist, was a matter of ' indifference.' He remonstrated against the concession which the Pope was willing to make; he said, that it was a thing dishonourable to the church, and highly prejudicial to the claims of the English crown: And he added, with great shew of reason, 'that the Scottish ' nation would naturally conclude, that the Pope intended to acknow- ' ledge the *right*, where he had given the *title*.' Neither did Edward omit to retort the maxim of Papal policy, ' that no alteration in the ' condition of the parties ought to be made during the subsistence of ' the truce.'

Ford. xiii. 5. A son was born to the King of Scots, [at Dunfermline, 5th March 1323-4], and named *David*. The court-poets of those times foretold, that

1323.

that this infant would, one day, rival his father's fame, and prove victorious over the English *.

1324.

Edward, the son of John Balliol, had resided for many years on his paternal estate in Normandy, neglected by England, and forgotten by the Scots. The English King now required his presence at court †. It is impossible to discover the purpose of this requisition: The presence of the representative of the rival family could not serve to facilitate the negotiations for a peace between England and Bruce.

The Scottish commissioners for treating of this peace were W. de Lamberton, Bishop of St Andrews, and Randolph. On the part of England, the two D'Espensers, who had all power at that time, and nine more commissioners were appointed, [at Yorke, 8th November].

In the course of the negotiations at Yorke, the English fondly insisted on the claim of feudal sovereignty; but *this* the Scots would not admit ‡; neither would they listen to the insidious, though plausible proposal, of having the contraverted matters argued in presence of the Pope.

The

*Fœd. iv. 61.
81.*

Fœd. vi. 70.

Fœd. iv. 141.

* ' Filius hic Regis, post patrem lumina legis
  ' Diriget, augebit, populum probitate fovebit,
  ' Iste manu fortis Anglorum ludet in hortis.'

  Fordun, L. xiii. c. 5.

† ' Cum dilectus et fidelis noster Edwardus de Baliolo de partibus transmarinis, ad ' nos, *de mandato nostro,* in Anglia sit venturus ;' *Fœdera,* T. iv. p. 62. [2d July.] *Fœdera,* T. iv. p. 81. 2oth August]

‡ Such I understand to be the import of what Edward wrote to the Pope, [8th March 1324 5] *Fœdera,* T. iv. p. 141. ' Scoti, in tractatu illo, nulla alia obtulerunt, ' nisi quae prius in aliis tractatibus obtulerant, quae *absque exhaeredatione* manifesta ' Regiae nostrae coronae, prout alias deliberato consilio fuerit judicatum, concedi ali- ' quatenus non valebant.'

1324.

Ford. lv. 168.
176. Mar. 62.
The Scots had made themselves masters of Berwick, in contempt of the Papal truce, and they still maintained possession of that fortress. When they sought to be reconciled to the church, Edward prevailed on the Pope to reject their prayer, until restitution should be made. But the Scots chose rather to remain under the sentence of excommunication, than to yield up Berwick.

1326.

Ford. xiii. 11.
A parliament was held at Cambuskenneth. The Clergy, Earls, Barons, and all the nobility of Scotland, together with the people, there assembled *, took an oath for performance of fealty and homage to David the King's son, and his issue; whom failing, to Robert Stewart.

Ford. xiii. 12.
At this time, Andrew Moray of Bothwell, the companion of Wallace, obtained in marriage Christian, sister of the King of Scots, and widow of Sir Christopher Seton †.

Ford. xiii. 12.
Barbour, 402.
Walter Stewart, the King's son in law, died, [9th April]. Had he lived, he might have equalled Randolph and Douglas: But his course of glory was short.

Ford. iv. 243.
Edward II. resigned ‡ his crown to his son Edward III. a youth in his fifteenth year, [24th January 1326-7.]

Ford. iv. 270.
271.
Edward III. renewed the negotiations for peace with Scotland, [4th March], and ratified the truce which his father had made, [9th March].

He

* ' Una cum populo ibidem congregato;' *Fordun*, L. xiii. c. 12.

† It was one part of the policy of Robert Bruce, to strengthen his family by matrimonial alliances.

‡ Some historians say, that he was *deposed*; but the difference seems merely verbal. *Tyrrel*, vol. iii. B. 9. p. 317 says, That ' Edward was, *by sentence of parliament, and by* ' *his own solemn resignation, deposed and laid aside.*'

1327.

He received intelligence that the Scots having assembled their for- *Ford. iv. 181, 187.*
ces on the borders, had resolved to infringe the truce, and, if peace
was not instantly concluded, to invade England. Edward discontinued
not the negotiations for peace, yet he summoned his barons to meet
him in arms at Newcastle upon Tine, [5th April]; and made every
preparation for opposing the enemy. At an exorbitant expence he
contracted with John Lord of Beaumont, brother of the Count of *Ford. iv. 290, 294, 357.*
Hainault, for a body of heavy-armed cavalry *, [18th May, 29th
June]; and, with uncommon precaution, he fortified Yorke, [15th *Ford. iv. 296.*
July]: And he even appears to have invited Edward Balliol from
France, that there might be a pretender to the Scottish crown, to be
employed at any fit opportunity, [12th July]. *Ford. iv. 305.*

Historians give different accounts of the causes which moved the *Ford xiii. 12.*
Scots at this time to disregard the truce. Fordun says, in general, *Barbour, 402.*
that they had detected the bad faith of the English †. According to
Barbour,

---

* This *John of Hainault*, as he is commonly called, had a pension for life from Edward III. of 1000 marks yearly; *Fædera*, T. iv. p. 292. He had been a chief instrument in the late revolution, when Isabella invaded England, and dethroned her consort Edward II.—14000 pounds were paid to John of Hainault for the horsemen whom he brought over. Their number is uncertain. The English historians generally say *five hundred*; but Froissart adds, ' Si le suyvit chacun vou'ontiers, selon son pouvoir,
' ceux qui furent mandés, et moult d'autres qui ne furent point mandés: Pourtant
' que chacun pensoit en rapporter autant d'argent comme les autres avoyent fait, qui
' avoient esté en l'autre chevauchée en Angleterre avec lui ;' T. 1. c. 16.

† ' Detectâ eorum fraude ;' *Fordun*, L. xiii. c. 12. *Barnes*, life of Edward III. p. 5. rejects this insinuation, ' because *the English* nation was never noted so much for fineness and subtlety as for downright honesty and blunt valour.' As if the conduct of the sovereign and his counsellors were the standard of the manners and dispositions of the English nation! It is not to be supposed that so prudent a person as Bruce would have involved himself in war with England, unless for weighty causes. Although there had been no other ground of complaint, the machinations of Edward II. which
prevented

ROBERT I.

1327.

Barbour, the English had seized some Scottish ships bound for the low countries, slain the mariners, and refused to make satisfaction.

Ford. xiii. 11.
Froissart, i. 16.
Randolph and Douglas invaded England *, [15th June 1327], on the side of the western borders. Their army was chiefly composed of cavalry, and amounted to about 20,000 men.

Froissart, l. 16.
Edward III. led an army, amounting, at the lowest computation, to 50,000 men, against the invaders, and arrived at Durham, [13th July] †.

Froissart, i. 17.
On the 18th of July, the English descried at a distance the smoke of the flames kindled by the Scots in their cruel progress. They marched out in order of battle, and proceeded towards the quarter from whence the smoke issued. Having marched for two days without receiving any further intelligence, they concluded that the Scots were about to retire. Disencumbering themselves of their heavy baggage,

---

prevented the Pope from granting a temporary absolution to the Scots, would have justified the renewal of hostilities; and, perhaps, it is to this that Fordun alludes in the words, ' Detecta eorum fraude.' On the authority of a chronicle quoted by Stow, *Barnes*, p. 5. and *Tyrrel*, vol. iii. B. 9. p. 340. say, that the Scots commenced hostilities on the very day of the young King's coronation, [1st February,] by attempting to storm the castle of Norham. But this is a gross error. We have seen that Edward ratified the truce, 8th March, and renewed the negotiations for peace, 23d April. Besides, it appears from *Fœdera*, T. iv. p. 287. that the Scots had not commenced hostilities on the 25th April 1327. The first mention of their having invaded England is to be found in an instrument dated at Yorke 17th June; *Fœdera*, T. iv. p. 293. This agrees exactly with Fordun, who says, That the Scots invaded England 17. kal. Jul. or 15th June; l. xiii. c. 12. The attempt against the castle of Norham was made in Autumn 1327; *Leland*, vol. i. p. 551.

* *Tyrrel*, vol. iii. B. 9. p. 340. says, That ' this army was commanded by the Earl of ' Moray and the Lord Thomas Randolph, two experienced commanders.'. Is it possible that Tyrrel wrote the history of Edward II. without discovering that *Lord Thomas Randolph was Earl of Moray?*

† A more particular account of this campaign may be seen in the Appendix.

1327.

gage, they refolved, by a forced march, to reach the river Tine, and, by taking poft on the north banks of that river, to intercept the Scots on their return. With wonderful celerity, the Englifh preffed on through woods, moraffes, and wild deferts. The cavalry, leaving the foot foldiers behind, croffed the river at Haidon, [20th July]. Before the infantry could come up, the river, fwollen by inceffant rains, was no longer fordable; and thus the army remained divided for feveral days, without any accommodation of quarters, and in exceeding want of provifions and forage. The troops now began to murmur; and they hefitated not to affirm, that falfe traitors had led the King and his army into a remote corner, there to perifh through fatigue and famine, without ever encountering an enemy. A new plan of operations was formed, and it was again refolved to march fouthwards. The King proclaimed a reward of lands, to the value of one hundred pounds yearly, for life, to the perfon who fhould firft difcover the enemies ' on dry ground, where they might be attacked.' Many knights and efquires fwam acrofs the river, and fet out upon this fingular fearch. *Froiffart, i. 17. Scala Chron. ap. Leland, i. 551.* *Ford. iv. 912.* *Froiffart, i. 19.*

The army continued to march for three days without receiving any intelligence of the Scots. On the fourth day, Thomas Rokefby, an efquire, brought certain accounts of them. He reported, ' that the ' Scots made him prifoner, but that their leaders, underftanding his ' bufinefs, had difmiffed him, faying, that they had remained for ' eight days on the fame ground, no lefs ignorant of the motions of ' the Englifh, than the Englifh of theirs, and that they were defirous ' and ready to combat.'

With Rokefby for their guide, the Englifh army came in view of the Scots. The Scots were advantageoufly pofted on the fide of a rifing ground, having the river Were in front, and their flanks fecured by rocks and precipices, [1ft Auguft]. The Englifh difmounted and advanced. They hoped to allure the Scots from their faftneffes; but the Scots moved not. Edward fent a herald to Randolph and *Froiffart, i. 20.*

1327.

and Douglas. In the style of those times, he said, 'Either suffer me to
'pass the river, and leave me room for ranging my forces, or, do you
'pass the river, and I will leave you room to range yours, and thus
'shall we fight on equal terms.' But the Scottish commanders scornfully answered, 'We will do neither: On our road hither we have
'burnt and spoiled the country, and *here* are we fixed while to us it
'seems good; and, if the King of England is offended, let him come
'over and chastise us.'

Two days passed in this manner, and the armies continued in sight
of each other. The English, understanding that provisions began to
fail in the camp of the enemies, resolved to maintain a close blockade,
and to reduce the Scots by famine.

Froissart, i. 31.
31. *Knyghton,*
2552. *He-*
mingf. li. 268.
Barbour, 411.
412.

On the morn the English saw, with astonishment, that the Scots
had secretly decamped, and taken post two miles further up the river,
in ground still stronger, and of more difficult access, and amidst a
great wood. The English placed themselves opposite to them, near
Stanhope park. At dead of night, Douglas, with two hundred horsemen, approached the English camp. Under the guise of a chief
commander making the rounds, he called out, 'Hah! St George, is
'there no watch here?' and thus eluding the centinels, passed on undiscovered to the royal quarters. His companions shouted, a Dou-
'glas, a Douglas! English thieves, you shall all die.' They overthrew whatever opposed their passage, and furiously assaulted the
King's tent. The King's domestics made a bold stand to save their
master. His chaplain * and others of his houshold were slain, and
himself hardly escaped. Douglas, disappointed of his prey, rushed
through

---

* *Hemingford,* T. ii. p. 268. calls him 'Vir *audax et armatus,*' which may imply a
censure of the brave chaplain of Edward III.; but, when an ecclesiastic draws his sword
to protect a benefactor and a sovereign, he may, with Hemingford's good leave, be
forgiven, although he should become *canonically irregular.*

1327.

through the enemies, and, with inconfiderable lofs, retreated *, [4th August.]

Next day the English learned from a prifoner that general orders had been iffued for all men to hold themfelves in readinefs that evening to follow the banner of Douglas. The English apprehending a night-attack, made themfelves ready for battle, lighted up great fires, and kept moft vigilant watch. *Froiffart,l.32.*

On

* In relating this celebrated *camifade* of Douglas, I have carefully followed the narrative drawn up by Froiffart, from information which feems to have been communicated by officers who had ferved under John de Hainault.—Had I leifure or inclination to criticife on former hiftorians, I might obferve, that there is a writer who fays, that *Douglas left the greateft part of his followers*; and, in proof of this, quotes various authors, who mention nothing of the lofs fuftained by Douglas, and Froiffart, who moft expresfsly afferts that his lofs was very fmall, ' Perdit aucuns de fes gens ' à la retraite, mais ce ne fut mie grandement;' vol. 1. p. 21. *Barbour*, p. 411. &c. fays, That Douglas had 500 horfemen with him; that they cut the tent-poles, and flew the English as they came out of their tents naked and unarmed. It appears from his account, that Douglas came in upon the rear of the English, and, if I miftake not, upon the rear of the right wing or firft battle. Barbour relates a little incident which I fhall give in his own words:

   ' And as they near were approuchand,
   ' An Englishman that lay *beekend*
   ' Him by the fire, faid to his *feer*,
   ' I wit not what may tide us here,
   ' But right a great *growing* me *tais*,
   ' I dread fore for the Black Douglas.
   ' And he that heard him, faid, *perfay*
   ' You fhall have caufe if that I may;
   ' With that, with all his company,
   ' He rufhed in on them hardily,
   ' And the *palzions* down he bare,' &c.

Beekend, bafking, warming; *feer*, companion; *growing*, fhuddering; *tais*, takes; *perfay*, by my faith; *palzions*, pavilions, tents.

1327.

Froissart, i. 32. On the morning two trumpeters were brought in prisoners. They reported that the Scots had decamped before midnight, and were returning to their own country. The English would not credit this strange and unwelcome report. They remained in order of battle during several hours, and still hoped and looked for the appearance of the enemy. At length some scouts having crossed the river, returned with certain intelligence, that the Scottish camp was totally deserted, [6th August.]

Barbour, 419 &c. Barbour relates, that there was a morass in the rear of the Scottish camp, which he calls the *two mile moss*; that the Scots made a road with brush-wood through the morass, and having thus passed over, removed the brush-wood, lest the English should pursue them.

Hemingford, ii. 268. Scala Chron. ap. Leland. i. 551. When the young King heard that the enemy had escaped out of his toils, he wept bitterly.

Froissart, i. 32. To pursue the Scots, already many miles distant, would have been in vain; and, indeed, the cavalry of Edward were so worn out by long marches and scanty sustenance, that they could hardly move to Durham. After having rested there for some days, Edward marched to Yorke, and then disbanded his army, [15th August.] The soldiers

Ford. lv. 304. of Hainault also were dismissed. They procured horses to convey themselves to the south of England, for their own horses had all died, or had become unserviceable, in the course of a three weeks campaign, [20th August.]

Thus, after foreign auxiliaries had been hired at an enormous expence, and the whole power of England had been exerted against the Scottish invaders, the enterprise of Edward III. terminated in disappointment and dishonour.

Hem. ii. 268. Various causes were assigned for the bad success of the northern expedition. Some men censured the auxiliaries of Hainault, and said that those foreigners were remiss in the public cause, through jealousy

of

1327.

of the renown which the English would have acquired by overcoming their enemies.

Others suspected treachery, and said, that some of the English commanders having been won by bribes, permitted the Scots to escape from Stanhope park. Mortimer, in particular, has been charged as the prime contriver of this treason, and as having received twenty thousand pounds from the Scots for his reward [a].

But all this is the language of pride and disappointment. The troops of Hainault had no cause to be jealous of the glory in which they themselves, who led the van, would have eminently shared; and, indeed, they appear to have suffered more by laborious marches, than probably they would have done, had they encountered the enemy. That Mortimer should have contributed to blast the honour of his own administration, is not to be lightly credited; and, although he had been willing to accept of a bribe of twenty thousand pounds, it was a sum which the King of Scots could not have bestowed. Froissart, who has given an ample account of the campaign 1327, never insinuates that the Scottish army was permitted to retire through any treachery of the English commanders. And, notwithstanding what has been said by Murimuth, and his many transcribers, it does not appear that 'the having connived at the escape of the Scots' was made one of the articles of Mortimer's impeachment; and this is the more remarkable, because the impeachment contains some articles of a nature less heinous.

Mortimer,

[a] 'Causæ verò mortis dicti Comitis Marchiæ; quæ imponebantur ei, fuerunt infra scriptæ —Secunda causa imposita fuit, quod ipse impedivit honorem Regis et regni apud *Stanhope park*, ubi Scoti fugerunt, qui capi et interfici potuerunt faciliter, si ipse, qui fuit major de consilio Regis, Anglicos cum Scotis hic congredi fecisset, ipse item, quia recepit XX mille libras a Scotis, illos tunc permisit evadere;' *A. Murimuth*, p. 77. *Walsingham* transcribes the words of Murimuth, *Hist. Angl.* p. 131. and *Tpud. Neust.* p. 511. To the same purpose, the Anonymous writer of the reign of Edward III. speaks, p. 398.

ROBERT. I.

1327.

Knyghton.
Brady, Tyrrel,
ut sup.

Mortimer, indeed, was charged in parliament, as guilty of embezzling the money paid by the Scots to England, in consequence of a treaty concluded in 1328; and it is not improbable, that this circumstance might have given rise to a general report, that he had received money from the Scots for aiding them in England.

The causes of that disgrace which befell the English in the summer 1327, may be easily discovered.

Without guides, and without intelligence of the motions of the enemy, they resolved, at all hazards, to pursue and attack the Scots, active, and accustomed to sudden predatory incursions, and led by able commanders. Former events had taught the English not to despise their adversaries; they now erred through excess of caution, and began, even from the gates of Durham, to march in order of battle. In a country uneven and difficult, their motions were slow, and ill suited to the rapidity of the course of that enemy whom they had to encounter.

No measures had been taken, and perhaps none could have been taken, for supplying the troops with provisions and forage.

The forced march to the banks of the Tine appears to have been ably planned; and, if the English army could have maintained itself in those quarters, it would have been exceedingly difficult for the Scots to retreat home, without engaging in a general action at great disadvantage. But it was not easy to find sustenance for an army of 50,000 men in the interior parts of Northumberland; and it was still harder to persuade bold-spirited and impatient barons to endure every sort of hardship in obscure and inactive cantonments, and quietly to wait for that enemy whom they were eager to seek. Troops, ill disciplined, and unaccustomed to fatigue, are apt to murmur at the delays of war: In such circumstances, the commanders of armies are often obliged to prefer the popular wishes to their own judgment; and, therefore, if the event proves disastrous, they are rather to be pitied than censured.

Every

ROBERT I.

1327.

Every thing which befell the English after they quitted the banks of the Tine, must be ascribed to the superior skill and vigilance of the Scottish commanders. What wonder that an inexperienced monarch of sixteen, a court favourite, some foreign officers, unacquainted with the country, and a croud of barons equally unfit to command or obey, should have been foiled by Douglas and Randolph!

Douglas and Randolph having returned expeditiously into Scotland, [9th August], the King of Scots resolved to lead his army against the eastern borders. He besieged the castle of Norham, which was gallantly defended by Robert Maners *. Douglas and Randolph were detached to make an attempt on the castle of Alnwick; but having failed in their enterprise, they returned to the King, who still lingered before Norham.

Ford. xiii. 12. Scala Chron. ap. Leland. L. 551.

So exhausted was the English treasury, that the demands of the foreign auxiliaries could not be discharged. Violent animosities prevailed among the great Lords, and the power of the Queen-mother, and Mortimer, who ruled the young King, was not firmly established. The events of the late campaign had been singularly unfortunate; and there were, in truth, no reasonable hopes of more prosperous success in the prosecution of the war. These considerations induced the English government to entertain serious thoughts of peace. William de Denoun, a lawyer, was sent to the King of Scots at Norham, with some proposals for the marriage of the Princess Johanna of England, and

Froissart, L. 19.

Scala Chron. ap. Leland. i. 551.

---

* ' In eadem obsidione apud Norham, Wilielmus de Monte-alto, Johannes de Clapham, et Malisius de Dobery, cum aliis propriâ inertiâ interfecti sunt;' *Fordun, L. xiii. c. 12.* This probably means that they were negligent in duty, and suffered themselves to be surprised. In *Scala Chron. ap. Leland. T. i. p. 551.* W. de Monte-alto is called *Mauhand*, i. e. *Mowhand*, now pronounced *Mowat*. Clapham seems to be the same as *Clapham*. I can form no conjecture as to *Dobery*; that person, from his appellation of *Malife*, appears to have been a native of Scotland. Boece being at a loss, as I am, turned *Dobery* into *Dunbar*.

126   ROBERT I.

1327.

and David, the only son of the King of Scots. This alliance was intended to be the basis of a treaty. Soon after, William de Denoun,
and Henry de Percy, were appointed plenipotentiaries for concluding
a peace with Scotland, [9th October]. To them other plenipotentiaries were added, [23d November]. But the persons who chiefly
managed this important business were Douglas and Mortimer.

Elizabeth, the consort of Robert Bruce, King of Scots, died, [26th
October]. She was buried at Dunfermline.

The commissioners for the treaty met at Newcastle, and drew up
certain articles of pacification. The English King summoned a parliament to meet at Yorke on the 8th of February 1327-8, for deliberating on those articles, [10th December]. Meanwhile, a short
truce was concluded with Scotland, [25th January 1327-8].

In the parliament at Yorke, the important preliminary, of renouncing all claim of superiority over Scotland, appears to have been ad-
justed*. Edward ' willed and consented, that the said kingdom, ac-
' cording

Ford. iv. 314.
Ford. iv. 315.
Ford. xiii. 18.
Ford. iv. 318.
Ford. iv. 337.

* This instrument is printed in *Fœdera*, T. iv. p. 337. from a copy, as I understand, in the Chronicle of Lanercoſt. *Tyrrel*, v. iii. p. 350. supposes this to be the
only copy extant; but he is mistaken; there is another in *Fordun*, L. xiii. c. 12. and
one more accurate than either, in an instrument under the hand of Wardlaw Bishop
of St Andrews, an. 1415. Mr Goodall, the editor of Fordun, has published this inſtrument according to Wardlaw's copy; its concluſion is more accurate than in *Fœdera*: ' Et ad præmiſſa omnia plenè, pacificè, et fideliter perpetuis temporibus obſer-
' vanda, dilectis et fidelibus noſtris Henrico de Percy, conſanguineo noſtro, et Willelmo
' le Zouſch de Aſſeby, et eorum alteri, ad ſacramentum in animam noſtram inde
' præſtandum, per alias literas noſtras patentes, plenam dedimus poteſtatem ac man-
' datum ſpeciale. In cujus rei teſtimonium, has literas noſtras fecimus patentes. Dat.
' ap. Ebor. primo die Martii, anno regni noſtri ſecundo,' i. e. March 1ſt 1327-8. This
William de la Zouche was a *Mortimer*; his father Robert married a lady of the family
of *de la Zouche*. William aſſumed the name of his mother, on obtaining a grant of
the barony of Aſhbie in Leiceſterſhire. See *Burton*, Leiceſterſhire, p. 19. The renunciation of all claim to the ſuperiority of Scotland was made before the peace, probably

ROBERT I.

1327.

'cording to its antient boundaries observed in the days of Alexan-
'der III. should remain unto Robert King of Scots, and unto his heirs
'and successors, free and divided from the kingdom of England, with-
'out any subjection, right of service, claim, or demand, whatever;
'and that all writings which might have been executed at any time
'to the contrary, should be held as void and of no effect.' [Yorke,
1st March 1327-8].

1328.

Peace with Scotland was concluded in a parliament held at Nor- *A. Murim. 71.*
thampton, [April 1328].

The original treaty is not extant, neither is there any transcript *Calendars of*
of it to be found; yet, from a careful examination of public instru- *Antient Char-*
ments, and of the writings of antient historians, it may be collected, *ters,* intr. 56.
that the chief articles of the treaty were these following:

I. There shall be a perpetual peace between the two kingdoms of *Fœd. iv. 337.*
England and Scotland. *Fœd. xiii. 11.*

II. The stone on which the Kings of Scotland were wont to sit at *Calendars of*
the time of their coronation, shall be restored to the Scots *. *Antient Char-*
ters, intr. 58.

III. The King of England engages to employ his good offices at *Fœd. iv. 350.*
the Papal court for obtaining a revocation of all spiritual processes de-
pending

bably that the two Kings might treat upon an equal footing, as sovereign and independent Princes.

* We owe the knowledge of this singular circumstance to the industrious author of
the Introduction to *The Calendars of Antient Charters*. He has discovered a writ under the privy seal, 1st July 1328, by Edward III. to the Dean and Chapter of Westminster, reciting, 'That his council had, in his parliament held at Northampton, a-
'greed that this stone should be sent to Scotland; and requiring the Dean and Chap-
'ter, in whose custody it was, to deliver it to the sheriffs of London, who were to cause
'it to be carried to the Queen-mother.'

1329.

pending before the Holy See against the King of Scots, or against his kingdom or subjects *.

Fœd. iv. 397. 410. &c.

IV. For thefe caufes, and in order to make reparation for the ravages committed in England by the Scots, the King of Scots fhall pay 30,000 merks to the King of England †.

Fœd. iv. 373. 467.

V. Reftitution fhall be made of the poffeffions belonging to ecclefiaftics in either kingdom, whereof they may have been deprived during the war ‡.

Fœd. iv. 384.

VI. But there fhall not be any reftitution made of inheritances which have fallen into the hands of the King of England, or of the King of Scots, by reafon of the war between the two nations, or through the forfeiture of former poffeffors ‖.

VII.

---

* To this purpofe Edward III. addreffed the Pope and the Cardinals in a more earneft ftrain than mere benevolence to the King and nation of Scotland would have excited; *Fœdera*, T. iv. p. 350.

† From the different paffages in *Fœdera*, referred to, it feems that this fum was to be paid at the rate of 10,000 merks, annually, on St John Baptift's day. Whether that day was fixed upon by accident, or whether the Englifh chofe to have this pecuniary acknowledgement made on the *Anniverfary of Bannockburn*, I know not.

‡ ' Quod viris ecclefiafticis utriufque regni, fuper poffeffionibus fuis per guerram oc-
' cupatis, nulletenus præjudicetur;' *Fœdera*, T. iv. p. 467. It appears from *Fœdera*,
T. iv. p. 373. that this article was, *bona fide*, executed by both nations. For Edward III. acknowledged that the King of Scots had made the ftipulated reftitution, and he, on his part, ordered reftitution to be made to the Abbeys of Jedburgh, Melrofs, Kelfo, and Dundrenan.

‖ Such a provifion was either expreffed or implied with refpect to Scotfmen. This appears from a grant in *Fœdera*, T. iv. p. 384. by Edward III. to Sir James Douglas :
' Sciatis, quod *de gratia noftra fpeciali* dedimus, conceffimus, et reddidimus.—Jacobo
' Douglas militi, manerium de Faudon, cum pertinentiis, in comitatu Northumbriæ,
' et omnes alias terras, &c. quæ Willielmus Douglas pater fuus habuit in Anglia, et
' quæ occafione guerræ inter Dominum E. quondam Regem Angliæ, avum no-
' ftrum, et tunc Regem Scotiæ, motæ, in manum ipfius avi noftri, tanquam fibi forif-
' factæ,

ROBERT I.

1328.

VII. But Thomas Lord Wake of Ledel, Henry de Beaumont Earl of Buchan, and Henry de Percy, shall be restored to their lordships, lands, and estates, whereof the King of Scots, by reason of the war between the two nations, had taken possession [a].

VIII.

---

[a] '[sese], capta fuerunt, et sic ad manus nostras devenerunt;' (ap. Ekham 12th May 1329.) *Abercrombie*, v. 1. p. 626. says, 'Though Englishmen were not to be repossessed 'of those estates Edward I. had given them in Scotland, yet Scotsmen were reponed 'to those he had taken from them in England; for which reason the lands of Fawdon 'in Northumberland, that had belonged to Sir William Douglas before the war first 'broke out, were now restored to Sir James Douglas, his son;' *Fordera*, T. iv. p. 384. Thus Abercrombie, thinking to do honour to his native country, has mistaken the plain import of the grant to Sir James Douglas, and has represented the treaty of Northampton as a treaty partial and unjust. Words cannot be plainer than those in the grant by Edward III. to Douglas; it is a restitution *through special favour* alone; and, indeed, it is impossible that different rules should have been established with respect to Englishmen in Scotland and Scotsmen in England. Modern historians have enlarged and embellished this article according to their own imaginations, and ancient historians have hardly mentioned it at all. There is some allusion to it in the following passage: ' But these Lords, Percy, Wake, Beaumont, and Zouche wald not agre 'upon this condition that the Englishmen should lefe such lands as they held by in-'heritance in Scotland;' *Scala Chron.* ap. Leland. T. i. p. 552.—It is provided by Statute 7. Parl. 1. James III. 'That na Englishman have *benefice secular* or religious 'within the realme of Scotland, *after the forme of the all maid thereupon by King Ro-*'*bert the Bruyse*.' No such act exists; for c. 24. Robert I. is of a less extensive import; it can hardly be supposed that *benefices seculars* comprehended all land-estates. It will be observed, that, by the treaty of Northampton, the King of Scots, in effect, renounced all claim to his paternal inheritances in England.

[b] *Henry de Beaumont*, in right of his wife, an heir pariener of the Earl of Buchan. *Thomas Lord Wake* of Ledel, or Lidel, was proprietor of that lordship. *Henry de Percy* had possessions in Galloway and Angus. The lands of *Vere* in Galloway and of Redcastle in Angus were his property. These lands formerly belonged to Henry de Balliol; they descended to his daughter and heir Constance, and from her, to her son Henry de Fishbarn, who sold them to Percy. *Dugdale*, T. i. p. 273. I have doubts as to the word *Vere*, which is in Dugdale. For further particulars, see *Dugdale*, articles *Beaumont*, *Wake*, and *Percy*.

1328

Fœd. iv. 354. VIII. Johanna, sister of the King of England, shall be given in marriage to David, the son and heir of the King of Scots.

Fœd. iv. 354. IX. The King of Scots shall provide the Princess Johanna in a jointure of L. 2000 yearly, secured on land and rents, according to a reasonable estimation †.

Reg. Ar. 2560. X. If either of the parties fail in performing the conditions of this treaty, he shall pay two thousand pounds of silver to the Papal treasury.

Such appear to have been the chief articles of a treaty, honourable for the Scots, and necessary for England.

The English historians, indeed, term the peace of Northampton *ignominious*, and the marriage of the Princess Johanna, *that base marriage*; because, on that occasion, Edward III. renounced a claim of superiority which the bloody and ruinous wars of full twenty years had in vain attempted to establish.

They who censure pacific measures, are generally persons exempted by their condition from the toils and dangers, and intolerable expence of war. No peace is ever adequate to the sanguine expectations of the vulgar: And, through some strange fatality, the expectations of the vulgar are no less sanguine after a long series of disasters, than after the most signal and uninterrupted success.

There were many causes which concurred to render the peace of Northampton necessary. England, at that period, was miserably divided by factions, under the dominion of a youth of sixteen, and, through the prodigality of the former reign, so impoverished, as hardly to be capable of paying for the feeble aid obtained from foreign mercenaries.

---

† ' Duo millia librarum terræ et reddituś per annum, per rationabilem exentum;' *Fœdera*, T. iv. p. 354. We may presume that the next yearly produce would be ascertained by an inquest, and this would produce a new *extent* of great part of the crown lands and rents.

1328.

mercenaries *. There were no able and experienced commanders to oppose against Bruce, Randolph, and Douglas: And, however harsh it may now found, it is acknowledged by the antient English historians, that, in the course of a twenty years war, the spirit of Scotland had attained an astonishing ascendant over the English.

That motives of private interest, also, induced Queen Isabella and Mortimer to precipitate a peace with Scotland, will not be denied. All the misfortunes which might have ensued in the prosecution of the war, would have been ascribed to the errors of their administration, while Edward alone would have reaped the glory of any successful enterprise: And, indeed, a young King, if bred up in camps, and constantly surrounded by his barons, could not have been long detained in a state of tutelage favourable to the ambition of Isabella and Mortimer.

Fortunate it is for a nation when the selfish views of its rulers chance to coincide with the public interest.

In consequence of the treaty of Northampton, David, Prince of Scotland, married Johanna, the daughter of Edward II. [at Berwick, 12th July].

1329.

Robert Bruce, the restorer of the Scottish monarchy, departed this life [at Cardross, 7th June 1329].

He had long laboured under an inveterate disease, which, in those days, was termed a leprosy †. He died at the age of 55. His remains

---

* Of the 14,000 marks due by treaty to John of Hainault, the first moiety was not discharged before the end of June 1328. *Fœdera*, T. iv. p. 357. The other moiety was advanced by some Florentin merchants, and Edward III. bestowed a gratuity of two thousand pounds on them for their good services, [25th May 1349.] *Fœdera*, T. iv p. 387.

† ' Lepra percussus.' *W. Hemingford*, T. li. p. 270. ' Chargé de la *grosse maladie* ce ' disoit on ;' *Froissart*, T. i. 24.

1329.

mains were interred, near thofe of his confort, in the middle of the choir at Dunfermline.

*Barbour, 437.
Ford. iv. 480.*

Bruce, in his laſt hours, requeſted Douglas, his old and faithful companion in arms, to repair with his heart to Jeruſalem, and humbly to depoſit it at the ſepulchre of our Lord [*].

Some authors aſcribe this requeſt to motives of policy, and obſerve, that, although Douglas and Randolph had hitherto harmoniouſly exerted their abilities in the public cauſe under their common ſovereign, yet that, after his death, emulation and diſſenſions might poſſibly have ariſen between thoſe high ſpirited men, who were equal in merit and popularity; and, therefore, that, to remove Douglas from Scotland, was a judicious contrivance for obviating the evils apprehended.

Nevertheleſs, when we recollect the notions of thoſe times, it is not improbable that Bruce had indeed reſolved to carry his arms into Paleſtine, and, by honourable and meritorious ſervice againſt the Saracens, to compleat his military glories, and make expiation for all his offences, and that now, diſappointed of this hope, he requeſted Douglas to convey his heart to Jeruſalem, as a teſtimony to the Chriſtian world of his penitence, faith, and zeal.

*Ford. xii. 29.
Charter of
Sutherland,
24. October
1347. Crawford, Peerage,
2. 377.*

Robert I. married Iſabella, the daughter of Donald, tenth Earl of Marre. By her he had iſſue a daughter, Marjory, married to Walter the Stewart of Scotland. His ſecond wife was Elizabeth, the daughter of Aymer de Burgh, Earl of Ulſter. By her he had iſſue, *David* II. Margaret, married to William Earl of Sutherland [†]; Matildis, married to

---

[*] Edward III. granted a paſſport to Sir James Douglas on his journey: ' Verſus ' Terram Sanctam in auxilium Chriſtianorum contra Saracenos, cum corde Domini ' R. Regis Scotiae nuper defuncti,' [1ſt Sept. 1329.] *Fœdera,* T. iv. p. 400.

[†] She had a ſon *John,* who died in England; *Fœdera,* T. v. p. 724. *Fordun,* L. ix. c. 13. L. xiv. c. 25. Fordun ſays, that the Counteſs of Sutherland died ſoon after the birth of her ſon: ' Mater poſt partum ſtatim ex hac luce migravit.'

1329.

to an Esquire, one Thomas Isaac *; [Elisabeth, married to Sir Walter Oliphant of Gask †.]

DAVID II.

IN consequence of the act of settlement 1318, Randolph assumed the character of Regent.

Indefatigable

* ' Quae nupsit cuidam armigero, nomine *Thomas Isaac*.' She had two daughters, Johanna married to John Lord of Lorn, and Catharine who died unmarried; *Fordun*, L. xiv. c. 7. *Crawfurd*, Peerage, p. 72. has thus perverted the passage in Fordun, ' Quae ex *Thoma de Tyack* habuit filiam,' &c. His intention was to conceal the mean marriage of the daughter of Bruce, and therefore he suppressed the words *quidam armiger*, [a certain esquire,] and he changed the name of *Thomas Isaac* into *Thomas de Tyack*, which has the appearance of a more dignified appellation, assumed from lands. There is a singular passage in *Fordun*, L. ix. c. 13. ' De Matilde penitus tacco, quia ' nihil egit memoriâ dignum ;' i. e. ' I chuse to be altogether silent as to Matilda, ' for she did nothing which deserves to be remembered.' Whether this passage only alludes to her mean alliance with Thomas Isaac, or whether it also implies a particular censure on her character, I know not.

† *Crawfurd*, Peerage, p. 72. is positive as to the existence of this *Elisabeth*; he says, ' I have seen a charter in the custody of Oliphant of Gask, bearing date on the 11th ' of January 1364, whereby King David erects the lands of Gask into a barony ; *Di-* ' *lecto et fideli suo* Waltero Olyfant *et* Elisabethae, *sponsae suae, dilectae sorori nostrae*.' In the MS. collections of Sir Alexander Seton, [Lord Pitmedden,] the charter is quoted as containing these words, ' Dilecto et fideli nostro Waltero Oliphant pro ' bono servitio suo nobis impenso, et Elisabethae sorori nostrae.' Here the word *dilectae* is omitted. Not having had any opportunity of inspecting this charter, I must still hesitate. The silence of Fordun and his continuator is remarkable ; every one conversant in antient deeds knows that *filius, filia, frater*, are words which do not necessarily imply legitimate relation. To remove all doubts, the charter itself, if extant, ought to be deposited in the Register-house.

Robert Bruce had a natural son, *Robert*, of whom mention will be made hereafter ;

1329.

Indefatigable in discharging the duties of his station, he secured the public tranquillity by wise ordinances, and distributed speedy and severe justice.

Ford. xiii. 18.
One example of the fortitude of his administration is too singular to be passed over in silence. A certain man having slain a priest, went to the Papal court, obtained absolution, and boldly returned to Scotland. Randolph ordered him to be tried, and, on conviction, to be executed: 'Because, although the Pope may grant absolution as to 'the spiritual consequences of sin, he cannot screen offenders from 'civil punishment *.'

1330.

Froissart, i. 21.
Ford. xiii. 20.
Barbow, 433.
Meanwhile Douglas, having the charge of the heart of his dear master, set sail from Scotland with a numerous and splendid retinue, [June]. He anchored off Sluys in Flanders, the great emporium of the Low Countries, where he expected to find companions in his pilgrimage †. He there learnt, that Alphonsus XI. the young King of Leon and Castile ‡, waged war with Osmyn, the Moorish commander in Granada.

The

---

* ' Quamvis sufficienter ostensum est, ipsum fore absolutum à *culpa*, tamen oportuit 'eum plecti pro *offensâ*;' *Fordun,* L. xiii c. 18.

† *Froissart,* T. i. c. 21. says, that Douglas had in his train a knight bearing a banner, [probably Sir William St Clair of Rosslin,] and seven other knights, and twenty six esquires, all 'comely young men of good family,' besides many attendants of inferior rank; that he kept open table, [tinel,] with trumpets and timbals, as if he had been King of Scotland, and that he was served in gold and silver plate. Froissart adds, that all persons of condition who visited him on shipboard were well entertained, with two sorts of wine, and two sorts of spice. ' Et sachez que tous ceux qui le 'vouloyent aller veoir, estoient bien servis de deux manieres de vins et de deux ma-'nieres d'espices.'

‡ *Froissart,* T. i. c. 21. says, ' Alphonsus IV. King of Arragon;' but that is a mistake, however implicitly followed by many historians: For we learn from *Mariana,*

L.

DAVID II.   135

1330.

The temptation of bearing arms against the enemies of the Christian faith was too violent to be resisted. In the judgment of those times, it was a holy warfare; and it seemed, in some measure, to correspond with the purposes of the journey which Douglas had undertaken: He therefore resolved to visit Spain, and combat the Saracens in his progress to Jerusalem *.

Douglas and his companions were honourably entertained by Alphonsus †. *Barbour, 433.*

The Spaniards came in view of the enemy near Theba ‡, a castle on the frontiers of Andalusia, towards the kingdom of Granada. *Mariana, xv. 21.* Osmyn the Moor ordered three thousand horsemen to make a feigned attack on the Spaniards, while, with the rest of his army, he took a circuit, with the intent of falling on the rear of the camp of Alphonsus. The King, having received intelligence of this stratagem, opposed some troops to the Moorish cavalry, and stood prepared in his camp to encounter Osmyn. Osmyn attacked the Spaniards, was repulsed and discomfited. The King, improving his victory, advanced, and won the camp of the enemies.

The

L. xv. c. 21, that the King of Arragon, although joined in alliance with the King of Castile against the Moors, did not bring his troops to the field.

* It is probable, however, that Douglas had projected this expedition before he quitted Scotland. His passport from Edward III. [dated 1st September 1329] is to him on his journey, ' Versus Terram Sanctam in auxilium Christianorum contra Sa-
' racenos cum corde Domini R. Regis Scotiae nuper defuncti;' *Foedera*, T. iv. p 400.

† It is reported, that, in the army of Alphonsus, there was an officer having his face altogether disfigured with the scars of wounds received in battle: ' It astonishes me,' said he, petulantly, to Douglas, ' that you, who are said to have seen so much service, ' should have no marks of wounds on your face:' ' Thank Heaven,' answered Douglas, ' I had always an arm to protect my face.' *Barbour*, p. 434

‡ Or *Teva*. *Fordun*, L. xiii. c. 21. quotes a metrical epitaph on Douglas, which says, ' Apud castrum Tibris.'

136   D A V I D II.

1330.

Barbour, 435.
—458.
Ford. xiii. 21.

The detached troops fought with equal advantage, and the Moorish cavalry fled. Douglas, with his companions, eagerly pursued the Saracens. Taking the casket which contained the heart of Bruce, he threw it before him, and cried, ' Now pass thou onward as thou wast ' wont, and Douglas will follow thee, or die !' The fugitives rallied. Surrounded and overwhelmed by superior numbers, Douglas fell [*]. [25th August].

Barbour, 441.

His few surviving companions found his body in the field, together with the casket, and reverently conveyed them to Scotland. The remains of Douglas were interred in the sepulchre of his forefathers, [†] and the heart of Bruce was deposited at Melros.

David

---

[*] While attempting to rescue Sir William St Clair of Roslin, he shared his fate; *Barbour*, 437. Robert and Walter Logan, both of them knights, were slain with Douglas. His friend Sir William Keith, having had his arm broke, was detained from the battle; *Barbour*, p. 439.

[†] Douglas was interred in the church of Douglas. His natural son Archibald Douglas erected a marble monument to his memory; *Barbour*, p. 441. But his countrymen have more effectually perpetuated his name by bestowing on him the appellation of ' the good Sir James Douglas;' *Fordun* reports, L. xiii. c. 21. that Douglas was thirteen times defeated in battle, and fifty seven times victorious. There are who quote Fordun as reporting ' that Douglas was *thirteen* times victorious over the Sara' cens.' *Boece*, L. xv. fol. 311. b. confidently asserts, that Douglas, after having buried the King's heart at Jerusalem, waged war with the Saracens in Palestine, and obtained many victories over them: That, in his return homewards, he was driven by a tempest on the coasts of Spain, where he died in battle. Boece had the works of Barbour and Fordun before his eyes when he invented this tale.

Perhaps my readers will not dislike to see the portrait of Douglas drawn by *Barbour*, p. 13.

' In visage was he some deal gray,
' And had black hair, as I heard say,
' But then of limbs he was well made,
' With bones great and shoulders braid.

' His

1331.

David II. and his confort Johanna, were anointed and crowned [*], *Ford. xiii. 11.* [24th November, at Scone].

About this time, an incident, unimportant in itfelf, is faid to have *Ford. xiii. 20.* been productive of mighty confequences. One Twynham Lowrifon was enjoined by William Heckford, official of the Bifhop of Glafgow, to do penance for adultery; he difregarded the fentence, and was excommunicated.

Twynham, with his profligate affociates, way-laid and cruelly beat the official, and extorted from him a large fum of money. After having committed this outrage, he fled into France, and there, as is reported, he found accefs to Edward Balliol; and, by difplaying the internal weaknefs of the Scottifh government, excited him to re-affert his claim to the crown.

Such is the account propagated from Fordun by our later hiftorians. But, in truth, there needed not the fuggeftions of an obfcure out-law for perfuading Edward Balliol to revive the pretenfions of his family.

1332.

The circumftances of this part of our national hiftory are momentous and interefting.

By

' His body well made and lenzie,
' As they that faw him faid to me.
' When he was blyth he was lovely
' And meek, and fwert in company;
' But who in battle might him fee,
' Another countenance had he,
' And in his fpeech he lifpt fome deal,
' But that fet him right wonder well.'

[*] By James Ben Bifhop of St Andrews. In the Advocates library at Edinburgh, there is extant an original Bull of Pope John XXII. addreffed to Robert Bruce, which impowers the Bifhop of St Andrews, and failing him the Bifhop of Glafgow, to a noint and crown the Kings of Scotland.

1332.

Ford. iv. 461.

By the treaty of Northampton, in the year 1328, it was provided, 'That Thomas Lord Wake of Ledel, Henry de Beaumont, called 'Earl of Buchan, and Henry de Percy, should be restored to their 'lordships, lands, and estates, whereof the King of Scots, by reason 'of the war between the two nations, had taken possession.'

Ford. iv. 461. 471. 518.

The article was performed as to Henry de Percy, but not as to Lord Wake and Henry de Beaumont; and, although Edward repeatedly complained of this delay of justice,* [1st December 1330, 24th February 1330-1, and 22d April 1332], yet he obtained no satisfaction.

Hume, History of England, ii. 163.

For this our historians have offered no specious excuse. Vainly do they say, that the inheritances of Lord Wake, and Henry de Beaumont, had been bestowed on the followers of Robert Bruce, and could not, without difficulty, be wrested from them †; for those inheritances, instead

---

* By some strange error, the requisition of the 22d April 1332, is limited to the estates of Lord Wake; although it appears from that very instrument, that Henry de Beaumont had not been restored.

† Such is the hypothesis of Mr Hume, v. ii. p. 163. he says, ' It had been stipula-
' ted in this treaty, that both the Scottish nobility, who, before the commencement of
' the wars, enjoyed lands in England, and the English who inherited estates in Scot-
' land, should be restored to their several possessions ; *Rymer*, v. 4. p. 384. But though
' this article had been executed pretty regularly on the part of Edward, Robert, who
' saw the estates claimed by Englishmen much more numerous and valuable than the
' other, either esteemed it dangerous to admit so many secret enemies into the king-
' dom, or found it *difficult to wrest from his own followers the possessions bestowed on
' them as the reward of their fatigues and dangers*; and he had protracted the perfor-
' mance of his part of the stipulation,' &c. Errors are crowded into this short para-
graph. 1. There was no article in the treaty of Northampton concerning a general and
reciprocal restitution. See *Annals*, p. 127. &c. 2. There is no evidence that Robert Bruce
protracted the performance of the treaty on his part, or that Edward III. ever complained of *his* delays. It is strange that Mr Hume should have quoted *Fœdera*, T. iv.
p. 384. and yet have said, that *Robert Bruce protracted the performance on his part,
while the article had been pretty regularly executed on the part of Edward III.* for the
instrument

1332.

instead of having been given away, did still, in all probability, remain with the crown. At the same time, it is undeniable, that, even laying aside all considerations of good faith, and of the sanctity of treaties, the true interest of the Scots led them to maintain the peace of Northampton inviolated; and, it is equally undeniable, that their true interest could not have been overlooked by Randolph, a politician of mature and exquisite judgment.

The delays and evasions of the Scottish regency seem to have proceeded from causes which I shall now attempt to explain.

By the treaty of Northampton, all the claims of the English barons to inheritances in Scotland were disregarded, excepting those of Henry de Percy, Thomas Lord Wake of Ledel, and Henry de Beaumont. Percy procured satisfaction; but the others did not.

Henry de Beaumont, in the reign of Edward II. had associated himself with the nobility against the D'Espensers, and, on that account, had suffered imprisonment and exile. He aided Queen Isabella in the invasion

Dugdale, ii. §§. 541. Knyght. 2549. Leland, i. 553.

instrument quoted from *Fædera*, however much it may have been misunderstood in other particulars, certainly proves that Edward III. made a grant to Douglas on the 24th of May 1329, in consequence, as Mr Hume supposes, of the treaty of Northampton. Now, Robert Bruce died on the 7th June 1329, just *nine* days after the date of the grant by Edward III. to Douglas; and thus the delay ascribed to Bruce, when opposed to the regular performance by Edward III. could not have been a delay of more than *nine* days. 3. The claimants under the treaty of Northampton were not many; they were only *two*, Thomas Lord Wake and Henry de Beaumont. 4. There is no probability that the lands which they claimed had been bestowed on the followers of Bruce; on the contrary, there is every reason for supposing, that, in 1332, the lordship of Ledel, claimed by Lord Wake, and the lands in Buchan claimed by Henry de Beaumont, were still enjoyed by the crown: For, in 1341, David II. made a grant of the former to Sir William Douglas, [See the Charter in *Douglas*, Peerage, p 489.] And Robert II. made a grant of the latter, as is universally acknowledged, to Alexander Stewart, his fourth son. But of any previous royal grant of either there is no vestige.

1332.

invasion which proved the cause of the depolition, captivity, and death of her husband. Although, under the administration of Mortimer, he had obtained a share in the partition of the spoils of the D'Espensers *, he persisted in opposing the measures of the new favourite; and, although his own interests were secured by the treaty of Northampton, he boldly exclaimed against the injustice done to the other barons by that treaty. He joined the Princes of the blood-royal in their attempts to rescue the young King from the hands of Isabella and her minion, and place him in their own; and, on the failure of that ill advised conspiracy, he again took refuge in foreign parts. It appears that Lord Wake, having followed the political opinions of Henry de Beaumont, was involved in like calamities and disgrace. While the Queen dowager and Mortimer retained their influence, the claims of those two barons were altogether overlooked: But, within forty-eight hours after the execution of Mortimer †, a peremptory demand was made by Edward III. to have their inheritances restored.

The demand was unexpected and alarming. Made at the very moment of the fall of Isabella and Mortimer, and in behalf of men who had loudly protested against the treaty of Northampton, it indicated a total and perilous change in the system of the English.

Randolph, of late years, had beheld extraordinary vicissitudes in England. The D'Espensers alternately persecuted and triumphant, and at length abased in the dust: The fugitive Mortimer elevated to supreme authority, victorious over the Princes of the blood-royal, and then dragged to a gibbet. Hence it was natural for Randolph to wish,

---

* 'He obtained a grant of the manor of Loughborough, in general taile, part of ' the possession of Hugh de le Despenser Earl of Winchester, then attainted,' 1. Edward III. *Dugdale*, Baronage, T. ii. p. 51.

† Mortimer was executed 29th November 1330. Edward III. made the requisition in favour of Lord Wake and Henry de Beaumont 1st December 1330.

1332.

wish, and even to look for some new revolution, which might prove more favourable to the Scottish interests. Meanwhile, with great reason, and good policy, he delayed the restitution of the inheritances claimed under the treaty of Northampton, in behalf of the avowed opposers of that treaty *.

Besides, it was necessary for Randolph to be assured, that the English, while they urged the performance of one article of that treaty, did, on their part, sincerely purpose to perform its more important articles, by continuing to acknowledge the succession in the house of Bruce, and the independency of the Scottish nation.

Of this, however, there was much reason to doubt. For the English King had taken Balliol under his protection, and had granted him a passport to come into England, with permission to reside there during a whole year, [10th October 1330]. These things had no friendly or pacific appearance.

Ford. iv. 452.

Be this as it will, the event too fatally justified the apprehensions of Randolph; for, while Edward III. was demanding restitution of the estates reserved by the treaty of Northampton, his subjects were arming in violation of that treaty †.

Ford. iv. 511. —512.

Having

---

* In consequence of this resolution, Lord Wake would have had an entrance into Scotland by the western marches, and Henry de Beaumont would have been master of the coasts of Buchan. Their establishment in Scotland would have facilitated the entrance of the disinherited barons, whose cause they had espoused. It might be matter of inquiry, whether they had any right to claim under *one* article of the treaty of Northampton, while they protested against *another*.

† It is remarkable, that, on the 24th March 1331-2, Edward appears to have known of the hostile association of the *disinherited* barons: His words are, ' Quia ex relatu ' accepimus plurimorum, quod diversi homines de regno nostro, et alii [meaning Balliol and his attendants,] pacem inter nos, et Robertum de Brus, nuper Regem Scotorum, initam et confirmatam infringere machinantes, diversas congregationes hominum ad arma indies faciunt, et, *per marchias regni nostri*, dictam terram Scotiae,

' ad

1332.

Leland.i 552.
Ford. xiii. 32.
15.

Having Balliol at their head, and guided by the counsels of Henry de Beaumont, the *disinherited* barons resolved to invade Scotland, vindicate their antient possessions, and subvert that government which the valour and policy of Robert Bruce had established.

Leland.1 553.
Knyght. 2510.
Walsing. 131.
Ford.iv. 511.

The whole force assembled on this mighty enterprise consisted of four hundred men at arms, and of infantry three thousand *.

At first, the barons intended to have entered Scotland by the marches, after the mode of avowed enemies in legitimate and national war. But Edward would not permit them. Although he favoured their undertaking, he dissembled until the event should be seen; and, as he could not pretend ignorance of their preparations, he published a specious order, ' that no one should presume to infringe ' the peace of Northampton,' (24th March 1331-2.]

Leland,i.553.

This obliged the barons to vary their plan of operations. They determined to invade Scotland by sea: And, without any obstacle, they embarked at Ravenshere in Holderness †.

Knygh. 1560.
Hem. li. 273.
Murim. 79.
Leland,l.478.
553.Ford.xiii.
25.

Among the *disinherited* or the *claimants* ‡, these were the principal: Henry de Beaumont, Gilbert de Umfraville, Thomas Lord Wake of Ledel, David de Strathbogie, Richard Talbot, Henry de Ferrers, and his

---

* ' ad eam modo guerrino impugnandum, ingredi intendunt ;' *Fœdera*, T. iv. p. 511. And yet, on the 22d April following, he demanded restitution of the Inheritance of Lord Wake, one of the Barons in arms; *Fœdera*, T. iv. p. 518.

** ' Having a 400 men of arms with him ;' *Scala Chron.* ap. Leland. v. i. p. 553. ' Cum trecentis armatis et tribus mille de omni genere peditum ;' *Knyghton*, p. 1560. ' Cum 1500 armatis et peditibus ;' *Walsingham*, p. 131.

† Called also *Ravenspur* and *Ravensburgh*, at the mouth of the Humber. The place does not exist, having been overwhelmed by the sea many centuries ago. According to conjecture, it stood near that point now called *the Spurn head.* See *Camden* Britannia, p. 740. and *Gibson's* additions, p. 747.

‡ They are sometimes called *les querelleurs*, which implies *claimants*.

1332.

his two brothers, William de la Zouche, and Henry the brother of Edward Balliol.

Historians also mention John, Alexander, Geffroy, and William de Moubray, Walter Comyn, Fulk Fitz-Warine, and Roger de Swinerton*.

Randolph,

* The claims of the chief of the difinherited barons will be underſtood, in ſome meaſure, from the following narrative.

HENRY DE BEAUMONT claimed the earldom of Buchan, by reaſon of his marriage with Alicia one of the heirs of Comyn 5th Earl of Buchan, and conſtable of Scotland. Dugdale, Baronage, T. ii. p. 50. ſays ' That ſhe was one of the couſins and heirs of ' John Earl of Buchan :' But T. ii. p. 685. that ſhe was his niece; and with this laſt opinion Burton, Leicesterſhire, p. 37. concurs. He ſuppoſes that ſhe was the daughter of Alexander who was the brother of John Earl of Buchan. Genealogiſts who examine the different paſſages in Dugdale will find ample matter for doubt.

GILBERT DE UMFRAVILLE claimed the earldom of Angus, of which his predeceſſor Robert had been deprived by forfeiture in the late reign; Cobs, 4. inſt. p. 47. Dugdale, T. ii. p. 505. He had a like right to the ſuperiority, [Actus dominii,] of the barony of Dunipace in Stirlingſhire, which Bruce had granted to William de Lindeſay; Rolls, Robert I. No. 88.

THOMAS LORD WAKE had right of inheritance in the lordſhip of Ledel or Lidel, through his grandmother Johanna de Stuteville. He now ſought to regain that poſſeſſion, of which he had been deprived in the courſe of the wars with Scotland; Dugdale, T. I. p. 273.

John Comyn of Badenoch, ſlain by Bruce at Dumfries, left a ſon John, and two daughters, Johanna and Eliſabeth. John died without iſſue, 19. Edward II. being then ſeized of the manor of Tiſſete in Tindale. He was called ' of Badenoch in Tindale ;' Dugdale, T. ii. p. 686. His Engliſh eſtates and his pretenſions in Scotland devolved on his two ſiſters. The eldeſt, Johanna, married David de Strathbogie, [or Haſtings,] Earl of Athole, who forfeited in 1323. She was the mother of David de Strathbogie, who, in England, retained the title of Earl of Athole; Dugdale, T. ii. p. 95.

Hence DAVID DE STRATHBOGIE claimed one half of the eſtates of Comyn of Badenoch, in right of his mother.

Eliſabeth, the younger ſiſter of the laſt John Comyn, married Sir Richard Talbot, called of Godrick caſtle in Herefordſhire, in right of his wife, as it ſeems; Dugdale,

T.

1332.

Randolph, in consequence of the English preparations, assembled an army, and advanced to Colbrandspath, on the frontier of East Lothian; but having received intelligence of the naval armament, he marched northwards, to provide for the defence of the interior parts of the kingdom.

T i p. 326. 686. and hence SIR RICHARD TALBOT claimed the other half of the estates of Comyn of Badenoch, in right of his wife.

HENRY DE FERRERS of GROBY had pretensions to lands in Galloway and elsewhere, through his grandmother Margaret de Quinci, one of the co-heirs of Roger de Quinci Earl of Winchester; *Dugdale*, T. i. p. 262. 267. It appears that Bruce made a grant of the superiority of the lands of Lambrachtoun and Grugure in Cuningham, to Robert de Cuningham, which had belonged to Alan de la Zouche and William de Ferrers, [the father of Henry,] *Rolls*, Robert I. No. 53. This was plainly a part of the de Quinci succession.

It is probable that the claim of WILLIAM DE LA ZOUCHE was founded on a grant made to him by his cousin Alan de la Zouche, of some part of the lands which had anciently belonged to Roger de Quinci, Earl of Winchester, the great grandfather of Alan. See *Burton*, Leicestershire, p. 19. and *Dugdale*, T. i. p. 153. T. li. p. 688. 689. What I have to offer on this subject is merely in the form of plausible conjecture.

Roger de la Zouche had two sons, Alan and William; Alan the eldest married Helen de Quinci, daughter and co-heir of Roger Earl of Winchester; he had a son Roger, who had a son Alan.

The lands of Tranent [anciently *Tranirnentis*,] in East Lothian, which belonged to Alan de la Zouche, were granted by Bruce to Alexander Seton; *Rolls*, Robert I. N. 56.

William, the second son of old Roger de la Zouche, left Joyce his daughter and heir married to Robert de Mortimer of Ricards castle; she had two sons, 1. Hugh. 2. WILLIAM.

Alan de la Zouche, the chief of the family, having no issue-male, settled the manor of Ashbie and other lands on his cousin WILLIAM DE MORTIMER, who assumed the name of *de la Zouche*. He, in all probability, is the WILLIAM DE LA ZOUCHE mentioned by historians as one of the disinherited barons. My conjecture is, that Alan, together with the manor of Ashbie, settled on WILLIAM the estates in Scotland which had belonged to Helen de Quinci; and, indeed, as matters then stood, it was an alienation not greatly to the detriment of the daughters of Alan.

The

1332.

kingdom. Amidst the excruciating pains of a confirmed stone, he ceased not to discharge the duties of his office with activity and vigilance.

The preceding narrative will be best understood by *a genealogical tree*.

Roger de la Zouche.

2. William de la Zouche.	1. Alan Lord of Ashbie.	= Helen de Quinci.
Robert de Mortimer. = Joyce.	Roger de la Zouche.	
2. WILLIAM, called DE LA ZOUCHE. 1. Hugh.	Alan de la Zouche, who made the settlement on William de Mortimer.	

No other hypothesis occurs to me which can connect WILLIAM DE LA ZOUCHE of Mortimer with any estates in Scotland.

Knyghton, p. 2560. relates, that William de la Zouche did not claim in person, but that [Ralph] Lord Stafford claimed for him. We may learn the reason of this from *Dugdale*, T. i. p. 153. William de la Zouche of Mortimer was at that time justice of the forests south of Trent, and constable of the tower of London. The duties of those offices, it is probable, prevented his personal attendance in the Scottish expedition; and, besides, it would not have been decent for a man possessed of such high employments to have appeared in arms against the Scots, while his sovereign affected to disapprove of the war.

Roger the father of JOHN DE MOUBRAY forfeited in the late reign. His estates were Eckford in Rokesburghshire, Keily in Fife [or perhaps Kello in the Merse,] and Methven in Perthshire. They were all granted to the Stewart of Scotland. See *Nisbet*, Heraldry, T. I. p. 287. and *Abercrombie*, T. ii. p. 149. These facts, however, must rest on the authority of the writers quoted, for I have seen no evidence of them on record.

Fordun, L. xiii. c. 25. gives the appellation of *Strathbolgie* to John de Moubray. It is observed by *Dugdale*, T. ii. p. 95. ' That when David de Strathbolgie, for 5,000
' merks, purchased, from Ralph de Monthermer, the estate of Athole, which had belong-
' ed to his ancestors, John de Moubray was one of the persons who entered a recog-
' nisance with him for the price.' Perhaps David de Strathbolgie, on this account, mortgaged his lands of Strathbolgie to JOHN DE MOUBRAY.

ALEXANDER

VOL. II.   T

146   D A V I D   II.

1332.

lance. He expired on the march * [20th July.] A man he was, to be remembered while integrity, prudence, and valour, are held in esteem among men.

The

ALEXANDER DE MOUBRAY was the brother of John; *Fordun*, L. xiii. c. 29. It is probable that he, and the other persons of that name, having no claim for antient inheritances, engaged as adventurers in the Scottish expedition.

WALTER COMYN was, in all likelihood, the son or representative of William Comyn of Kilbride in Lanerkshire, who forfeited in the last reign. His lands also had been granted to the Stewart; *Remarks on Ragman's Roll*, p. 10. subjoined to *Nisbet*, Heraldry, v. ii. But I do not vouch for the truth of this, not having discovered any thing to that purpose on record. There was a Walter Comyn who held seven pounds and six pennies of the lands of Brankholme, in the barony of Hawick, [Selkirkshire,] *Rolls*, Robert I. No 24. Two persons bearing the name of *Walter Comyn* followed the fortunes of Balliol; the one was killed at Annan 26th December 1332, and the other was killed in the forest of Kilblain, September 1335; *Fordun*, L. xiii. c. 25. c. 36.

HENRY DE BALLIOL was the younger brother of Edward, who now asserted his pretensions to the crown of Scotland. A person of that name had a grant of the lands of Brankholme, with the exception of the parcel granted to Walter Comyn; *Rolls* Robert I. No 24.; but whether he was the same person, I know not.

FOLK FITZ WARINE and ROGER DE SWINERTON are barons well known in English history; but what were the estates in Scotland to which they laid claim, I have not been able to discover.

* At Musselbargh, five miles to the east of Edinburgh. It is said, *Fordun*, L. xiii. c. 19. that he died on the 13th of August. But this is a mistake of the transcriber; for the Earl of Marre was chosen guardian in his room, 2d August; *Fordun*, L. xiii. c. 22.—*Barbour*, p. 442. says, that Randolph was poisoned by a friar; *Fordun*, L. xiii. c. 19. says, by his chaplain, an English friar; and he adds some circumstances, implying, that Edward III. was then on the borders of Scotland, and was privy to this base deed; *Boece*, L. xv. fol. 310. 311. adds many more circumstances to the same purpose; and yet he confesses that Randolph was afflicted with a confirmed stone. This popular story has been examined, *Remarks on the history of Scotland*. c. iv. In support of what is there observed, I have to add, that *Edward III. during the course of the summer and autumn 1332, was never within 100 miles of the Scottish borders*. He resided at Woodstock, near Oxford, from 2d May to 28th July; *Fœdera*, T. iv p. 520—526. at Wigmore in Herefordshire, 7th August; *ibid*. p. 529.; at Kidderminster in Worcestershire,

1332.

The Scottish parliament assembled at Perth for electing a Regent. After great diversity of opinions, it was agreed, that Donald Earl of Murre, nephew of the late King, should be intrusted with that important charge *, [2d August]. An unhappy choice! His connection with the royal family appears to have been the principal merit of the person elected to supply the place of Randolph. The Earl of Marre, while a child, had been conveyed into England by Edward I. and remained in captivity for many years. After his release, he seems to have established his chief residence in England †. No military service of his is known, except a subordinate command which he held during the short campaign in the year 1327. Having, probably, small knowledge of his native country, and being destitute of civil abilities, and experience in war, he assumed the reins of government at a most critical juncture, and amidst perils which it would have required the genius of Douglas, Randolph, and Bruce, effectually to oppose.

After

---

shire, 18th August; *ibid.* p. 530.; at Westminster 13th and 20th September; *ibid.* p. 531.—533. From examining dates, it is natural to draw this conclusion, that Edward III. was upon a progress through the interior parts of his kingdom, and that having heard of the changes in Scotland, he repaired to London.

* ' Omnes magnates, tam ecclesiastici quam laici, apud Perth, quarto nonas Augusti ' congregati, post plures altercationes, et varias dissensiones, Donenaldum Comitem de ' Mar unanimiter elegerunt in regni custodem;' *Fordun*, L. viii. c. 22. It was indeed difficult to make a fit and unanimous choice. Most of the surviving companions of the victories of Bruce were far advanced in years; his grandson, the Stewart, was under age, and the pretensions of the other great Lords were nearly equal.

† He was present at the parliament of Scone 1318; but his name does not appear in the letter to the Pope 1320. This, of itself, affords reasonable evidence that he was not then in Scotland. There is a remarkable passage in *Scala Chron.* ap. Leland, T. I. p. 550. ' Donald Earl of Marre in Scotland was made, by King Edwarde, gardian of ' the castel of Bristow, the which be delyverid to the Quene, and so repaired into Scot- ' land.' This was in summer 1326; *Kyngston*, p. 2545.

DAVID II.

1332.

Ford. iv. 519.

After *the difinherited Lords* had embarked at an English port, in order to invade Scotland, Edward impowered Henry de Percy to punish all his subjects who should presume to array themselves in contempt of his prohibition: And, because he understood that the Scots were arming, he impowered Percy to arm for repelling them, [9th August]. This tardy zeal for maintaining peace, and this pretext of self-defence, were thin disguises to cover the hostile intentions of the English government against an unhappy nation, now bereaved of its chief supports, and rendered feeble by the minority of its Sovereign.

Ford. xiii. 22.
Hem. ii. 273.

Edward Balliol, and his associates, appeared in the Frith of Forth, [31st July]. He landed in the neighbourhood of Kinghorn *, [6th August], and routed the Earl of Fife, who opposed his landing with some troops hastily assembled. In this conflict, Alexander Seton, the son, was slain †.

Ford. xiii. 23.
Hem. ii. 173.

Balliol marched next day to Dunfermline; and having ordered his fleet to sail round the east coast of Fife, and wait for him at the entrance of the river Tay, he proceeded northwards, and encamped on the Millar's acre at Forteviot, with the river Earn in front, [11th August].

Ford. xiii. 23.

The Earl of Marre encamped with a numerous army on the opposite bank of the river Earn, in the neighbourhood of Duplin. Another army, nearly as numerous, under the command of the Earl of March, had advanced from the southern parts, through the Lothians and Stirlingshire,

---

* Although historians say *Kinghorn*, yet I suppose that *Wefter-Kinghorn*, now called *Brentifland*, was the place where Balliol landed. The ground about Kinghorn would have been exceedingly inconvenient for the disembarkation of cavalry.

† *W. Hemingford*, T. ii. p. 173. says, that the Earl of Fife opposed the landing of Balliol with a body of 10,000 men, out that 900 Scots were slain in the action; but *Fordun*, L. xiii. c. 12. says, ' Cui Alex. oder Seton filius cum paucis ei in facie refiftens, ' eodem die cum tribus aut quatuor ibidem occubuit.' The three or four mentioned by Fordun, were probably men of some rank. As to this Alexander Seton, the son, See *Appendix*.

1332.

lingshire, and had fixed its quarters at Auchterarder, eight miles to the west of Forteviot *.

No situation could be more perilous than that of Balliol: Within view of one army greatly superior in numbers to his own, and most advantageously posted, and, at the same time, hourly in hazard of seeing another formidable enemy advance on his flank. To retreat, in such circumstances, through Fifeshire, would have been impracticable; and, although it had been practicable, would have availed him nothing, for he had ordered his fleet to depart from the Frith of Forth; neither would the danger have been less imminent, or the hopes of success more probable, had he marched towards the mouth of the river Tay, in the uncertain expectation of meeting his fleet.

He took the desperate resolution of crossing the river, and attacking the Regent in his camp.

Andrew Murray of Tullibardin directed the English to a ford †.

The Scots kept no watch, but abandoned themselves to intemperance and riotous mirth, while at midnight, the English, led by Alexander de Moubray, crossed the river. They ascended a rising ground, came unperceived on the right flank of the Scottish army, and made a pitiless slaughter. At the first alarm, young Randolph, Earl of Moray, hasted with three hundred men at arms to oppose the enemy.

Ford. xiii. 23.
25.
Ford. xiii. 23.
Hem. ii. 273.
Knyght. 2560.
-2. Mar. 79-

Being

* Historians differ as to the force of the armies. Fordun, L. xiii. c. 23. says, That the regent had 30,000 men under his command, and the Earl of March as many; and L. xiii. c. 22. that Balliol had between 500 and 600 armed men, that is, horsemen, completely armed. W. Hemingford, T. ii. p 273. reckons each of the Scottish armies at 40,000, and Balliol's at 500 armed men. Knyghton, p. 2560. says, That Balliol, when he landed in Fife, had 300 armed men, and 500 more of different form; ' De ' omni genere peditum,' and that he had with him 2500 in all, at his camp on the banks of the river Earn.

† He fixed a stake in the river to direct them, ' fixit palum in le Dernford aqua ' de Erne;' Fordun, L. xiii c. 25.

1332.

Being gallantly feconded by Murdoch Earl of Menteth, Alexander Frafer, and Robert Bruce, a natural fon of the late King, he checked the Englifh impetuofity, and maintained the combat on equal terms. But the Regent, and the whole multitude, rufhed to battle without order or difcipline, and at once overwhelmed Randolph and his companions. In a moment all was unutterable confufion; and, while thofe behind ftill preffed on, the foremoft were thrown down and trodden under foot, and fuffocated. The Englifh flaughtered without controul. The carnage and purfuit lafted for many hours *, and the remains of this mighty army were utterly difperfed, [12th Auguft †.] Never did the Scottifh nation receive an overthrow fo difgraceful; and, indeed, the Englifh themfelves ftood aftonifhed at their eafy victory ‡.

Ford. xiii. 24.
Hem. ii. 275.
Knygh. 2560.
-1.

In the action of Duplin moor, there were flain many Scotfmen of eminent rank. Donald Earl of Marre, the Regent, whofe ignorance of military difcipline was the chief caufe of this national difafter ‖.

Thomas

* Ab orta folis ufque ad altam primam diei;' *Knyghton*, p. 2561. ' ad horam nonam;' *W. Hemingford* T. ii. p. 273.

† According to *Fordun*, L. xiii. c. 22. 23. Balliol came to the river Earn on the eve of St Laurence, or 9th Auguft, and fought on the next day, or the 10th; and yet Fordun afterwards mentions the 11th of Auguft as the day of the battle. Knyghton fays, that the battle was fought ' Die Mercurii poft feftum Sancti Laurentii;' that is, if I miftake not, on the 12th of Auguft.

‡ ' Virtute divinâ reverâ non humanâ;' *W. Hemingford*, T. ii. p. 273. To the fame purpofe, *Fordun*, L. xiii. c. 24. ' Quos utique non vis humana, fed ultio proftravit ' divina, quod in hoc patet, quod multo plures ex collifione corporum, emfricatione ar' morum, et proftratione equorum, fe invicem opprimentium, fine vulnere cecidierunt, ' quàm qui telo vel gladio jugulati funt;' and c. 23. he applies to the Scots that faying of one of the antients, ' Nunquam in folido ftetit fuperba felicitas.'

‖ *Barnes*, Edward III. p. Co. fays, on the credit of a MS. Chronicle, ' That the ' Earl of Marre had fecretly combined with Balliol;' and he relates a converfation
which

1332.

Thomas Earl of Moray, Murdoch Earl of Menteth, Robert Earl of Carrick *, Alexander Frafer †, and Robert Bruce ‡; the flaughter made of the men at arms, and of the infantry, was very great ‖. Of the

which paſſed on that fubject, during the battle, between the Earl of Marre and the Earl of Carrick, erroneouſly called the baſtard of Robert Bruce. It is grievous that a man ſhould be charged as unfaithful to that cauſe in which he died. Nothing, indeed, can be more improbable than a charge which fuppoſes that the nephew would have betrayed the fon of Robert Bruce, at the expence of his own authority as well as of his honour; beſides, the circumſtances related by Barnes, at too great length to be tranſcribed, are utterly abſurd.

* He was the natural fon of Edward Bruce, and had received the title of Earl of Carrick from the late King.

† Chamberlain of Scotland. He married Mary the fiſter of Robert Bruce. He was anceſtor of the Lords Lovat and Saltoun. See *Crawfurd*, Officers of State, p. 274.

‡ A natural fon of the late King. The Engliſh hiſtorians mention Nigel and Alexander Bruce among the flain; *Knyghton*, p. 2561. *Walfingham*, p. 131. I know nothing concerning them. They alſo ſpeak of an *Earl of Athole* among the flain. The perſon meant is John Campbell Earl of Athole; but he was killed at Halidon in the following year.

‖ 'Ad hominum tria millia;' *Fordun*, L. xiii. c. 24. But this muſt be a miſtake, unleſs he means *men at arms*. *W. Hemingford*, T. ii. p. 273. ſays that twelve Barons were flain, with 800 knights, probably a miſtake of the tranſcriber for 86, 2000 men at arms, and 13,300 foot foldiers.

In deſcribing the diſaſter at Duplin moor, Boece has furpaſſed himſelf, L. xv. fol. 312. 313. the ſtory, as related by former hiſtorians, is juſt within the bounds of credibility. Boece, however, reſolved to add a little of *his own marvellous*.

Of Balliol's harangue to his troops, I ſay nothing, although it would have enabled any ſingle deſerter to diſcloſe the whole plan of operations, whoſe ſucceſs depended on the utmoſt ſecrecy. Neither will I ſay any thing of the ſecond harangue made at midnight, to his officers, when not a moment was to be loſt in the parade of words; becauſe I know, that, for ſuch things, there are precedents, antient and modern.

What I have ſtill to obſerve, is concerning a downright fiction of Boece. He literally hurries his readers into the midſt of things; and he affects, that the firſt attack of the

1332.

the men at arms, under the particular command of the Earl of Fife, three hundred and sixty were slain; the Earl himself having been made prisoner, submitted to the conqueror.

On the English was on the rear of the center of the Scottish camp, and that they surprised the Regent's tent, and killed him while he lay asleep, [' Jamque ubi in media castra ' ad praetorium pervenerant, nec quisquam adventum perceperat, ibi praetorio dejecto ' ducem imprimis dormientem confodiunt.']

He next remarks, that ' all unwarlike men, and especially the English,' are of a mer- ' ciless disposition towards the vanquished, [quum omnes homines imbelles, tum prae- ' sertim Anglorum gens, nimis in victos ac superatos impotentes nulli parcunt.'] This is, indeed, an extraordinary remark to be made by a Scotsman, in a narrative of the battle of Duplin. Bellenden, the paraphrast of Boece, has judiciously omitted it.

In numbering the slain, Boece has given free reins to his imagination. ' Three ' thousand gentlemen, and an innumerable multitude of the common sort,' far ex- ceeds any English account of the slain.

When he comes to particulars, he is singularly unfortunate. ' William Hay con- ' stable of Scotland was slain, and the race would have been extinguished, had be ' not left his wife pregnant.' ' Una dies Fabios,' &c This is an old fable often repeat- ed in our histories. What Boece relates is altogether fabulous. 1. There is no rea- son for believing that Sir Gilbert Hay of Errol, whom Boece calls William, was slain at Duplin. 2. That the line of the family was carried on by a posthumous child, is im- possible. David the son of Sir Gilbert, constable of Scotland, was witness to a char- ter in 1344, Chart. Aberbrothoc, and was killed at the battle of Durham in 1346, as Boece himself acknowledges, fol. 325. a. To say that the constable of Scotland was killed at the head of an army in the 14th year of his age, is a contradiction. But, 3. which is completely fatal to the hypothesis of Boece, Thomas, the son of this David, was a commissioner sent to England in 1353; that is, according to Boece, *twenty-one years after the birth of his father!* Should it be said, that *Thomas* might have been the brother of *David*, I can only answer, that there is no authority for the assertion, and that it is contrary to the received opinion; and besides, that it will not aid Boece's story, unless we also suppose that the widow of the constable brought forth twins, David and Thomas.

Boece says, that, at Duplin, Robert Keith the marshal was slain, with most of his kindred. If this was so, it is strange, that neither Fordun, nor any of the English hi-

storians

DAVID II.   153

1332.

On the side of the English there fell two knights, John de Gourdon, *Knygh. 2561.*
and Reginald de la Beche, with thirty-three esquires; and, of common
men, an inconsiderable number.

Next day Balliol took possession of Perth. Apprehending an at- *Hem. II. 275.*
tack from the Earl of March, he ordered the ditch to be cleared, and *Knygh. 2561.*
the town to be inclosed with palisadoes *.

A soldier coming from the carnage at Duplin, met the Earl of
March, shewed his mortal wounds, and expired. This was the first
intelligence that the Scottish army received of the overthrow of their
countrymen. On their advancing to the field of battle, it was sadly
confirmed.

florians should have mentioned it, while they made mention of the death of persons
less distinguished.

He adds, that David Lindesay of Glenesk was slain, with 80 gentlemen of his kindred. There is a great sameness in the narrative of Boece; and, I presume, that the
80 gentlemen were thrown in for the sake of variety. There was no such person as
David Lindesay of Glenesk in 1332. The person then in possession of that barony was
Alexander de Lindesay, and he was slain in 1333, at Halidon. If Boece means to
speak of David Lindesay, the head of the family, it is certain that he was not killed at
Duplin in 1332, for he was alive in 1346, when his son was killed at Durham. Fordun, L. xiv. c. 3. reckons among the slain at that battle, ' David de Lindesay filius et
' haeres D. David de Lindesay.'

Boece gives the names of many knights slain at Duplin; but I have neither leisure
nor opportunity to examine this part of his narrative. It is probable, however, that
he has not been more accurate in his account of persons of inferior rank, than in his
account of more eminent persons.

* ' Fortificaverunt villam cum larga fossura et de palo, suppoentes & infra breve
' habit·ros indigentiam defensionis,' *Knyghton*, p. 2561. This circumstance is mentioned, because many historians of both nations have considered Perth as a place of
strength at that time, have mentioned its *surrender*, and have pointed out the causes
of its making no resistance. Perth appears to have been dismantled by Robert Bruce,
in consequence of a favourite maxim of his policy, which, however specious in theory,
served to accelerate the conquests of Balliol.

VOL. II.   U

1332.

confirmed. Eager for revenge, they hurried on to Perth. While they were descending from the neighbouring heights, 'Courage,' cried Henry de Beaumont, ' those men will not hurt us.' Whether he said this merely to animate the English, or whether he formed his conjecture from the disordered motions of the enemy, or whether he, indeed, discerned the banners of some noble persons, who secretly favoured Balliol, is uncertain. Certain, however, it is, that the hasty resolution of assaulting Perth, was as hastily abandoned, and that the slow operations of a blockade were preferred. The Scots hoped by investing the town, and cutting off all communication with the sea, to reduce the English to the extremities of famine, and force them to capitulate.

Hem. ii. 173.
Knygh. 2561.

John Crabbe, a Flemish mariner, had eminently distinguished himself at the defence of Berwick. Attached to the service of Scotland, he continued for many years to cruise on the eastern coasts, and exceedingly annoyed the English commerce *. While the Scots blockaded Perth, he came with ten vessels to the entrance of the river Tay: He took the ship which belonged to Henry de Beaumont; but soon after, in a general engagement, his whole fleet was burnt, [24th August.]

Ford. xiii. 24.
Scola Chron.
ap. Leland,
i. 553.

The Earl of March, after this disaster, saw that his own numerous forces were in imminent hazard of perishing through want of provisions †, while the English, now become masters at sea, received abundant

---

* ' Qui multa mala saepius per mare pluribus annis Anglis intulerat;' *W. Hemingford*, T. ii. p. 273.

† This circumstance is mentioned in *Scala Chron.* ap. Leland, T. i. p. 553. ' Cam an infinite numbre out of al partes of Scotland afore S. John's toune, and soue after, ' for lak of vitayle, were constraynid to recoyle and dispatchle themselves.' *Fordun*, L. xiii. c. 24. either not knowing, or not remarking this circumstance, has censured

the

1332.

dant supplies. He therefore relinquished the blockade, and ordered the Scots to disperse themselves. His orders were instantly obeyed: And thus, within the space of three weeks from his landing, Edward Balliol saw himself in quiet possession of Scotland.

He was crowned at Scone, [24th September *,] in presence of the clergy and people of Fife, and of the low country of Perthshire, who had submitted to a power which they could not resist. Duncan Earl of Fife, and William Sinclair Bishop of Dunkeld, assisted at this solemnity. The former had, a few weeks before, opposed Balliol in the field, and the latter, in the reign of Robert Bruce, for his valiant opposition to the English invaders, had merited the title of *The King's Bishop*. *Ford. xiii. 24.*

Immediately after his coronation, the new monarch repaired to the southern parts of Scotland, having intrusted Perth to the custody of the Earl of Fife. *Knyght. 2562. Ford. xiii. 25.*

James Fraser, Simon Fraser, and Robert Keith, surprised Perth, and razed its fortifications, [7th October.] The Earl of Fife, and his family and vassals, were made prisoners. Andrew Murray of Tullibairden, who had directed the English to a ford on the river Earn, was taken at Perth, and punished as a traitor. The English historians report, *Ford. xiii. 25. Knyght. 2562.*

the conduct of the Earl of March in abandoning the blockade of Perth. Many circumstances in the conduct of that noble person admit not of apology; in particular, his negligence, and his ignorance of the motions of the enemy at Duplin, are inexcusable; and it must be admitted, that his behaviour was often ambiguous, and resembling that of an opulent man, who means to save his own fortune out of the public wreck; yet, after the destruction of Crabbe's fleet, it does not appear that the blockade of Perth was any longer practicable.

* *W. Hemingford,* T. ii. p. 273. places the coronation of Balliol on the 27th September.

1332.

port, that the Earl of Fife, the governor, betrayed the town to the Scots*.

Ford. xiii. 25. Such of the Scots as still adhered to their infant sovereign, conferred the office of Regent on Sir Andrew Murray of Bothwell, husband of Christian the sister of Robert Bruce. But he, although brave and active, had not force sufficient to attempt ought considerable.

Ford. iv. 539. 540. On the news of the sudden change of affairs in Scotland, Edward III. repaired to Yorke, having been counselled by his parliament, *for the safety of the realm,* to draw near the Scottish frontiers †.

Ford. iv. 536. —539. Meanwhile, Balliol came to Rokesburgh, and *there* made a solemn surrender of the liberties of Scotland. He acknowledged the English King for his *liege Lord*; and, as if that had not been sufficient, he became bound to put him in possession of the town, castle, and territory of Berwick, and of other lands on the marches, extending in all to the yearly value of L. 2000, ' on account, as the instrument bears, of ' the great honour and emoluments which we have procured through ' the *sufferance* ‡ of our lord the King, and by the powerful and ac-' ceptable aid which we have received from his good subjects.'

Moreover,

---

* ' Idem Comes se Scotis contulit, villamque illis proditiosè tradidit;' *Knyghton,* p. 2562. It may seem strange that Balliol placed such confidence in the Earl of Fife, so lately an enemy. But the forces of Balliol were not numerous, and he could not leave an English garrison in Perth: He, therefore, judiciously entrusted that town to a Lord whose territories lay open to the incursions of the English fleet. This circumstance might either serve to insure his fidelity, or afford means of chastening his bad faith.

† It appears from *Fœdera*, T. iv. p. 535.—550. that Edward III. remained at Yorke, and in his neighbourhood, from 26th October 1332 to 9th March 1332-3.

‡ ' La suffrance.' It was necessary to use *sufferance* in the translation. *Permission* implies more than Balliol meant to express; and *connivance* would be an improper word to use where a sovereign prince is concerned.

1332.

Moreover, Balliol offered to marry the Princess Johanna, whom he considered as only betrothed to David Bruce, and to add L. 500 of land-rent to her original jointure, and this under the extravagant penalty of L. 10,000, to be appropriated as a portion to the young lady, or otherwise disposed of for her behoof.

He further engaged to provide for the maintenance of David Bruce, as the King of England should advise.

And, *lastly*, he became bound to serve Edward in all his wars, excepting in England, Wales, and Ireland, for the space of a year together, with 200 men at arms, and all at his own charges, and he bound his successors to perform the like service, with an hundred men at arms, [23d November.]

Edward having engaged to maintain Balliol in possession of Scotland, Balliol engaged to serve him in all his wars without exception, [23d November.]

At this season there was a duplicity in the conduct of Edward III. *Foed.* iv. 535. which can neither be accounted for nor justified. With much earnestness he solicited the papal court to prefer Robert de Ayleston, Arch-deacon of Berks, to the vacant see of St Andrews, and he urged that it was necessary to have, in that office, a person of pacific dispositions, and well affected to England, 'the plighted fidelity of the 'Scots being frail, and their friendship dubious [*];' but he industriously avoided any mention of the revolution in Scotland, [26th October.]

In another despatch to the Pope, he expressed his fears lest his *Foed.* iv. 540. conduct in Scottish affairs should be misrepresented; and, while he spake of the enterprise, victories, and coronation of Balliol, he kept a profound

---

[*] 'Cum sit fragilis et dubia proes nos et regnum nostrum Scotorum promissa fides 'et amicitia;' *Foedera*, T. iv. p. 535.

1332.

profound silence with respect to the submission made by Balliol to him as his liege lord, [15th December.]

Fœd. iv. 540. And, which is the most singular of all, he, at the very fame time, appointed plenipotentiaries to treat with ambassadors from the Regent and barons of Scotland, [14th December.]

Scala Chron. ap. Leland, L 553. 554. It is said, that, when the Scottish ambassadors implored the assistance of Edward in behalf of their sovereign, Edward made answer, 'That he could give no assistance to those who had deprived his subjects of their estates.' But it is not probable that this evasive answer was made, after Edward, by receiving the homage, had acknowledged, and had become bound to support the title of Balliol.

Perhaps the concessions made at Rokesburgh by Balliol were, for a season, kept secret. If this conjecture be admitted, the conduct of Edward, however unjustifiable, will appear consistent.

Fœd. xiii. 25. Many of the Scottish barons, either through despair, or from antient attachment to the Balliol line, submitted to the conqueror, and acknowledged his title.

Hem. il. 273. The Earl of March and Archibald Douglas obtained a truce from Balliol until the second of February, by which time it was proposed to have all controversies settled in a general convention.

John, the second son of Randolph, now become Earl of Moray by the death of his brother: Archibald, the youngest brother of the renowned Douglas, together with Simon Frafer, assembled a body of horsemen at Moffat in Annandale, and suddenly traversing the country, assaulted Balliol at Annan, where he lay in thoughtless security. Henry, the brother of Balliol, gallantly resisted the enemy; but at length, being overpowered by numbers, he was slain. With him there fell many other persons of distinction*. Balliol escaped almost naked,

* Particularly, Walter de Comyn, John de Moubray, and Richard Kirby, *Knyghton.*

1332.

naked, and with hardly a single attendant, and took refuge in England, [16th December.]

That the Scots perfidiously violated a truce then subsisting, is averred by the English historians; but this charge is certainly too general. The Earl of March, whose estates lay exposed to the enemy on all quarters, might judge it expedient to temporize, and request a truce; but no convention between Balliol and him could bind the Earl of Moray.

Walsing. 132. *Knyght.* 2562.

Alexander Earl of Carrick, a natural son of Edward Bruce, had lately submitted to Balliol, and was found in arms at Annan. The moderation and prudence of the young Earl of Moray saved him from the punishment of a traitor [*].

Ford. xiii. 25.

Balliol, now an exile, appointed commissioners to swear in his name to the faithful performance of whatever he had promised to the King of England, [at Burgh, 12th February 1332-3.]

Ford. iv. 54.

The Scots began to make excursions into the English borders. Edward issued a proclamation, in which he solemnly averred, that the Scots, by their hostile depredations, had violated the peace of Northampton, [23d March 1332-3.] And he repeated this averment, [30th March 1333.]

Ford. iv. 55.

Balliol,

---

tom, p. 2562. *Fordun,* L. xiii. c. 25. *Barnes,* Edward. III. p. 67. says, ' surely the
' Lord John Moulray of England was not now slain, as Hector Boece falsely affirms;
' for we find, by undoubted records, *Dugdale,* v. i. p. 127. that he died not till twen-
' ty nine years after this time.' Mr Ruddiman, *aut. ad Buchanan.* p. 156. attempts to
justify Boece, by observing, that if the authority of Dugdale is relied on, we must admit that *Boece,* and almost all our other historians, and also Knyghton, an English
writer, are mistaken; the better answer is, that Boece mentions not ' the *Lord* John
' Moubray of England,' and that he and Dugdale speak of different persons.

[*] This seems to be the sense of the passage in *Fordun,* L. xiii. c. 25. ' In quo con-
' flictu captus fuit Comes de Carrick per Comitem Moravine, et a morte liberatus.'

1332.

Balliol, 'by the fufferance of the Englifh King and the aid of Eng-
'glifhmen,' had invaded Scotland, overcome its armies, and feated himfelf on the throne of Bruce. In gratitude for this fufferance and aid,
he ceded part of the Scottifh dominions to England, and furrendered
the independency of the reft: Yet, after all thefe events, Edward complained that the Scots had violated the peace of Northampton. Hiftory records not a more flagrant example of a royal manifefto offering infult to the common fenfe of mankind.

Hem. li. 274.
Knyght. 2562.
Walfing. 131.

Balliol, having been joined by many Englifh barons, returned to
Scotland, [9th March 1332-3.] He took and burnt a caftle where
Robert de Colville commanded *, and eftablifhing his quarters in the
neighbourhood of Rokefburgh, began to make preparations for be-
fieging Berwick.

Walfing. 131.

Juft after the return of Balliol, Archibald Douglas †, with 3000
men, invaded England on the fide of the weftern marches, wafted the
whole diftrict of Gillefland, and brought off much booty, and many
prifoners.

In

---

* It is probable that the perfon here meant is Robert Colville of Ochiltree, and the
caftle, Oxnam in Teviotdale, which belonged to him. *Knyghton,* p. 2562. fays, 'Ce-
' perunt unam forfalam, in qua invenerunt Dominum Robertum de Colvyll cum X.
' armatis, cum multis dominabus et feminis de patria, et plures alios homines;' which
paffage *Barnes,* Edward III. p. 73. thus paraphrafes, ' They took a certain fonrefs,
' wherein they found the Lord Robert Colvile *prifoner, whom they releafed,* with many
' other Englifh gentlemen, and feveral great ladies of the country, *all whom they re-
' leafed.*'

† Sir James Douglas, called *the good Douglas,* was never married; his eftate went to
his Brother Hugh, who probably laboured under fome imbecillity either of body or of
mind; for his name never appears in hiftory, and feldom on record. His brother
Archibald was the perfon who, at that period, maintained the renown of the houfe of
Douglas. He was commonly called *Tineman,* implying, as may be conjectured, *Tiny,*
or *flender little man.*

1332.

In revenge, Sir Anthony de Lucy made an inroad into Scotland. *Walfing.* 131. *Ford* xiii. 27. This enterprise, in itself unimportant, had fatal consequences; for Sir William Douglas, famous in our story, under the appellation of *The knight of Liddesdale*, encountered de Lucy, was totally defeated, and made prisoner *, [near Lochmaben, towards the latter end of March.]

1333.

Edward commanded the knight of Liddesdale to be put in irons. *Ford.* iv. 593. *Ford.* xiii. 27. His captivity endured for two years.

About the same time Sir Andrew Moray of Bothwell, the Regent, *Ford.* xiii. 27. resolved to attack Balliol before the arrival of reinforcements from England. A sharp conflict ensued at the bridge of Rokesburgh. Ralph Golding, a resolute soldier, having advanced before his companions, was thrown to the ground. The Regent generously attempted to rescue him; but, ill seconded by his troops, he fell into the power of the enemies. Disdaining to be their prisoner, he cried, 'I 'yield to the King of England, conduct me to him.' He was conducted to Edward at Durham, and detained in close custody †.

And

---

* William Barde and one hundred more were made prisoners, one hundred and sixty were slain. Among the slain are mentioned Sir Humphry de Bois, Sir Humphry Jardine, and William Carlyle, [probably of Torthorald.] It may be conjectured, that Sir Humphry de Bois was the ancestor of Hector Boece. That historian says, L. xv. fol. 323. a. 'proavus meus Hugo Boetius, cujus pater ad Duplin occubuerat, *Baro Drifdalae*,' &c. Drisdale is a territory in Annandale. Boece supposed that his ancestor was slain at Duplin; it is more probable that he was slain at Lochmaben, with his countrymen.

† The English historians seem to place this event in the former year, immediately after the coronation of Balliol. Fordun, however, places it in the beginning of 1333, and he relates the circumstances with much precision, L. xiii. c. 27. Edward III. came to

1333.

And thus Scotland, in an evil hour, was deprived of the services of two of its ablest commanders, Sir Andrew Moray of Bothwell and the Knight of Liddesdale.

Ford. xiii. 27. Archibald Douglas now became Regent, whether by a regular election, or by the general wish of the nation, is uncertain [*].

Ford. iv. 552. Edward avowed his hostile intentions towards the Scots. He ordered an army to assemble at Newcastle upon Tine, within a month from the 4th of April †, [30th March.] He desired that public prayers might be put up for himself and his troops engaged in the defence and preservation of the kingdom, [23d April,] and he request-
Ford. iv. 556 ed the Earl of Flanders to prohibit his subjects from giving aid by sea to the rebellious Scots, [27th April.]

Ford. iv. 557. The King of France had formerly solicited Edward in behalf of the Scots, and had received an ambiguous and courtly answer. Edward now threw aside all disguise, and declared, that the Scots had violated the peace, and that he was resolved to chastise their outrages, and seek redress for the wrongs done, in such manner as to himself should seem good, [7th May.]

Ford. iv. 558. There was another circumstance in the conduct of Edward which shewed that he meant to circumscribe the territories of Scotland, as well as to chastise the Scots. He ordered possession to be taken of
the

---

to Durham about the 8th of April 1333; *Fœdera*, T. iv. p. 553. This may contribute to ascertain the date of the Regent's disaster.

* ' Interea vero Archibaldus de Douglas, qui *Tyneman* dictus est, statim post captionem Domini Andreæ de Moravia custodis, gardianus effectus est,' *Fordun.* L. xiii. c. 27.

† ' A die paschae proximè futuro in unum mensem ad ultimum,' *Fœdera*, T. iv. 552. In 1333, Easter-day fell on the 4th of April. This is a material date, and serves to correct a common error of historians as to the duration of the siege of Berwick.

1333.

the Isle of Man, in his name, [20th May,] and soon after he made it over to William de Montague, who had some claim of inheritance in it, [9th August.]

The chief purpose of the English King was to gain the town and castle of Berwick, already ceded to him by Balliol.

To the Scots the preservation of Berwick appeared no less important. The Earl of March was appointed to the command of the castle, and Sir William Keith to the command of the town. *Ford. iv. 564. 566.*

Balliol with his forces came before Berwick. Edward arrived soon after with the English army, and established his quarters at Tweedmouth, opposite to Berwick, on the south bank of the Tweed, [May]*. *Hem. II. 274. Ford. iv. 558.*

The siege was vigorously prosecuted on the quarter towards the sea, as well as by land. Although the Scots made an obstinate defence, and were successful in burning great part of the English fleet, yet, *Ford. xiii. 27.*

---

* Edward appears to have been at Belford on his march northwards, 7th May, *Fœdera*, T. iv. p. 557. So that it is probable, that, in a day or two after, he came to Berwick. Froissart relates, v. l. c. 27. that Edward III. leaving Balliol with his forces before Berwick, invaded Scotland, wasted the country, penetrated as far north as Dundee, and from thence marched across the island to the neighbourhood of Dunbarton. That he took the castles of Edinburgh and Dalkeith, and placed garrisons in them, and that, after having employed six months in this expedition, he returned to the siege of Berwick. This story has been transcribed by divers historians, who could not distinguish when Froissart was well informed, and when not. Froissart has placed, in 1333, events, which, as to many particulars, occurred afterwards. This *course of six months* is an impossibility; for Edward did not come to the siege of Berwick before May, and the place surrendered on the 20th of July. Besides, it appears from *Fœdera*, T. iv. p. 558.—564. that Edward was in the neighbourhood of Berwick 27th and 30th May 2d, 4th, 5th, 6th 8th, and 26th June, 2d, 4th, and 15th July; so that he never could have been three weeks absent; and, indeed, it is not probable that he was ever absent from the siege. An invasion of Scotland at that time could have served no purpose of conquest, and, by dividing the army, might have had fatal consequences.

1333.

yet, unless relief arrived, they must, at last, have surrendered. The English historians aver that the garrison amused the besiegers with deceitful proposals of capitulation.

Hem. ii. 215. Murim. 80.

At length the Regent appeared with a numerous army in the neighbourhood of Berwick, [11th July.] He endeavoured to convey succours into the town, or to provoke the enemies to quit the advantage of the ground, and engage in battle. But all his efforts were vain; the English obstructed every passage, and stood on the defensive.

Hem. ii. 215. King's 2363 Walsing. 132. Ford. xiii. 27.

The Regent then entered Northumberland, wasted the country, and even assaulted Bamburgh castle, where Philippa, the young Queen of England, had her residence *. He fondly imagined that Edward III. would have abandoned the siege of Berwick, after the example of his father, in circumstances not dissimilar. Edward nevertheless persevered in his enterprise.

Yp Neuf 511. Ford. xi. i. 26.

During a general assault, the town was set on fire, and in great measure consumed. The inhabitants, having experienced the evils of a siege, and dreading the worse evils of a storm, implored the Earl of March and Sir William Keith to seek terms of capitulation. A truce was obtained; and it was agreed, that the town and castle should be delivered up on terms fair and honourable, unless succours arrived before the hour of vespers on the 19th July †.

Ford. xiii. 27.

Ford. iv. 564. —568.

It was specially provided, ' that Berwick should be held as relieved,

' in

---

* In support of the facts here related, Tyrrel quotes the MS. chronicle of Lanercoft. Walsingham, *Ypod Neuftrias*, p. 511. supposes the attempt on Bamburgh castle to have been made after the main army returned to Scotland; but this is exceedingly improbable.

† The articles of capitulation are to be seen in *Fœdera*, T. iv. p. 564. —568. They are curious, and present a detail singularly minute; but they cannot be abridged, and they are too diffuse to be transcribed.

1333.

' in cafe two hundred men at arms, in a body, fhould force their paf-
' fage into the town.'

By the treaty, Sir William Keith was permitted to have an interview with the Regent. He found him with his army in Northumberland, urged the neceffity of his return, and fhewed him, that Berwick, if not inftantly relieved, was loft for ever. Perfuaded by his importunities, the Regent refolved to combat the Englifh, and either to fave Berwick or lofe the kingdom.

On the afternoon of the 19th of July the Regent prepared for battle. He divided his army into four bodies: The *firft* was led by John Earl of Moray, the fon of Randolph; but as he was young and inexperienced in war, James and Simon Frafers, foldiers of approved reputation, were joined with him in the command. The *fecond* body was led by the Stewart of Scotland, a youth of fixteen, under the infpection of his uncle Sir James Stewart of Rofyth. The *third* body was led by the Regent himfelf, having with him the Earl of Carrick and other Barons of eminence. The *fourth* body, or referve, appears to have been led by Hugh Earl of Rofs.

The numbers of the Scottifh army on that day are varioufly reported by hiftorians. The continuator of Hemingford, an author of that age, and Knyghton, who lived in the fucceeding age, afcertain their numbers with more precifion than is generally required in hiftorical facts.

The continuator of Hemingford minutely records the numbers and arrangement of the Scottifh army. He fays, that, befides Earls and other Lords, or great Barons, there were 55 Knights, 1100 men at arms, and 13,500 of the commons, lightly armed, amounting in all to 14,655.

*Hem. ii. 275.
276.*

With

1333.

Knyght. 2563. 2564. With him Knyghton appears to concur, when his narrative is cleared from the errors of ignorant or careless transcribers *.

It is probable, however, that the servants who tended the horses of persons of distinction, and of the men at arms, and the useless followers of the camp, were more numerous than the actual combatants.

The English were advantageously posted on a rising ground at Halidon, with a marshy hollow in their front. Of their particular disposition we are not informed, further than that Balliol had the command of one of the wings.

Ford. xiii. 28. It had been provided by the treaty of capitulation, 'That Berwick 'should be considered as relieved, in case two hundred men at arms 'forced their passage into the town.' *This* the Scottish men at arms attempted; but Edward, aware of their purpose, opposed them in person, and repulsed them with great slaughter. The Scottish army rushed on to a general attack; but they had to descend into the marshy hollow before mounting the eminences of Halidon. After having struggled with the difficulties of the ground, and after having been incessantly galled by the English archers, they reached the enemy. Although fatigued and disordered in their ranks, they fought as it became men who had conquered under the banners of Robert Bruce. The English, with equal valour, had great advantages of situation, and were better disciplined than their antagonists. The Earl of Rofs led the reserve to attack in flank that wing where Balliol commanded; but he was repulsed and slain. There fell with him, Kenneth Earl of Sutherland, and Murdoch Earl of Menteth †.

In the other parts of the field, the events were equally disastrous. The Regent received a mortal wound, and the Scots every where gave

* See Appendix.
† *Knyghton*, p. 2562. says, that the Earl of Strathern was killed; but he is mistaken. See *Fœdera*, T. iv. p. 595.

gave way. In the field, and during a pursuit for many miles, the number of slain and prisoners was so great, that few of the Scottish army escaped.

Besides the Earls of Rofs, Sutherland, and Menteth, there were among the slain Malcolm Earl of Lenox, an aged Baron, he had been one of the foremost to repair to the standard of Robert Bruce, and he now paid the last duties to his country; Alexander Bruce Earl of Carrick, who atoned for his short defection from the family of his benefactor; John Campbell Earl of Athole, nephew of the late King; James Frafer, and Simon Frafer, John de Graham, Alexander de Lindefay, Alan Stewart, and many other persons of eminent rank.

The Stewart had two uncles, John and James. John was killed, and James mortally wounded and made prisoner [*].

The Regent, mortally wounded, and abandoned on the field of battle, only lived to see his army difcomfited and himself a prisoner.

This victory was obtained with very inconfiderable lofs. It is related by the English historians, that, on the side of their countrymen, there were killed one knight, one esquire, and twelve foot soldiers. Nor will this appear altogether incredible, when we remember that the English ranks remained unbroken, and that their archers, at a secure distance, incessantly annoyed the Scottish infantry.

Ford. iv. 568, Tp. Neuf. 511.

According to capitulation, the town and cattle of Berwick furrendered. The English King took twelve hoftages for fecuring the fidelity of the citizens of Berwick.

Ford. iv. 581.

Whether he put to death any of the hoftages whom he had formerly

---

[*] *Fordun, L. xiii. c. 28. relates, that Sir James Stewart was ſlain; the English hiftorians, that he was mortally wounded and made prisoner. It may be remarked, that at Halidon two Stewarts fought under the banner of their chief; the one Alan of Dreghorn, the paternal ancestor of Charles I. and the other James of Bosfyth, the maternal ancestor of Oliver Cromwell.*

1333.

merly received, is an historical problem, which will be considered in a separate dissertation *.

Knyghton. 2563.
Ford. iv. 570.

Edward not only granted his protection to the Earl of March, [26th July,] but he also received him into favour, and appointed him to a distinguished command on the borders of the two kingdoms.†

Anonymous,
Ed. III. 402.

' And now,' says an English historian, ' it was the general voice, ' that the Scottish wars were ended; for no man remained of that na- ' tion who had either influence to assemble, or skill to lead an army.'

Ford. xiii. 18.

Some castles, however, still remained in the possession of the friends of Scotland. Malcolm Fleming having escaped from the carnage at Halidon, secured the castle of Dunbarton. Alan de Vypont held the castle of Lochleven, Robert Lauder the castle of Urquhart in Inverness-shire, and Christian Bruce the castle of Kildrummy in Marre. This venerable matron was the sister of Robert I. and mother of the Earl of Marre, Regent, flain at Duplin in 1332.

Ford. xiii. 18.

There was also a strong hold in Lochdown, on the borders of Carrick, where John Thomson, a man of low birth, but approved valour, commanded ‡.

Froisart, i. 34.

In such circumstances, it became necessary to provide a safe place of refuge for the young King and his consort. Malcolm Fleming found

---

* See Appendix.

† *Fordun*, L. xiii. c. 28. says, ' In crastino verò justu Rex Angliae omnes *examinari*, ' multi tamen tam nobilium quàm aliorum innoceū refervantur.' It is not probable that Edward III. would have ordered all the prisoners taken at Halidon to be put to death; and it will be remarked, that Fordun has not mentioned the name of any person who suffered in consequence of an order equally cruel and impolitic.

‡ ' Fortalicii de Louchdown, quod tunc Anglicè vocabatur *Pele*, custos erat vulnus ' *vernaculus*, Johannes videlicet Thomae;' *Fordun*, L. xiii. c. 28. He was probably the same *John Thompson* who led home the broken remains of the Scots after the battle of Dundalk. See *Annals*, vol. ii. p. 81. 82.

1333.

found means to convey them from the castle of Dumbarton into France, where they were honourably entertained †.

Balliol held a parliament, [about the beginning of October 1333.] To it many Englishmen, now become possessed of estates in Scotland, repaired. The English King appointed commissioners to require from Balliol and his parliament the ratification of the treaty of Rokesburgh. Nothing, however, was concluded at this time.

Anonymous, Ed. III. 405. Fœd. iv. 578.

Edward summoned Balliol to his parliament; but Balliol excused himself by reason of the unsettled state of Scotland ‡.

Anonymous, Ed. III. 405.

Balliol held a parliament at Edinburgh, [10th February 1333-4.] Geffrey Scrope, chief justice of England, demanded, in the name of Edward III. that the treaty between Balliol and his liege Lord should be ratified; and to this Balliol and his parliament consented. Balliol became bound to serve, with all his forces, in the wars of Edward; and for performing, in part, the conditions covenanted, he made an absolute surrender of the town, castle, and territory of Berwick, to be annexed for ever to the English crown. These things were concluded on the 12th February 1333-4. With so much precipitancy did the assembly

Fœd. iv. 590. &c.

---

† Whether David II. was conveyed into France after the battle of Duplin in 1332, or after the battle of Halidon in 1333, is a question of little importance. Our later authors have decided in favour of 1333, and not without probable reasons; the chief is, that Balliol, 23d November 1332, offered to marry Johanna, the infant consort of David Bruce; *Fœdera*, T. iv. p. 536.—539. which he would not have done, had she been conveyed into France immediately after the battle of Duplin, 11th August 1332. This is a more specious argument than any thing drawn from the chronicle of Froissart, where dates and facts are strangely misplaced and confounded, as the manner is in colloquial history.

‡ This is said on the Authority of the anonymous author of the life of Edward III. subjoined to the edition of W. Hemingford by Hearne. Henry de Beaumont and William de Montague are mentioned as Balliol's attornies, p. 405.

1333.

assembly at Edinburgh dismember the kingdom, and yield up the national liberties *.

The

* There is an Instrument in *Fœdera*, T. iv. p. 590. &c. which relates the whole circumstances of this disgraceful transaction; from it we learn the names of the principal persons present.

BISHOPS.

John de Lindsay Bishop of Glasgow.
Alexander de Kynynmound Bishop of Aberdeen.
William [Sinclair] Bishop of Dunkeld.
Henry ———— Bishop of Galloway.
John ———— Bishop of Ross.
Maurice ———— Bishop of Dumblane.
Adam ———— Bishop of Brechin.

BARONS.

Henry de Beaumont Earl of Buchan.
David de Strathbolgie Earl of Athole.
Patrick de Dunbar Earl of March.
Richard Talbot Lord of Marre.
Alexander de Seton.
Alexander de Moubray.
William de Keith, Stewart of the houshold.

William Brithain Chancellor of Scotland.

The Instrument adds, ' et aliis compluribus Baronibus, magnatibus, proceribus, et hominibus tam clericis quàm laicis.' Impartiality constrains me to mention, that there is too much ground for supposing that *William Bishop of Dunkeld* was the courageous prelate whom Robert I. termed *his Bishop*. See *Keith*, Catalogue of Scottish Bishops, p. 51. 52. and that *Maurice Bishop of Dumblane* was *that* Maurice abbot of Inchaffray who, at the battle of Bannockburn, ' passed along the front of the Scottish army bare-
' footed, and bearing a crucifix in his hands, and exhorted the Scots in few and for-
' cible words to combat for their rights and their liberty;' See *Annals*, vol. ii. p. 47. the same person now concurred in voting the annihilation of those rights and that dear-bought liberty. The Earl of March had been newly reconciled to the English interest;

Fœdera,

1334.

The humiliation of the unhappy kingdom became complete when Balliol, by a solemn instrument, surrendered great part of the Scottish dominions to be annexed for ever to England.

In this instrument Balliol said, that he had formerly become bound *Fœd. iv. 614,* to make a grant to Edward of lands on the marches to the amount of —616. *two thousand pound lands*, that the Scottish parliament had ratified his obligation, and that he had accordingly surrendered Berwick and its territory; and now, for completely discharging his obligation, he made an absolute surrender to the English crown of the forests of Jedburgh, Selkirk, and Etrick; of the counties of Rokesburgh, Peebles, and Dumfries; together with the county of Edinburgh, and constabularies

Fœdera, T. iv. p. 570. As to *Seton* and *Keith*, it is not altogether certain who they were. The other Barons mentioned in the instrument were all of the number of the *disinherited* or *claimants*. *Tyrrel*, vol. iii. p. 381. observes, ' that Edward III. went to ' Edinburgh about the beginning of February 1333-4, where Balliol then held a par- ' liament, who, in the presence, and by the assent of the prelates, &c. did homage to ' King Edward in French, as it is expressed in the charter.' He adds, ' that the origi- ' nal is still preserved in a box, entitled *Scotia tempore Regis Edwardi III.* in the old ' chapter-house at Westminster. And that this rather deserves our notice, because ' none of our historians, either in print or manuscript, say any thing of this charter, nor ' mention any homage to have been done by this Balliol to our King Edward.' This is utterly erroneous, though delivered with the self-sufficiency which distinguishes the works of Tyrrel. The homage of which he speaks was performed at Rokesburgh 23d November 1332; *Fœdera*, T. iv. p. 530. and there is a transcript of it in the instrument of the notary reciting the proceedings of the parliament at Edinburgh 10th and 12th February 1333-4; *Fœdera*, T. iv. p. 590. &c. That instrument, as well as the other writings in *Fœdera*, demonstratively prove that Edward III. did not appear at Edinburgh in person in February 1333-4; his commissioners Geffrey Scrope, and others, acted in his name. It is strange that Tyrrel should have said, that no historians mention any homage done by Edward Balliol to Edward III. when all the more antient historians mention it, and when he himself pretends to confute Walsingham and Murimuth for having asserted that Balliol did homage to Edward III. at Newcastle in June 1334.

1334.

laries of Linlithgow and Haddington, and of all the towns and castles belonging to the several territories thus surrendered, [at Newcastle upon Tyne, 12th June 1334.]

Foed. iv. 616.—618.

Edward immediately regulated the government of his new dominions: He appointed a sheriff for each district, a chamberlain, or general steward, and a justiciary of Lothian [a], [15th and 21st June.] Although the territories, thus acquired, were of greater extent than that Lothian which England had formerly claimed; yet it was politic to impose the antient name on the whole territory, that it might seem to have been *resumed* rather than *acquired*.

Rym. ii. 977. Wolsing. 133. A. Mur. 74. Scala Chron. ap. Leland. i. 554.

Balliol presented himself before his liege Lord; did homage and swore fealty ' for the *whole* kingdom of Scotland and the isles adjacent,' [at Newcastle upon Tyne, 18th June 1334.]

Foed. iv. 618.

The surrender of the southern part of Scotland had been made with such precipitation, and in terms so general, that the private estate of Balliol

---

[a] The partition of the country, and the names of the persons who were to bear rule in the different districts, are thus recorded in *Foedera*, T. iv. p. 616—618. *Rokesburgh*, Geffrey de Moubray; *Edinburgh*, John de Kingston; *Peebles*, Gilbert de Bourgdon; *Dumfries*, Peter Tilliol; *Jedburgh town*, *with Selkirk and Etrick*, Robert de Maners; *Jedburgh castle and forest*, William de Pressen; *Chamberlain of the new acquisitions*, John de Bourdon; *Justiciary of Lothian*, Robert de Lowedre. Geffrey de Moubray, who had the charge of the district of Rokesburgh, married Isobel Stewart, the widow of Donald Earl of Marre, slain at Duplin in 1332. Soon after his appointment, he claimed the offices of Sheriff of Rokesburgh and keeper of Selkirk forest, in right of his wife; *Foedera*, iv. 622. But what was the nature of her claim, I cannot discover; perhaps her father, Alexander Stewart of Bonkill, held those offices heritably.

The justiciary of Lothian was required to do all things ' secundum legem et ' consuetudinem regni Scotiae.' These were the dictates of sound policy. Edward and his ministers knew that the people of a subjugated province dislike the laws of their new rulers, however superior in excellence they may be to the former usages of the nation, and that a change, even to the better, must be imperceptibly accomplished, and rather by the wish of the subjects, than by the avowed will of the lawgiver.

1334.

Balliol was comprehended under the words of the inftrument. Edward, therefore, iffued a declaration, importing, that the lands of Botel, Kenmore, and Kirkandrews, were not to be underftood as falling within the furrender. He faid, that, having already received fatisfaction in full, he had too much reverence for God, juftice, and good faith to man, that the ceffion fhould be prejudicial to the private rights of the King of Scots, [at Newcaftle, 18th June 1334.]

The *difinherited Lords*, to whofe fortunate valour Balliol owed fo much, had the chief fhare in his favour. A quarrel now arofe among them, which, from flight beginnings, produced extraordinary confequences. The brother of Alexander de Moubray died [*], leaving daughters, but no iffue-male. Moubray having claimed to be preferred to the daughters of his brother, Balliol countenanced his fuit, and, as it appears, put him in poffeffion of the inheritance. Henry de Beaumont, Earl of Buchan, and David de Strathbolgie, [or Haftings], Earl of Athole, efpoufed the caufe of the heirs general. Perceiving that their folicitations were not heard, they left the court in difguft, and retired to their caftles, [about the end of Auguft.] Balliol foon became fenfible that it was dangerous to exafperate two Barons, haughty and independent, the Lords of the extenfive territories of Athole, Badenoch, and Buchan; and, therefore, he difmiffed Moubray; and, as an earneft of his favour, conferred on David de Strathbolgie the whole eftates of the young Stewart of Scotland. But that which conciliated the favour of Buchan and Athole, alienated Moubray from the fervice of Balliol.

About this time, Sir Andrew Moray of Bothwell having been fet at liberty, returned to his native country; and, with his antient zeal for

Ford. xiii.

Ford. xiii.

[*] Probably John de Moubray, flain at Annan 16th December 1332. See *Annals*, vol. ii. p. 58.

1334

for the public, began to assemble the surviving friends of Scotland. Moubray, dreading the power and violence of his adversaries, joined himself to Sir Andrew Moray. Geffrey de Moubray also, whom Edward had appointed governor of Rokesburgh, revolted to the Scots *.

Scala Chron.
ap. Leland,
L. 554.
Walsing. 134.
Ford. xiii. 40.

Richard Talbot was in the north when these disturbances began. He endeavoured to pass into England; but he was intercepted by Sir William Keith of Galston, defeated and made prisoner †.

Ford. xiii. 39.

Sir Andrew Moray and Alexander de Moubray marched into Buchan, and besieged Henry de Beaumont in his castle of Dundarg. Beaumont, despairing of relief, capitulated, and obtained liberty to depart into England ‡.

Ford. xiii. 39.

The Stewart of Scotland had lain concealed in Bute ever since the battle of Halidon; he now found means to pass over to the castle of Dunbarton, and resolutely stood forth in the public cause.

Ford. xiii. 39.

Assisted by Dougal Campbell of Lochow, he made himself master of the castle of Dunoon in Cowal. His tenants of the island of Bute attacked and slew Alan de Lile, the governor, and presented his head to

---

* His wife Isabella, Countess-dowager of Narre, retired into England, and obtained from Edward a grant of her husband's whole chattels in England, and estates in the county of Northumberland, [22d February 1335-6.] *Fœdera,* T. iv. p. 635.

† There is some confusion in the dates of the great variety of events which occurred in this busy period. I have endeavoured to arrange them in that order which appears most probable. In the following year Richard Talbot was ransomed for 2000 marks; *Anonym.* Edward III. p. 408. *Fordun.* L. xiii. c. 40.

‡ In *Tyrrel. N. Ruffrias,* p. 512. it is said, that the castle of Dundarg was relieved by the English. Fordun's account is more consistent with probability, and is confirmed by *Scala Chron.* ap. Leland. T. i. p. 554.

1334.

to their master [a]. John the son of Gilbert [b] was made prisoner in the action where De Lile fell. This man was governor of the castle of Bute; he ordered the garrison to surrender, and attached himself to the Scottish interest. Encouraged by these successes, the Stewart invaded the territory of Renfrew [c], his antient inheritance, and by military execution compelled the inhabitants to acknowledge the sovereignty of David [d].

Godfrey de Ross, the governor of Airshire, either from considerations of interest, or through necessity, submitted to the Stewart. *Ford. xiii. 33.*

Fordun thus describes the Stewart: 'He was a comely youth, tall 'and robust, modest, liberal, gay, and courteous; and, for the innate 'sweetness of his disposition, generally beloved by true hearted Scots-'men [e].' *Ford. xiii. 32.*

The Earl of Moray had escaped into France after the battle of Halidon; he now returned to Scotland. The Scots acknowledged him and the Stewart as Regents under the authority of their infant and exiled sovereign. The Earl of Moray speedily collected a body of troops, *Ford. xiii. 33.*

---

[a] *Fordun, L. xiii. c. 32.* calls those men *the Brandanes of Bute,* and says, that, as a reward for their services, they asked and obtained a perpetual exemption from payment of *multures.* It is to be presumed, that they sought to be freed from the obligation of bringing their corn to be grinded at the mill of the barony, not that it should be grinded gratuitously.

[b] 'Johannes Gilberti,' *Fordun. L. xiii. c. 32.*

[c] The district called the *Stewart-lands,* or the *barony. Fordun. L. xiii. c. 33.* says, that the Stewart was joined by Thomas Carruthers and his relations from Annandale, and by Thomas Bruce from Kyle.

[d] 'Ad fidem Scoticanam convertunt;' *Fordun. L. xiii. c. 33.* Literally, 'the parti-'sans of the Stewart converted the inhabitants of Renfrew to the Scottish faith.'

[e] I would have said *universally* instead of *generally,* had it not been for an expression in Fordun, L. xiii. c. 32. 'a cunctis fere populis,' &c.

176   DAVID II.

1334.

troops, invaded the country of the Earl of Athole, and constrained him to retire into Lochaber. Athole, deprived of all means of subsistence, was compelled to surrender. Ambition or levity of mind induced him to embrace the party of the conquerors *.

Hem. ii. 177.
Ford. iv. 628.

On this rapid change of things, Balliol again retired into England, and implored the protection of his sovereign. At an unfavourable season for military operations, Edward led his troops against the insurgents, [14th November.] With one part of the army Balliol wasted Avondale and the adjacent territories, [December.] He celebrated Christmas in royal state at the castle of Renfrew, and distributed lands and

For f. xiii. 19.

* It is difficult to account for the motives which induced Athole to join the partisans of David II. By the late revolution he had been restored to his paternal inheritance, and had obtained possession of great part of the estate of the Comyns, in right of his mother, the eldest daughter of John Comyn slain at Dumfries. By the prodigal liberality of Balliol, he had received a grant of the whole estates of the Stewart. In his own right, and in right of his mother, he had ample possessions in England. Although the fate of war now deprived him of every thing in Scotland, and reduced him to the necessity of laying down his arms; yet there appears not to have been any necessity for his resuming them again to combat against his party, and against Balliol his benefactor. It is reasonable to suppose, that the Scots would have given such conditions to him, as they gave to Henry de Beaumont, and would have permitted him to depart into England. On the other hand, he had every thing to fear from the resentment of Edward III. and, accordingly, we find, that the King immediately confiscated the English estates of Athole ; *Dugdale,* Baronage, vol. ii. p. 96. It is true, that, at an after period, Athole pretended, that, ' what he had done was not out of any evil ' intentions towards the King, but for his honour, and to save his own life ;' *Dugdale,* ibid. These are the common pretences of unsuccessful traitors, which, although they may find place in the narrative of a pardon, are never believed. The most probable reason for the conduct of Athole seems to be, that, in the right of John Comyn, he had all the claims of the Balliol line to the crown of Scotland, supposing Edward Balliol to be set aside, whom his submissions to England had rendered odious. Athole, amidst the confusions of war, might possibly have hoped to assert such ambitious pretences.

1234

and offices among his guests *. The person in whom Balliol placed his chief confidence, was William Bullock, an ecclesiastic of eminent abilities. He was appointed Chamberlain of Scotland, and he had the custody of the castles of St Andrews and Coupar, and of other fortresses entrusted to him.

Edward led the rest of his army into the Lothians, seized certain men whom the English historians term 'evil doers,' put their leaders to death, and ruled at pleasure in a desolate and defenceless country. *Rem. ii. 277.*

At this perilous juncture, Patrick Earl of March formally renounced the fealty which he had sworn to England †. *Hem. ii. 277.*

There were great motives urging him to a resolution so desperate. Balliol had ceded to Edward that part of Scotland where the estates of the Earl of March lay, and the Earl foresaw inevitable ruin to himself, and to the power of his family, should England be left in possession of the Lothians; for, although the English Kings had hitherto, by their protection, maintained the house of March in an independency dangerous to Scotland, yet it was obvious that they would never permit it to continue formidable on the new frontier.

1335.

We have seen that Alan de Vipont held the castle of Lochleven against the adherents of Balliol. That castle, built on a small island, was strong from its situation, and of difficult access. John de Strive- *Ford. xiii. 30. 31.*
lin

---

* Such appears to be the meaning of *Fordun*, L. xiii. c. 29. ' ad Renfrew, villam ' regiam, pervenit, ubi *regio more festum faciens*, convivia suis terras et officia distri- ' buit.'

† ' Redeuntibus verò Regibus versus Berewicum, Comes Patricius, qui fidelitatem ' juraverat et homagium fecerat, ab eis recedendo, quanquam Rex Angliae multas cu- ' rialitates sibi fecerat, suum homagium per literas suas eis remisit;' *W. Hemingford*, T. ii. p. 277. *per literas suas eas*, is an idiom of old French, *par les siennes lettres*.

Vol. II. Z

1335.

lin * blockaded it, erected a fort in the neighbouring cemetery of Kinros, and, at the lower end of the lake, where it forms *the water of Leven*, he raised a strong and lofty bulwark. By means of it he hoped to lay the island under water, and to constrain Vypont to surrender. Four men of the garrison approached in silence, and, after much labour and perseverance, pierced the bulwark. The sudden inundation swept away the enemies who were quartered on that side. Confusion arose in the English camp. The garrison of the castle landed at Kinros, and stormed and plundered the fort. It chanced that John de Strivelin was absent, with many of his soldiers, celebrating, at Dunfermline, the festival of Margaret Queen of Scotland †, [19th June.] On his return, he passionately swore, that he would never desist from his enterprize until he had rased the castle, and put the garrison to the sword. Yet, after some vain attempts, he retired, ' with the im-
' putation of perjury,' says Fordun, as if the offence had consisted, not in swearing rashly, but in failing to accomplish what was impracticable ‡.

Meanwhile

* Probably the same John de Strivelin who had been made prisoner at Halidon. There were with him many barons whom the English had received into favour, particularly Michael and David de Wemyss, Richard de Melvil, and Michael de Arnot. A. de Vypont was assisted by James Lambyn, [probably Lamy,] a citizen of St Andrews; *Fordun*, L. xiii. c. 30.

† ' Nundinae Fermolinodunenses etiamnum celebrantur 18 die Junii, pridie festum ' *translationis* D. Margaritae, i. e. 19. Junii, juxta Extract. Dempsterum et Camera-
' rium,' *Ruddiman*, not. ad Buchanan, p. 159. See *Annals*, vol. I. p. 503. Mr Ruddiman suspects that the siege of Lochleven happened in some other year than 1335. His chief reason is, that, from the 4th April to the 24th June 1335, there was a truce between the two nations; and, to prove the existence of the truce, he refers to an instrument in *Foedera*, T. iv. p. 640. But that instrument only shows that proposals for a truce had been made, not that a truce had been concluded.

‡ Fordun ascribes the success of the Scots to the interposition of St Servanus, the tutelary

1335.

Meanwhile the Stewart, and the Earl of Moray, Regents, assembled a parliament at Dairsy, [near Coupar in Fife,] April 1335. There appeared at that assembly, the Earl of March, Sir Andrew Moray of Bothwell, Alexander de Moubray, William Douglas of Liddesdale, and many other barons. The Earl of Athole also appeared, having a formidable train of attendants, and bearing himself with a haughtiness of demeanour which the Scottish Lords could ill brook. This ambitious and fickle young man set up his party in opposition to the Earl of Moray, and wrought on the inexperience and facility of the Stewart, to join with him in perplexing and thwarting the national counsels. The deliberations of the parliament were influenced by private interests, animosities, and mutual disgusts; and, at length, the barons, without having concerted any general plan of defence, separated themselves in confusion *.

Through the mediation of France, some overtures had been made for a treaty with the Scots; but the English parliament rejected all terms of peace, and Edward again invaded Scotland †, [11th July.] Whilst

tutelary saint of that district. He, it seems, thus chastised the impiety of John de Strivelin and his army, who had erected a fort on consecrated ground; and yet Queen Margaret failed to protect John de Strivelin, who had left his post that he might pray at her shrine.

* Of this parliament Fordun speaks, L. xiii. c. 34. ' Ubi, propter tyrannidem Da-
' vidis Comitis Atholiae, nihil aliud uſtam est nisi derisione dignum. Hic Seneſcallo
' adhaerens, qui tunc non magnâ regebatur sapientiâ, sed Comitem Moraviae et Willi-
' elmum de Douglas despectui habens, omnibus ibi existentibus factus est infestus;
' Sed circumspecta praenominatorum prudentia immanem ipsius saevitiam callidè de-
' clinavit.' In justification of the Stewart, Mr Goodall observes, not. ad Fordun. ' at
' quid mirum, si infra aetatem juvenis senibus astutià cedat.' It is to be regretted, that Fordun has not been more explicit in his narrative; one may easily discern that he had some particular circumstances in view which he could have explained.

† Knyghton, p. 2566. says, that Edward III. invaded Scotland by the west marches,
and

180   D A V I D II.

1335.

Whilst he cruelly ravaged the country, Balliol and Earl Warenne, on another quarter, profecuted the war with equal inhumanity *. The two Princes arrived in the neighbourhood of Glafgow, and, having united their forces, marched to Perth.

Ford. xiii. 35.
Ford. iv. 654.
Scala Chron.
ap. Leland.
l. 555.

Soon after the arrival of Edward in Scotland, Count Guy of Namur landed at Berwick with a confiderable body of men at arms, in the fervice of the Englifh, [30th July.] Imagining that Edward had left no enemies in his rear, he advanced to Edinburgh, at that time an open place, and having its caftle difmantled. Scarcely had he arrived there, when the Earls of Moray and March, and Sir Alexander Ramfay, appeared in the neighbourhood with a powerful force. They fought on *the Borough muir* with obftinate valour. Richard Shaw, a
                                                                            Scottifh

and croffed the Solway on the 11th July 1335. This has the appearance of great accuracy; and, indeed, Knyghton relates many minute particulars as to the progrefs of Edward's army, which feem to have been tranfcribed from fome military journal of thofe times Fordun, L. xiii. c. 34. fays, that the navy of Edward was feen in the frith of Forth, 6th July 1335. This does not contradict Knyghton; for Edward might have marched his army on the one fide, while his fleet with provifions and military ftores advanced on the other fide of the ifland. His grand father Edward I. followed a like plan of operations; but *here* lies the difficulty; in *Fædera*, T. iv p. 655.—57. there are different orders iffued by Edward, dated from Carlifle 18th, 25th, 26th, and 28th of July 1335. This appears inconfiftent with Knyghton's account. I incline, however, to believe that the public bufinefs continued to be tranfacted in the King's name at Carlifle, even after he was perfonally in Scotland: And, what confirms me in this opinion, is, that an order, which, from its nature, muft have been iffued by the King himfelf, is dated from Erthe [Airth on the Forth,] 3d Auguft 1335; *Fædera*, T. iv. p. 658. Now, it is not probable that Edward could have marched an army from Carlifle to Airth, between the 28th July and the 3d of Auguft, efpecially as he went by Glafgow or its neighbourhood.

* *Knyghton*, p. 2566. fays, that Balliol and Earl Warenne made themfelves mafters of the caftle of *Combernauth* belonging to the Earl of Athole, and this circumftance is repeated by many hiftorians. The true name of the caftle is preferved in *Scala Chron.* ap. Leland, vol. i. p. 555. ' Balliol got the caftle of Combernauld by affaulte.' Cumbernauld

1335.

Scottish esquire, was singled out by a combatant in the army of the Count of Namur. They were transfixed with each other's spears, and both slain. On the body's being stripped of its armour, the brave stranger was discovered to be a woman. Victory was about to declare for the enemy, when William Douglas came down from Pentland hills with a re-inforcement. The troops of Namur gave way, yet still maintained the fight in retreating. At length, Count Guy was compelled to take refuge among the ruins of the castle. Having ordered all his horses to be killed, he formed a temporary parapet of their bodies. Nevertheless, thirst and hunger soon obliged him to capitulate. The Earl of Moray paid due respect to the valour of the strangers, and allowed the Count of Namur, and his troops, to depart unmolested, on their promise not to serve against David in the Scottish wars [*].

The Earl of Moray, accompanied by William Douglas, and his brother James, escorted Count Guy of Namur to the borders. On his return, William de Prefsen, warden of the castle and forest of Jedburgh,

Ford. xiii. 35.
Hem H. 278.
An. Edw. III.
408. Marim.
16.

bernauld in Stirlingshire had belonged to John Comyn, and had been granted to Malcolm Fleming by Robert Bruce; it was now in the possession of the Earl of Athole as one of the co-heirs of Comyn.

[*] *Fordun*, L. xiii. c. 35. says, that one reason which induced the Earl of Moray to shew such courtesy to the conquered, was that he imagined it would be an agreeable service to Philip King of France. This Count Guy of Namur was the second son of John de Dampierre Count of Namur. John de Dampierre had for his first wife Margaret the daughter of Robert de Clermont or Bourbon, sixth son of Lewis IX. King of France. Although Margaret left no children, the alliance established a connection with the royal family of France. Fordun supposes that the Count of Guelders, also a leader in Edward's army, was the person made prisoner. In *Fœdera*, T. iv. p. 658. there is a passport from Edward III. to the Count of Namur returning home [dated at Perth 11th August 1335.]

1335.

burgh, attacked and routed his party *. James Douglas was slain, and the Earl himself made prisoner, and conveyed into England †.

The

* This is the account given by Fordun, and it seems the most probable one. *Knyghton*. p. 2566. gives a very different account; he says that the Scots, to the number of 10,000 men, under the command of the Regent, marched to besiege the castle of Bamborgh, where the English Queen resided, that, by this diversion, they might oblige the English to withdraw their troops from Scotland: That they were encountered by a body of 5000 English, and defeated, with the loss of 19 Knights, and 500 men, [it is afterwards said 5000, which may be an error of the transcriber] That the English took the Earl of Moray prisoner, and conducted him to Bamburgh castle, and that they themselves lost 400 men. This story is of very dubious credit; for the earlier writers make no mention of it. See *Hemingford*, T. ii. p. 278. *Anonym*. Edw. III. p. 408. *A. Murimuth*, p. 86. Besides, there is a grant made by Edward III. *Foedera*, T. iv. p. 670. [10th October 1335,] which seems inconsistent with the narrative in *Knyghton*; from it we learn that the Earl of Moray was made prisoner, ' in quodam ' conflictu,' by William de Pressen, ' et quidem alii fideles nostri in sua comitiva ex- ' istentes.' Now, if 5000 English had attacked and defeated 10,000 Scots, this would not have been called ' a conflict between the Scots and William de Pressen, and cer- ' tain others of Edward's subjects in his company.' The words plainly imply such a skirmish as Fordun describes. In the same sense, it is said, *Scala Chron*. ap. Leland. T. i. p. 555. ' The Count of Murref was by chance taken yn the marches by one Wil- ' liam Pressen.' It is conjectured by *Barnes*, p. 97. that this English army was commanded by John of Eltham Earl of Cornwall, brother of Edward III. who, with the troops of the northern counties, penetrated by Galloway and Airshire into the western parts of Scotland, and then marched through Lenox, Menteth, and Stratherne, to the head quarters at Perth. That this army should have encountered a Scottish army on its rout from Edinburgh to Bamburgh castle, is a wonderful circumstance indeed! Edward III. rewarded the good services of William de Pressen by a grant of the estate of Edrington near Berwick, until he should be provided with twenty pounds of land yearly, in some other place; *Foedera*, T. iv. p. 670.

† The Earl of Moray was committed by Edward III. to the custody of the Sheriff of Yorke, and then ordered to the castle of Notingham [13th August 1335] this warrant is dated at Perth.] *Foedera*, T. iv. p. 660.; removed to Windsor 19th December 1335; *Foedera*, T. iv. p. 662.; to Winchester 25th May 1336; *Foedera*, T. iv. p. 700.

and

1335.

The captivity of the one Regent, and the inexperience of the other, seemed to precipitate the ruin of the Scottish nation. Alexander de Moubray, Geffrey de Moubray, and certain other persons *, having, as they said, full powers from the Earl of Athole, and Robert the 'Stewart of Scotland,' concluded a treaty with Edward III. [at Perth, 18th August 1335.]

By this treaty it was provided, that the Earl of Athole, all the other barons, and all persons of the community of Scotland, on submitting themselves to the English King, should receive pardon, and have their lands, fees, and offices within the kingdom secured. But an exception was made of those who, *by common assent*, [in parliament,] should be denied the privilege of this indemnity.

The liberties of the Scottish church were to be preserved on their former establishment; and the laws, and antient usages of Scotland, as in the days of King Alexander, were to continue in force.

Further, it was provided, that all offices in Scotland should be held by natives of that kingdom, with this exception, that the Sovereign might name whatsoever persons he pleased to offices within his royal domains †.

The

*Ford. xlfd. 36.
Hem ii. 278,
Knight. 2588.
Tyrr. iii. 387.*

and to the tower of London 28th September 1336; *Fœdera,* T. iv. p. 708. He did not recover his liberty till 1341, when he was exchanged for the Earl of Salisbury, a prisoner with the French; *Fœdera,* T. v. p. 250.

* The other persons were Geffrey de Root, Eustace de Loreyne, and William Bullock, an ecclesiastic; to all appearance, he is the same man on whom Balliol conferred the office of Chamberlain. As there is no reason for believing that William Bullock had, at this time, ever revolted from Balliol, we may conclude that he acted as attorney for the persons who were absent.

† Or, as it is more generally expressed, his *regalities*. *Tyrrel*, vol. iii. p. 387. thus translates the passage, ' Yet, that the King of Scotland of his royalty may make such ' officers as he pleases, and of what nation soever.' The ambiguity in this translation leaves

1335.

The other articles of the treaty of Perth respect the particular persons therein named, who had estates in England, and principally, indeed, the Earl of Athole.

Fæd. iv. 664.
Færd. xiii. 36.

Edward III. granted a special pardon to the Earl of Athole, restored him to his English estates, [at Perth, 24th August 1335,] and conferred on him the office of Lieutenant in Scotland *.

Ford. xiii. 36.
Hem. ii. 278.
Anonym. Ed.
III. 408.
Tyr. Nrv. 511.

Athole required all men to acknowledge the authority of Balliol, and, with the zeal of a new convert, arbitrarily and severely punished the partizans of that cause which himself had deserted. With 3000 men he besieged the castle of Kildrummy, hitherto the asylum of the royalists. There still remained three barons, says Fordun, who had not made their submission to England; the Earl of March, William Douglas of Liddesdale, and Sir Andrew Moray of Bothwell. They kept themselves in lurking places, not without the connivance of the English lords. Sir Andrew Moray resolved, at all hazards, to attempt the

---

leaves it uncertain whether Tyrrel understood the original; but there is no uncertainty as to Barnes, who says, p. 98. ' Yet so, as that the King of Scotland, of *his prero-*
' *gative royal,* may, at any time, according to his pleasure, advance to places of office,
' men of any nation whatsoever.' *Abercrombie,* vol. ii. p. 49. follows the paraphrase of Barnes, which just amounts to this, that all offices shall be enjoyed by Scotsmen, saving the good pleasure of the King to bestow them on the men of any other nation.

* I here transcribe a passage from *Scala Chron.* ap. Leland, T. i. p. 555. ' Edwarde
' the 3d cam from S. John's tounne to Edingburgh, whither cam Robert the Seneschal
' of Scotland, onto hys peace. This Robert was sunne to the doughter of Robert
' Bruse King of Scotland.' Edward III. was at Edinburgh from the 16th to the 20th September 1335. *Foedera,* T. iv. p. 667. 669. It appears from Leland's manner of spelling, that, in the days of Henry VIII. the English had much of that pronunciation which is now termed *Broad Scotch.* Thus he writes *cam* for *came, sunne* for *son,* and *doughter* for *daughter.* The word *his* is still pronounced in the south east parts of Scotland *hes;* whether the sound of *hys* was the same, I cannot say. This observation might be enlarged and inforced from the common spelling of words so late as the reign of Queen Elisabeth, and from other examples, which would astonish many of my readers.

1335.

the rescue of his wife and family *. He and the Earl of March, with William Douglas, had collected 800 men, natives of the Lothians and Merse, and they were joined by 300 from the territory of Kildrummy, under the command of John Craig †. They surprized Athole in the forest of Kilblain. His troops, seized with a panic, fled and dispersed themselves ‡. Abandoned by his dastardly soldiers, and disdaining quarter, Athole was slain §. Thus perished, in the flower

* Fordun, L. xiii. c. 36. says, 'petiit licentiâ et obtentâ a D. Willelmo de Monte- 'cuto Regis Angliae tunc principali consiliario.' If William de Montagu, (afterwards Earl of Salisbury,) gave any such permission, it is a striking example of the consequences of jealousy and emulation among the great.

† Probably the vassals of the earldom of Marre, whereof Kildrummy was the capital messuage, not a detachment from the garrison of that castle, as later authors have imagined. Fordun calls the commander quidam Johannes Crag, which plainly shows that he did not mean to speak of John Crabbe the Fleming, whom he had formerly mentioned; yet later authors suppose them to have been the same.

‡ ' Subito dissipatâ ejus comitivâ ;' Tped. Newst. p. 512.

§ According to Fordun, L. xiii. c. 36. Athole was slain 30th November 1335, [prid. kal. Decemb.]; according to English historians, ' post festum S. Michaelis,' which, literally taken, implies the 30th September, but may mean some time between that feast and another. Abercrombie, vol. ii. p. 51. shews from Foedera, T. iv. p. 711. that, on Thursday the 12th of September 1335, Balliol granted to John of the Isles the ward of the heir of David Earl of Athole deceased. This evidence is cogent, and yet it seems strange, that Athole should have procured the pardon and forgiveness of Edward III. taken possession of his new office, collected a body of troops, besieged Kildrummy, and died in battle, all between the 18th August and the 9th September 1335; for if his death was known, and the ward of his son granted on the 12th September at Perth, it follows that he could not have been killed at Kilblain later than the 9th September. Should this seem improbable, we might conjecture that the instrument in Foedera, T. iv. p. 711. which is a copy, not an original, bears Thursday 12th September, instead of Thursday 12th December, from a mistake of the transcriber; the difference between the two words would be very minute in the original manuscript. What strengthens this

1335.

flower of his age, David de Haſtings, of royal deſcent, nobly allied, and poſſeſſing eſtates above the rank of a ſubject *. He was brave and enterprizing, but ambitious withal, inſolent and unſteady. Robert Brady, Walter Comyn, and three other knights, died in the field with Athole. Thomas, the brother of Walter Comyn, having been made priſoner, was beheaded.

Ford. xiii. 35. The Earl of Moray had been engaged, juſt before the time of his captivity, in negociating a treaty with John, Lord of the Iſles. That Lord, deſcended from the famous Somerled, was not powerful enough to be altogether independent of Scotland; yet the extent of his territory, and its remoteneſs, had enabled him hitherto to remain in a ſtate of dubious allegiance.

Fœd. iv. 711. Balliol, by mighty offers of advantage, won him over to acknowledge himſelf the vaſſal of Scotland. A contract, in form of indenture, was executed between Balliol and the Lord of the Iſles. By it Bailiol,

---

this conjecture is, that Edward III. in the terms of accommodation offered to the King of France, expreſsly ſays, that the Scots ſlew the Earl of Athole during a truce; *Fœdera*, iv. p. 806. and the ſame thing is ſaid by *A. Murimuth*, p. 87. and by *Walſingham*, p. 136. Now, it is certain, that it was not until the 8th November 1335 that Edward granted a truce to Sir Andrew Moray and his adherents, *Fœdera*, T. iv. p. 675. and T. v. p. 161. I obſerve, by the way, that Edward appears to have unjuſtly charged the Scots as guilty of a violation of the truce; for he had granted it under the expreſs condition that the Scots ſhould proclaim it on their ſide; *Fœdera*, T. iv. p. 677. and it is not probable that they would have done this while Athole remained in arms, and held Kildrummy beſieged.

* He was deſcended from Donald, ſurnamed Bane, the brother of Malcolm III. King of Scots. He held in England the caſtle of Mitford, the Manor of Grinſborough in Lincolnſhire, of Holkeham in Norfolk, and many other manors; *Dugdale*, Baron. vol. ii. p. 95. In Scotland, the Earldom of Athole, and great part of the extenſive eſtates of the Comyns, Lords of Badenoch. To theſe Balliol added the lands which belonged to the Stewart. He was only twenty-eight at his death; *Dugdale*, ut ſup.

1335.

Balliol, 'as far as in him lay *,' yielded to John, Lord of the Isles, and his heirs and assigns, the islands of Mull, Sky, Ila, and Giga, the lands of Cantire and Knapdale, with other islands and territories, and also the wardship of the heir of the Earl of Athole, at that time a child of three years old. *Dugd. ii. 96.*

On account of which conceffions, the Lord of the Isles bound himself, and his heirs, to be the liege men of Balliol, and his heirs, and to aid them at all times, to the utmost, against all their enemies. He also became bound ' to swear to the performance of the premises on the ' eucharist, on the cup of the altar, and on the missal;' and, *for farther security*, to grant hostages, if required †, [at Perth, 12th September, probably 12th December 1335. Confirmed by Edward III. 5th October 1336.]

Thus did Balliol, in order to secure the fidelity of the Lord of the Isles, increase his power and influence, and extend it even unto Athole, the center of Scotland.

Edward, on his side, endeavoured to strengthen himself in his new acquisitions, by making grants of them to his principal lords. With this view, he bestowed the town and sheriffdom of Peebles, the town, sheriffdom, and forest of Selkirk, and the forest of Etrick, on William de Montague, and his heirs ‡, [10th October 1335.] *Fœd. iv. 671. 672.*

In the former year, he had acquired from Henry Percy the Pele of Lochmaben, with Annandale and Moffatdale, and had given him *Dugd.Baron. i. 274.*

in

---

* ' Quantum in se est,' *Fœdera,* T. iv. p. 711. This shows that Balliol had a slender hold of the estates which he yielded up.

† ' Pro quibus quidem conceffionibus.' In this deed no mention is ever made of the words *dare* or *confirmare*.

‡ William de Montague was to pay a yearly acknowledgement of L. 20 for Selkirk, and as much for Peebles; *Fœdera,* T. iv. 671. 672.

1335.

in exchange, the town, castle, constabulary, and forest of Jedburgh, with some other places in that neighbourhood *.

Fœd. iv. 674. 676. Edward lent L. 300 to Balliol, [16th October 1335,] and soon after bestowed on him a daily pension of five merks, to be enjoyed during pleasure †. [27th January 1335-6.]

Fœd. xiii. 36. After the death of the Earl of Athole, Sir Andrew Moray assembled a parliament at Dunfermline, and was acknowledged by that assembly in the character of Regent ‡.

Meanwhile,

---

* *Dugdale,* Baronage, vol. ii. p. 274. says, ' Henry Percey had a grant from Balliol
' of the inheritance of the Pele of Lochmaban, as also of Annandale and Moffetdale
' in as ample manner as Thomas Randolph, some time Earl of Moray, ever had them;
' which castle, lands, &c. then valued at 1000 merks *per an.* he did, the year follow-
'ing, 8. Edward III. surrender to Edward III. in exchange for the castle and consta-
' bulary of Jedburgh, and towns of Jedburgh, Benjedburgh, Hassenden, and the forest
' of Jedburgh, together with 500 merks, to be received out of the customs of Berwick,
' as also the custody of the castle of Berwick, with the fee of 100 merks for that ser-
' vice in time of peace, and 200 pounds *per an.* in time of war.'

† He made several other donations to Balliol as his necessities required. Thus, he gave him ten tons [dolia] of flour, and ten of wine, 30th December 1335; L. 200 for paying his north-country debts, [in partibus borealibus,] and L. 100 besides, 24th March 1335-6. L 200, and wine and provisions of the value of L 100, 3d October 1336. And L. 20, 3d January 1337 8. See *Fœdera,* T. iv. p. 683. 694. 710. 834.

‡ Two remarkable events concerning Scotland are recorded by some of the English writers as having happened about this time; they must not be altogether overlooked, although both of them are fictitious: The *first* is mentioned by *Knyghton,* p. 2568. it is said, ' that the Scottish Lords having been constrained to submit to the English
' power, took a solemn oath that they, together with David Bruce and his wife, would
' appear in the English parliament at Michaelmas, and stand to the determination of
' Edward and his council; and that it was agreed that David Bruce and his wife
' should reside in England until the death of Balliol, and, in the mean time, that the
' Scots should perform due homage to Edward. Nevertheless, that by the machinations
' of France the Scots were prevailed upon not to appear.' This narrative is somewhat abrupt; for it does not mention what was to be provided for David Bruce *after* the death

1335.

Meanwhile, the Papal and French ambassadors were inceſſantly ſoli- *Fœd.* iv. 676.
citing Edward in behalf of the Scots. A ſhort truce had been granted *Hem.* II. 178.
to them, [8th November 1335,] and commiſſioners appointed to treat
of peace *. The truce was renewed from time to time †, but it does
not appear that it ever took full effect; for Sir Andrew Moray kept *Fœd.* xiii. 36.
the field during the winter, and blockaded the caſtle of Coupar in 37. *Fœd.* iv.
Fife, which William Bullock held, and the caſtle of Lochindorp, where 694.
Catherine de Beaumont, the widow of the Earl of Athole, reſided;
and, therefore, when Edward granted a renewal of the truce, [8th *Fœd.* iv. 690.
March

of Balliol. Tyrrel, however, vol. iii. p. 388. ſupplies the blank by a conjecture of his
own, but without mentioning it as a conjecture. He ſays, ' That the Scots ſubmit-
' ted to King Edward, upon condition that they would obey Balliol during his life;
' and, in the mean while, David Bruce and his Queen *were to have a royal mainte-
' nance in England; but that if* Balliol *died without iſſue, as he had none at preſent, that
' then* David *was to ſucceed him.*" *Barnes,* p. 99. tells the ſame ſtory, with this variation, ' that David and his Queen were to reſide *privately,* but *honourably,* at Lon-
' don;' for this *he,* too, quotes Knyghton, and even diſtinguiſhes the paſſage with inverted commas; and *this* it is to write hiſtory! The narrative in Knyghton is inconſiſtent with the whole ſtrain of the tranſactions of that winter.

The *ſecond* circumſtance, is a charter of homage granted to Edward III. by David
Bruce, in a parliament held at Edinburgh on the 1ſt November, in the 5th year of his
reign. This is printed by Dr Brady, *Appendix,* No 85. It is a ſenſeleſs forgery; for
David Bruce was certainly in France on the 11th November 1333, and for many years
after. Beſides, a Scottiſh parliament could not meet at Edinburgh, which had now become a part of the Engliſh dominions.

* Edward appointed William de Montague, and others, to treat with Sir Andrew
Moray. 1ſt November 1335; *Fœdera,* T. iv. p. 674. and Geffrey Scrope, and others, to
treat with David Bruce, 10th November 1335; *Fœdera,* T. iv. p. 675. The Scottiſh
commiſſioners were Andrew Moray, William de Keith, Robert Lauder, and William
Douglas, 23d November 1335; *Fœdera,* T. iv. p. 677.

† Truces were granted 8th, 16th, and 27th November, 21ſt December, 22d, and
26th January 1335-6, and 8th March 1335-6; *Fœdera,* T. iv. p. 675. 677. 681. 684.
685. 690.

1335.

March 1335-6,] he did it under this exprefs condition, that the Scots fhould defift from blockading the caftles of Coupar and Lochindorp, and that they fhould not undertake the fiege of any other fortrefs.

1336.

Ford. iv. 687. Edward began to fufpect that the Scots held fecret intercourfe with the French King, and that a powerful armament, prepared in France under pretence of the holy war, was deftined againft England *. He *Ford. iv. 691.* appointed Henry of Lancafter to the command of his troops in Scotland, [7th April 1336,] and intrufted him with the moft ample powers for receiving the Scots to pardon and favour, [10th April.] Embarraffed with important affairs on the continent, he appears to have been averfe to carry on the Scottifh war with vigour; and, therefore, *Ford. iv. 699.* he authorifed the General, and other Lords †, to confent to a new truce with the Scots until the latter end of June, [4th May.]

Hem. ii. 278. Anonymous, Ed III. 404. 410 Scala Chron. ap Leland, i. 556. Ford. iv 706. Ford. xiii. 37. The Englifh army lay at Perth, when Edward unexpectedly appeared there. For now the King of France had avowedly taken the Scots under his patronage, and no longer concealed his intentions of invading England. It therefore became neceffary to crufh the Scots before they could receive any affiftance from their allies. Edward led his army into the north ‡, [Auguft,] raifed the fiege of Lochindorp, wafted

---

* This partly appears from a proclamation iffued by Edward 16th February 1335-6; Foedera, T. iv. p. 687 where the following ambiguous expreffions are ufed, ' auribus ' noftris eft intimatum, quòd quidam homines de Scotis quafdam alligationes et con- ' foederationes in partibus exteris, cum quibufdam hominibus partium earundem faci- ' unt, et ea de caufa ipfi homines alienigenae ad arma fe parant, et naves in magna ' copiofitate fupra mare congregare nituntur, et de guerra muniri, ad invadendum ' hoftiliter regnum noftrum,' &c.

† The other commiffioners were Thomas de Beauchamp Earl of Warwick, Henry de Beaumont Earl of Buchan, and William de Bohun; Foedera, T. iv. p. 659.

‡ Edward was at Berwick 16th June; Foedera, T. iv. p. 702. At Perth 4th, 6th, and

1336.

wasted Moray, and penetrated to Inverness *. He attempted to force the Scots to a general action; but Sir Andrew Moray remembered the military lessons of his old master, and took refuge amidst forests and morasses, from which Edward could not dislodge him.

While Edward, in the vain pomp of triumph, over-ran the north, Thomas Rosheme, a knight in his service, landed at Dunoter, not many miles from Aberdeen. The citizens of Aberdeen attacked him and were defeated, but Rosheme fell in the action. Edward, on his return, severely chastised the temerity of the citizens, and laid the town in ashes. *Scoto Chron. ap. Leland, l. 555 Fordsill. 37. Hem. ii. 274.*

The enemies had been dispersed, but not subdued †; and, therefore, Edward attempted, according to the policy of his grandfather, to curb their incursions by a chain of fortresses. He put in a state of defence the castles of Dunoter, Kinclevin ‡, Lawrieston, Stirling, Bothwell, Edinburgh, and Rokesburgh, and he greatly augmented the fortifications *Ford. xiii. 39.*

and 18th July, 24th August, 1st and 3d September; *Fordera.* T. iv. p. 703.—707. Hence we may, with sufficient certainty, place his expedition into the north of Scotland, between the 18th of July and the 24th of August 1336.

* * Per multa millia ultra quàm unquam fuerat avus suus; *W. Hemingford,* T. ii. p. 278. This confirms what was observed, *Annals,* vol. I. p. 275. that Edward I. did not march into Caithness.

† *Barnes* observes, p. 90. that ' King Edward passed as far as Elgin and Inverness, ' where Scotland is bounded by the sea, in pursuit of the enemy, to see if by any means he ' could bring them to a battle. Yet, for all their assistance from France, *they durst not* ' *look him in the face.*' It is probable, that, in the days of Edward III. the vulgar had the like notions of the geography of Scotland and of the victories of the English King. But *A Murimuth,* p. 88. h.s given the sentiments of a dispassionate bystander; *fecit bonum quod potuit,* says he. Indeed, as the necessities of Edward's situation required an offensive war, it was the policy of the Scots to stand on the defensive. This is a simple rule, but which has been frequently transgressed through pride, temerity, or impatience.

‡ Called also *Kynnef* by *Fordun,* L. xiii. c. 38.

1336.

cations of Perth *. Having left a considerable body of troops at Perth with his brother John, surnamed of Eltham, Earl of Cornwall, he departed into England. The Earl of Cornwall died soon after †, [at Perth, about the end of October.]

Scarcely had Edward departed, when Sir Andrew Moray came forth from his fastnesses, and besieged the castle of Stirling ‡. [October 1336.]

Hem. ii. 279.
Anonym. t d.
III. 210. A
Alurm. RB.
Scala Chron.
ap. Leland,
i. 556.

* With gates and towers of hewen stone, which Edward commanded to be built at the charges of the monasteries of St Andrews, Dunfermline, Lindores, Balmerinoch, Aberbrothock, and Coupar in Angus. There were three towers and three great gates. [*portae majores*.] There was, it seems, a tower over each gate. Fordun says, that the monasteries were in a manner ruined by this expence. He adds, that John de Gowry, prior of St Andrews, paid 280 merks to the workmen for building one of the towers, L. xiii. c. 38. This chain of fortified places, from Dunoter to Stirling, appears weak; the castles, so far distant from each other, could not afford mutual support; and therefore, it may be conjectured, that there were intermediate castles formerly erected, which served to complete and strengthen the chain, such as Inverbervie, Brechin, and Forfar. In this line of fortifications, three miles to the west of Glamis in Angus, there are the vestiges of a castle, of which the name is forgotten; but, in its neighbourhood, there is a hamlet called *Ingliston*; this seems to point out the origin of the castle.

† ' Sine bello ;' *Anonym.* Edward III. p. 410. ' of fayr death ;' *Scala Chron.* ap. Leland. vol. i. p. 556. But *Fordun*, L. xiii. c. 38. gives a different account of his death; he says, that the Earl of Cornwall had burnt the priory and church of Lesmahago in Clydesdale, together with many unhappy persons who had fled thither as to a sanctuary; that Edward III. meeting with his brother before the great altar at Perth, reproached him for his cruel and sacrilegious deed; and, on his making a haughty reply, stabbed him to the heart. Fordun relates this strange tale rather in the way of applause than blame. Edward III. was at Nottingham 29th September 1336; *Foedera,* T. iv p. 709. and 3d October, ibid. p. 710.; at Bishop Aukland, 5th and 18th October, ibid. p. 712, 714.; and at Newcastle upon Tyne, 28th October and 3d November, ibid. p. 715. The Earl of Cornwall was born in 1316, so that he was twenty at his death; Dugdale, Baron. v. ii. p 109.

‡ According to *Fordun*, L. xiii. c. 41. the siege of the castle of Stirling happened in summer 1337. He admits, however, that accounts vary as to the year that event is placed

1336.] Edward made haste to relieve that important post. He was young and brave, and his motions were rapid. Sir Andrew Moray earnestly pressed on the siege; but Sir William Keith, the favourite of the army, having been slain *, the Scots abandoned their enterprise.

Edward returned into England †, and Sir Andrew Moray again took the field, made himself master of the castles of Dunoter, Lawrieston, and Kinclevin, and, during the winter, harrassed the territories of Kincairdine and Angus. *Ford. xiii. 39.*

While the Lord Berkeley was leading a convoy of provisions from Edinburgh to the castle of Bothwell, the knight of Liddesdale lying in wait at Blackburn assaulted him, but was utterly discomfited, and escaped, almost alone, through the favour of the night. *Scala Chron. ap. Leland, i. 556. Ford. xiii. 44.*

The Scottish royalists were not inattentive to the means of annoying the enemy, even on his own coasts. At Genoa, they hired some gallies to act against the English; but the Genoese regency seized and burnt them. This was a service which Edward considered as meriting a special letter of thanks. *Foed. iv. 709.*

With

placed in October 1336, because there is evidence from *Fœdera*, that Edward was not in Scotland during the summer 1337; and because it is certain from *Fœdera*, T. iv. p. 716. &c. that he returned to Scotland about the beginning of November 1336, and actually came to Stirling. As he had left Scotland in September, it must have been something unexpected and important which induced him to make so sudden a journey thither in the winter season; and, unless we suppose it to have been the siege of the castle of Stirling, it will be difficult to account for it.

* This Sir William Keith is said, but without evidence, to have been the younger son of Sir Robert Keith the Marishal. He was killed by his own lance, says *Fordun*, L. xiii. c. 41. ' propriâ lanceâ interfectus, non minus infeliciter, quàm mirabiliter.'

† Edward was at Stirling in the beginning of November 1336; *Fœdera*, T. iv. p. 716.; and at Bothwell castle 28th November, 3d, 4th, 11th, 12th, 15th, and 16th December; ibid. p. 716.—725. The next account which we have of him is from Doncaster 22d December; ibid. p. 726.

194   D A V I D II.

1336.

Fœd. iv. 721. With more prosperous fortune, a naval armament, fitted out in France by the partizans of David Bruce, infested the English coasts, made captures of many ships near the isle of Wight, and plundered Guernsey and Jersey. There is no doubt that those hostilities were committed with the connivance, and even with the aid of the French King [*].

Fœd. xiii. 39. Sir Andrew Moray, joined by the Earls of March and Fife, and William Douglas, made an inroad into Fife, cast down the tower of Falkland, took the castle of Leuchars, and, after a siege of three weeks, made himself master of the castle of St Andrews, [28th February]. Not having a force to maintain remote garrisons, he destroyed it. The only

---

[*] *Tyrrel*, vol. III. p. 393. says, that the fleet was *under the command of David Bruce, and Barnes*, p. 106. less ambiguously, that *the admiral of this navy for the French was David Bruce*; and he quotes *Ashmole*, History of the Garter, T. ii. p. 677. The single evidence to which Ashmole, Barnes, and Tyrrel appeal, is *Rot. Scotiæ* 10mo, Edw. III. m. 3. That instrument is printed in *Fœdera*, T. iv. p. 721. and the words from whence it is inferred that David Bruce acted as admiral of the fleet are these: ' Nu-
' per, ut pro certo intelleximus, David de Bruys, et nonnulli alii de Scotia, hostes nostri,
' *et sibi adhærentes*, copiosam navium et galearum multitudinem, in diversis locis so-
' pra mare, et etiam in aliis locis et portubus exteris, *congregare fecerunt*, et merca-
' tores et alios regni nostri per mare transeuntes hostiliter aggrediuntur, tum naves et
' bona et res ipsorum subditorum nostrorum quàm quasdam alias naves, prope littora
' Insulae Vectae jacentes ancboratas, mercatoribus et marinariis in dictis navibus existen-
' tibus acquiter interfectis, plures ceperunt et secum abduxerunt,' &c. [dated at Bothwell in Scotland 11th December 1336.] Surely these words do not import that David Bruce commanded the fleet in person; yet *Abercrombie*, vol. ii. p. 55. observes,
' That King David was now about fourteen years of age, yet was thought capable of
' very great matters: A proof that God Almighty, through his wisdom and goodness,
' *for the most part*, forms the very nature of sovereigns for rule and government, and
' that he endows them, from their infancy, with those qualifications which are o-
' thers the product of aged experience and painful study.' The amiable English casu-
ist has well expressed the sentiment of Abercrombie, where he says, ' that all maids
' of honour have beauty—by their place.'

1336.

only fortress in that quarter which resisted his arms, was the castle of Coupar, where William Bullock commanded *.

The castle of Bothwell was next besieged and taken by the Scots †. [March 1336-7.]

Hem. ii. 279. Anonymous, Ed. III. 410. Ford. xiii. 39.

1337.

Having thus secured the passage of the Clyde, Sir Andrew Moray invaded Cumberland, and wasted the country in the neighbourhood of Carlisle. On his return, he invested the castle of Edinburgh. The English on the borders hastened to relieve it ‡. William Douglas encountered them at Crichton in Mid-Lothian. Many were slain on each side; and, although the Scots appear to have maintained the field, yet they had no cause to boast of victory, for Douglas their commander

Scala Chron. ap. Leland. L. 556 Hem. ii. 280.

Scala Chron. ap. Leland, L. 557. Ford. xiii. 44.

---

* 'Excepto castro de Cupro, *valida virtute* Domini Wielmi Bullok defenso;' Fordun, L. xiii. c. 39. This brave man, who checked the career of the successors of the Regent, was an ecclesiastic, and is therefore called by Barnes ' Dr William Bullock.' In 1336, Edward paid L. 20 to Bullock for repairing the works at Coupar, and presented him with a gratuity of 100 merks; Fœdera, T. iv. p. 694.

† *Fordun*, L. xiii. c. 30. mentions Stephen Wiseman as slain at this siege on the Scottish side, and Giksin de Villers on the English. He observes, that the Scots owed much of their success to a military engine which he calls *boufleur*.

‡ 'The marchers of England hering of the sege of Edenburge, cam to rescue it; 'so that the [Scots] cam thens to Clerkington, and the Englischemene cam to Krethmore, where, betwixt them and the Scottes was a great fighte, and many slayne on 'both parties. Then the Scottes made as they wold go yn to England, and loged 'themselff at Galufchel, and the Englishbe went over Twede.' *Sc. la Chron.* ap. Leland. v. i. p. 556, 557. The motions of the two armies are accurately described in this passage. Had the Scots been worsted, it is not probable that they would have marched to Galasbiels after the battle. It seems that the English took the direct road from Crichton to Roxburgh.

1337.

der was grievously wounded, and Sir Andrew Moray judged it expedient to relinquish the siege *.

Hem. ii. 180. The military operations against the Scots began now to languish. Edward, busied in preparing for war with France, could not bestow much attention on the affairs of Scotland. Henry de Beaumont, in-
Ford. xiii. 38. deed, who appears to have commanded in the north, occupied himself in revenging the death of Athole, his son-in-law, and slew all Scotsmen whom he suspected to have been present in the action at Kilblain, whenever they fell within his power. But this served rather to exasperate the nation, than to reduce it under the dominion of Balliol and the English.

Ford. xiii. 39. Scotland, at this time, was visited by a grievous famine, the consequence of the desolations of war. Many persons died of want; and many, abandoning their native country, emigrated into other lands.

Hem. ii. 180.
Knygt. 2570.
Walsing. 135.
Ford. iv. 727.
While the war raged, the wives and children of many of the Scottish barons had sought an asylum in Flanders. On the first appearance of public tranquillity, they embarked, to return, in two vessels under the guidance of John de Lindesay, Bishop of Glasgow. At that time, John de Ros, the English admiral, was escorting home the ambassadors whom Edward had employed in his continental negotiations †;

he

---

* *Fordun*, L. xiii. c. 41. insinuates, that the Regent was obliged to raise the siege through the treacherous practices of some Scotsmen. Douglas was run through the body by a spear: 'Per corpus transfianceatus;' *Fordun*, L. xiii. c. 44.

† There is a passage in *Scala Chron.* ap. Leland. v. l. p. 557. which deserves to be transcribed, although it relates not to Scottish affairs: 'The Erle of Sarisberi, that was 'nere of privy counsel with King Edwarde, tolde hym, that *his alliaunce with th' Empe-* '*rour and the Alemayn, was very costly, and to a smaul profite to hym.*' Thus, there is nothing new under the sun! In *Fœdera*, T. iv. p. 754. and 756. there are to be found contracts for military services, and subsidies between Edward III. and the valarous knights, (strenui milites,) Henry de Graischaf, and Arnold de Bagheim, and the noble

1337.

he encountered the Scottish ships, and, after a gallant resistance, took them. The Bishop was mortally wounded, and many persons of distinction were slain. What added greatly to this disaster was, that the King of France had sent warlike stores by these vessels, together with a considerable sum of money, to his allies the Scots *, [August 1337.]

Edward publicly asserted his claim to the crown of France, [7th October 1337.] The apparent, and the real causes of the war which ensued between France and England, are foreign to the subject of these annals. It must, however, be observed, that, at this particular juncture, it was of mighty importance to the Scots that Edward occupied himself in foreign wars, and, on that account, relaxed his military operations against his weaker neighbours †.

Fœd. iv. 818.

In

---

noble and potent personages [nobiles et potentes viri,] Henry de Gemenith, Ernest de Malenarken, and Wimunde de Dunzenchoyen, and many others, whose names are equally uncouth to an English ear.

* *Walsingham,* p. 135. places this event in 1335, and *Keith,* Catalogue of Scottish Bishops, p. 145. observes, from the Chartulary of Paisley, that the successor of John de Lindesay was Bishop of Glasgow in 1335. Nevertheless I have placed this event in 1337, not only on the authority of *Hemingford,* T. ii. p. 260. but on that of *Fœdera,* when compared with Walsingham himself. Walsingham says, that the Scottish ships were taken by the Earls of Salisbury and Huntington, when returning from their German embassy; now, it is certain from *Fœdera,* T. iv. p. 789. that they were in the Low Countries 19th July 1337, and that they returned to England in the following month; *ibid.* p. 808. If a successor was appointed to John de Lindesay so early as 1335, it must have been owing to this, that the greatest part of his diocese was within the dominion of the English, and that he had revolted to the Scots.—Hemingford says, that 250 were made prisoners: Of that number he mentions John Stewart, David de la Hay, Hugh Gifford, John de la More, William Baillie, and Alexander Frisel [or Fraser,] ' filii nobilium.'

† Bowmaker, the continuator of Fordun, says, L. xiii. c. 41. ' incepta est guerra inter Reges Franciae et Angliae satis atrox et dira; feliciter tamen pro Scotis; nam, 6
' Rex

1337

Parl. iv. 810. 814.

In the present situation of the affairs of England, it became necessary that the Scots should be amused with the hopes of an armistice, or a peace; and, accordingly, negotiations to that effect were renewed, [7th and 15th October 1337.] It was proposed, and with no injudicious policy, that two treaties should be carried on at the same time, the one with David Bruce, and the other with the royalists in Scotland. Edward also invested the Earls of Arundel and Salisbury with the most ample powers for receiving to pardon and favour all Scotsmen who might be willing to accept of terms, [15th October 1337.]

Parl. iv. 814.

Hem. E. 281. The negotiations, however, proved fruitless, and the Earl of Salisburgh laid siege to the castle of Dunbar [a], [28th January 1337-8.]

Dunbar

---

[a] 'Rex Angliae praedictus guerram in Scotiae continuasset, ipsam *ex toto, et sui distinctis*
cultatis, quantum ad humanum spectat judicium, obtinuisset.' These expressions, it might be admitted, are too strong; yet it ought to be remembered, that the principal fortresses of Scotland were in the hands of the English; that they were masters at sea; that there was a famine in the land; and, that the Scots were far from being unanimous in defence of their liberties. To heroes of romance, nothing is difficult; but Sir Andrew Moray and his associates were not heroes of romance; they were only brave men struggling under mighty disadvantages with a powerful enemy. And surely, even to such men, so circumstanced, a foreign war, which removed from them the weight of the English arms, was a most acceptable event. Yet, Mr Goodall observes, *not ad Fordun* 'Neque erit quare adeo timeret ne Edwardus III. tunc Scotos potius
'subjugaret, quàm cum antea a multis retroactis annis, et ipse ac pater avusque suus,
'qui totis viribus in id incubuerint frustra, ut et ipse postea, temporibus Scotis non
'minus adversis.'

[b] Most historians suppose the siege to have been undertaken about the beginning of the year 1337, according to the modern computation. This has involved them in obscurity and contradictions, which they themselves perceive not, but which an attentive reader must. It is not merely the authority of Hemingford which fixes that siege about the beginning of the year 1338, according to the modern computation; for there is another proof of it; which seems conclusive: All historians agree, that William de Montagu, Earl of Salisbury, was at that siege: That the siege began about January,
and

DAVID II.

1337-8.

Dunbar was the chief post which the Scots possessed on the eastern coast, and it preserved their communication with the continent. Its castle, situated on a rock, almost surrounded by the sea, and newly fortified, was strong, as well by art as nature. The Earl of March chanced to be absent when the English laid siege to his castle of Dunbar. His spouse, the daughter of Randolph, undertook to defend it in the absence of her Lord. The Countess of March, from her dark complexion vulgarly termed *Black Agnes*, performed all the duties of a vigilant commander; animated the garrison by her exhortations and munificence, and braved every danger with the intrepidity of a Randolph,

and lasted until the beginning of June. Now, we learn from *Fœdera*, T. iv. p. 726. that William de Montague was, on the 24th January 1336-7, appointed to command on the coasts of England, from the mouth of the Thames *westward*: That, soon after, he was appointed an ambassador in foreign parts, 15th, 18th, and 19th April, 1337; *Fœdera*, T. iv. p. 744, 745, 747. It appears that he had gone abroad 29th April; ib. p. 749. and that he continued in the Low Countries, and in the neighbourhood, during the months of May and June; ib. p. 789. and he appears to have returned in August 1337; ib. p. 808. Thus, we see, that if the siege of Dunbar had been carried on in 1337, the Earl of Salisbury could not have commanded at it. There is a circumstance mentioned by *Fordun*, L. xiii. c. 41. which, when compared with a passage in *Fœdera*, will tend greatly to support what has been already observed: He says, speaking of the siege of Dunbar, "Habebat eo tempore Comes duas permaximas galeas 'de Janua—ad observandum ne quid eis ad subsidium per mare adventaret.' Now, it appears from *Fœdera*, T. iv. p. 835. that on the 3d of January 1337-8 Edward granted a commission to John Doria and Nicolas Biauco [called de Flisco or Fiesco, T. v. p. 83.] to sail with two gallies, as they are called, to the coasts of Scotland, 'ad perscrutandum 'mare.' That they were Genoese vessels, is plain from the names of their commanders, *Doria* and *Fiesca*. The business in which they were employed, and the date of their commission, precisely coincide with the hypothesis, that the siege of Dunbar was undertaken in January 1337-8 *Fordun*, L. xiii. c. 40. says that the siege began 'on 'the 13th January.' *Knyghton*, p. 2570. ' after Epiphany,' which is a few days later. *Walsingham*, p. 136. ' on the 28th of January.' It is probable, that Walsingham speaks of the time when the warlike operations began, and the other historians of the time when the English first appeared before the castle.

1337-8.

dolph. When the warlike engines of the besiegers hurled stones against the battlements, she, as in scorn, ordered one of her female attendants to wipe off the dust with a handkerchief; and, when the Earl of Salisbury * commanded that enormous fabric called *the Sow* † to be advanced to the foot of the walls, she scoffingly cried out, 'Beware, Montague, thy sow is about to farrow,' and then ordered a huge rock to be let fall upon it, which crushed it to pieces. Such little circumstances may seem beneath the dignity of historical narrative, yet they are characteristical of those times, exhibiting a picture of bold unpolished manners.

Ford. xiii. 41. A certain man, who had the charge of one of the gates, agreed with the English to leave it open. Salisbury resolved to lead the party which by this treason was to surprise the castle. He found the gate open; but while he was entering in, John Copland, one of his attendants, hastily pressed on before him; the portcullis was let down, and Copland, mistaken for his Lord, remained a prisoner. The person with whom Salisbury held correspondence had disclosed the whole machination to the Scots.

1338.

Ford. xiii. 41. The English, thus unsuccessful in their attacks, turned the siege into a blockade, closely environed the castle by sea and land, and strove to famish the garrison. Alexander Ramsay heard of the extremities to which Dunbar was reduced. He embarked with forty resolute men,

* Richard Earl of Arundel commanded the English forces in Scotland; but, it appears, that the conduct of the siege had been committed to the Earl of Salisbury.

† There is an attempt to describe the nature of this engine, in the account of the siege of Berwick, vol. ii. p. 89. That obvious witticism of *the sow's farrowing*, was employed by the Scots on the former occasion, according to Barbour. As, however, the same observation is ascribed to the Countess of March, it is repeated here.

1338.

men, eluded the vigilance of the English, and, amidst the silence of a dark night, entered the castle by a postern next the sea. He sallied out, and attacked and dispersed the advanced guards. The English commanders, disheartened by so many unfortunate events, at length withdrew their forces, after having remained before Dunbar during nineteen weeks, [about 10th June.] They even consented to a cessation of arms *; and, departing into the south, entrusted the care of the borders to Robert Manners †, William Heron, and other Northumbrian barons. The failure of the enterprise against Dunbar was, in all its circumstances, held exceedingly disgraceful to England ‡.

Although the English remained masters of Edinburgh, the adjacent territory was infested by bands of the Scots. Alexander Ramsay concealed himself in the caves of Hawthornden with a company of resolute young men ||, and issuing out from thence as occasion presented

Rym. T. 180. Knyght. 1570. Scala Chron. ap. Leland, L 557.

Scala Chron. ap. Leland, l. 557.

Fœd. viii. 48.

---

* ' Acceptis sub certis conditionibus treugis ;' *W. Hemingford*, T. ii. p. 281. The Earl of Arundel had a commission from Edward III. to make truces, and even to conclude peace with the Scots, [25th April 1338.] *Fœdera*, T. v. p. 32.

† Probably Robert Manners of Etale in Northumberland, ancestor of the Duke of Rutland ; *Dugdale*, Baron. Vol. ii. p. 109.

‡ ' Post longam moram in obsidione ibidem factam relicta obsidione recesserunt
' abinde, *in eorum opprobrium non medicum*,' says *Knyghton*, p. 2570. ' Quæ quidem
' obsidionis dimissio et treuga majoribus Angliæ et multis ibidem congregatis displi-
' cuit ; *fuerat enim, ut ferebatur, ipsa dispendiosa, nec honorifica, nec secura, sed Scotis
' utilis atque grata*,' says *Walsingham*, p 136. In *Scala Chron.* ap. Leland, Vol. i.
p. 557. there is a very aukward apology for the English commanders. ' The lords
' being at a point of rendering the castel of Dunbar, hering that they that letted the
' King's passage into Fraunce for prosecuting his title thereof, should be counted as
' traditors, disloggit themsell thense with treuves, lest they should have been counted
' as letters of the Kingges passage.' All this adds to the renown of Black Agnes.

|| *Fordun* mentions the names of some of them, viz. Haliburton, Heryng, Heries, Dunbar, and Disbington. He adds, that ' to be of Alexander Ramsay's band,' was
considered

202   DAVID II.

1338.

entrd itself, he pillaged the neighbourhood, and even extended his inroads to the English borders. Returning out of Northumberland with much booty, he was encountered by Robert Manners at Preston, near Werk castle. By a feigned flight he led the English into an ambush, attacked, and totally defeated them. Robert Manners was made prisoner, and William Heron wounded. So compleat was the victory, that hardly any Englishmen escaped.

Scala Chron. ap. Leland, l. 517.
Ford. xiii. 48.

While Alexander Ramsay thus distinguished himself, the knight of Liddesdale, by his valour and perseverance, expelled the English from Teviotdale *.

Ford. xiii. 43.

About this time, Sir Andrew Moray, Regent of Scotland, died. When very young, he was joined in command with Wallace; and, during a course of forty years, in an age of heroes and patriots, had been eminent for intrepidity and public spirit †. Robert, the Stewart of Scotland, succeeded him in the office of Regent.

Ford. xiii. 43.

Ford. xiii. 45.

The new Regent began his administration by preparing for the siege of Perth. That town had been the head quarters of the English for many years: As Balliol had chosen it for the place of his usual residence, it might be termed the seat of government, and it was a post of exceeding importance. There were mighty obstacles to be overcome before the Scots could have any hopes of winning a fortress, which,

considered as a branch of military education, requisite for all young gentlemen who meant to excel in arms.

* ‘ Hoc in tempore, D. Willelmus de Douglas, per incredibiles conflictus et la-
‘ bores Tevidaliam ad pacem Regis, expulsis Anglicis, reduxit.’ *Fordun, L. xiii. c. 44*
relates several other gallant actions performed by him.

† *Fordun, L. xiii. c. 43.* blames him for the cruel manner in which he waged war, by desolating the country, and reducing the inhabitants to the extremities of famine. But this is to be ascribed rather to the savage manners of those times, than to the natural disposition of Sir Andrew Moray; for the historian himself admits, that ‘ he
‘ was a just and beneficent person.’

DAVID II.   203
1338.

which, according to the skill of those times, had every defence of art, and which, by reason of its vicinity to the sea, maintained a constant intercourse with England.

The Regent despatched the Knight of Liddesdale into France to represent the state of affairs, and to implore the aid of the French King. *Fœd. iii. 45.*

Edward had intelligence of the preparations made by the Scots, and he provided for the security of the fortresses, which lay most exposed to their assaults *. Having already experienced the fidelity of William Bullock, he continued him in the government of the castle of Coupar. But he appears to have entertained suspicions of the persons whom Balliol might entrust with the defence of Perth, and, therefore, he required him to commit the custody of that place to Thomas Ughtred †, a commander in whom the English had entire confidence, [4th August 1338.] *Fœd. v. 68.*

Balliol

---

* It appears from *Fœdera*, T. v. p. 68. that there had been a scandalous neglect in supplying the English garrisons with provisions; and that many men who adhered to the English interest had, in quest of subsistance, abandoned the fortresses where they were stationed. Edward ordered ample supplies to be sent both to Perth and Coupar, [30th July.] The particulars are as follows:

PERTH.	COUPAR.
600 Quarters of wheat,	100 Quarters of wheat.
700 Quarters of barley,	120 Quarters of barley,
300 Quarters of oats,	200 Quarters of oats,
30 Tons [dolia] of wine.	6 Tons [dolia] of wine.

From the minutes of the 13th parliament of Edward III. it is plain, that, by *dolia*, tons are understood.

† Balliol, in the first year of his government, bestowed on Thomas Ughtred the barony of Bonkill, and all the other estates of Sir John Stewart, [at Rokesburgh, 20th October.] *Fœdera*, T. v. p. 170. This grant was confirmed by Edward III. 8th April 1340. *ib.*

1338.

Ford. v. 109. 131. Balliol obeyed the commands of Edward, left Perth, and fixed his residence in England *.

1339.

Ford. xiii. 45. The Stewart appeared before Perth with his army. He had under him William Earl of Ross, Patrick Earl of March, Maurice Moray Lord of Clydesdale, William Keith †, and many other barons. Alan Boyd, and John Stirling ‡, commanded the archers.

Ford. xiii. 45. Froissart, i. 34. Hemilt. 215. At this juncture, the knight of Liddesdale returned from his embassy in France. He brought with him five ships of force, commanded by a Frenchman, whom our writers term *Hugh Hautpyle*, and many knights and soldiers compleatly armed. Among them there were Arnold d'Audeneham ||, afterwards a Marshall of France, and the Lord of Garencieres.

Ford. xiii. 45. Hitherto the Scots had endeavoured to maintain the contest with England by force alone; but the Stewart sagaciously employed policy as well as force.

William Bullock, promoted by Balliol to high honours, held the castle of Coupar. It had baffled the arms of the late Regent, and was thought to be a post of great consequence. The

---

* This may be inferred from different circumstances in *Fædera*. See T. v. p. 109. and p. 131.

† *Fordun, L. xiii. c. 45.* calls him William Keith of Galston. He must not be confounded with that William Keith who distinguished himself at Berwick, and was accidentally slain at the siege of Stirling.

‡ *Fordun, ib.* terms them *valentes armigeri*.

|| *Froissart, vol. I. c. 34.* calls him *d'Audregicm*; but I follow more correct authors. *Fordun, L. xiii c. 45.* makes mention of two esquires among the French, whom he terms *famefores*, viz. Giles de la Husa and John de Braisi. He has omitted the other names, which are here restored from Froissart.

1339.

The Stewart founded this man. He discovered him to be selfish and avaritious; and, fatiating his predominant passion by an ample grant of lands, won him over from his duty. Bullock abandoned and betrayed his benefactor, yielded up the fortress committed to his charge, and, with his numerous adherents, swore fealty to David.

Men in all ages have rewarded treason; but in that age men were wont to put confidence in traitors. Bullock was received into as great trust with the Scots as he had ever enjoyed under Balliol; and he seems to have acted with zeal and fidelity in support of that cause which he had so dishonourably espoused.

The Stewart, assisted by the counsels of Bullock, laid siege to Perth. *Fœd. xiii. 45.* Ughtred, the governor, made a gallant resistance. Alan Boyd, and John Stirling, who commanded the Scottish archers, were slain, and the knight of Liddesdale was dangerously wounded. The Earl of Ross, by the artifice of a mine, diverted the water from the fosse. The Scots prepared to storm Perth; Ughtred capitulated, and was conducted with his garrison into England, [17th August *.]

The Stewart conferred honourable rewards on his French auxiliaries, and dismissed them. *Fœd. xiii. 46.*

His next enterprise was against the castle of Stirling, which was feebly defended. Thomas Rokesby, the governor, despairing of succours from Edward, accepted conditions similar to those which had been granted to the governor of Perth †. *Fœd. xiii. 46. Froissart, i. 74.*

The

* The conduct of Thomas Ughtred became the subject of an inquiry in parliament. His justification of himself had so fair a shew, that the Regent, in absence of the King, ordered him *to be restored to his good name*, [pristinæ restitui famæ suæ,] until the King should return to England and appoint a more exact inquiry, *Fœdera*, T. v. p. 131. (29th October 1339.) Ughtred was employed in an office of trust 18th February 1339-40; *Fœdera*, T. v. p. 167. and, by a grant which Edward III. made to him, 8th April 1340, *Fœdera*, T. v. p. 177. it appears that he was restored to favour.

† *Froissart*, T. i. c. 74. says, that the Scots employed cannon at this siege, ' par en-
' gins et canons.'

1339.

The Stewart having thus dislodged the enemy from every post to the north of the Frith of Edinburgh, undertook a progress through Scotland, administered justice, redressed grievances, and established good order.

Ford. v. 124.
Knygbt. 1575.
Meanwhile Edward occupied himself in asserting by force of arms his title to the French crown. He entered the territories of France, [26th September,] and was opposed by Philip, his adversary, in person. The armies of the two nations remained for some days in fight of each other, and then, as of mutual consent, withdrew, [at Vironfosse, in the Cambresis, about the end of October.]

Home, hist. of Eng. ii. 175.
'Such was the fruitless, and almost ridiculous conclusion of all
'Edward's mighty preparations; and, as his measures were the most
'prudent that could be embraced in his situation, he might learn from
'experience in what a hapless enterprise he was engaged.'

Froissart, l. 57.
It is reported by Froissart, that David King of Scots was in the French army.

1340.

Knygbt. 1578.
Ford. v. 206.
Edward unsuccessfully besieged Tournay. A truce was concluded between France and England, [25th September,] to endure until 24th June 1341. The Scots were to be comprehended in this truce. If they did not accede, Philip, and his allies, became bound to with-hold succours from them.

Scoto Chron. ap Iceland. l. 55.
Knygbt. 1577.
While Edward remained before Tournay, the Scots, under the command of the Earls of March and Sutherland, made an inroad into England. They were encountered and repulsed by Thomas de Gray.

1341.

Ford. xiii. 46.
The fortresses of Edinburgh, Rokesburgh, Berwick, Jedburgh, and Lochmaben, with several less considerable castles in the south, still remained under the power of the English.

The

1341.

The castle of Edinburgh was surprised by a device of William *Ford. xiii. 47.* Bullock. According to his appointment, one Walter Curry of Dundee privately received into his ship the Knight of Liddesdale, with William Fraser, Joachim of Kinbuck, and two hundred resolute men. Curry cast anchor in Leith road; he pretended to be an English shipmaster having a cargo of wine and provisions, and agreed to furnish the commander of the castle * with whatever was requisite for his garrison. He brought his barrels and hampers to the entry of the castle, suddenly threw them down, obstructed the closing of the gate, and slew the centinels. At a signal given, the knight of Liddesdale, and his companions, who lurked in the neighbourhood, appeared, and overpowered and expelled the garrison, [17th April.]

David II. with his consort Johanna, landed from France, [at Inver- *Ford. xiii. 49.* bervie in Kincairdineshire, 4th May 1341 †.]

Alexander

---

* From the minutes of the 13th parliament of Edward III it appears that Thomas Rokesby was governor of both the castles of Stirling and Edinburgh. Whether he continued to command at Edinburgh, after having yielded up Stirling, is uncertain. *Froissart*, T. I. c. 56. says that Richard Limosin, an Englishman, was governor of the castle of Edinburgh. Froissart, ib. gives a long narrative of the surprise of that castle; in the chief circumstances it agrees with the account in Fordun. The Knight of Liddesdale appointed his bastard brother to the command of the castle of Edinburgh. He is called *William Douglas senior*, by *Fordun*. L. xiii. c. 47. This circumstance ought to be remembered; for, as will be hereafter seen, it serves as a guide to the proper interpretation of several passages in our national history.

† It has become a received opinion, that David Bruce did not arrive from France until 1342. The words of Fordun certainly import that he arrived in 1341, and I see no reason why his authority should be disregarded, merely to make way for the reports of foreign or more recent historians. *Knyghton*, p. 2581. places this event in 1341; but there is a manifest confusion in the dates of that part of Knyghton's work; thus, for example, he mentions the return of David to have happened in 1342, and yet he says, p. 2580. that David invaded Northumberland in 1340. There is a passage in *Scala Chron.* ap. Leland. T. i. p. 559. which confirms the narrative of Fordun:

'This

1342.

Ford. xiii. 49. Alexander Ramfay of Dalwolfy took the ftrong fortrefs of Rokefburgh by efcalade [a], [30th March 1342.] The King, as a reward for this important fervice, injudicioufly beftowed on Ramfay the charge of fheriff of Teviotdale, which William Douglas, *the knight of Liddefdale*, then held. From that moment, Douglas, once the friend and companion in arms of Ramfay, became his implacable enemy.

Ford. xiii. 50. According to the duty of his office, Ramfay held courts in the church of Hawick, expecting the wonted attendance of the crown's vaffals. Douglas came with an armed retinue, and was courteoufly welcomed by the noble-minded and unfufpicious Ramfay. Equally regardlefs of the reverence due to magiftracy, and of the fanctity of the place, Douglas dragged him from the judgment-feat, and conveyed his prey, bleeding, and loaded with chains, to the caftle of Hermitage, [Friday, 20th June;] and *there* he immured Ramfay in a remote apartment. It is related, that, above the place of his confinement,

---

[a] This feafon, *David Belfed* [plainly a miftake of the tranfcriber for *Bruce*,] came out of France, and ye *the winter after, about Candlemas*, made a rode into the Englifh marches, and brent much corne and houfes, and ye *foner after*, he made a rode ynto Northumberland into Tyne.' Both thefe inroads are mentioned by Fordun as having happened in 1342. If the two inroads were made, the one about Candlemas, and the other in the fummer after the arrival of David II. as *Scala Chronica* circumftantially relates, it follows, that David arrived from France in 1341; for it is plain from hiftory, that there were no military operations on the frontiers of England in fummer 1343, and thus the feries of events is perfpicuous. David arrived from France in May 1341. About February 13; 1-2, he accompanied the Earl of Moray, or fome other commander of the Scottifh army, in his invafion of the weftern marches; on the 30th or 31ft March 1342, Alexander Ramfay furprized the caftle of Rokefburgh; this, at once, facilitated the invafion of Northumberland in fummer 1342, and fecured a retreat.

[b] *Fordun,* l. xiii. c. 49. fays, that the enterprife was fuggefted by one *Hado Ednam*. Fordun places this event on Eafter-eve, [30th March 1342.] But *Scala Chron.* ap. Leland, T. i. p. 518.—p. on the morning of Eafter-day, [31ft March.] ' At the very houre ' of the refurrection:' It is added, ' but all they that were capitaynes of this covyne ' dyed after an ll death.'

1342.

finement, there lay a heap of corn, and that, with some grains which dropt down through the crevices in the floor, Ramsay supported a miserable life for seventeen days. Thus perished one of the bravest, and worthiest, and most fortunate leaders of the Scottish nation, to the everlasting infamy of him who perpetrated the murder, and to the disgrace of that feeble government which durst not avenge it.

About the same time ensued the fall of William Bullock. That able and sagacious person, after having betrayed and abandoned the cause of Balliol, acquired great honours under the King of Scots, and became his favourite and chief counsellor. Having been invidiously accused of treasonable practices, he was thrust into the castle of Lochindorp, with the meanest criminals, and *there* expired through extremity of cold and hunger [*].

A *Scottish* historian, who records the fate of those two eminent persons, Ramsay and Bullock, adds this singular observation: 'It is an 'antient saying, that neither the wealthy nor the valiant, nor even 'the wise, can long flourish in Scotland, for envy obtaineth the 'mastery over them all [†].'

Bullock, it is probable, fell unpitied by his contemporaries, and was speedily forgotten; but a grateful nation remembered the virtues and meritorious services of Ramsay, and cried aloud for vengeance.

The

---

[*] ' Invidiâ procerum et aliorum multorum apud Regem de infidelitate delatus, de ' mandato ejus per David Barclay capitur, et cum Molmaran et aliis iniquis deputatus ' in Lochindorp, custodiae mancipatur, et fame et frigore ad modum dicti Alexandri ' de Ramsay defecit.—Post quorum mortem tristia felicibus in regno successerunt;' *Fordun*, L. xiii. c. 50. It is plain from this passage, that Fordun viewed Bullock in the light of an innocent and oppressed man.

[†] ' Antiquitùs proverbialiter dici solet de Scotis, quod neque dives, neque fortis, ' sed nec sapiens Scotus, praedominante invidiâ, diu durabit in terra;' *Fordun*, L. xiii. c. 50.

1342.

The young King fought to execute justice on the offender, but could not. At length, through the intercession of the Stewart, he received Douglas into favour; appointed him keeper of Rokesburgh castle, which Ramsay had won from the English, and restored him to the office of sheriff of Teviotdale. Thus increasing his honours and influence, the King of Scots put Douglas in possession of the middle marches.

And thus was the first Douglas who set himself above the law, pardoned through the generous intercession of the Stewart.

Ford. xiii. 49.
Scala Chron.
ap. Leland,
L. 559.

During this year, England was infested by frequent inroads of the Scots. The Earl of Moray * entering on the side of the western marches, wasted the country, and burnt Penreth, [February 1341-2.] David served as a volunteer under him. In summer, David erected the royal standard, liberally distributed the honours of knighthood, and led his numerous forces into Northumberland. But from such mighty preparations nothing memorable ensued. Several of the new knights fell into an ambush which Robert Ogle had laid for them †, and David ingloriously retreated. A third invasion was undertaken; but Balliol, lieutenant to the north of Trent ‡, obliged the Scots to desist from their enterprise.

The

---

* He had been exchanged for the Earl of Salisbury, made prisoner by the French in the neighbourhood of Lisle; *Fordun,* L. xiii. c. 48. *Scala Chron.* ap. Leland. T. I. p 558. The French would not release Salisbury unless he made oath never to bear arms in France; and Edward III. consented to this extraordinary condition, [20th May 1342.] *Fœdera,* T. v. p. 313.

† *Fordun,* L. xiii. c. 49. has recorded their names, viz. Stewart, Eglinton, Boyd, Craigie, and Fularton. As four of the five appear to have been from the shire of Air, and as the fifth, Stewart, might have been from that neighbourhood, there is reason to believe that the number of Knights created at that time was exceedingly great.

‡ All persons, who, on account of felony, had taken refuge in sanctuaries, were pardoned by royal proclamation, under condition of serving, at their own charges, in the army

1342.

The Scots besieged the castle of Lochmaben in Annandale, where Walter Selby commanded. Henry de Lancaster, Earl of Derby, with many other great Lords, and a numerous army, went to succour Lochmaben; but before their arrival, Selby, aided by John Kirkeby, Bishop of Carlisle, and Thomas de Lucy, had constrained the Scots to retire. Edward III. issued a proclamation, bearing, that, for himself, and his allies, he had consented to a truce with Philip of France, and his allies, to endure until Michaelmas in the year 1346, [20th February 1342-3.] At what time it was that the King of Scots formally acceded to this truce is not known *. It appears, however, that, on all sides, the military operations were suspended †.

Walsing. 160. 161.

Fœd. v. 357.

Edward

army of Balliol, [5th July 1342;] *Fœdera*, T. v. p. 318. They are denominated *Gritbmen*, i. e. *Girthmen*. Froissart, T. i. c. 75. gives a very circumstantiated account of this campaign. According to him, David assaulted Newcastle, took and plundered Durham, laid siege to Werk-castle, and raised the siege; but all this seems to be fabulous, and to have been invented by some person who meant to impose on the inquisitive credulity of Froissart. It cannot be reconciled with known historical dates, with the characters and condition of the persons therein mentioned, or with the general tenor of authenticated events. Had David violated the patrimony of St Cuthbert, in the savage manner related by Froissart, the English histories would have teemed with declamations on an enormity, more heinous, in the opinion of those days, than any crime prohibited by the decalogue. Besides, the sacking of Durham, related by Froissart, was an event too singular and momentous to be altogether omitted; and yet the English historians make no mention of it, neither does Fordun, whose simple narrative I have chosen to follow.

* The French King had written to David II. desiring him to accede to the truce; but had received no answer, [19th May 1343;] *Fœdera*, T. v. p. 365. That David afterwards acceded to the truce, is evident from commissions relating to that subject, which Edward III. issued 20th May, 18th August, and 1st December 1343; *Fœdera*, T. v. p. 367. 379. 391.

† *Froissart*, T. i. c. 90. says, that Edward led an army to Berwick, celebrated Easter there, and remained in that part of the country for three weeks. Edward did not arrive

1343.

Fœd. v. 379. Edward employed this season of tranquillity in seducing William Douglas, the knight of Liddesdale, from the duty which he owed to his King and his benefactor. We have seen that Douglas, instead of being punished for the murder of Alexander Ramsay, had obtained additional honours and authority. He now entered into a treasonable negotiation with England, either because he dreaded the vengeance of the partisans of Ramsay, and looked for a more powerful protector than his own sovereign, or because, after having committed an enormous crime, he had become lost to every sentiment of virtue.

Fœd. v. 379. Henry de Percy, Maurice de Berkeley, and Thomas de Lucy, were appointed commissioners by Edward III. 'with full powers,' as the record bears, ' to treat of, and conclude a treaty with William Dou-
' glas, to receive him into our faith, peace, and amity, and to secure
' him in a reward,' (18th August.)

Whether the commissioners concluded any treaty with Douglas at that time is uncertain: But the very proposal for a treaty shews that his reputation was tainted *.

1344.

Fœd. v. 414. The Scots becoming weary of the truce, made inroads on the marches.

---

rive in London, from an expedition into Britanny, till the 4th of March 1342-3; *Fœdera*, T. v. p. 357. he appears to have been there on the 14th, 17th, and 21th March; *Fœdera*, T. v. p. 350.—360. In 1343, Easter-day fell on the 13th April. Edward appears to have been at London on the 18th April 1343; *Fœdera*, T. v. p. 361. and on the 1st and 12th May; *ib.* p. 362.—364. If, then, Edward went to Berwick, it must have been before Easter, and he must have returned with exceeding expedition immediately after Easter.

* Mr Roddiman, *not. ad Buchanan*, p. 430. Imagines that David II. had received intelligence of this treason, and that, *to secure the fidelity of Douglas*, he then appointed him to the offices of governor of Rokesburgh and sheriff of Teviotdale. There appears not any authority for this fanciful hypothesis.

1344.

marches [*]. Balliol, with the forces of the north of England, was appointed to oppose them, [25th August.]

1345.

Edward III. declared that Philip of France had violated the truce; and he ordered hostilities to be re-commenced, [24th April.] *Fœd. v. 419. 452. et p. st.*

He particularly charged Philip with having aided the Scots, contrary to the conditions of the truce, [15th March 1345-6.] *Fœd. v. 448.*

1346.

While the English King was occupied in foreign wars, David, at the instigation of France, resolved to invade England. He appointed his army to assemble at Perth; with the other Scottish barons, William Earl of Ross, and Raynald of the Isles †, appeared at the rendezvous; the Earl of Ross assassinated Raynald in the monastery of Elcho, abandoned the King's host, and led back his followers to their mountains. This seemed an omen of impending national calamities. *Ford xiv. 1. Walsing. 167.*

David stormed the castle of Lidel, and beheaded Walter Selby the governor. Selby, according to the usage of those loose times, seems to have been both a robber and a warrior, alternately plundering and defending his country ‡. *Ford. xiv. 1. Scala Chron. ap. Leland, p. 561.*

After

---

[*] *Walsingham*, p. 165. mentions a skirmish in which a Scottish commander, whom he calls *Alexander Strachan*, was defeated and slain, by the Bishop of Carlisle and Robert Ogle; and this, with great pomp of words, he has magnified into a battle.

† The parentage of this Raynald continues, if I mistake not, to be matter of very serious controversy among the different septs of the M'Donalds.

‡ He was one of the band of robbers so famous in English story, who, under their leader Gilbert Middleton, robbed two Cardinals and the Bishop of Durham. He afterwards held out the castles of Mitford and Horton against his sovereign; Scala Chron. ap. Leland, T. l. p. 561. Yet *Packinton*, ap. Leland. T. i. p. 470. says, 'David King 'of Scotts caused *the noble knight* Walter Selby capitayne of the Pyle of Lydelle, to 'be slayne afore his owne face, not suffering hym so much as to be confessid.'

1346.

After the Scots had advanced thus far, the Knight of Liddesdale counselled the King to abandon his enterprise against England, and to dismiss his army. 'What,' cried the Scottish Barons, 'must we 'fight merely for *your gain*? you have profited by the spoils of Eng-'land, and do you now envy us our share*! Never had we such an 'opportunity of taking vengeance on our enemies. Edward and his 'chief commanders are absent, and we have none to oppose our pro-'gress except ecclesiastics and base artisans.'

Ford. xiv. 2. The counsels of Douglas were slighted, and David proceeded on his enterprise. At Hexham he numbered his forces, consisting of two thousand men at arms, compleatly accoutred, and of a very great multitude of light armed infantry. David crossed the river Tyne at Ryton, above Newcastle, and urged his way into the bishoprick of Durham, cruelly wasting the country, and not even sparing the hallowed patrimony of St Cuthbert. He pitched his camp at Bear-park †, within view of Durham, [16th October, at nine in the morning.] At this critical juncture Edward III. lay before Calais with the flower of his troops.

Ford. v. 514. In his absence the English regency issued a proclamation of array, and appointed William le Zouche Archbishop of Yorke, Henry de Percy,

---

* 'Tu satis abundas de bonis Anglorum, nec velles in lucro socios habere, (ed) in 'bello;' *Jordan,* L. xiv. c. 2. The expression is highly characteristical, but the full force of it could not be conveyed in the narrative; the castle of Lidel was connected with the territory of W. Douglas, and it served as a frontier garrison to his castle of Hermitage. The meaning of the Barons was this: 'By our valour in storming the 'castle of Lidel, you have rounded, as it were, and secured your own territories, and 'now your ambition is satisfied.'

† Called by *Fordun,* L. xiv. c. 2. *Beau repair;* by *Walsingham,* Ypod. Neustriae, p. 517. *Bewrepeir;* and by *Knyghton,* p. 2590. *Beal repair.* The place is well known.

1346.

Percy, and Ralph de Nevil, or any one of them, to the command of all the forces of the northern parts of England *, [20th August.]

The Archbishop and his colleagues assembled their forces at Bishop-Aukland. It is remarked, that their army was chiefly composed of ecclesiastics; but, in this there is somewhat of monastic exaggeration, in honour of the clerical order; for it is certain that the sheriffs of the northern counties, and many of the most powerful and popular Barons of those parts, were at the rendezvous.

A. Murim. ennuis. 10%. Welfing. 167.

The English marched towards Sunderland bridge, with the view, as it seems, of occupying an advantageous post, and of checking the further progress of the invaders. The Knight of Liddesdale advanced with the men at arms, to procure forage and provisions; he unexpectedly encountered the whole English army on its march, near Ferry of the Hill. He attempted to avoid an engagement; but he was pursued, attacked, and discomfited †. His natural brother William Douglas

Fœd. civ. 2. 5.

---

* Froissart supposed that Philippa, the consort of Edward III. was their leader; and in this he has been implicitly followed by the later historians of both nations. A young and comely Princess, the mother of heroes, at the head of an army in the absence of her Lord, is an ornament to history. Yet no English writer of considerable antiquity mentions this circumstance, which, if true, they would not have omitted. Balliol also is said to have been next in command to Queen Philippa; yet the antient English writers say nothing of it; and the whole strain of *Fœdera* is inconsistent with the hypothesis of his having had any such command. *Barnes*, p. 378. says, that the English were ' in number 1100 men at arms, 3000 archers, and 7000 footmen, be-' sides a choice band of expert soldiers, newly come from before Calais, the whole a-' mounting to 16,000 complete;' for this he quotes *Giov. Villani*, the Florentin historian, L. xii. c. 75. Villani's account of the battle of Durham is exceedingly superficial; and, which is remarkable, he says nothing of what Barnes quotes as from him. See *Muratori*, Scripta. Ital. T. xiii. p. 959.

† ' Rex—de approximatione Anglorum nihil conscius, misit de mane Dominum ' Willelmum de Douglas ad depopulandam terram ecclesiasticam de Durham, et ad ' praedas

DAVID II.

1346.

Douglas was made prisoner [a]. 500 of his best men were slain, and he himself, with the remains of his party, hardly escaping, carried the alarm and panic into the camp of the Scots.

Ford. xiv. 3. On this sudden intelligence of the approach of the enemy, the Scots hastily prepared for battle. Their right wing, or van, was commanded by the Earl of Moray and the Knight of Liddesdale; the center by the King in person, and the left by the Stewart and the Earl of March. The ground on which the army formed, was intersected by ditches and inclosures †.

Ford. xiv. 2. The English advanced to Nevil's cross. In their front, a crucifix was borne, amidst the displayed banners of the nobility.

Ford. xiv. 3. Graham ‡, a Scottish officer, offered to attack the English archers in

---

[a] 'praedas exercitui suo reficiendo corrogandas. Qui infcios in hoftes irruens, obviaverunt fibi, tam fubitó quam mutuó, ad locum qui vulgariter dicitur *le Ferry of the Hill.* Sed quia non fuppetiit dicto Domino Willelmo de Douglas copia congrediendi cum tanta multitudine adverfariorum, ad regem cum fuis fugam iniit, in qua quingenti de Scotis viris validioribus amifi in loco qui *Sunderlandis* nuncupatur: Sed et ipfe Douglas manus eorum feliciter evafit. Quod audientes Scoti mirabiliter confternati,' &c. *Fordun,* L. xiv c. 3. This paffage in Fordun fufficiently authenticates every circumftance in my narrative. Fordun fays, that Douglas met the enemy at *Ferry of the hill,* but that the carnage enfued at *Sunderland.* This fhews that Douglas, in his attempt to retreat, had been overtaken by the enemy.

[b] *Knyghton,* p. 2590. fuppofes that Douglas himfelf was made prifoner. ' Dominus Willelmus Douglas cum fuis praecefferat exercitum Scotiae, et Angli inopinati fupervenerunt fuper eum, et captus eft per unum armigerum *Domini le Deyncourt.*' But the true fact appears from *Faedera,* T. v. p. 531. where William Deynecourt is faid to have made prifoner William Douglas l'eifne [i. e. *l'aifne,* or *the elder.*] We have had occafion to fee in *Fordun,* L. xiii. c. 47. that *William Douglas the elder* was the baftard brother of the Knight of Liddesdale.

† ' Inter foffata et fepes ;' *Fordun,* L. xiv. c. 3. *fepes* is tranflated *inclofures,* not *hedges*; becaufe in modern language a *hedge* is generally underftood to imply a *quickfet*; but in thofe days fences were made of ftakes and fmall boughs of trees, in wattled work.

‡ *Fordun,* L. xiv. c. 3. calls him *John de Graham:* Perhaps he means Sir John de Graham

1346.

in flank, if an hundred men at arms were put under his command; 'but, to confess the truth,' says Fordun, ' he could not procure a single 'man on that service*, either, because the attempt was too hazardous, or because the spirit of the men at arms had funk under their recent disaster.

The English began the attack on the right wing of the Scots where *Ford. xiv. 5.* the Earl of Moray commanded†. The Scots, entangled among ditches and inclosures, had not room to act. The Earl of Moray was slain, and the Knight of Liddesdale made prisoner. The Scots, bereaved of their leaders, gave way, and were totally routed on that side. The English attacked the center, where David commanded, not only in front, but also with their archers on the flank, now exposed by the defeat of the right wing. The archers of the enemy, without intermission, annoyed the Scots; yet the contest, even on terms so unequal, was obstinately maintained for several hours. The chief officers of the crown, and many of the nobility, fell at the side of their Sovereign. He, although dangerously wounded ‡, still encouraged his few surviving

---

Graham who assumed the title of *Earl of Menteth*, as in right of Mary his wife. Among the prisoners, *Fœdera*, T. v. p. 533.—5. mention is made of *David de Graham*, ancestor of the Duke of Montrose; perhaps Fordun or his transcriber has written *John* for *David*.

* ' Jussit Dominus Johannes de Graham centum equestres lanceatos ad interrum-
' pendum Anglorum sagittarios, ut vel sic expeditiùs hostes Rex invaderet. Sed, ut ve-
' rum fatear, nec unum quidem obtinere potuit ;' *Fordun*, L. xiv. c. 3. Some MSS. add,
' quòd nullus se tanto discrimini ausus est committere.' A movement like that proposed by Graham, decided the battle of Bannockburn. It was the English archery which proved fatal to our countrymen at Halidon.

† This is expressly affirmed by *Fordun*, L. xiv. c. 3. ' agmen illud cui Comes Mora-
' viae praeficiebatur, impetiit.'

‡ He was wounded in the head by an arrow; *Knyghton*, p. 2591. He received another

DAVID II.
1346.

ving companions, and fought like the son of Bruce. At length, John Copland, a gentleman of Northumberland, difarmed him. The King, while ſtruggling to difengage himſelf, with his gauntlet wounded Copland*; yet he was overpowered and made priſoner †.

The Stewart and the Earl of March, who commanded the left wing, made their retreat good, although not without loſs ‡.

Such other wound; the arrow pierced ſo deep, that its point could not be extracted; *Fordun*, L. xiv. c. 3. Fordun relates, that David was miraculouſly cured while he prayed at the ſhrine of St Monan, and that, in grateful remembrance of the ſaint, he erected and endowed a church to his honour. As to that church, or rather chapel, See *Spotiſwood*, Religious Houſes, c. 15. *Major*, L. v. c. 19. relates the ſame ſtory; but he has aſcribed to St Ninian the honour which was due to St Monan.

* ' Prius tamen duobus de ſuis dentibus ictu Regis evulſis;' *Fordun*, L. xiv. c. 3.

† *Knyghton*, p. 2591. ſays, that the King of Scots having abandoned the field, was taken at Neryngton, by a ſervant of John Copland. Neryngton is conſiderably to the ſouth of Durham. It is impoſſible to imagine that the King, if he had left the field, would have paſſed forward into England.

‡ In this narrative of the battle of Durham, the account given by Fordun, ſimple, and, to all appearance, impartial, has been followed. From it we may learn the immediate cauſes of the defeat of the Scots. They were, in effect, ſurpriſed, and they fought on diſadvantageous ground. The death of the Earl of Moray, the captivity of the Knight of Liddeſdale, and the diſcomfiture of the right wing, brought on the ruin of the center, and thus the battle was loſt. *Boece*, L. xv fol. 324. b. has been pleaſed to aſſert, ' that The Stewart and the Earl of March, perceiving that the forces under ' their command were diſpirited, and unwilling to fight any longer, withdrew them to ' a place of ſafety.' He adds, ' that this retreat was the cauſe of all the diſaſters which ' enſued.' There are who believe Boece, and yet vindicate the Stewart! The proper vindication of the Stewart is, ' that the narrative of Boece is fabulous.' Although not altogether of his own invention, it has no warrant from Fordun, or from any Engliſh hiſtorian of conſiderable antiquity. That the Stewart fought, and that he did not retire without loſs, is evident from the number of the Barons of the name of *Stewart* who were either killed or made priſoners For, it muſt be preſumed, that ſome of them, if not all, fought under the banners of the chief of their family. Beſides, two Mahlands,

1346.

Such was the disastrous event of the battle fought in the neighbourhood of Durham, on the 17th of October 1346.

The loss of the vanquished was exceedingly great. Among the slain there were the Earls of Moray and Strathern, David de la Haye Constable, Robert Keith the Marshall, Robert de Peebles Chamberlain, and Thomas Charteris Chancellor of Scotland, together with many Barons of eminence.

Besides the unfortunate David Bruce, there were made prisoners, the Earls of Fife, Menteth, and Wigton, the Knight of Liddesdale, and about fifty other Barons.

Of the common sort slain or made prisoners, there is no certain computation.

'That day,' says Walsingham, 'would have been the last of Scottish rebellion, had the English, neglecting the spoil, and the making of captives, urged the pursuit of the fugitives, and cut off from the land of the living that nation which has ever been rebellious*.'

The English commanders, allured by the lucre of ransoms, connived at the escape of many of their prisoners. This practice became so prevalent, and seemed of such hazardous example, that it was prohibited by proclamation, under pain of death † [20th November.]

The Maitlands, and Adam de Whitsom were slain, and Patrick de Polwarth made prisoner; and it is probable, from their names, that they were with the forces under the command of the Earl of March. In the Appendix, the reader will find a list of the killed and prisoners, collected from all the probable information that could be procured.

* 'Et revera bis dies fuisset ultimus obstinatae Scotorum rebellionis, si praedis et captivis tunc omnino neglectis, Angliae gentem ab antiquo rebellem persequendo de terra viventium delevissent;' *Walsingham*, hist. Angl. p. 167. We can now smile at the pious regrete of Walsingham, a regrete which has been impatiently reiterated on other occasions.

† Notwithstanding the proclamation, it appears that Gerard de Widdrington, and others, persisted in this traffic; *Foedera*, T. v. p. 594. [18th October 1347.]

1346.

Ford.v.537.9.
Knyght, 2592.

The King of Scots, with his faithful and favourite servant Malcolm Fleming Earl of Wigton, was conducted to a long and dreary captivity in the tower of London *, (2d January 1346-7.)

Ford. v. 530.

Meanwhile the English regency, studious to improve the success at Durham, appointed commissioners to pardon the Scots, and receive their fealty †, (20th October 1346.)

Ford. v. 542.

John Copland who took the King of Scots, and Robert de Bertram who took the Knight of Liddesdale, were amply rewarded ‡.

Ford. xiv. 5

The English entered Scotland: The fortresses on the borders made no resistance. Eustace Lorain, keeper of Rokesburgh castle, yielded it to Henry de Percy. The castle of Hermitage surrendered, and the English became masters of the whole country on the borders from the east to the west sea, and advanced their posts to the neighbourhood of the vale of Lothian ‖.

Balliol

---

* *Knyghton*, p. 2592. relates, that by the command of Edward III. David Bruce was conducted to the Tower, under an escort of 20,000 men well armed: That the different companies of London, in their proper dresses, were present at the procession; and that David Bruce sed on a tall black horse, so as to be seen of all men.

† Walter de Bermingham, Justiciary of Ireland, was impowered to proffer conditions of peace to John of the Isles; and, if they were refused, to wage war against him, *Fordera*, T. v. p. 530. 4th November 1346.

‡ Copland was made a Banneret, with a salary of L. 500 yearly, to him and his heirs, until lands of the like yearly amount should be bestowed on him. He obtained a pension for life of L. 100, under condition of furnishing twenty men at arms, *Fodera*, T. v. p. 542. [20th January 1346-7.] He was also made warden of Berwick; *Fodera*, T. v. p. 557. Besides all this, it appears that he obtained the office of sheriff of Northumberland, and keeper of Rokesburgh castle; *Fodera*, T. v. 756. 760. ‖ Robert de Bertram obtained a pension of 200 merks to him and his heirs, until the King should provide him in lands of an equal value,' *Fodera*, T. v. p. 713.

‖ ' In tantum fines suos dilataverunt, ut infra breve marchias ad Colbrandspeth et ' Soltrè pertingant : Deinde usurpando ad Karlyulippes, [Qu. Carlops,] et Crossecryne'. Qu. *Fordun*, L. xiv. c. 6.

1346.

Balliol resided in Galloway, in a corner of his nominal kingdom. Having been joined by Henry de Percy and Ralph Nevil [*], he led the men of Galloway into the Lothians, penetrated to Glasgow, and returned through Cuningham and Niddesdale, wasting the country in his cruel and impolitic progress.

Ford. xiv. 6. Fœd. v. 545.

The Stewart was elected to the office of Regent [†]; and, notwithstanding the national calamities, he supported the cause of his absent sovereign, and maintained a shew of civil government in Scotland.

Ford. xiv. 6.

William Lord Douglas, son of Archibald, surnamed *Tineman*, had been educated in France. At this disastrous season, he returned home, expelled the English from Douglas-dale, and took possession of Etrick forest. John Copland governor of Rokesburgh hastily assembled forces to protect Teviotdale; but the men of Teviotdale joined themselves to Douglas, and expelled Copland.

Ford. xiv. 6.

John de Graham Earl of Menteth had formerly sworn fealty to the English King [‡]; and Duncan Earl of Fife had sworn fealty to Balliol, the vassal of England. Notwithstanding these engagements, they went over to the party of David Bruce, and were made prisoners with him at Durham. Edward determined their death; and accordingly he issued an order for trying them; and, together with that order, he transmitted to the judges ' a schedule containing the sentence of con-
' demnation,'

Fœd. v. 549. Knyght. 2592.

---

[*] Henry de Percy had 100 men at arms, and 100 archers on horseback: Ralph Nevil 80 men at arms, and 80 archers on horseback. They were hired to serve under Balliol for a year, 20th January 1346-7. *Fœdera*, T. v. p. 545.

[†] The title which he assumed runs thus: ' Robertus Seneschallus Scotiae, locum te-
' nens Gerenissimi principis David, Dei gratia Regis Scotiae illustris;' *Fœdera*, T. v. p. 831.

[‡] ' Qui ad effundum de consilio nostro et nobis in omnibus fidelia, corporale prae-
' stitis juramentum;' *Fœdera*, T. v. p. 549. John de Graham had assumed the title of Earl of Menteth in right of his wife Mary, according to the practice of that age.

1346.

'demnation *,' [22d February 1346-7.] They were condemned. The Earl of Menteth suffered as a traitor; but sentence against the Earl of Fife was not executed †.

1347.

Knight. 1595.
Fœd. v. 575.
588. 623.
629 660.671.
725.761.781.

Edward III. won Calais, after a tedious siege, [4th August.] He concluded a truce with France to endure until June 1348; and by various prorogations, until the 1st of April 1354. Scotland was comprehended under this truce, [28th September.]

1348.

Fœd. v. 618. Negotiations were commenced for obtaining the liberty of the King of Scots ‡, [16th April.]

Fœd. v. 647. Johanna, a Princess of England, obtained permission to visit her consort, the King of Scots, after he had remained in durance for two years, [10th October.]

1349.

Fœd. xiv. 7. *The great pestilence*, which had long desolated the continent, reached Scotland.

---

* 'Mittimus vobis praesentibus inclusam quandam cedulam continentem judicium ' in eis proferendum, per nos et concilium nostrum apud Caleys ordinatum;' *Fœdera*, T. v. p. 549.

† Probably on account of his relation to the Royal family of England. His mother Mary de Monthermer was the niece of Edward I.

‡ The commissioners from Scotland were numerous, viz. William de Landales Bishop of St Andrews, John Pilmore Bishop of Murray, Adam Bishop of Brechin, Thomas de Fingask Bishop of Caithness, Thomas Earl of Marre, David Lindesay of Crawford, Robert Erskine of Erskine, William de Meidrum [called Dominus de Ba*chynaneshet*, a corrupted word which I understand not,] Alexander de Seton Master of the hospitalers in Scotland, Sir Andrew Douglas, Friar Walter of Blantyre, and William Wigmer burgess of Edinburgh; *Fœdera*, T. v. p. 618. 625. 632. 634. 646. 657.

1349.

Scotland. The historians of all countries speak with horror of this pestilence. It took a wider range and proved more destructive than any calamity of that nature, known in the annals of human kind [*].

1350.

John St. Michael and his accomplices assassinated Sir David Berk- *Ford. xiv. 7.*
ley, [at Aberdeen, on Shrove Tuesday.] The Knight of Liddesdale, then a prisoner in England, is reported to have hired the murderers, to revenge the death of his brother Sir John Douglas, whom Berkley had assassinated.

Philip King of France died, [23d August.] He was succeeded by *Ford v. 68a.*
his son John. *Hemed. 103.*

A treaty with Scotland was carried on for releasing the King of *Ford. v. 686.*
Scots from his captivity, and for establishing perpetual peace between *659.700.711.*
the two nations. Against this Balliol ineffectually protested; he was, however, permitted to be present at the conferences, [5th March 1350-1.]

1351.

In consequence of an agreement between Edward III. and certain *Ford. v. 711.*
commissioners from Scotland, the King of Scots was enlarged, and *722 734 787.*
permitted to visit his dominions, on his making oath to return into custody. Seven youths of the first rank were given as hostages for the performance of his oath [†], [4th September.]

From

---

[*] *Barnes*, p. 428.—441. has collected the accounts given of this pestilence by many historians; and hence he has, unknowingly, furnished materials for a curious inquiry into the populousness of Europe in the fourteenth century.

[†] 1. John, son and heir of the Stewart, afterwards King of Scots, under the assumed name of *Robert III*. 2. John Dunbar, son and heir of the Earl of March. 3. John, son and heir of the Earl of Sutherland; his mother was the sister of David II. 4. Thomas Fleming, grandson (nepos) of the Earl of Wigton. 5. James Lindesay, son and heir of

David

1352.

Fœd. v. 737. From an instrument preserved in *Fœdera Angliae*, it appears that the English were engaged in some mysterious negotiations with the King of Scots and Lord Douglas.

The instrument is of the following tenor: ‘ Besides the instructions
‘ publicly given to Roger de Beauchamp, concerning the business of
‘ Scotland, he is charged with this secret commission.

‘ That, in case the treaty should fail, and it should be thought, af-
‘ ter conference (*examinement*) with the Lord David Bruce and the
‘ Lord William Douglas *, that the work might be accomplished in
‘ another way [*exploit se purra faire par autre voie,*] and if they have
‘ founded the dispositions of their friends, and if the commissioners for
‘ England are of opinion, that the return of the Lord David to the
‘ south would be a hinderance to the business; then it is the King's
‘ pleasure, that the Lord David do remain at Newcastle or at Berwick,
‘ in the choice of the commissioners, until the King receive more in-
‘ formation, and until his further commands be made known.

‘ Moreover, in case the commissioners shall judge that the setting at
large the person of the Lord David will tend to promote the business,
‘ and

David Lindesay. 6. Hugh Ross, brother and heir presumptive of the Earl of Ross.
7. Thomas Moray, brother and heir presumptive of John Moray Lord of Bothwell.

* *Boece*, L. xv. fol. 324. a. erroneously asserts, that David II. bestowed the title of *Earl* on Lord Douglas, just before the fatal expedition to Durham: ‘ Priusquam iter Rex in-
‘ grederetur, solennibus ceremoniis Wilhelmum Douglas Comitem Douglassiae crea-
‘ vit.’ This error has been transplanted into our genealogical histories, has taken root, and will flourish. Although we have been long reformed from popery, we are not yet reformed from Hector Boece. There is every reason to suppose that Lord Dou-
glas did not return to Britain till after the battle of Durham; it is certain that he con-
tinued to bear the name of *Lord Douglas* for several years after that unhappy event; and hitherto no man has pointed out either authentic instrument, or credible history, in which he is called *Earl of Douglas* before 1357. Yet all this avails not; Hector Boece has said, ‘ that he was solemnly created *Earl of Douglas* in 1346.’ As fast as the cobwebs of fictitious history are brushed away, they will be replaced.

1352.

'and if they can have sufficient security by hostages, oaths, cove-
'nants, or otherwise, from him, and from those who are willing to
'accede to his agreement, [*que veullent estre de son accord*], then it is
'the King's pleasure that the commissioners be impowered to prolong
'the time of his re-delivering himself, and to permit him to remain
'at large, until some limited day between this and Whitsunday next,
'at farthest, that, in the interval, it may be seen what he can accom-
'plish in the premises,' [*quel exploit il en purra faire*.]

An English historian reports, that the King of Scots, having him- *Knygh.* 1603.
self sworn fealty to Edward, engaged to procure the acquiescence of
his people in the long contested claim of feudal superiority; but that
the Scots, with one voice, declared, ' that they would joyfully pay the
' ransom of their sovereign, and that no consideration whatever should
' induce them to renounce their independency.'

Whether the mysterious instructions to Roger de Beauchamp establish, in any measure, the truth of what the historian relates, I determine not.

The negotiations, whatever might have been their tendency, proved *Ford.* v. 746.
unsuccessful, and the King of Scots was remanded to prison. *Ford.* xiv. 15.

But the English King concluded a singular treaty with his prisoner *Ford.* v. 738,
the Knight of Liddesdale.

By it, the Knight of Liddesdale bound himself, and his heirs, to
serve the English King, and his heirs, in their wars against all persons
whatever, excepting his own nation. But this strange proviso was
added, ' that he might, at pleasure, renounce the benefit of the ex-
' ception.'

He shall furnish, says the treaty, ten men at arms, and ten light
horsemen, for three months service, on his own charges.

Should the French, or other foreigners, join the Scots, or the Scots
join the French, or other foreigners, in invading England, the Knight

1352.

of Liddefdale fhall do his utmoft endeavours to annoy all the invaders, 'excepting the Scots.'

He fhall not, either openly or in fecret, give counfel or aid againft the King of England, or his heirs, on behalf of his own nation, or of any others.

The Englifh fhall do no hurt to his lands, or his people, and his people fhall do no hurt to the Englifh, unlefs in felf-defence.

He fhall permit the Englifh, at all times, to pafs through his lands without moleftation.

He fhall renounce all claim to the caftle of Liddel [*].

In cafe the Englifh, or the men refiding on the eftates of the Knight of Liddefdale, injured each other, by fetting fire to houfes or ftackyards, by pillaging, or by committing any like offences, it was declared, that the treaty fhould not be thereby annulled, but that the parties contracting fhould forthwith caufe the damage to be mutually liquidated and repaired.

Edward, on his part, engaged to releafe the Knight of Liddefdale from his captivity, and to make a grant to him of the territory of Liddefdale and of Hermitage Caftle, together with fome lands in the interior country of Annandale [†]. But it was fpecially provided, that his heirs fhould hold the eftates thus granted, under condition of fulfilling the articles of this treaty, and no otherwife.

It was ftipulated, that the Knight of Liddefdale fhould make oath for the due performance of every thing incumbent on him, under pain of being for ever held 'a difloyal and perjured man, and a falfe 'liar,' and that he fhould give his daughter and his neareft heir-male

---

[*] Said in the inftrument to have belonged to Lord Wake, and now to be the inheritance of the Earl of Kent; *Fœdera*, T. v. p. 739.

[†] Half of the town of Moffat, Corbenci, [Corehead], Newton, and Grannem-Polborby in Moffat-dale; *Fœdera*, T. v. p. 739.

1352.

male [*], as hostages, to remain in the custody of the English King for two years.

Nevertheless, in the same base instrument, he made professions of his purpose to yield due service to his liege Lord the King of Scots [†], in every thing that might be consistent with the articles of this treaty, [London 17th July.]

And thus, in an evil hour, did Sir William Douglas at once cancel the merit of former atchievements, and, for the possession of a precarious inheritance, transmit his name to posterity in the roll of timeservers and traitors.

1353.

Duncan M'Dowal, a powerful chief in Galloway, was the hereditary

Ford. xiv. 15.

---

[*] James, the son of Sir John Douglas, afterwards known by the name of *Lord of Dalkeith*. By inheritance, by marriage, and by royal grants, he became possessed of very ample estates. See *Douglas*, Peerage of Scotland, p. 490. I have some reason to suspect that Froissart mistook him for *the Earl of Douglas*; if so, the confident assertion of that writer, who pretended to have been personally acquainted with the Earl of Douglas, has led me into an error. See *Remarks on the History of Scotland*, c. 3.

[†] ' Et est l'entencion que le dit Monsieur William puisse tous jours faire son devoir ' devers son Seigneur lige, et toutes choses qui ne sont contraires a cestes alliances;' *Fœdera*, t. v. p. 739. It would have puzzled the most able sendist to discover what that devoir could be; for Sir William Douglas had agreed to fight the battles of the King of England and his successors, even against the auxiliaries of his liege Lord, and never to give counsel or aid against the King of England, even in behalf of his own nation. He had expressly stipulated a neutrality for his own estate; he had virtually engaged to facilitate the entry of the English into Scotland at all times; and he had submitted to hold his lands of the English King. These were feudal delinquencies inconsistent with the service of his liege Lord. Some readers may think that there was no occasion for entering into so minute a detail of a private covenant between Edward III. and a Scottish Baron; but the articles of this singular treaty could not be abridged, and they tend to explain the policy of Edward III. and the real character of the Knight of Liddesdale.

Ff 2

1353.

ary enemy of the house of Bruce, and bound by fealty to England. William Lord Douglas penetrated into Galloway, and either by force or persuasion, induced M'Dowal to renounce England for ever, and to acknowledge the sovereignty of the King of Scots. Edward ordered the estates of M'Dowal to be seized, and his goods confiscated *, [18th August.]

Fœd. v. 756. Knygh. 2606. The treaty for the release of the King of Scots was renewed. By permission of Edward he came to Newcastle, where commissioners from the two kingdoms held fruitless conferences. It is said that the Scots suspected that their King, under the influence of English counsels, was prone to barter the national independency for his own freedom. And it is added, that they refused to contribute to his release, unless he consented to withdraw himself from evil advisers, and to grant an ample indemnity for all offences committed in Scotland since his captivity. This last report has a probable appearance, for there were many and mighty offenders who had cause to dread the restoration of their Sovereign.

Ford. xiv. 8. The Knight of Liddesdale, while hunting in Etrick forest, was waylaid and assassinated by his kinsman and godson William Lord Douglas, in revenge, as was said, for the murder of Ramsay and Berkley, [August, at a place called *Galvord*.] Fordun bestows this eulogy on the

* *Fordun*, L. xiv. c. 15. says, ' Willelmus de Douglas—collectâ multitudine non ' medicâ armatorum, secessit in Galweciam, ubi sic finaliter tractavit, quod Dovenaldum ' M'Dowall, et totam terram Galwelae, ad fidem Regis retraxit.' He adds, that M'Dowal swore fealty to the King of Scots in the church of Cumnock, in presence of the Stewart, and that he faithfully persevered in his allegiance. Fordun seems to place this event in 1356; but I have placed it in 1353, on the authority of an instrument in *Fœdera*, T. v. p. 750. which begins thus, ' Quia Duncanus [in Fordun Dovenaldus] Magdowaill, contra fidelitatem et sacramentum nobis per ipsum praestita, ' Scotis inimicis nostris contra nos jam adhaesit.' &c. [18th August 1353.] By *Galweia* in this place is to be understood the interior Galloway, called sometimes by our writers, *Insula Scotis inimica*.

1353.

the Knight of Liddesdale: 'A hardy soldier he was, and one who
'had endured much in defence of the liberty of the kingdom: Skilled
'in war; faithful to his promise; the scourge of the English; and a
'wall of defence to Scotland.' So little suspicion had Fordun of the
foul alliance with Edward III.

There are no descendants of the Knight of Liddesdale.

1354.

At length a treaty for the ransom of the King of Scots was concluded, [Newcastle 13th July.] The ransom was fixed at 90,000 merks Sterling, to be paid at the rate of 10,000 merks annually, for nine years: During that space, there was to be a truce between the two nations, and in it all the allies of England, and especially Balliol, were included.

Twenty young men of quality were to be given as hostages. It was provided that the King of Scots, the bishops, and prelates, and all the nobles of Scotland, should become bound after the strictest form that could be devised *, as well for payment of the ransom, as for

---

* 'En la meilloar manere et fourme comme homme favera plas feurement deviser
' par rafon;' *Fœdera*, T. v. p. 793. This treaty contains many provisos respecting
the hostages, which would not afford entertainment or instruction to the reader. One
clause, however, is of a singular nature, and deserves to be remembered. It was provided, that, on payment of the first moiety of the ransom, [2d February 1354-5.], the eldest son of the Earl of March, as hostage, should be exchanged for the eldest son of
the Stewart, and that, on payment of the second moiety, the eldest son of the Stewart
should be exchanged for his brother Walter, if alive, and if not, for another of the sons
of the Stewart [un autre de les fils.] This seems to imply, that, in 1354, the Stewart
had, at least, four sons. The English commissioners engaged to use their good offices
for procuring the liberty of Walter de Haliburton, David de Annand, and Andrew
Campbell, without ransom. The reader cannot fail to remark, that the merchants and
burgesses of Aberdeen, Perth, Dundee, and Edinburgh became bound not only for
themselves, but for all the merchants in Scotland.

1354.

for obfervance of the truce; and, in like manner, the merchants and burgeſſes of Aberdeen, Perth, Dundee, and Edinburgh, for themſelves, and for all the other merchants in Scotland.

In caſe of any delay in payment, additional hoſtages were to be given; and, in caſe of failure in performance, the King of Scots was to be delivered back to the Engliſh.

Fœd. v. 811. This treaty was ratified by commiſſioners from Scotland, [12th November,] and by Edward III. and his ſon the Prince of Wales, [5th December.]

Fœd. v. 768. It is certain, that, about this time, the Engliſh King negotiated with Balliol, as well as with David Bruce; but to what particular end is unknown.

Fœd. v. 760. 804. He obtained poſſeſſion of Hermitage Caſtle by treaty with Eliſabeth, the widow of Sir William Douglas of Liddeſdale *, [8th October.]

About this time, the Scottiſh government injudiciouſly debaſed the coin.

* Edward had appointed commiſſioners to treat with her, 14th October 1353; *Fœdera*, T. v. p. 760. The treaty, however, was not adjuſted until October 1354. Edward made a grant to her of Liddeſdale and Hermitage Caſtle for life; and he promiſed, if ſhe married an Engliſhman, to enlarge the grant to her and her huſband, and to the heirs of the marriage. And thus the heirs of the Knight of Liddeſdale were excluded, contrary to the treaty between him and Edward III. while the heirs of his wife by another huſband were let in. The lady did homage, and ſwore fealty to Edward, and conſented to admit and pay an Engliſh garriſon. But it was provided, that, if ſhe married an Engliſhman, he ſhould have the command of the garriſon. Not long after, ſhe married Hugh Dacre, brother of William Lord Dacre. He was appointed keeper of Hermitage Caſtle, 1ſt July 1355; *Fœdera*, T. v. p. 818.

Edward alſo became bound, on his attaining the ſovereignty of Scotland, to put the Lady in poſſeſſion of whatever lands belonged to her of right, (probably, as the daughter and heireſs of Sir John Graham of Abercorn.) Laſtly, it was covenanted, that the treaty with her deceaſed huſband ſhould be annulled, and that her daughter and the heir-male of her huſband, hoſtages for the performance of that treaty, ſhould be delivered back, [8th October,] *Fœdera*, T. v. p. 804.; but this laſt was ſuperfluous, for the term during which they were to remain as hoſtages had already expired.

1354

coin. Edward issued a proclamation forbidding its currency in England, and ordered it to be taken as bullion only, (12th March 1354-5.) The preamble of this proclamation will seem strange to those who are unacquainted with the state of the two nations about the middle of the fourteenth century. 'The antient money of Scotland,' says Edward, 'was wont to be of the same weight and alloy as our Sterling money 'of England, and, on that account, had currency with us; yet, of late, 'money, bearing the resemblance of the antient money, has been 'coined in Scotland of less weight, and of baser alloy, and begins to 'have currency, whereby the English nation will be deceived and 'wronged *,' &c.

1355.

A truce between the two nations, for the long term of nine years, *Fœd.* xiv. p. would have proved prejudicial to France; and therefore the French King employed his utmost endeavours to frustrate it. He sent Eugene de Garencieres to Scotland with a small but chosen body of soldiers †, and, which was of more importance, with a considerable sum of money ‡. This

---

* ' Licet antiqua moneta Scotiae ejusdem ponderis et allaiae, ficut fuit moneta nof-
' tra Sterlingi Angliae, ante haec tempora esse confueverit, propter quod in regno
' nostro Angliae habuit cursum suum ; quia tamen quaedam moneta, dictae antiquae
' monetae similis et conformis, quae in pondere minor et allaiâ debilior exiftit, in die-
' to regno Scotiae de novo est cussa, et in regno nostro suum cepit cursum,' &c. *Fœdera,* T. v. p. 813.

† ' Post festum Paschae venit quidam miles nobilis et expertus armis, nomine Eu-
' genius de Garenceria, cum quibusdam militibus praeelectis et valentibus armigeris,
' numero sexaginta ;' *Fordun,* L. xiv. c. 9.

‡ Ten thousand marks, according to *Scala Chron.* ap. Leland. T. i. p. 564.; but, according to *Fordun,* L. xiv. c. 9. forty thousand gold *mutons.* This gold coin had the impression of the *Agnus Dei,* which the vulgar mistook for a sheep; hence it got the ridiculous name of *munton. Gugein,* Hist. L. ia. fol. 152. b. says, ' Mutonus, id enim
' monetae

1355.

This money was to be diftributed among the Scottifh nobility, on condition of their renewing the war, [April.] 'The Scots,' fays Fordun, ' are wont, for the fake of any prefent gain, to overlook all fu-
' ture inconveniencies *.' They accepted the French offers, and confented to diffolve the truce, and invade England.

Ford. xiv. 9. Scala Chron. ap. Leland, i. 364.

The Earl of March, who had affifted at the treaty with England, appears to have been fingularly active in forwarding the negotiations with France, whether from ambition, or avarice, or levity of mind, is uncertain.

The Northumbrian borderers had made a predatory incurfion into the territories of the Earl of March. Eager to feize any fair pretext for hoftilities, the Earl ordered Sir William Ramfay of Dalwolfy to enter England, pillage Norham, and lay wafte the adjacent country. Ramfay obeyed, and infultingly drove off his fpoils, in view of Norham caftle. The keeper, Sir Thomas Gray, fallied out with a body of cavalry to chaftife the fpoilers. Ramfay fled; Gray purfued him acrofs the Tweed, and fell into an ambufh which the Earl of March and the French commander Garencieres had laid in concert with Ramfay. Gray, perceiving himfelf befet on every fide, commanded his horfemen to difmount, and led them on to a defperate attack. But perfonal valour, admired and praifed even by enemies †, could not break through

---

* ' monetae aureae nomen erat, quia *arietis* effigiem, quem *moutoun* Franci dicunt,
' fculptam haberet ;' he fuppofes that it had the impreffion of a ram ; *mouton*, in propriety of fpeech, is a wedder. This coin was originally of the value of 12 fols 6 deniers of fine filver.

* ' Qui crebrò per denarium aminant folidum ;' *Fordun*, L. xiv. c. 9. literally, ' who
' often for a penny lofe a fhilling.'

† ' Animas fuas in propriis manibus committebant, Scotis viriliter refiftentes ;' *Fordun*, L. xiv. c. p. ' Yet for al that, Gray with his men lighting upon foot, fet upon
' them with a wonderful corage, and killed mo of them than they did of the Englifh
' men ;' *Scala Chron.* ap. Leland, T. i. p. 565.

1355.

through those toils in which rashness had entangled him. He was made prisoner, together with his eldest son, and James Dacre, and many other brave men. Few of the English escaped. Of the Scots, John de Haliburton, a commander of approved fidelity and courage, was slain, [August, at Nisbet.]

Thomas Stewart Earl of Angus, having collected some ships, approached Berwick in the night, landed his forces silently, and scaled the walls on the side next the sea, while, on the land side *, the Earl of March, with the French auxiliaries, seconded the attack. The inhabitants fled into the castle, and abandoned to pillage a town become opulent through the tranquillity of twenty years, [about the beginning of November †.] The tower called *Douglas Tower* still remained in the possession of the English. John Copland, who commanded on the eastern borders, attempted, in consequence of the access by *Douglas Tower*, to dislodge the Scots from their new conquest. The Scots repulsed him, and won the tower. Elated with this success, they assaulted the castle; but that enterprise far exceeded their strength. The Regent came to Berwick, and provided, as well as the situation of affairs could allow, for its defence. He thanked the French auxiliaries

Ford. xiv. 10.
Scala Chron.
ap. Leland,
L 565.

---

* 'By treason,' says a MS. in the library of Peters house, Cambridge; ap. *Leland*, T. i. p. 479.

† All historians seem agreed that the surprise of the town of Berwick happened about the beginning of November. In *Scala Chron.* ap. Leland, T. i. p. 565. this event is placed *twenty-one days* after the ambush at Nisbet. Holding this computation to be just, the ambush at Nisbet ought to be brought down to the beginning of October, instead of being placed in August, as has been done on the authority of Fordun. Hector Boece has comprehended the history of Scotland, between the battle of Durham and the surprise of Berwick, in a single page, T. xv. fol. 325. a. The little that he says is taken from Fordun; but he has varied the narrative according to his own fancy. Thus, for example, he speaks of the Knight of Liddesdale having been assassinated by *one* William Douglas;' 'a Wilhelmo *quodam* Douglas.'

1355.

liaries for their good services, and dismissed them to their own country.

It appears singular that the Regent thus dismissed the French auxiliaries, after they had performed good service at Nisbet, as well as at the storming of Berwick, and especially at a juncture so critical, and in the depth of winter. An English historian accounts for it, by observing, that 'the French could not submit to live after the country 'fashion*.' And, indeed, the French, although eminently skilled in the elegancies of life, have seldom acquired the important art of appearing easy while from home.

Knygh. 2608.

Edward III. having returned from France, [18th November,] assembled an army for recovering Berwick, before the Scots could have leisure to strengthen its fortifications. He invested the town: Articles of capitulation were speedily adjusted, and the Scots had liberty to depart with all their effects, [13th January 1355-6.]

Barnes, 486. Ford. v. 828. Ford. xiv. 11. Tynd. Neust. 511.

Balliol, weary of being the nominal sovereign of a people among whom he had no authority, resolved to renounce Scotland for ever.

He made an absolute surrender to Edward III. of all his private estates in Scotland, [at Rokesburgh, 20th January 1355-6 †.]

Fæd. v. 855.

On the same day, he made an absolute surrender to Edward III. of the kingdom and crown of Scotland, 'by delivery of a portion of the 'earth

Fæd. v. 852.

---

* 'Nescientes vivere secundùm morem patriae, citò repatriaverunt;' *Knyghton,* p. 2608. In writing history, I have industriously avoided the refinements of conjecture; and, therefore, I shall, on this occasion, barely hint, that the Stewart might possibly have wished to rid himself of the French auxiliaries. They were particularly connected with the Earl of March, in whom the Stewart could place no confidence; and their remaining in Scotland would have proved an obstacle to the renewal of the negotiations with the English.

† His principal estates lay in Galloway; *Fædera,* T. v. p. 833. He had also some lands in Annandale; and he held Lauderdale by virtue of a grant from Edward III.; *Fædera,* T. v. p. 632.

1355.

'earth of Scotland, and also by delivery of his golden crown.' These were confidered as the proper feudal fymbols of poffeffion given, [at Rokeſburgh, 21ſt January 1355-6.]

Balliol judged it incumbent on him to publiſh to the world the reaſons which occaſioned this furrender. They are here collected from the various inſtruments drawn up at that time, and they are *eleven* in number.

1. The many great favours, and diſtinguiſhed marks of honour, beſtowed on him by the Engliſh King. 2. Balliol's eſpecial affection towards the Engliſh King. 3. The near relation by blood in which they ſtood to each other [*]. 4. The ingratitude, and the obſtinate rebellion of thoſe his relations who ſtood next in ſucceſſion to the crown. 5. That his own right to the crown might not altogether periſh. 6. That its oppoſers might not eſcape with impunity. 7. The various and imminent dangers, ſpiritual as well as temporal, in which his ſubjects were involved through the prevalency of rebellion. 8. The feebleneſs of his body by reaſon of the approach of old age. 9. The evils which might ariſe from a diſputed ſucceſſion after his death. 10. His expectation, that, through the valour of Edward, the wicked would at length be overcome; and, through his wiſdom and clemen-

Fœd. v. 831.
834. 839.

cy,

[*] The nature of their relation will be diſcerned from the following pedigree:

1355.

ey, the good protector. And, *lastly*, in order to promote union, for the mutual strength, safety, and advantage, of the two nations.

Fœd. v. 831. To this instrument of surrender, a clause was added of the following import: 'And we, and our heirs, shall warrant against all mortals, 'for ever, the said kingdom and crown of Scotland, the Isles, and all 'other the premises, with their whole pertinents, to the said Edward 'our cousin, and his heirs and assigns *.'

It must appear exceedingly strange, that Balliol, when deprived of the possession of the kingdom of Scotland, and despairing to regain it, should have made it over to another, ' with absolute warranty.'

Fœd. v. 836. In return for this surrender, Edward became bound to pay five thousand merks to Balliol, and to secure him in an annuity of two thousand pounds Sterling, [at Bamburgh, 20th January 1355-6 †.]

The fate of Edward Balliol was singular. In his invasion of Scotland, during the minority of David Bruce, he displayed a bold spirit of enterprise, and a courage superior to all difficulties. By the victory at Duplin he won a crown; some few weeks after, he was surprised at Annan, and lost it. The overthrow of the Scots at Halidon, to which he signally contributed, availed not to his re-establishment. Year after year he saw his partisans fall away, and range themselves under the banners of his competitor. He became the pensioner of Edward III. and the tool of his policy, assumed and laid aside at pleasure: And, at last, by the surrender at Rokesburgh, he did what in him

* ' Et nos et haeredes nostri, dicta regnum et coronam Scotiae, Insulas, et omnia
' alia praedicta, cum suis pertinentiis universis, praefato Domino et consanguineo nos-
' tro, haeredibus et assignatis suis, contra mortales omnes warrantizabimus et in perpe-
' tuum defendemus ;' Foedera, T. v. p. 833.

† From the instruments executed on this memorable 20th January 1355 6, it appears that Edward III. and Balliol were, on the same day, at Rokesburgh and Bamburgh. It is probable, that the treaty was concluded at Bamburgh, and that the parties afterwards went to Rokesburgh to give and to receive livery and saisine.

DAVID II.   237

1355.

him lay to entail the calamities of war on the Scottish nation, a nation already miserable through the consequences of a regal succession disputed for threescore years. The remainder of his days was spent in obscurity; and the historians of that kingdom where he once reigned, knew not the time of his death. He died childless, [1363.]

Abercrombie,
ii. 109
Knyght. 1627.

Edward, after having received the solemn surrender of Balliol's rights, remained at Rokesburgh for some days. He suffered himself to be amused with hopes of the submission of the Scottish barons; but perceiving at length that they only sought to gain time, and that they had no purpose of acknowledging his authority, he resolved to extort their obedience, and he led his numerous forces into East Lothian. The Scots had not failed in their wonted precaution of driving off the castle, and removing every sort of provisions beyond the reach of the enemy. Edward ordered a fleet of victuallers to attend him in the frith of Forth; but his ships were dispersed by a tempest, and many wrecked. As he advanced, his difficulties increased. Flying parties of the Scots infested him on all sides, and embarrassed his march. Edward, enflamed by disappointment and rage, desolated the country, and laid every town, village, and hamlet, in ashes. More resembling the frantic JOHN, than the conqueror at Cressy, he spared not the edifices consecrated to religion *. It behoved him to retreat; and, while part of his army was passing by the borders of Etrick forrest, Lord Douglas set upon them, and slew great numbers. This inroad

Knyght. 2611.
Ford. xiv. 13.

* * 'Combusto burgo et toto monasterio, ac solemni ecclesia Fratrum Minorum de
' Hadington, opus certè quod sumptuosum erat, mirique decoris, ac totius patriae illius
' solatium singulare, cujus chorus quidem, ob singularem pulchritudinem et luminis
' claritatem, *Lucerna Laudoniae* communiter vocabatur, direxit iter suum per Laudo-
' niam, circumquaque cuncta comburens et devastans, et nihil pro posse salvans, usque
' ad burgum de Edinburgh perveniret. A quo abcedens, et omnia combustibilia in-
' cinerans, propterea vulgò *le Burnt Candlemas dies* datur, ad propria sine honore re-
' meavit.'

238   D A V I D II.

1355.

inroad happened about the time of the feast of the purification; and hence it was long remembered as an æra among the vulgar in Scotland, under the name of *the burnt Candlemas*.

Ford. v. 846. After having been thus foiled, Edward issued an ostentatious proclamation, intimating, that he was resolved, as sovereign of Scotland, inviolably to maintain the antient laws, and the usages of that kingdom, [15th March 1355-6.]

1356.

Ford. xiv. 15. After Edward's retreat, the Scots expelled his partisans from the west marches. Roger de Kirkpatrick stormed the castles of Dalswinton and Carlaverock, and obtained possession of Nithsdale: And John Stewart, eldest son of the Regent, obliged the inhabitants of Annandale to yield submission to the Scottish government. About this

---

‘ removit ;’ *Fordun,* L. xiv. c. 13. To the same purpose the English historians speak : ‘ King Edouarde went beyond Lambremore in Lownes, destroying the country on to ‘ Edinburg ;’ *Scala Chron.* ap. Leland. T. I. p. 566. ‘ Super hoc Rex carpit iter ver‘ sus Edynsborg cum iii aciebus, et destruxerum patriam per viii leucas in circuitu, ‘ et succenderunt ignes et flammas ;’ *Knyghton,* p. 2611. Some of the English historians, as Walsingham and the Continuator of Murimuth, have altogether suppressed this savage and inglorious expedition. As to the fact of Edward having burnt churches, Barnes bluntly says, ‘ I believe it not, because of that notable success which followed ‘ his arms this year in France ;’ *Edward III.* p. 491. Mr Hume says, ‘ Balliol attended ‘ Edward on this expedition ; *but finding* that his constant adherence to the English ‘ had given his countrymen an unconquerable aversion to his title, and that he him‘ self was declining through age and infirmities, he finally resigned into the King's ‘ hands his pretensions to the crown of Scotland ;’ *History of England,* v. ii. p. 216. If there is no inaccuracy in the language of the historian, he erroneously imagines that Balliol made the surrender *after* the expedition into Scotland. That Balliol attended Edward into Scotland, is exceedingly improbable, and it is a circumstance not recorded by the old historians of either nation. Barnes, indeed has asserted it, but without quoting any authority ; p. 491. And Tyrrel has transcribed the passage from Barnes, without even quoting him, V. iii. p. 592. Thus is history written!

1356.

this time, also, according to Fordun, it was that Lord Douglas reduced Interior Galloway.

The affairs in France required the whole attention of Edward. He *Ford. v. 847.* now expressed his willingness to enter into a treaty with the Scots, not only for the ransom of their King, and for a cessation of hostilities, but also for a perpetual peace °. William de Bohun, Earl of Northampton, warden of the marches, with others, were appointed commissioners, [25th March 1356.]

Lord Douglas made a treaty with the warden. He became bound *Ford. v. 849.* not to molest the English while they abstained from hostilities against his estates, and those of the Earl of March, [17th April.] This cessation of arms was to continue until the ensuing Michaelmas. Within that period he might have accomplished a pilgrimage which he had undertaken into foreign parts. Other objects, however, more suited to his temper, and his profession of arms, diverted him from this fashionable expiation for crimes.

The eyes of all men were turned towards France. The Black *Ford. xiv. 16.* Prince had imprudently penetrated into that country with forces disproportioned to those of his antagonist. John, the French King, assembled a formidable army to intercept him in his retreat. The Scots, who at that time enjoyed a momentary tranquillity at home, crowded from every quarter to the French standard. Lord Douglas, forgetful of his religious pilgrimage, offered his sword to the French King. He was received with distinguished honours †, and his service was *Scoti Chron.* accepted. *ap. Leland. 1. 567.*

° ' Ad tractandum et concordandum cum praelatis, nobilibus, et popularibus regni
' Scotiae, adversariis nostris, de redemptione et de liberatione David de Bruys, priso-
' narii nostri, ac de treugis sive suffereneiis guerrae, et *de finali pace, ac legis et perpe-*
' *tuis amicitiis, inter nos et ipsos nostros adversarios nostras ineundis;*' *Foedera,* T. v.
p. 847.

† ' Was made knight of his hands;' *Scoti Chron.* ap. Leland, T. l. 567. To say
' that a person received the honour of knighthood,' is, in modern language, uninterest-
Ing.

1356.

accepted. The French and the English encountered in the vineyards of Maupertuis, not far from Poictiers, [19th September.] The event of that day is well known. Great carnage was made of the Scots. Lord Douglas, after having been wounded, was forced off the field by his surviving companions *. Archibald Douglas, a warrior eminent in our history, fell into the power of the enemy; but, by the extraordinary presence of mind of Sir William Ramsay of Colluthy, he was concealed, and escaped unknown †.

Ford. xiv. 17.

In-ing, and sometimes it is ludicrous. This must always be the case when names and ceremonies are retained, while, from a total change of manners, that which gave dignity to such names and ceremonies is forgotten by the vulgar.

* Froissart, T. i. c. 162. says, that Lord Douglas left the field as soon as he perceived that the English had the advantage, ' because he dreaded being their prisoner ;' " car nullement ne vouloit estre prins des Anglois, ains eust plus cher estre occis.'

† The story, as related by Fordun, is curious. It shall be translated, as nearly as possible in his own manner. ' Archibald Douglas having been made prisoner along ' with the rest, appeared in more sumptuous armour than the other Scottish prisoners, ' and, therefore, he was supposed by the English to be some great Lord. Late in the ' evening after the battle, when the English were about to strip off his armour, Sir ' William Ramsay of Colluthy happening to be present, fixed his eyes on Archibald ' Douglas, and affecting to be in a violent passion, cried out, You cursed, damnable ' murderer, how comes it, in the name of mischief, [ex parte Diaboli], that you are thus ' proudly decked out in your master's armour ? Come hither and pull off my boots. Douglas approached trembling, kneeled down, and pulled off one of the boots. Ramsay ' taking up the boot, beat Douglas with it. The English bystanders imagining him ' out of his senses, interposed, and rescued Douglas. They said, that the person whom ' he had beaten was certainly of great rank, and a Lord. What ? he a Lord,' cried Ramsay, ' he is a scullion, and a base knave, and, as I suppose, has killed his master. ' Go, you villain, to the field, search for the body of my cousin, your master, and when you ' have found it, come back, that, at least, I may give him a decent burial. Then he ' ransomed the feigned serving-man for forty shillings, and having buffeted him smartly, he cried, Get you gone ; fly. Douglas bore all this patiently, carried on the deceit, and was soon beyond the reach of his enemies.' This story, as to some of its circumstances, may not seem altogether probable ; yet, in the main, it has the appearance

1356.

In a parliament held at Perth, the Scots appointed the Bishop of *Ford. v. 851.*
St Andrews, and the Bishop of Brechin, Sir William Livingston, and
Sir Robert Erskine, commissioners to treat with England, not only for
the ransom of the King, but also for peace between the two nations *,
[17th January 1356-7.]

1357.

A truce for two years was concluded between Edward III. and the *Ford. vi. 3.*
French King, [at Bourdeaux, 23d March 1356-7.] It was provided,
that the Scots might take the benefit of this truce: But the Scots
chose to negotiate for themselves; and concluded a truce for six *Ford. vi. 15.*
months with England, [8th May 1357.]

During

pearance of truth. Had I been at liberty to vary the narrative, I would have made
Ramsay suspect, that the feigned serving man had stript his master, after he had been
slain, or mortally wounded. This Archibald was the natural son of the renowned Sir
James Douglas, slain by the Saracens in Granada; *Fordun,* L. xiv. c. 16.

* The commission granted in consequence of this appointment is sealed by the
Stewart, Regent, in his own name, by two Bishops for the whole clergy, by Patrick
Earl of March, Thomas Earl of Angus, and William Keith, the Marshal, for the nobility, [nomine et vice procerum et baronum,] and with the common seals of the
boroughs of Aberdeen, Dundee, Perth, and Edinburgh, for all the burgesses, and
whole community, [nomine et vice omnium bergensium, et totius communitatis.]
The commission is granted ' de unanimi et expresso consensu et assensu omnium
' procelatorum, procerum, ac totius communitatis Regni nostrae.' The commissioners
are persons whose names generally appear in the negotiations about that period; William Landales, Bishop of St Andrews, Patrick de Leuchars, Bishop of Brechin, and
Chancellor of Scotland; *Krith,* Catalogue of Scottish Bishops, p 95.; Sir William
Livingston, and Sir Robert Erskine, afterwards Chamberlain of Scotland. They obtained a passport from Edward III. 28th March 1357; *Foedera.* T. vi p. 12. Rymer
has printed their commission as if it had been granted in January 1355 6, instead of
January 1356 7. This error in a single date has occasioned considerable confusion.
Abercromble, Vol. II. p. 119. did not remark the error; and, by that means, he has
exceedingly perplexed his narrative.

VOL. II.   H h

1357.

Ford. xiv. 10. During this season of public tranquillity, when no enemies were to be dreaded on the borders, Roger de Kirkpatrick chanced to entertain Sir James Lindesay as his guest at Carlaverock castle. After an evening passed in friendship and jollity, Kirkpatrick retired to rest. Lindesay burst into his chamber, and murdered him. Lindelay rode off precipitately. The darkness of that night seemed to favour his escape. Having continued his course until day-break, he perceived himself still in the neighbourhood of the castle. Bewildered by guilt, he was seized. He was tried, and instantly executed *, [about 24th June.]

Knygh. 2617. Some Scotsmen, impatient of peace, equipped three vessels, and sent them well armed to cruise against the English in the east seas. Their course was short: They were forced by a tempest to take shelter at Yarmouth, with the English ships which they expected to seize, and they were confiscated.

Ford. vi. 51. This incident, however, did not interrupt the negotiations between the two kingdoms. David Bruce was conveyed to Berwick, where the commissioners held their conferences, [August.]

The English insisted that one hundred thousand marks Sterling should be paid as the ransom of the King of Scots.

A

---

* *Fordun,* L. xiv. c. 20. remarks, that Lindesay and Kirkpatrick were the heirs of the two men who accompanied Robert Bruce at the fatal conference with Comyn. If Fordun was rightly informed as to this particular, and as to the time of the murder of Kirkpatrick at Carlaverock castle, an argument arises in support of a notion which I have long entertained, that the person who struck his dagger in Comyn's heart was not the representative of the honourable family of Kirkpatrick in Nithsdale. Roger de Kirkpatrick was made prisoner at the battle of Durham in 1346; Roger de Kirkpatrick was alive on the 6th August 1357; for, on that day, Humphrey, the son and heir of Roger de Kirkpatrick, is proposed as one of the young gentlemen who were to be hostages for David Bruce; *Fœdera,* T. vi p. 35. Roger de Kirkpatrick, Miles, was present at the parliament held at Edinburgh, 20th September 1357; *Fœdera,* T. vi. p. 43. And he is mentioned as alive, 3d October 1357; *Fœdera,* T. vi. p. 48. It follows, of necessary consequence, that Roger de Kirkpatrick, murdered in June 1357, must have been a different person.

DAVID II.

1357.

A parliament was held at Edinburgh, [26th September.] The nobility, the clergy, and the boroughs, consented to the demand of the English. The Regent, and the nobility present, became bound for the payment of this exorbitant sum; and they declared, that their obligation should be effectual against all persons of that estate. In like manner, the Bishops, having obtained the consent of their respective chapters, bound themselves, and all the rest of the clergy; and the commissioners of the boroughs bound themselves, and all the burgesses and merchants of Scotland *. To the four ambassadors already

Foed. vi. 39, —46.

---

* As the transactions in this parliament are curious, and throw considerable light on the history of those times, it may be proper to enter into a detail of circumstances: It appears, that, at first, the Scots prelates granted powers to certain persons to act for them in parliament at Edinburgh, and to concur in every thing which might be requisite for effecting the deliverance of their Sovereign. The Bishop of Aberdeen named three commissioners, one of them was John Archdeacon of Aberdeen, [John Barbour the metrical historian.] Like commissions were granted by the Bishop and Chapter of Murray, of Glasgow, and of Dunkeld, by the Bishop of Argyle, by the Chapter of Ross, by the Prior and Chapter of St Andrews, and by the Abbot and convent of Scone; *Foedera*, T. vi. p. 39. 40. These are preserved in *Foedera*, and it is probable that there were others, although now lost. It seems that this form was laid aside, and that it was judged more proper that the Bishops should become bound personally in parliament, for the whole clergy. The nobles present in the parliament at Edinburgh 26th September 1357, were

Robert, Stewart of Scotland, the King's lieutenant.

William Earl of Ross	David Graham Lord of Dundaff
Malcolm Earl of Wigton	William More Lord of Abercorn
Donald Earl of Lenox	Roger Kirkpatrick
William Douglas, [Lord Douglas]	John Maxwell
William Keith, Marshall of Scotland	Thomas Bisset
James Lindesay Lord of Crawford	Patrick Ramsay

They, ' de consensu et voluntate omnium Comitum, procerum, et Baronum, et com-
' munitatis regni Scotiae,' appointed commissioners to appear at Berwick, and treat
with the English, namely, Patrick Earl of March, Thomas Earl of Angus, William Earl

of

1357.

ready appointed, the parliament added Patrick Earl of March, and Thomas de Fingalk, Bishop of Caithness. Each of the three estates granted a separate commission to certain persons to appear at Berwick, and to treat with the English.

Fœd. vi. 46. —52.

The treaty, which had been in agitation for so many years, was at length concluded, [at Berwick, 3d October 1357.] By it the King of Scots was released, after a captivity of *eleven* years. The Scottish nation agreed to pay one hundred thousand marks sterling as the ransom of their Sovereign, by yearly payments of ten thousand marks, [on the 24th June.] Twenty young men of quality, and among them the eldest son of the Stewart, were to be given as hostages; and, for further

of Sutherland, Thomas Moray of Bothwell, William Livingston, and Robert Erskine, [in *Fœdera*, T. 6. p. 43. he is called *de Griffin*; but I suppose that to be one of the numberless errors in transcribing, which disgrace the *Fœdera Angliæ*.]

The Bishops present were

William Bishop of Glasgow
John Bishop of Dunkeld
Alexander Bishop of Aberdeen
          John Bishop of Moray
          Alexander Bishop of Ross
          William Bishop of Dunblane
Martin Bishop of Argyle.

It seems that Michael Bishop of Galloway was not present; but he afterwards acceded, *Fœdera*, T. vi. p. 61.

They appointed William Bishop of St Andrews, Thomas Bishop of Caithness, and Patrick Bishop of Brechin, to be their commissioners.

There were delegates present in parliament from seventeen boroughs, ranged in the following order:

1 Edinburgh
2 Perth
3 Aberdeen
4 Dundee
5 Inverkeithing
6 Crail

7 Coupar
8 St Andrews
9 Montrose
10 Stirling
11 Linlithgow
12 Hadinton

13 Dumbarton
14 Rutherglen
15 Lanerk
16 Dumfries
17 Peebles.

They appointed eleven commissioners, the same men who were the delegates in parliament for the boroughs of Edinburgh, Perth, Aberdeen, and Dundee.

1357.

further security, three of the following great lords were to place themselves in the hands of the English: The Stewart, the Earls of March, Marre, Rofs, Angus, and Sutherland, Lord Douglas, and Thomas Moray of Bothwell. It was provided, that a truce should continue between the two nations until compleat payment of the ransom. The King of Scots, the nobility, and the boroughs, ratified this treaty, [5th October:] And the Bishops ratified it on the following day, [6th October.] *Fœd. vi. 51. —65.*

David, immediately after his release, summoned a parliament *; laid the treaty before the three estates, obtained their approbation, and then ratified the treaty anew, [at Scone, 6th November.] *Fœd. vi. 68.*

1358.

The King of Scots had undertaken to apply to the Pope for his ratification of the engagement which the Scottish Bishops had come under, subjecting the ecclesiastical revenues in payment of the ransom. But the Pope declared, that such obligations might prove ruinous to the church, and that he could not, in conscience, ratify them by his authority; and, therefore, he peremptorily rejected the request †, [21st June 1358.] *Fœd. vi. 89. 90.*

It appears that the King of Scots inclined to reside in the country where he had been so long a prisoner. After having remained at liberty for a few months, he procured permission from Edward III. to visit England, [14th July.] This permission was to continue in force until February 1358-9. In the course of his reign, he made many expensive, unprofitable, and impolitic visits of the like nature. *Fœd. vi. 98.*

Ambassadors

* So I understand the words, 'in pleno concilio nostro apud Sconam ;' *Fœdera*, T. vi. p. 68.

† Nevertheless, Edward III. by an instrument dated 24th June 1358, seems to acknowledge that the Scottish Bishops had obtained that permission which the Bull itself refuses to grant; *Fœdera*, T. vi. p. 90. Perhaps he only meant to acknowledge, that they had done every thing in their power to obtain such permission.

1359.

Ford. xiv. 11.

Ambassadors were sent to the Pope for procuring a grant of the tenth of the ecclesiastical revenues in Scotland towards payment of the King's ransom. The Pope consented to make the grant for three years, under condition that nothing more, on account of that ransom, should be exacted from the Scottish clergy.

Alliances between France and Scotland, 20—31. MS. Adv. Libr.

Sir Robert Erskine, and Norman Lesley [*], plenipotentiaries appointed by the King of Scots, entered into a negotiation with plenipotentiaries appointed by Charles the Dauphin, Regent of France.

'Our nation,' said the Scottish plenipotentiaries, 'has maintained a long and disastrous war against England. After our Sovereign was made prisoner in battle, he might, by renouncing the French alliance, have obtained his own liberty, and peace to his people; but he rejected liberty and peace on such conditions. In full confidence of aid from France, he agreed to lay down a ransom of one hundred thousand marks Sterling, by annual payments of ten thousand marks: He gave hostages of the chief of his nobility; and he concluded a truce with England until the ransom-money should be discharged. Of this sum only ten thousand marks have been paid; and, until the remainder is paid, the hostages cannot be relieved, or war re-commenced. The Scottish nation is not only willing, but most able to carry on the war with vigour †, yet cannot, conveniently ‡, discharge the ransom before the terms appointed, unless by the aid of France.'

The

---

[*] Sir John le Grant was in the commission [dated at Edinburgh 10th May 1359] but it does not appear that he ever acted. The King calls Norman Lesley *Armiger noster*.

† 'De la quelle guerre ils avoient tres grand desire faire *bonne et forte*, et la pourront faire.'

‡ 'Le quel payement nostre dit Seigneur le Roi D'Escosse et son Royaume ne pourroient faire *bonnement* devant les termes dessus dits.' *Abercrombie*, vol. II. p. 124.—126. refers to this negotiation; but in many particulars he has misunderstood it. He says,

1359.

The Scottish plenipotentiaries reminded the French of the alliance which subsisted between France and Scotland; and concluded, by engaging, 'that the Scots should instantly, and vigorously, and at their 'own charges *, make war against the English, if the Regent, and 'kingdom of France, afforded the aid necessary for discharging the 'ransom †.'

The French, by their plenipotentiaries, professed their regard for the faith of treaties; and they gently insinuated, that the Scots themselves had overlooked the terms of the alliance, by omitting to include France in the truce. They said, that, while their country was exposed to the ravages of war, and their own Sovereign a captive, they could not, *conveniently*, pay so large a sum; nevertheless, if the Scots made war against England, they would afford whatever assistance was in their power.

Although,

---

says, that Erskine and Lesley ' were commissioned to renew *the old league*, so it is expressly called, hitherto inviolably observed between the two nations.' The words of the commission by David II. are: ' Quod cum quaedam confaederatio amicitiae inter ' illustres Reges Franciae, *et progenitorum nostrum*, ac nos, populumque ipsorum et nos- ' trum, ab olim facta fuit, et inviolabiliter observata diutius, &c.' This *old league* must imply the treaty concluded at Corbeil, 16th April 1326, between the King of France and Robert Bruce, unless the words of the commission are egregiously and wilfully misconstrued.

* The Scottish plenipotentiaries observed, that the King of France had formerly become bound to furnish to the King of Scots, during war with England, the pay of five hundred armed horsemen and five hundred archers, but that the Scots were willing to release him from that obligation.

† ' Neanmoins si tost comme le Roy et le royaulme d'Escosse feront guerre au Roy ' et au royaume d'Angleterre nostre dit Seigneur le Regent et le royaulme de France ' les aideront et conseilleront en tout ce qu'ils pourront bonnement.' This general clause is transcribed from the treaty of Corbeil, 16th April 1326. But the words *comme loyaux alliez*, which occur in the treaty of Corbeil, are omitted in that of Paris; *Alliances*, MS. fol. 19. See also *Additions to Annals*, Vol. II. 116.

248   DAVID II.

1359.

Although, at first, the one party demanded so much, and the other offered so little, it was finally agreed, that, on Easter day 1360, the French should pay fifty thousand marks Sterling to the Scots; and that the Scots should renew the war with England. A ratification of the former alliance between France and Scotland was also reciprocally stipulated, [at the Louvre, *near* Paris, 29th June 1359.]

1360.

Fœd. vi. 178.—196. The French and the English concluded a treaty of peace, [at Bretigny near Chartres, [8th May 1360.] By it the French King 're- 'nounced every alliance with Scotland, and engaged for himself and 'his successors, that they should not, in time coming, aid, comfort, 'or favour the King, kingdom, or subjects of Scotland, or make any 'new alliance with them to the prejudice of the English.*'

The English King, on his part, renounced every alliance with the people of Flanders.

Fœd. vi. 265. But both Kings afterwards protested, that these renunciations should only take place in the event of the articles of the peace being reciprocally fulfilled, [24th October.]

Fœd. vi. 107. 108. A treaty for a final peace with the Scottish nation was commenced, [20th August.]

In

---

* This ought to be perpetually remembered; it is the 32 article. See *Fœdera*, T. vi. p. 192. 'Concordatum est, quòd Rex Franciae, ex suna primogenitus, regens, pro 'ipsis et pro haeredibus suis, Regibus Franciae, In quantum fieri potest, dimittent et 'recedent in toto de alligantiis, quas habent cum Scotis; et promittent, in quantum 'fieri potest, quòd nunquam illi, vel haeredes sui, nec Reges Franciae qui pro tem- 'pore erunt, dabunt vel ferent Reg) nec regno Scotiae, nec subditis ejusdem, praesenti- 'bus vel futuris, auxilium, consolamen, vel favorem contra dictum Regem Angliae, 'nec contra haeredes et successores suos, nec contra suum regnum, vel subditos suos, 'quocunque modo; et quòd ipsi non facient alias alligantias cum dictis Scotis, in fu- 'turum, contra dictum Regem et regnum Angliae.'

DAVID II.

1360.

In this year a singular incident occurred. David Bruce, during his captivity, had an unlawful intercourse with one Catharine Mortimer, a native of Wales. She came to Scotland with him, and continued for several years to be his favourite concubine. She became obnoxious to some of the nobility. They conspired against her life. Two wretches, Hulle and Dewar, went to her residence, pretending that they had orders to convey her to the King. She committed herself to their guidance. On the road between Melros and Soltra, they murdered her. Great suspicions arose that Thomas Stewart Earl of Angus, a turbulent and profligate person, had instigated the murderers. The King imprisoned him in the castle of Dunbarton; and honourably interred his beloved Mortimer in the chapel of the abbey of Newbottle.

Ford. xiv. 24. Scala Chron. ap. Leland, L. 57b.

1361.

The plague broke out again in Scotland, with redoubled violence, and continued its ravages through this year. It was computed, that one third of the people perished in this general calamity; among them were many persons of distinction. The Earl of Angus died in his prison at Dumbarton, and some of the hostages died in England [*].

To avoid the infection, the King, with many of his nobles, retired into the northern parts of Scotland. Some differences arose between him and the Earl of Marre. The King besieged and took the castle of Kildrummie, the principal residence of that nobleman, and placed a garrison in it. The Earl obtained leave to quit the kingdom; but he was soon received into favour again.

Ford. xiv. 24.

Ford. xiv. 24.

Our

---

[*] The King's nephew, son of the Earl of Sutherland, died of the plague at Lincoln; Fordun, L. xiv. c. 25. Fordun adds, that *Thomas Earl of Moray* died of the plague in England 1361. But there existed no such person at that time. Fordun probably meant 'Thomas Moray Lord of Bothwell.'

1361.

Fœd. vi. 119. Our historians are silent as to the cause of the King's displeasure against a nobleman nearly allied to the royal family: But it was probably this: The Earl of Marre had lately become bound, for a pension of six hundred marks Sterling, to serve Edward III. 'in his wars, 'and elsewhere, against all men, his liege lord only excepted.' It was natural for the King to be displeased at such a treaty between one of his own subjects, and a Prince still at enmity with Scotland; and he appears to have seized the first convenient opportunity of expressing his displeasure.

1362.

Walsing. 179. Johanna, Princess of England, the consort of David Bruce, died * childless.

1363.

Ford, xiv. 25. The King of Scots, in a parliament at Scone, proposed to the three estates, that, in the event of his dying without issue, they should choose for their King one of the sons of Edward III. And he earnestly expressed his wish that the choice might fall on Lionel Duke of Clarence.

---

* There is a strange diversity among historians concerning the time of the death of this ill fated lady; *Fordun,* L. xiv. c. 18. says, that she went to England in 1357, and died after she had remained there for some time, [aliquanto tempore commorata.] In *Scala Chron.* ap. Leland. T. l. p. 568. it is said, ' The Quene of Scotland, sister to ' King Edward, cam oute of Scotland to Wyndesore to speke with him, and after was ' with her mother Quene Isabel at Hertford, and ther dyed.' This imports that she died, either before her mother, or soon after her. It is certain that her mother died in autumn 1358.—Fordun, and the author of Scala Chronica, are in a mistake.—Queen Johanna must have lived beyond the year 1357 or the year 1358; her husband speaks of her as alive on the 21st February 1358-9; *Fœdera,* T. p. vi. 118. Nay, more, on the 2d May 1362, a passport is granted by Edward III. to John Heryng ' the servant of ' Johanna Queen of Scotland, oor sister;' *Fœdera,* T. vi. p. 364. and, therefore, I incline to follow *Walsingham,* p. 179. who places her death in 1362.

1363.

Clarence. This, he said, would be the means of establishing perpetual tranquillity: That the Duke of Clarence would be able to maintain the national liberties; and that the English King would renounce for ever all pretensions to the sovereignty of Scotland.

The estates instantly, and unanimously, made answer *, ' that they
' would never permit an Englishman to reign over them: That the
' proposition made by the King was ill-advised: That, by acts of
' settlement, and solemn oaths of the three estates, in the days of Ro-
' bert Bruce, the Stewart had been acknowledged presumptive heir of
' the crown; and that he, and his sons, were brave men, and fit to
' reign.' The King appeared to be sensible of the force of their arguments, and desisted from his proposition †.

But such a proposition, having been once made, could not be forgotten. Jealousy and distrust arose in the minds of a people who prized the national independency above all things. Many of the nobility entered into associations for their mutual support; and they resolved to force the King to disclaim his proposition, or, on his refusal, to expel him. The Stewart, in particular, entered into associations with the Earls of March and Douglas, the most powerful of the southern barons; and, which is remarkable, he formed a confederacy with his own sons. We are ignorant of the precise tenor of those instruments: We may, however, presume, that they aimed at maintaining the legal succession to the crown.

Neither

---

* ' Cui breviter et sine ulteriore deliberatione aut retractione responsum fuit per u-
' niversaliter singulos et singulariter universos de tribus statibus;' *Fordun*, L. xiv. c. 25.
that is, ' generally by each man, and particularly by all.'

† Something has been said on this subject in *Remarks on the history of Scotland*, c. 5.
But a more accurate attention to dates has enabled me to place the transactions of this
year 1363 in a clearer light. By some strange inadvertency, I quoted *Barnes*, p. 426.
427. Instead of *Foedera*, T. vi. p. 416. 417. See *note* p. 116.

1363.

Neither did the malecontents rest satisfied with such precautions: They took up arms, seized the persons whom they suspected of favouring the political views of the King, plundered the estates of the supposed traitors, and divided the spoils as if they had been in an enemy's country.

Personal intrepidity distinguished the character of David Bruce. Undismayed at the hostile appearances which he beheld on every side, he called on his people to protect their Sovereign; and he issued a proclamation, commanding his barons to desist from their rebellious attempts. His proclamation having been received with scorn, the King had recourse to arms. Many resolute men stood forth in defence of the throne *. The insurgents now perceived the hazards to which they had exposed themselves and their country, and they sued for peace. A general amnesty was granted, under condition that the barons should renounce their associations, become bound to abstain from such private confederacies in time coming, and renew their oaths of fealty.

Ford. xiv. 17. Fordun has preserved the form of the obligation executed by the Stewart. It is under the penalty of forfeiting for ever all right and title to the crown of Scotland, as well as to his own inheritances, and of being held a perjured man, and a false and dishonoured knight †, [at Inchmurdoch, 14th May 1363.]

And

---

* *Fordun, L. xiv. c. 25.* says that the King of Scots expended large sums of money in paying the forces which he had drawn together, ' in stipendiis illorum exposita multâ ' pecuniâ.' This, if true, is singular; the finances of David Bruce must have been very low at that time; and it is hardly possible to imagine, that he could have commanded any considerable sum of money, without assistance from England.

† *Fordun, L. xiv. c. 27.* says, that the other nobles came under like obligations, *mutatis mutandis*. ' Sub isto tenore juraverunt caeteri, mutatis tamen certis terminis, pro- ' ut personarum qualitas expostulavit.' Pity that he had not been more explicit; for then we should have seen who they were that engaged in this insurrection, and what confederacies

1363.

And thus a dangerous insurrection, which the extravagant proposals at Scone had excited, was quelled by the fortitude and clemency of the King.

Scarcely was the public tranquillity restored, when this capricious Prince repaired to London, and again involved himself in secret negotiations with Edward III.

*Ford. vi. 416.
487.*

The two Kings were present at a conference held by their privy-counsellors, (23d November 1363.)

The heads of this conference were committed to writing; but it was anxiously premised, that the whole should be viewed merely in the light of a scheme or plan, and that nothing should be understood as having been either proposed on the one side, or agreed to on the other.

This singular historical curiosity is still preserved, and is of the following import:

L

confederacies they had formed. It is probable that the obligations were granted, either in parliament, or at a convention, ' convocatis omnibus regni optimatibus ;' *Fordun,* ib. The following persons appear to have been present:

- William bishop of St Andrews
- Patrick Bishop of Brechin, Chancellor
  John Abbot of Dunfermline
- Walter Wardlaw Archdeacon of Lothian, Secretary
- Gilbert Armstrong Prior of St Andrews
- Robert Erskine Chamberlain of Scotland
  Archibald Douglas   }
  Robert Ramsay   } Knights
- Thomas Faulde
- Norman Leslie
  Alexander Lindesay.

There were others present whose names are omitted by *Fordun.*

From this list one may form a tolerable conjecture as to the persons who, at that time, enjoyed the chief confidence of the King. Those marked with an asterisk, appear to have been employed in the secret negotiations with England.

DAVID II.

1363.

I. In default of the King of Scots, and his issue-male *, the King of England, for the time being, to succeed to the kingdom of Scotland.

II. If this was agreed to, then the town, castle, and territory of Berwick, to be forthwith delivered to the Scots.

III. As also the castles of Rokesburgh, Jedburgh, and Lochmaben, with their respective territories.

IV. And also, in general, all lands occupied by the King of England, or those under his government, in which the late King Robert was vested and seized at the time of his decease.

V. The whole ransom-money doe by the Scots to be discharged, their obligations for payment cancelled, and the hostages set at liberty.

VI. The King of England to make satisfaction to the Earl of Athole, the Lords Beaumont, Percy, and Ferrars; to the heirs of Sir Richard Talbot, and to all who claim lands in Scotland, whether by the gift or grant of the King of Scotland, since he became a prisoner, or otherways, so that the present possessors may enjoy such lands without any manner of challenge against them, or their heirs.

VII. The King of Scotland to be put in possession of the greatest part of the lands and rents which his ancestors held in England, and to have an equivalent, in a suitable place, for the remainder; he performing service to the King of England for such lands only.

VIII. The name and title of *kingdom of Scotland*, to be preserved with due honour, and proper distinctions, no union or annexation being made with England; and the King to be styled, in all public instruments, and others, *the King of England and of Scotland*.

IX.

---

* The original bears, ' sans heir engendre de son corps.' But the expression at the end of this conference, ' heir masle engendre son corps,' shews, that issue male was understood.

1363.

IX. The King, after having been crowned King of England, to come regularly to the kingdom of Scotland, and to be crowned King at Scone, in the royal chair, which is to be delivered up by the English: The ceremony of the coronation to be performed by persons whom the court of Rome shall depute for that purpose.

X. Every parliament concerning the affairs of the kingdom of Scotland, to be held either at Scone, or in some other place within that kingdom.

XI. The King, at his coronation, to make oath, that he will maintain the freedom of the holy church of Scotland, so that it shall not be subjected to any Archbishop, nor to any one else, saving the Papal see.

XII. Also, to make oath, that he will maintain the laws, statutes, and usages, of the kingdom of Scotland, established under its former Kings.

XIII. Also, to make oath, that he will, in no sort, summon the people of Scotland, or force them to appear in any court, unless within the kingdom, according to their own laws and usages.

XIV. Also, to make oath, that he will never consent that the Bishopricks, ecclesiastical dignities, or other benefices of the holy church of Scotland, be conferred on any except natives.

XV. The Chancellor, Chamberlain, and Justiciary, the sheriffs, provosts, bailies, governors of towns and castles, and other officers, to be natives of the kingdom of Scotland only.

XVI. The Prelates, Earls, and Barons, and other freeholders, whether antient or new, in the kingdom of Scotland, to be fully maintained in their privileges, lands, revenues, and offices, according to their infeftments and their possession.

XVII. The Earl of Douglas to be restored to the estates in England to which his father and uncle had right, or to receive an equivalent in a suitable place.

XVIII.

1363.

XVIII. No grants to be revoked which have been made by the present King of Scotland, or any of his predecessors.

XIX. The merchants of Scotland to use their liberties in merchandizing, and not to be obliged to go to Calais, [then the staple town for the sale of wool] or elsewhere; and to pay to the general customs, only half a mark for each sack of wool [*].

XX. The English King to make oath never to alienate the kingdom of Scotland, or to make over any part of it to be held of the King of England, or any one else, but to preserve the kingdom free and entire, as in the days of King Robert.

XXI. His only counsellors, as to Scottish affairs, to be Peers, and Lords of Scotland.

XXII.

---

[*] ' Que les marchans d'Escose useroient leur franchises de marchander, et qu'ils ne ' seroient constrainz a aler a Cales, ne ailleurs, fors a leur voloir, et qu'ils ne paient ' fors demi mare du sac de laine a la grant coustume ;' *Fœdera,* T. vi. p. 427. Not being perfectly certain as to the meaning of this article, I have added the words as they stand in the original, leaving my readers to judge for themselves. *Abercrombie,* v. ii. p. 131. has given a translation of this article, which I imagine to be erroneous: It runs thus, ' That the merchants of Scotland should have full liberty of commerce and trade ' with the English, and that they should not be obliged to go any where, not even to ' Calais, the then staple port for English wool, which was their grand, and, perhaps, ' only commodity, but might purchase wool in England itself, upon paying but half ' a mark custom for the sack of it.' He adds, in his commentary, ' the Scots are in-' vited to share in the commerce and wealth of flourishing and triumphant England.' The expression ' useroient leur franchises de marchander,' seems to imply no more than that the Scottish dealers, as well in buying as in selling, should have their former privileges referred to them. They might have full liberty of commerce and trade with the English ; but this could only mean in such a way as was consistent with the system of commerce established in England. If the Scots were to have full liberty to purchase, the English would have had full liberty to sell ; and *this* would at once have annihilated the favourite institution of Staple. Hence I incline to conclude, that the mention of a duty of half a mark Sterling on the sack of wool, respects what was to be paid as a duty on Scottish wool, not what was to be paid on the purchase of English wool. The difference is exceedingly material.

1363.

XXII. To impose no taxes whatever, others, or otherwise, than what were wont to be imposed in the days of the former Kings of Scotland.

XXIII. The people of Scotland not to be called out to military service, otherwise than of old. After the term of forty days, during which they are bound to serve on their own charges, to receive pay according to the rank of the persons who serve, and the nature and extent of the service.

XXIV. The abbeys, and other religious houses of both kingdoms, to be reciprocally restored to their lands, revenues, and benefices.

XXV. Indemnity to all who, after fealty performed to the English King, have revolted.

XXVI. The treaty founded on this conference, to be read in presence of the people and the King, whenever he is crowned, and the King to make oath for observing all its conditions.

XXVII. The King of England to advise with his council, as to granting and confirming whatever other points, conditions, and articles, shall be demanded by the three estates * of Scotland, for the general good of the kingdom, and for the more firm establishment of lasting tranquillity †.

XXVIII.

* ' Les trois communaltes ;' *Foedera*, T. vi. p. 427.

† *Abercrombie*, V. ii. p. 132. thus translates the xxvii. article: ' That the King of ' England was willing to grant, by the advice of his council, whatever else the three ' communities of the kingdom of Scotland should ask for their farther security and ' satisfaction.' But ' se voudra aviser à granter,' is far short of such a meaning. In truth, the article is merely illusory. It only implies that Edward III. would grant any other conditions that might be agreeable to himself. By mentioning *the advice of his council*, he provided against the odium of refusing his assent to any equitable modifications of the treaty.

Vol. II.   K k

1363.

XXVIII. The King of Scots to found the inclinations of his people as to the subject of this conference, and to inform the English King, and his council, of the result, fifteen days after Easter next.

The two Kings having retired from the conference, their counsellors discoursed on the perplexing question of 'a recompense to be made for the castles and territories, which it was proposed to yield up to the Scots, in case the treaty should be frustrated by the King of Scots leaving issue-male.' What expedients were suggested on either side is unknown.

Happily for David Bruce, the secret of this conference was faithfully kept *. Had it been disclosed, the proposals, however cautiously expressed, would have raised a general alarm in the Scottish nation, and have proved the cause of a more formidable insurrection than that which had been lately quelled. It is probable that David, on his return to Scotland, was soon made sensible of the extravagance and impracticability of the plan digested in the conferences at Westminster.

It was, indeed, a plan equally extravagant and impracticable. It did not tend to establish the internal tranquillity, increase the importance, or secure any valuable interests of the nation; neither do the Scots appear to have stipulated advantages of moment with respect to their commerce.

According to the plan proposed, the King of England was to become the Sovereign of the Scots; and thus the line of regal succession, acknowledged in the reign of Robert Bruce, was to be broken, all the descendants of his daughter Marjory disinherited, and even the daughters of David Bruce, and all the descendants of those daughters, excluded from the throne.

No

---

* To the best of my recollection, this conference was not known till after the union of the two kingdoms, when Mr Rymer published it in the sixth volume of Fœdera Angliæ.

1363.

No national benefit * accrued from a treaty so humiliating, and of such obvious injustice, other than a discharge of the sums still due for the ransom of the King of Scots.

The only visible motives which could have induced the King of Scots to ratify such articles, are, the jealousy which he might have conceived of the Stewart, as a person who was more respected in Scotland than himself, and the impatient desire of securing his own liberty. It will be remembered, that he had come under the most solemn engagements to return to his prison, if the ransom was with-held; and he might possibly have discerned, that his subjects were either unable, or unwilling, to make regular payments of a sum so exorbitant.

As he had no children, the exclusion of his own daughters was a very distant contingency. And, if resentment, and the love of ease, were his motives, every distant contingency would be disregarded †.

About this time it was that the King of Scots married Margaret Logie, a woman of singular beauty ‡. This unequal alliance proved unhappy.

Ford. xiv. 28. Scala Chron. ap. Leland. L 379.

The

---

* I say, ' no other national benefit,' for it is evident from the difficulty suggested at the end of the conference, that the English would never have surrendered Berwick, &c. until the King of England had become possessed of his new kingdom. The reader will remark, in the minute of the conference at Westminster, an affected repetition of the phrase, *the kingdom of Scotland.* Perhaps the Scottish negotiators imagined, that the phrase was sufficient to secure the independence of their country. But the clause concerning military service, would of itself have had the consequence of rendering the Scottish nation dependent, and of exhausting all her force in the warlike enterprises of an English Sovereign.

† I formerly imagined, that the proposal made by David II. to his parliament was in consequence of the negotiations at Westminster in November 1363. But the dates are so distinctly marked in Fordun, and the argument from the nature of the obligation granted by the Stewart, in May 1363, is so cogent, that I do not see how that hypothesis can be supported.

‡ In one MS. of Fordun she is called *the daughter,* and in another *the widow* of John

1363.

Fœd. vi. 435. The King of Scots made another visit to England. [February 1363-4.] under pretence of performing his devotions at the shrine of the Virgin at Walsingham *.

1364.

The history of Scotland, from the year 1363 to the end of the reign of David II. affords few interesting occurrences; and even these are, in general, imperfectly related.

Knyghton, 1627. John King of France died, [at London 8th April.] He was succeeded by his son *Charles*.

1365.

At first, the annual payments of the ransom settled for the king of Scots, had been made with tolerable regularity †; but, for some years past,

---

John Logie. In the MS. of Fordun, which Hearne used in his edition, she is called ' magna domina, bonestis ac nobilioribus orta natalibus.' *Boece*, L. xv. fol. 327. 2. says, that her father was *Sir John Logie*. In *Fœdera*, T. vi. p. 576. there is a passport to ' Johannes de Logy de Scotia, cum xii equitibus,' [26th October 1367.] He her parentage what it will, all writers agree that she was exceedingly beautiful. The author of *Scala Chron*. ap. Leland, T. i. p. 579. says, ' the King of Scottes took to wife, ' by force of love, one Margaret de Logy.' Fordun, or rather his interpolator, on mention being made of Margaret Logie, runs out into an extravagant digression concerning bad wives; L. xiv. c. 28.—32. There are some passages in that digression capable of forcing a smile from the severest readers.

* At the same time, Margaret, his consort, obtained a passport to visit the shrine of Thomas à Becket, *Fœdera*, T. vi. p. 435. The King of Scots visited England almost every year. See *Fœdera*, T. vi. p. 451. 463. 497. 582. 613. 651. He had generally a numerous retinue. In January 1368-9, there were 100 horsemen in his train, and 60 in the train of his consort; *Fœdera*, T. vi. p. 582. Such frequent journies, undertaken in so great state, must have been exceedingly expensive. They were not fit to be undertaken by David Bruce, who ought to have studied, by frugality, to ease his affectionate and loyal subjects of the burden of his ransom.

† The following payments were made: 1358, 24th June, 10000 marks; *Fœdera*, T. vi. p. 92. 1359, 30th October, 3000 marks; *Fœdera*, T. vi. p. 141. 1359, 2d December, 2500 marks; *Fœdera*, T. vi. p. 151. Date uncertain, 4500 m; tho; *Fœdera*, T. vi. p. 197. 1360, 24th June, 10000 marks; *Fœdera*, T. vi. p. 202. In all 30000 marks.

DAVID II.

1365.

paft, they had ceafed. Probably the negotiations for a furrender of Scotland had made the Englifh King lefs importunate, and the Scottifh lefs attentive as to the ranfom; but the negotiations being now at an end, Edward demanded the arrears and the penal fums incurred through failure in payment.

This produced a new treaty, by which the King of Scots obliged himfelf to pay one hundred thoufand pounds Sterling *, at the rate of 6000 marks annually, on the 2d of February, until the whole fhould be cleared. The truce between the two nations was prolonged to the 2d of February 1370-1, [12th and 20th June 1365.]

Fœd. vi. 488

1367.

About this time, committees of parliament, with parliamentary powers, were introduced, under the pretence of general conveniency. From them the inftitution of *The Lords of the Articles* appears to have had its origin †.

Pitmedden, MS. Collections.

The

---

* It is probable, however, that this was of the nature of a penal fum, and that, if the King of Scots faithfully obferved the treaty on his part, the fum was to be reftricted to 80000 marks. Certain it is, that the method of accompting which enfued was on fuch principles. There is fome obfcurity in the tranfaction, owing to this, that *all* the mutual obligations between the two Kings have not been publifhed in *Fœdera*. In *Calendars of Antient Charters*, p. 226. 39000 Edward III. there is this title, *de quibufdam conditionibus contentis in treugis*. This is, probably, the inftrument wanting.

† ' A. D. 1367. ' Apud Sconam convocatis tribus communitatibus regni congre-
' gatis ibidem, certae perfonae electi fuerunt per eafdem ad parliamentum tenendum,
' data aliis *caufa autumni* licentiâ ad propria redeundi; quidam ex parte cleri, quidam
' ex parte baronum, quidam ex parte burgenfium, electi funt.
' Parliamentum apud Perth, 6. March 1368, cum fuper certis punctis praefens par-
' liamentum fuerit ordinatum teneri, electi fuerunt certae perfonae ad ipfum parlia-
' mentum tenendum, datâ licentiâ aliis recedendi.
' Parliamentum

DAVID II.

1369

Fœd. vi. 638. The truce between the two nations was prolonged for the farther space of fourteen years, and it was agreed that the residue of the ransom-money should be cleared by annual payments of 4000 marks [a], [20th July.]

Stat.DavidII. 18. In this year an act of parliament was made of the following tenor: 'No justiciary, sheriff, or other officer of the King shall execute any order, whether under the great-seal, privy-seal, or signet, if such order be against law; but, whenever it is presented to him, he shall indorse it, [or note it,] and in that form return it †;' (at Scone, 18th February 1369-70.

An

---

[a] Parliamentum apud Perth, 18. Feb. 1369, anno regni Davidis 40. Quum fuerit inexpediens quòd universalis communitas ad deliberationem intenderet seu expectaret, electi fuerunt quidam, ad generalem et unanimem consensum et assensum trium communitatum congregatarum, ad ea quae concernunt communem justitiam, judicia contradictoria et querelas alias, quae per parliamentum debeant determinari, discutienda, et alii *per eos communes et alias communitates* [Qu] electi ad tractandum et deliberandum super certis et specialibus ac secretis regni et regis Davidis negotiis, antequam veniant ad notitiam dicti concilii generalis, et quòd judicia contradictoria proponentur praeultimo die parliamenti vocatis partibus et facta de premissis relatione solenni sententialiter sit pronunciatum, secundum leges et consuetudines regni.'

[b] While the annual payments of the ransom were made at the rate of 6000 marks, according to the second treaty, there were paid the following sums: 1366-7, 2d February, 6000 marks; *Fœdera,* T. vi. p. 493. 1367-8, 2d February, 6000 marks; *Fœdera,* T. vi. p. 550. 1368-9, 2d February, 6000 marks; *Fœdera,* T. vi. p. 585. 1369-70, 2d February, 6000 marks; *Fœdera,* T. vi. p. 601. In all 24000 marks.

The King of Scots, in the third treaty, says, that 56000 marks were still due. 24000 marks added to that sum make up the 80000 marks, which I understand to have been exigible, according to the second treaty.

The 56000 marks were at length completely paid, and a discharge in full was granted by Richard II. in the 7th year of his reign, [1st December 1383.] *Fœdera,* T. vii. p. 417. For an account of the various payments, the reader may consult *Fœdera,* T. vi. p. 648. 689. 734. T. vii. p. 26. 40. 68. 113. 152. 208. 271. 417.

† ' Nullus justiciarius, vicecomes, aut aliquis alius minister Regis, faciet executionem

1369.

An act also was made revoking all late grants by which any persons were exempted from bearing their share in public burdens, and in the services due to the King [*]. *Chart. Moray. L. 80.*

The King of Scots, yielding to the suggestions of his consort, imprisoned the Stewart and his three sons, John, Robert, and Alexander. This imprisonment of *the heir presumptive* and his children is a singular event in a reign full of strange incidents, and yet it is mentioned by one historian alone [†]. *Ford. xiv. 34.*

1370.

The power of Margaret Logie over the uxorious but fickle monarch was of short endurance. Disgusts and bitter animosities arose between the King and his consort. He applied to the Scottish bishops and obtained a divorce [‡]. Margaret Logie escaped from Scotland, and found means *Ford. xiv. 34.*

---

[*] 'nemo alicujus mandati sibi directi, sub quocunque sigillo, magno, secreto, vel parvo, feu signeto in praejudicium juris. Sed, si quid tale fuerit praesentatum, indorset et indorsatum remittat ;' *Stat. David II. c. 18.* The date is added from a MS. in my possession.

[*] 'Statutum est a Rege David, ex deliberatione parliamenti, communi utilitate pensata, quod omnes libertates de novo concessae generaliter revocentur, sic scilicet quod ad servicia Domini Regis contribuant, conserviant, et opera subeant cum vicinis ;' *Chart. Murav.* Vol. i. fol. 80. Much might be learned from an accurate edition of the whole statutes of David II.

[†] 'Ad cujus suggestionem Rex nepotem suum Robertum Stewart, cum tribus filiis Johannem, Robertum, et Alexandrum, arrestavit, et in diversis munitionibus ad custodiendum deputavit ;' *Fordun,* L. xiv. c. 34.

[‡] *Fordun,* L. xiv. c. 34. says, ' circa festum carnisprivii, an. 1369.' In 1368-9, lent commenced in the third week of February. Fordun mistakes, if he means to place the divorce about the beginning of lent 1368-9. For it appears from *Fœdera,* T. vi. p. 582. that David, and his consort, obtained a passport to visit England in January 1368-9; and it is not probable, that, in the very next month, he procured a divorce from her. Fordun, therefore, must have meant to place the divorce in 1369-70. It is remarkable, that, in *Fœdera, T.* vi. p. 613. there is a passport, 10th March 1369-70, for David to visit England, in which no mention is made of his consort.

1370.

means to present herself to the court at Avignon. She appealed to Pope Urban V. from the sentence of the Scottish Bishops. The cause was warmly agitated, and depended long; the issue is not certainly known; but, as Fordun remarks that the Pope threatened to lay the kingdom of Scotland under an interdict, it is probable that the proceedings of the Scottish Bishops were judged to be irregular *.

On

---

* Fordun, who had seen a copy of the proceedings, is silent as to the grounds of the sentence pronounced by the Scottish Bishops; and, as to the reasons of appeal, he says, ' Liber Inde confectus, et notariorum signis signatus, praecellit in scriptura, judicio ' meo qui processum vidi et haec scripsi, continentiam literaturae quatuor psalterio-' rum;' L. xiv. c. 34. But, although he is so ridiculously accurate in recording the *size* of the writings, he says not a word of their *contents*. John Major, L. v. c. 23. honestly confesses that he was unacquainted with the merits of the cause. Boece, not inclining to be ignorant of any thing, observes, L. xv. fol. 327. a. that the King of Scots was reported to have married Margaret Logie, rather on account ' of her beauty, ' than with the wish of having children by her: That he repudiated her when she ' had entered into her twenty-fifth year, and he had no hopes of children by her. ' [Magis, ut j. Œlabator, specie captus, quàm quòd *sobolem* ex ea *ruperet*. Eam autem ' annum egressam vicesimum quartum, quum *nullam ex ea prolem speraret*, repudia-' vit.'] This is a singular story indeed! The King married without wishing for children, and repudiated his wife because he despaired of having children by her. And the reason of his despair was, that she had entered her twenty-fifth year! Belleaden, B. xv. fol. 231. a. perceiving, probably, that this story was absurd, has substituted another in its room, which, from its tenor, has the appearance of a popular tradition: ' He mariit ane lusty woman, namet Margaret Logy, and, within *thri* ' *monethis* after, he repentit, and was so sorowful, that he had degradit his blud ryal ' with sic obscure lynnage, that he banist hir, and all otheris that gave hym counsall ' thairto, out of his realme. At last this lady past, with ane certane hir freindis, to ' Avinion, quhaire the Paip held his seit for the tyme, and was so favorit, that scho ' gat finalie an sentence aganis King David, to annexe to hir as his lawchfull lady and ' wyffe. Thus suld the realme have cumyn under interdiction and gret truble, war ' nocht scho desissit be the way returnand hame.'

Much of this ill-told, and confused story, may be corrected from record. Margaret Logie was living with the King of Scots, and acknowledged as his wife, from 14th January

1370.

On the disgrace of Margaret Logie, the Stewart and his three sons *Fœd. xiv. 34.* were released from their prison, and re-instated in the favour of the King.

David II. died, [22d February 1370-1, in the castle of Edinburgh,] *Fœd. xiv. 34.* in

nuary 1365-6, to 4th January 1368-9; *Fœdera,* T. vi. p. 484. 497. 582. So that, instead of banishing her in *three months,* he lived with her *three years,* and, probably, for a longer space. The time of her death is uncertain; but we know that the survived her husband. She was at Avignon on the 23d June 1372. She is then styled ' egregia Domina, Domina Margareta, Regina Scotiae, uxor quondam Domini Da-' vidis Regis Scotiae illustris, jam defuncti ;' *Fœdera,* T. vi. p. 727. She obtained a passport from Edward III. 24th March 1373-4; *Fœdera,* T. vii. p. 35. Hence we may certainly conclude, that it was not her death which relieved Scotland from the apprehension of a Papal interdict. Fordun, it is true, says something like this; ' fi in-' pervixisset' But, to reconcile his expression with the truth of history, we must suppose that *Rex,* or *Papa,* is to be understood; that is, David Bruce, or Pope Urban V.

A worthy friend of mine, while at Rome in 1770, took the trouble of inquiring whether the proceedings on the appeal of David II. were to be found in the Papal archives. The *Abbate Corquelini,* the learned and industrious editor of the *Magnum Bullarium Romanum,* engaged in this search. It was laborious, and proved unsuccessful. I cannot express this so well as in his own words. After having mentioned his searches in the Vatican library, and elsewhere, he says, ' confugiendum fuit ad secre-' tius archivium Vaticanum, in quo regesta integra bullarum, brevium, ac literarum ' Pontificum Avenionensium asservari explorarum est, Romam a Cardinali Ursinio ' duobus abhinc sœculis adportata. Elias Baldius, Graecae Latinaeque linguae scriptor ' in laudata bibliotheca, et Johannes Marinius secretioris Vaticani scrinii pro-custos, ' pro sui fide asserentos, codices se singulos bibliothecae et archivii non regesta mole, ' sed schedas quoque quam diligentissime, nec sine magno dierum quinque impendio, ' perlustrasse, nullamque actae a Davide Rege, causae aut interpositae appellationis ' schedam vel indicium adinvenisse.' If, by any accident, this work should fall within the knowledge of the *Abbate Corquelini,* and his associates, they are requested to accept of my sincere thanks. I lament, that, when I wished to have the inquiry made, the precise date of the proceedings was not known to me. That would have greatly abridged the trouble of such a search. The proceedings must have been in 1370, or in the beginning of 1371, about the latter end of the Pontificate of Urban V.

VOL. II. L l

1370.

in the 47th year of his age, and the 42d of his reign. He was buried in the church of the abbey of Holyrood, before the great altar.

He was succeeded by his nephew ROBERT, the Stewart of Scotland.

When we acknowledge David II. to have been courteous and affable, and possessed of personal intrepidity, we complete the catalogue of his praise-worthy qualities *. But the defects in his character were many, and all of them were prejudicial to the public; he was weak and capricious, violent in his resentments, and habitually under the dominion of women.

The Scottish nation had an amiable partiality for the only son of their great deliverer, and his misfortunes excited universal pity. Hence it is, that the historians of our country are studious to draw a veil over the faults of David II. †.

Nevertheless, while we pity the early exile, and unfortunate valour, and tedious captivity of the only son of Robert Bruce, we ought not to forget, that he degenerated from the magnanimity of his father, and that, through the allurements of present ease, or through motives of base jealousy, he was willing to surrender the honour, security, and independence of that people whom God and the laws had entrusted to his protection.

MISCEL-

* *Fordun*, L. xiv. c. 34. says, that David II. by his policy, suppressed the robbers in the mountainous country of Scotland, and in the isles: That he set them against each other, rewarded those who destroyed their adversaries, and thus, insensibly, extirpated the disturbers of the public peace. It was a cruel policy, if indeed used. But it is probable, that, in this account, there is much exaggeration. For the remote parts of Scotland remained as uncivilized and disorderly after the reign of David II. as in elder times.

† It must, however, be admitted, that our historians were ignorant of the conferences at Westminster in November 1363. Fordun imagined, that the proposal made by the King to his parliament in the beginning of that year, was in consequence of a promise extorted from him during his captivity; L. xiv. c. 24. This good natured hypothesis, founded on an imperfect knowledge of facts, has been adopted by later historians, who had opportunities of being better informed.

MISCELLANEOUS

OCCURRENCES.

1306.

WILLIAM of Lambyrton Bishop of St Andrews, while a *Fordū.* 1015. prisoner in England, had a daily allowance for himself of six pence, of three pence for his serving man, of three half-pence for his foot-boy, and of three half-pence for his chaplain.

Elisabeth, the consort of Robert Bruce, while a prisoner in England, *Fordū.* 1013. had servants appointed to attend her, and particularly, ' a foot-boy ' for her chamber, sober, and not riotous, to make her bed *.'

1308.

John Duns Scotus †, called *doctor subtilis*, died; a person excessively admired by his contemporaries. He taught what, in those days, was
called

---

* ' Eit ele un garzon a péz, por demorer en sa chambre, tiel qui soit sobre, et ne un ' riotous, por son lit faire.'

† ' Descended from the family of *The Dunses* in the Merse;' *M'Kenzie*, Lives of Scots writers, Vol. i. p. 315. But *Camden*, Britannia, p. 861. says, that he was a native of Northumberland; because a note subjoined to a manuscript copy of the works of John Duns, in the library of Merton college, Oxford, has these words: ' Explicit ' lectura subtilis doctoris in universitate Oxoniensi, super libros sententiarum, Doc' toris Johannis Duns, nati in villa de *Emilden* vocata *Dunstan*, contracta *Duns*, in ' comitatu Northumbriae, pertinens ad domum scholasticorum de *Mertenhall* in Oxo' nio, ex quondam dictae domus socii.' This testimony is not sufficient to confute the
received

1308.

called *philosophy* and *theology*, at Oxford, Paris, and Cologne. It is reported that, at Oxford, thirty thousand pupils attended his lectures [*].

So received opinion: For, in its utmost latitude, it only implies, that an unknown, and illiterate transcriber of the works of John Duns, chose to make him a native of Emilden in Northumberland, called *Dunstan*, and, by a fanciful abbreviation, *Duns*. There was a more antient *Johannes Scotus*, distinguished by the appellation of *Erigena*, who flourished in the days of the Emperor Charlemagne. The Scots have laid claim to him also as their countryman; but upon less probable grounds. They translate *Erigena*, 'a native of the town of Air;' but, in order to justify this translation, they must suppose, that the town of Air existed in the days of Charlemagne! The obvious translation of *Erigena* is, 'a native of Ireland.'

[*] Anthony à Wood, *Antiquitates Universitatis Oxoniensis*, p. 147-ed an. 1303, says, ' Huc denuo tempestate exundare coepit scholarium frequentia—Oppidanis Brevi regio Sept. aiz. dato, stricte praecipitur ut hospitiorum scholasticorum possessione properè excederent, maximè eum academici lecturas jam essent resumpturi. Quod regem vero induxit, ut mandatis suis exequendis sedulò magis attenderet, erat Scotorum frequentia, quos Oxonii commorari jusserat; Malè enim metuens, ne gentis illius optimates, et ingenua pubes, si alibi educarentur, rebus novis maximè studerent; post Scoticas suas expeditiones, captivorum quemque eruditioni deditum Oxonium deduxit.' This inundation of *Scottish students* was, in all likelyhood, the foundation of the pupils of *John Duns Scotus*, called *Scoti*, from their masters, or from the sect to which they belonged. That they were Scotsmen of fashion, (optimates et ingenua pubes,) is exceedingly improbable.

James Vitalis says of John Duns,

——————— ' omnibus sophistis

' Argutus magis, atque capriosus.'

Which may be thus translated : ' The chief of quibblers."

Jacobus Latomus, in one of his epigrams, says,

' Quaecunque humani sacrosacra jurisque sacrasi

' In dubiom veniunt cuncta, vocante bruto.

That is, ' All laws to canvass, human or divine,

' Of all to doubt, great *Scottish Duns*, was thine!

I have only to add, concerning this singular personage, that Lucas Wading published a part of the works of John Duns in ten volumes in folio, A. D. 1639; and that many treatises of his composition are still in MS.

MISCELLANEOUS OCCURRENCES. 269

1310.

So great famine in Scotland, that many persons fed on horse-flesh. *Ford. xii. 10.*

1312.

Hugh Harding, an Englishman, challenged William de Seintlowe, a Scotsman, for bearing the coat armorial of Harding. To decide the controversy, they fought at Perth. William de Seintlowe was vanquished, and resigned the coat armorial, and the honour of the combat, to Hugh Harding, by open confession, in presence of Robert Bruce. The King, sitting on his throne, adjudged the coat armorial to Harding [a]. *E. Biss. in N. L'pronom, de andio militia. ri. Notæ 34.*

Five-

[a] ' Robertus, Dei gratia, Rex Scotiæ, omnibus ad quos praesentes literae pervenerint, salutem. Cum nos accepimus duellum apud nostram villam de Perthe, die confectionis praesentium, inter Hugonem Harding Anglicum, appellantem, de armis de Goules, tribus leporariis de auro colloree de B. et Willielmum de Seint'owe, Scotum appellatum, eisdem armis sine differentia inductum. Quo quidem duello percusso, praedictus Willielmus se finaliter reddidit devictum, et praedicto Hugoni remisit ac relaxavit, et omnino de se et haeredibus suis in perpetuum praedicta arma, cum toto triumpho, honore, et victoria, ore tenus in indicatio nostra. Quare, nos in folio nostro tribunali regali (undi) patris, cum magnatibus et dominio regni nostri personaliter sedentes, adjudicavimus et finaliter decretum dedimus, per praesentes, quòd praedictus Hugo Harding et haeredes sui, de cætero in perpetuum habeant et teneant, gaudeant et portent, praedicta arma integraliter, ab'que calumnia, perturbatione, contradictione, reclamatione, praedicti Willielmi seu haeredum suorum: In cujus rei testimonium, has literas nostras fieri fecimus patentes, apud dictam villam nostram de Perthe, secundo die Aprilis, anno regni nostri septimo, annoque Domini 1312.'

' Diploma hoc, genere et studiis nobilissimi Sampsonii Erdefwick, de quo vide Camdenum, adversariis debemus,' *E. Biss*, in N. U'pronum de studio militari notae, p 34. *Colloree de B:* is obscure; perhaps it may signify, that the greyhounds had blue collars. In plain language, the coat armorial was, ' three gold or yellow greyhounds, ' with [blue] collars, on a red field.' Harding won it, and, by the decree of the King of Scots, wore it. This certificate is singular in its style; I do not affirm it to be authentic, not having seen the original writing. Qu. Was this *Hugh* related to *John Harding* the forger?

1314.

Chart. Abrd.
ii. 12.
Five shillings supposed to be the value of a cow, and six shillings and eight pence, the value of an ox [*].

1327.

Barbour, 411.
Fire-arms were first employed by the English in their wars with Scotland. Barbour calls them 'crakys of war.'

Froissart, l. 18.
Froissart thus describes the manner of living of the Scots during their military expeditions. 'Their Knights and Esquires are well
' mounted on great coursers; the common sort, and the country people
' ride little horses. They take no carriages with them, by reason of
' the unevenness of the ground among the hills of Northumberland,
' through which their road lies, neither do they make provision of
' bread or wine; for, such is their abstemiousness, that, in war, they
' are wont, for a considerable space of time, contentedly to eat flesh half
' dressed, without bread, and to drink river-water, without wine: Nei-
' ther have they any use for kettles and caldrons; for, after they have
' flead the cattle which they take, they have their own mode of dref-
Froissart, i. 19. ' sing them.' [This he elsewhere describes to be, by fixing the hide to
four stakes, making it in the shape of a caldron, placing fire below,
and so boiling the flesh.] 'They are sure of finding abundance of
' cattle in the country through which they mean to go, and therefore
' they make no farther provision. Every man carries about the saddle
' of

---

[*] 'Affedatio terrarum de Dunnethyn,' by Bernard Abbot of Aberbrothock, to David de Maxwell—' Et fi dictus David amerciatus fuerit in curia Domini Abbatis, ' pro propria querela dabit pro amerciamento, quoties acciderit, *quinque solidos* vel *unam* ' *vaccam.*' *Ch. Aberbr.* vol. ii. fol. 12. Bernard, the Abbot, became Bishop of Sodor in 1328. The delivery of *four oxen* by the Earls of Lenox, was commuted, in 1317, into a payment of *two marks of silver.* So that, at that time, it appears that the price of an ox was *six shillings and eight pence.* The deed containing this commutation is so cautiously conceived, that we may conclude the bargain to have been fair; *Chart. Aberbroth.* ibid.

MISCELLANEOUS OCCURRENCES.

1327.

' of his horse, a great flat plate, and he trusses behind him a wallet
' full of meal; the purpose of which is this; after a Scottish soldier
' has eaten flesh so long that he begins to loath it, he throws this plate
' into the fire, then moistens a little of his meal in water, and when
' the plate is once heated, he lays his paste upon it, and makes a little
' cake, which he eats to comfort his stomach. Hence we may see,
' that it is not strange, that the Scots should be able to make longer
' marches than other men *.'

1329.

Thefts had become so frequent in Scotland, that husbandmen were *Ford.* xiii. 18.
obliged to house their plough-shares every night. Randolph, Regent
in the minority of David II. ordered that all plough-shares should be
left in the fields, and, if stolen, that the county should refund their value. A certain husbandman hid his plough-share, and pretending that
it had been stolen, obtained its value † from the sheriff of the county.
The cheat happened to be discovered, and the husbandman was hanged for theft.

1335.

Edward III. made a grant of the estate of Edrington near Berwick. *Fœd.* iv. 670.
This

---

* Here is a minute and long description of the method of *baking bannocks on a girdle.*
Froissart says, ' chacun emporte entre la selle de son cheval et *le panea*, une grande
' piece plat ·.' Sauvage, the publisher of Froissart, *annot.* 39. confesses his ignorance
of the sense of the word *panea* at this place. It probably implies *crupper.* As to the
caldrons made of the hides of cattle, Sauvage says, *annot.* 41. ' J'ay entendu de ceux
' qui disent avoir veu chose semblable en Ecosse, que les Escotois, apres avoir écorché les
' grosses bestes, attachent les peaux, par les pieds, à quatre fourchettes droites, & ceux
' en terre : Tellement qu'au milieu d'icelles peaux, ainsi suspendues, se fait un fond ;
' dedans lequel ils mettent bouillir et cuire ce qu'ils veulent, sur feu moyen, et si
' bien temperé, que c'est tout s'il brule seulement le poil, qui est tourné vers lui.'

† Fordun says, that the iron work of the plough was estimated at two shillings.

1335.

This grant is remarkable; because it determines a controverted point in the hiſtory of the law of Scotland. It proves that, antiently, *ſalmon-fiſhings* and *mills* were extended, that is, valued, for aſcertaining the rate of public taxations *, &c.

Fœd. iv. 711. By a treaty of alliance between Edward Balliol and John Lord of the Iſles, it was ſpecially provided, that the Lord of the Iſles ſhould have right to ſtand Godfather to any heir of Balliol's body †.

1336.

Fœd. xiii. 51. Alan of Winton forcibly carried off the young heireſs of Seton. This produced a feud in Lothian, while ſome favoured the raviſher, and others ſought to bring him to puniſhment. Fordun ſays, that, on this occaſion, a hundred ploughs in Lothian were laid aſide from labour.

Fœd. xii. 43. Henry de Lancaſter †, commander of the Engliſh forces, invited

the

---

* " Quae quidem villa [de Aderyton] piſcaria [de Edermuth] et molendina [vil-
" lae de Berewico] ad centum et ſeptem libras, tres ſolidos, et ſeptem denarios, *tempore*
" *pacis*, per dilectum clericum noſtrum Thomam de Burgh, Camerarium noſtrum de
" Berewico ſuper Twedam, de mandato noſtro *extenduntur*,' *Fœdera*, T. iv. p. 670.
Here alſo there is a new ſenſe of the phraſe *tempore pacis*, not implying any antient valuation, but only the rate at which the ſubjects might be reaſonably eſtimated in times of public tranquility.

† " Praeterea praefatus Dominus Rex vult et concedit, quòd quacunque tempore
" habeat haeredem de corpore ſuo legitimè procreatum, quòd *compaternitas* ejuſdem
" haeredis praefato Johanni concedatur." In *Du Cange*, v. *Compaternitas*, it is ſaid,
" *Compaternitas*, cognatio ſpiritualis quae inter compatres intercedit. *Compérage* Gal-
" lis. P. Damiani, L. ii. Epiſt. 17. *duo quidam viri qui et amicitiae invicem fœdere, et*
" *compaternitatis neceſſitudine, tenebantur*. Tharœz-us Reg. Hung. c. 66. *apud quem*
" *aliquamdiu commoratus* compaternitatis *vinculo Regi ſociatur*, vid. c. 1. et 3. *de cog-*
" *natione ſpirituali*."

‡ *Fordun*, L. xiii. c. 43. calls him *Earl of Derby*; but he did not obtain that title until 19th March 1337; *Knyghton*, p. 2568. The tournament at Berwick is placed at

the

1336.

the Knight of Liddesdale to combat with him in the lists at Berwick. In the first course, the Knight of Liddesdale was wounded by the breaking of his own spear. This accident having interrupted the sport, Henry de Lancaster requested Alexander Ramsay to bring twenty gentlemen with him to encounter an equal number of English. The request was complied with; and the sports continued for three days. Two of the English combatants were killed on the field: Nor was the loss of their antagonists less considerable. The point of a spear pierced the brain of William de Ramsay. After having been shrieved, he expired in his armour. John Hay, an eminent person among the Scots, received a mortal wound. At this juncture, Patrick Graham happened to arrive from abroad. An English knight challenged him. 'Brother,' said Graham, *pleasantly*, 'Prepare for death, and confess yourself, and then you shall sup in Paradise.' *And so it fell out*, says Fordun; for Graham transfixed him with his spear, and left him dead on the field. This story is related, as much as possible, in the style of Fordun. He appears not to have felt any horror at a scene, where brave men, without either national animosity or personal cause of offence, lavished their lives in savage amusement.

1339.

A great famine in Scotland, the poorer sort fed on grass, and many were found dead in the fields. *Ford. xiii. 46.*

1340.

At the siege of Stirling, in this year, the Scots employed cannon. *Freissart l. 74.*

Ten

the only season in which it could have been celebrated—during the truce in summer 1336.

1345.

Chartulary Aberdeen, 73.

Ten marks Sterling settled as a stipend on the vicar of Aberdeen [*].

1346.

Ford. xiii. 51.

Alexander Bruce, Earl of Carrick, fell at Halidon in 1333. A person, assuming his name, appeared in Scotland. He said that he had been made prisoner in the battle; that he had concealed his quality for a long course of years; and, at length, under the feigned character of a citizen of Aberdeen, had procured himself to be ransomed. His tale, related with many circumstances, imposed on numbers, and particularly on the meaner sort. After having undergone several examinations at court, he made his escape into Carrick, his supposed inheritance; but he was apprehended, tried by a special commission, convicted as an impostor, and hanged, [at Air. July.] Fordun says, that, according to the report of some, the judicial procedure against this adventurer was not formal; and hence there were who still believed that he had right to the title which he assumed.

1347.

Ford. v. 517.

Edward Balliol, and many others, were engaged to serve the King of England. The daily pay of Balliol was sixteen shillings; of a Banneret, four shillings; of a Knight, two shillings; of an Esquire, one shilling; and of an archer on horseback, fourpence. The Earl of Angus, [Umfraville,] and the other chief commanders, had the daily pay of eight shillings. Twenty-eight days were reckoned to the month, and ninety days to the quarter.

David

---

[*] In 1392, four marks were added to a prebend of six marks *per annum*, 'Quòd 'modernis temporibus sex marcae non sufficiunt annuatim ad sustentationem congru- 'am capellani.' It is added, 'qui prebendarius sibi de habitu quoties indigebit tene- 'bitur providere;' *Chart. Aberdeen,* fol. 108.

MISCELLANEOUS OCCURRENCES.

1349.

David II. while a prisoner, appeared in a tournament at Windsor, [23d April.] The harness of his horse was of blue velvet, 'with a pale 'of red velvet, and beneath, a white rose, embroidered thereon.' This is the earliest mention of *the Scottish white rose*, which, in process of time, became a party-badge. It appears to have had no connection whatever with the York rose, and to have been more antient than it.

Ashmole, History of the Garter, ii. 185.

The great pestilence reached Scotland. It proved mortal in forty-eight hours. The bodies of persons seized with the distemper swelled exceedingly. This pestilence was particularly fatal to the poorer sort.

Ford. xiv. 7.

1350.

A perpetual annuity of eight marks Sterling, secured on land, was purchased for one hundred and twenty marks. This appears to have been a deliberate bargain [*].

Chart. Morav. I. 76.

1354.

William Heron accused John Wallace and William Prudholm as horse-stealers. They offered to justify themselves according to the law and customs of Scotland, by single combat, against Heron or any person whom he should delegate. Heron obtained permission from Edward III. to send two men into Scotland as his champions for proving the charge.

Ford. v. 808.

After

---

[*] 'Carta fundationis de uno capellano super firmam terrae de Moyn.' By Alexander de Meaneteys, Dominus de Lambrlde, [an English name, converted by degrees into *Menyes*, and, by a false reading, into *Menzies*.] He says, 'Cùm Johannes de Innernys, cancellarius ecclesiae Moravien. volens in eadem ecclesia unum capellanam fundare pro anima sua, tradidisset mihi in pecunia numerata centum et viginti marcas Sterl. ad comparandum sibi et assignatis suis in perpetuum annuum redditum octo marcarum Sterlingorum,' &c. *Chart. Morav.* Vol. i. fol. 76.

1355.

Ford. xiv. 9. After the action at Nifbet in Berwickſhire, a certain Frenchman, who ſerved in the armies of Scotland, purchaſed ſome Engliſh priſoners, and, having conveyed them to a retired place, beheaded them, in revenge for the death of his father, whom the Engliſh had ſlain. I do not recollect a like example of ſentimental barbarity in the hiſtory of latter ages.

Ford. v. 8cll. Edward III. had permitted Balliol to hunt in the foreſt of Inglewood. The foreſt laws were ſo rigorouſly maintained in thoſe times, that it became neceſſary to grant a formal indemnity to all men who had hunted in company with Balliol.

1356.

Ford. v. 870. There is another Inſtrument of a like nature, but ſtill more ſingular, which mentions, that Balliol had caught of fiſh in the ponds of the Lordſhip of Haitfield, in Yorkſhire,

	Feet.	Inches.
2 Pikes of	3	6
3 Pikes	3	0
20 Pikes	2	6
20 Pikes	2	0
50 Pikerels	1	6
6 Pikerels	1	0
6 Breams and bremels		
109 Perch, roach, tench, and ſkelys.		

1358.

Ford. xiv. 11. On Chriſtmas Eve, there happened an inundation in Lothian, great beyond example. The rivers, ſwollen by exceſſive rains, roſe above their banks, and ſwept away many bridges and houſes. Tall oaks, and other large trees, that grew on the banks, were undermined by the waters, and carried off to the ſea. The ſheaves of corn laid out

1358.

to dry in the adjacent fields were utterly loft *. The fyburb of Hadington, called *the Nungate*, was levelled to the ground. When the water approached the nunnery at Hadington, a certain nun fnatched up the ftatue of the Virgin, and threatened to throw it into the river, unlefs Mary protected her abbey from the inundation †. At that moment the river retired, and gradually fubfided within its antient limits. 'This nun,' fays Fordun, 'was a fimpleton, but devout, although not according to knowledge ‡.' If, however, fhe perceived any abatement of the inundation before fhe uttered her threats, fhe was not a fimpleton.

1361.

The peftilence again in Scotland, with the fame fymptoms as in 1349. *Ford. xiv. 24.*

1362.

One hundred fhillings provided to the vicar of Cloveth and Kildrummy. *Chart. Aberdeen, 9.*

1370.

Andrew Dempfter of Caraldfton became bound to the Abbot and abbey of Aberbrothock, that he, and his heirs, fhould furnifh a perfon, refiding within the territory of Aberbrothock, to adminifter juftice in the courts of the abbey. An annual falary of twenty fhillings Sterling was allowed to the judge thus furnifhed. The falary to be paid out of the iffues of the courts ‖. *Chart. Aberbr. l. 1.*

APPEN-

---

* Hence it appears that harveft was not got in on the 24th December 1358.

† At this day, the Portugueze failors, direct their favourite St Antonio in a like form.

‡ 'Simplicitate quadam latus, fed mente, quamvis non fecundùm fcientiam, devotus,' *Fordun*, L. xiv. c. 21.

‖ 'Facient ipfis defu viti de officio judicis in curiis eorum per unum hominem eorundem refidentem in fchira de Aberbroth, qui jurabit fpecialem fidelitatem ad diétum officium faciendum;' *Chart. Aberbroth.* Vol. i. fol. 1.

APPENDIX.

No. I.

OF THE MANNER OF THE DEATH

OF

MARJORY, DAUGHTER OF ROBERT I.

ANNALS Vol. II. pag. 65.

IT is an opinion generally received, that Marjory the daughter of Robert I. while big with child, was thrown from her horse, and killed between Paisley and the castle of Renfrew, [on Shrove Tuesday, 2d March 1315-6]; and that her child was brought into the world by the Caesarean operation.

Hist. of Ren- Crawfurd thus relates the story: 'At this place, in the lands of
frew fo. p. 41. ' Knox, there is a high cross standing, called *Queen Blearie's cross*;
' but no inscription is legible. Tradition hath handed down, that it
' was erected on this occasion. Marjory Bruce, daughter of the re-
' nowned Robert I. and wife of Walter, great Stewart of Scotland, at
' that time Lord of this country, being hunting at this place, was
' thrown from her horse, and, by the fall, suffered a dislocation of the
' *vertebrae* of her neck, and died on the spot. She being pregnant,
' fell in labour of King Robert II. The child or *foetus* was a *Caesar*.
' The operation being by an unskilful hand, his eye being touched by
' the instrument, could not be cured; from which he was called *King*
' *Blearie*.

'*Blearie*. This, according to our historians, fell out in the year
'1317.'
   Such is the tradition which Crawfurd relates in a strange and embarrassed style.
   I cannot discover the origin of this story. Fordun, the author of *Ford* iii. 25. Excerpta e Chronicis Scotiae, and John Major, relate the birth of Robert Stewart, afterwards King of Scotland by the name of Robert II.; but they mention nothing of extraordinary circumstances attending his birth.

   Barbour, who wrote in the reign of Robert II. and Winton, who wrote soon after the death of Robert III. are silent as to the events related by Crawfurd, and so also are Bellenden, Lesley, and Buchanan.

   Boece not only omits any mention of this story, but speaks in a *Boec*, 305. strain inconsistent with it. His words are, ' Mortua eisdem ferè tem-
' poribus Marjora, Roberti filia, relicto filio adhuc puero Roberto
' Stewart.'' If Boece had imagined that Marjory lost her life in this extraordinary manner, he never would have said, ' That she died
' leaving a son *yet a child*.'

   It is said, in confirmation of the vulgar tradition, that, by the unskilfulness of the surgeon who performed the Caesarean operation, the infant received a wound in the eye, and that hence Robert II. was styled *Blear-eye*.

   That Robert II. when advanced in years, had a remarkable inflamma- *Froiss.* ii. 169. tion in one of his eyes, is certain. Froissart, who visited his court, speaks thus: ' Robert King of Scotland had one eye turned up, [or tucked
' up,] and red; it seemed like *sanders wood* [*].'

   But surely this affords no presumption that Robert II. received a wound in his eye when he was entering into the world, or that the inflammation was occasioned by that accident. A man bred up in war

---

[*] The words of Froissart are corrupted; but their sense is sufficiently intelligible:
' Le roy Robert d'Escoce, *avec ung yeux rouges rebaffez* li Rebbloit de sandal.' In those times *rouge comme sandal* was a common phrase for *exceeding red*.

as he was, might have had his eye hurt without the unskilfulness of a surgeon.

The chief argument in favour of the popular tradition, arises from the circumstance of a cross, or pillar, having been erected on the spot where the Princess Marjory is supposed to have died. That pillar has been removed within the memory of man; and it was known in the beginning of this century by the name of *Queen Blearie's cross* [*].

Popular tradition is the most inaccurate of all histories. It records, in Angus, every particular of the last days of M'Beth; and it points out the very spot where the fabled Hays turned the chance of the imaginary battle of Luncarty. By tradition, Wallace has been degraded into a hero of romance, a giant, and a combater with spirits: And, indeed, he is scarcely known to the vulgar under any other character.

The capital, and obvious absurdity in the tradition of the cross of *Queen Blear-eye* is this, that Marjory, the wife of the Stewart of Scotland, is supposed to have received the appellation of *Queen*. Fifty-seven years had elapsed after her death before her son Robert succeeded to the crown. Now, even supposing her to have been called a *Queen*, because her son became a *King*, it still follows, that she could not possibly have received that appellation until fifty-seven years after her death; and that she could not have received it from any one who knew so much of history as that Robert Stewart succeeded to David Bruce.

Besides

---

[*] I am assured by persons eminently skilled in the Gaelic language, that there are two words in that language, pronounced *Cuiné Blair*, which literally signify *Memorial of Battle*. The difference of sound between *Cuiné Blair* and *Queen Blearie*, as pronounced by the vulgar, is less than generally occurs between the Gaelic and the Saxon pronunciation of the same words. It is certainly less than between *Ard Saül* and *Arthur's Seat*, *Dunpendir* and *Troprain*. Holding this etymology to be just, we might conclude, that the origin of the name of the pillar, or monument in question, is to be sought for in times much more ancient than those of Robert I.

Besides, why should Marjory Bruce be called *Blear-eye* because her son was wounded in the Caesarean operation?

It has been remarked by a learned friend, 'that the cross might 'originally have been called *King Blearie's mother's cross*; and that, 'in process of time, this might have been changed into *Queen Blea-* 'rie's cross*.' That change must have been pretty violent, which, in a sentence of four words, omitted *mother*, the chief word, and turned *King* into *Queen*. But still the observation holds good, that the name of *Queen Blear eye* could not have been given to *the Princess Marjory* until *fifty-seven years* after her death: And, indeed, there is reason to believe, that the name of *Blear-eye* was not given, even to her son, for many years after.

Our ancestors did not distinguish their sovereigns who bore one common name, by the appellation of *first, second, &c.* Thus, on the Scottish coins, we have the general title of *Alexander Rex*, and *Robertus Rex*, while antiquaries are obliged, from the size of the coin, the fineness of the metal, and other circumstances, to determine whether *Alexander* II. or III. *Robert* I. II. or III. ought to be understood.

While Robert II. reigned, there was no occasion for distinguishing him by any peculiar epithet. To call him *King*, or *Liege Lord*, was a sufficient description. Neither is it probable, that, after the accession of his son Robert III. Robert II. would have been distinguished from Robert I. otherwise than by the name of *Robert Stewart*, in opposition to the name of *Robert Bruce*. Thus we know, that David II. was called *David Bruce*, or *David Rex modernus*, to distinguish him from *David I.*

After the death of Robert III. a distinction between Robert II. and Robert III. became necessary. Although our ancestors did not use the distinction of *first, second*, or *third*, when speaking of Kings who had the same name, yet they used another distinction, which was no less intelligible.

Every one knows that the epithet given to Robert III. was *Faranyeir:* But the import of the word is not generally known. *Faren, faran,* is *gone* or *paſt,* as *farand* is *going* or *paſſing.* Thus, *farand man* was used with us for a *traveller.* And *way-fairing man* continues to be a phrase in the Engliſh language. We ſtill retain *auld farand,* literally, *an old traveller,* but figuratively, a *perſon ſharp* or *verſatile.* For, while there was little intercourſe among nations, he who had travelled into foreign countries was ſuppoſed to have acquired, by experience, a knowledge of mankind, and a ſuppleneſs of manners, not attainable by thoſe who had always continued at home. Of the like import is the French expreſſion *vieux routier.*

Thus *faranyeir* means of *the paſt year,* or *late;* and *Robert Faranyeir* is preciſely *the late King Robert.* Robert III. ſometimes received the appellation of *John Faranyeir,* becauſe his baptiſmal name was *John.* And thus he was diſtinguiſhed from *John Balliol,* or *John the firſt.*

Our anceſtors having thus diſtinguiſhed Robert III. from the two former Roberts, took a ſeparate method for diſtinguiſhing between Robert II. and him. They called Robert II. *Blear-eye,* from the inflammation in his eye. That circumſtance could not fail of being generally remembered by the nation; becauſe the interval between his death, and the death of his ſon Robert III. was of fifteen years only.

Hence, it is probable, that, as Robert III. could not receive the appellation of *Faranyeir* till after the acceſſion of James I. ſo Robert II. did not receive the appellation of *Blear-eye* before the ſame period, when it became neceſſary to diſtinguiſh between him and *the late King Robert.*

Should this deduction be held juſt, it will follow, that Marjory the daughter of Robert I. could not poſſibly have received the appellation of *Queen Blear-eye,* or *Blearie,* till after the death of her grandſon Robert III. that is, about *ninety* years after her own death; and *this,* of itſelf,

itself, must greatly invalidate the evidence arising from a tradition, to which so confident an appeal is made.

I do not by this admit that she was known by that name at the distance of ninety years after her death; for hitherto I have not seen any evidence that she was known by that name, till near four hundred years after her death.

Many other circumstances in the vulgar tale are exceedingly improbable. 1. The Princess Marjory is supposed to have been hunting on horse-back when the time of the delivery of her first child approached. 2. The day appointed for this extraordinary hunting-party was *Shrove Tuesday*. The Protestants of Paisley, in whose neighbourhood this story may be said to have originated, cannot discern the difference betwixt *Shrove Tuesday* and any other Tuesday; but if a Roman Catholic Princess, even in our free times, should be invited to a hunting-match on Shrove Tuesday, she would be shocked at the profane invitation. 3. It is a singular circumstance, that the Princess should have dislocated the *vertebrae* of her neck, and yet that there should have been time to perform so successfully the Caesarean operation on her child. 4. It is extraordinary, that there should have been at hand any person so capable of performing the operation, as not to hurt the child any farther than by a flesh-wound in the eye-lid, or on the ball of the eye.

Of late years, the circumstances of the story have been somewhat varied, and it has been reported, that the Princess Marjory was not riding on a hunting-party, but was riding to Mass, when she lost her life.

The person who made this improvement on the story, knew that *Shrove Tuesday* was a day kept holy by the Romish Church for the purposes of solemn confession.

Another

Another story is now told in the neighbourhood of *Queen Blearie's cross*. It is said, that there were disturbances in the country; that the Princess Marjory rode from Renfrew towards Paisley, with the purpose of taking refuge there; but that she was thrown from her horse, and died of the fall.

This edition of the story seems calculated to soften the improbabilities of the former traditions. It supposes that the Princess Marjory rode on horseback at a period so critical, from necessity, not choice.

Having made these observations on the popular story of *Queen-Blearie*, I leave it with my readers, to form the conclusion.

No. II.

No. II.

JOURNAL OF THE CAMPAIGN

OF

EDWARD III.

1327.

ANNALS, Vol. II. *pag.* 118.

THE old English historians are brief in their accounts of the mighty preparations made by Edward III. in 1327, for repelling and conquering the Scottish invaders, and of the unsuccessful events of that campaign.

Froissart has supplied this defect in English history. His account, although not altogether accurate, is particular and ample. Any one who reads it with attention must perceive, that Froissart procured his information from some officer of the cavalry of John de Hainault, who served under Edward III. in 1327. And, it will be seen hereafter, that there is such an exactness in dates as could scarcely have occurred, unless a military journal had been kept at the time by the person from whom Froissart procured his information. It must be confessed, that the relator had an imperfect notion of the country through

through which the army marched; and, there is reason to believe, that, in some circumstances, Froissart has misunderstood his meaning.

From Froissart's account, explained by two or three occasional passages in English historians, and from the dates of events ascertained in *Foedera Angliae*, a journal of this campaign may be drawn up with reasonable precision.

Froiss. l. i. 16.
Foed. iv. 295. 196.

10th July 1327, Edward III. marched from Yorke with his army in three divisions, or *battles*, in the language of that age. The King led the first division, or van, and lay that night at Topcliff *. The auxiliaries, consisting of heavy armed cavalry, commanded by John de Hainault, were in the first division, and encamped near the King †.

Froiss. l. 16.
Foed. iv. 295. 296.

11th and 12th, Halted at Topcliff until the second and third divisions came up ‡.

Froiss. l. 16.

13th, Decamped before day-break, and, by a forced march, arrived at Durham §.

14th,

---

* Froissart, Vol. i. p. 16. says, '*six lieues au dessus de la dite cité.*' [Yorke.] This nearly corresponds with the distance between Yorke and Burrough-bridge. But, as it appears from *Foedera*, T. iv. p. 295. 296. that the King halted at Topcliff, it is more natural to suppose that he proceeded to Topcliff on the first day, than that he halted there, no more than six miles from Burrough-bridge, on the second day's march. We cannot expect great precision, as to distances, from Froissart, or any other foreigner on whom he relied. Besides, the next march was very long, even supposing the army to have set out from Topcliff; and there is no occasion to make it longer.

† Not so much to shew honour to them, as to keep them at a distance from the English archers, with whom they had had a fatal quarrel while the army was quartered at Yorke.

‡ In *Foedera*, T. iv. p. 295. 296. there are three instruments by the King, all dated at Topcliff, 12th July 1327.

§ A march, nearly, of 50 miles. The King was at Northallerton on the 13th July; *Foedera*, T. iv. p. 296. But, if Froissart is not mistaken, he did not stop there. Were it not for the authority of Froissart, I would lay down the rout thus: 10th July, *Topcliff*. 11th and 12th, halted. 13th, *Northallerton*. 14th, *Durham*. This last might still be called a forced march, being longer than either of the preceding marches.

14th, 15th, 16th, and 17th, Remained at Durham, expecting intelligence of the motions of the enemy *.

18th, The English descried at a distance the smoke of the flames kindled by the Scots in the country which they wasted in their progress. The army marched from Durham in order of battle, the infantry ranged in three bodies, with the cavalry on the flanks. They proceeded towards that quarter from whence the smoke appeared to issue, came to their ground in the evening, and encamped at a wood near a little river.

19th, At break of day decamped, and continued to march until the afternoon, always in order of battle. The march of this day was exceedingly fatiguing, as they had to pass through woods, morasses, and wild deserts †. Encamped in a position like the former one, at a wood near a little river. The King lodged in a mean monastery.

It was resolved in a council of war to leave the baggage of the army at this camp, and, by a forced march towards the north-west, to gain the Tine, and to intercept the Scots, who were now supposed to be about to return home, probably, because the smoke of their ravages had ceased. The army began to march at midnight.

20th, This day's march was the most laborious of all, and through very difficult ground; the army kept no order; every man pressed forwards without regarding his companions; and the cavalry left the foot soldiers behind. At the close of day the cavalry reached the Tine, and crossed it at Haidon ‡; they lay on their arms that night, in want of

---

* In *Fœdera*, T. iv. p. 300. there is an order by the King and council, dated at Durham 17th July 1327. This is an important date, and must be remembered.

† Froissart, Vol. i. p. 17. says, 'deserts sauvages.'

‡ Froissart does not mention the place. The only notice that we have of it, is in *Scala Chron.* ap. Leland, T. i. p. 551. 'The King after loggid at Eiden, [this must ' mean Haiden,] when they had cumpasit the batles of the Scottes.'

288   JOURNAL of the CAMPAIGN

of all neceffaries. It was reported that they had marched twenty-eight Englifh miles that day.

21ft, The infantry came up, but could not ford the river, which had become much fwollen by violent rains during the night.

Froiff. i. 18.   22d, The rains continued during this day [Thurfday], and throughout the week. The army fuffered much from want of fhelter for themfelves and their horfes, and from the exceeding fcarcity of provi ons.

Froiff. l. 18.   23d, Provifions and other neceffaries arrived from Newcaftle and the places in the neighbourhood *, but in fmall quantities, and fold at exorbitant prices.

Froiff. l. 19.   24th, 25th, 26th, and 27th, The army remained on the fame ground, without receiving any intelligence of the Scots. The troops now began to murmur at their fituation, and to charge fome of their leaders as falfe traitors, who had brought the King and his army into a remote corner where they were expofed to perifh through fatigue and famine, without ever encountering an enemy. It was now refolved to march again towards the fouth. The King proclaimed a *Fœd. iv. 315.* reward of lands to the value of one hundred pounds yearly, for life, to the perfon who fhould firft difcover the enemies 'on dry ground 'where they might be attacked †.'

Fifteen

---

* Froiffart fays ' from Newcaftle;' but it only be fuppofed that the different towns and villages on the banks of the Tine contributed in bringing provifions to the army. Froiffart feems to fay that the provifions arrived on the 22d; but this is inconfiftent with what follows in his narrative, that the army was without neceffaries for *three* nights.

† ' Rex, &c. falutis, quòd cum nuper, dum in partibus borealibus cum exercitu no-
' ftro faimus, proclamari feceriumus, quòd ille, qui nos perduceret ad vifum inimicorum
' noftrorum, ubi eos appropinquare poffemus, fuper terra ficca, pro facto ab eis habea-
' do, fibi faceremus habere centum libratas terrae per annum, *ad terminum vitae fuae*;
' ea dileCtus et fidelis nofter Thomas de Rokefby nos perduxerit ad vifum inimico-
' rum noftrorum praedictorum in loco duro et ficco, juxta proclamationem praedic-
' tam; Noveritis igitur,' &c. [at Lincoln 28th September 1327.] *Fœdera*, T. iv.
p. 315.

Fifteen or sixteen Knights and Esquires swam the river and set out *Froiſ. l. 19.*
upon this search.

28th, The army decamped, the cavalry went some miles up the ri- *Froiſ. i. 19.*
ver *, where they crossed, although with much difficulty; many
soldiers were drowned in the passage. The army thus re-assembled,
quartered at a neighbouring village which the Scots had burnt. Here
they found forage for their horses.

29th, Marched over an uneven country until noon, when they dis- *Froiſ. l. 19.*
covered some villages lately burnt by the Scots. There they found
corn and grass, and remained all day.

30th, Marched without receiving any intelligence of the Scots. *Froiſ. l. 19.*

31st, Marched again until about three o'clock in the afternoon, *Froiſſ. 19.20.*
when Thomas Rokesby, an esquire, brought certain accounts that the *Fœd. iv. 311.*
Scots were encamped about nine miles off, on the side of a bill. He
reported, ' That the Scots had made him prisoner; but, on hearing his
' business, dismissed him, and said, that they had been on that gr und
' for eight days, as ignorant of the motions of the English as the En-
' glish of theirs, and that they were ready and desirous to fight.' The
English army halted at Blanchland upon the river Derwen †, a place
belonging to the Cistertians.

1st

---

p. 312. *Froiſſart*, v. i. p. 19. ſays, ' cent livres de terre à *heritage*.' This miſtake, natural enough to be reported in the camp, has been careleſsly adopted by later hiſtorians, who had an opportunity of reading the grant made to Rokeſby.

* Froiſſart ſays ſeven leagues; but I preſume that he meant miles. As Edward lay
at Haidon, it is not probable that he would have marched 20 miles farther up the river. It ſeems that the Engliſh repaſſed the Tine ſomewhere about Beltingham, above
the junction of Allan and Tine; and, if ſo, then *the burnt village*, mentioned by Froiſſart, muſt have been Beltingham.

† Froiſſart ſays, v. i. p. 20. ' Une *Blanche abbaye* qu'on nommoit du temps du Roi
' Artus, la Blanche lande.' By *the days of King Arthur*, he means *from time immemorial*.
The place ſtill retains its ancient name.

1st August, With Rokesby for their guide, they advanced towards the Scottish army, and came in view of it about mid-day. The Scots were drawn up in three bodies on the side of a hill, having the river Were in front, and their flanks secured by rocks and precipices.

Froiss. vol. 1.

The English dismounted and advanced, hoping that the Scots would abandon their advantageous position, and cross the river; but the Scots moved not. Then the King sent a message to Randolph and Douglas the Scottish generals, of this import, ' Either suffer me to pass the river, ' and leave me room to range my forces, or, do you pass the river, and ' I will leave you room to range yours, and thus shall we fight on e- ' qual terms.' This message, of itself, would have determined the Scottish generals to remain on the defensive; and, therefore, they made answer in scorn, ' We will not accept of either proposal; we have ' burnt and spoiled the country on our road hither, and *here* are we ' fixed, during our pleasure; if the King of England is offended, let ' him come and chastise us *.' The English troops, although destitute of every accommodation, remained on their arms until morning. The Scots, after having placed their guards, returned to their camp. During the night, they kept great fires constantly burning, and sounded horns without ceasing †, ' as if,' says Froissart, ' all the fiends of hell ' had

---

* This message and the answer resemble not the manners and style of modern times; they may seem uncouth and improbable to readers who suppose that soldiers always thought and expressed themselves as they do in our days, after much of the antient pedantry of war has been exploded.

† Barnes, *Edward* III. p. 13. says, ' They made so many and so great fires of En- ' glish wood, as if they designed thereby to provoke their enemies *by wasting so prodi- ' gally that fuel of which they themselves had so little*.' This observation is ridiculous, and betrays gross ignorance. The intention of the Scots in lighting up great fires, and in sounding horns throughout the night, was, probably, in order to call in the parties who were occupied in pillaging the country. It is said in *Scala Chron.* ap. Leland, T. I. p. 552. ' At this tyme Archibald Douglas toke great prayes in the bi- '*shopricke* of Duresme, and encountered with a band of Englishmen at Darlington, and ' killed

'had been there.' And in this manner did both armies pass the night*.

2d August, The armies were again drawn out, as on the former day. Some English parties crossed the river, and skirmished with the Scots; but the English commanders saw that the Scots could not be provoked to quit their fastnesses; and therefore they called in the parties.

3d, Matters remained in the same situation. The English received intelligence that the Scots had no provisions left but cattle, which they slaughtered from day to day. The English resolved to keep the Scots closely blockaded in their camp, expecting soon to reduce them by famine.

4th, On the morning they perceived, with astonishment, that the Scots had decamped during the night. The Scots took post somewhat higher up the river Were, in ground still stronger, and of more difficult access, than what they had occupied before, and amidst a great wood. The English placed themselves on a hill opposite to the enemy: This was near the place called *Stanhope Park*. Douglas, with two hundred horsemen, crossed the river at some distance from the English camp. When he approached the out-guards, he cried, 'Ha! St George, no ward,' [guard,] and thus, under the appearance of

---

' killed many of them.' This must have happened while Edward III. was in the neighbourhood of the Tine.

* Froissart says, v. i. p. 21. ' Furent logés cette nuiɑ, *qui fut la nuit St Pierre, à l'entrée d'Aoust* de l'an. 1327; *jusqu' au lendemain, que les seigneurs ouirent messe*.' The festival of *S. Petri ad vincula*, [1st August,] is here meant. But it is not certain whether *la nuit S. Pierre* means the eve of St Peter, [31st July], or the night of his festival [1st August]. *Nox*, in the Latinity of the lower ages, sometimes means *eve*. But I know not whether *la nuit* has a like sense in French. The circumstance of hearing mass next day would lead us to suppose that *eve* is here meant. If so, we must hold that the English remained about Haidon one day less, and about Stanhope Park one day more, than this journal supposes.

of an English officer of distinction making the rounds, he came undiscovered at dead of night to the royal quarters. His companions called out 'a Douglas, a Douglas, English thieves, you shall all die,' overthrew whatever opposed them, and furiously attacked the King's tent. The King's domestics made a brave stand to protect their Sovereign. His chaplain, and others of his household, were slain; and he himself with difficulty escaped. Douglas, thus disappointed of his prey, rushed through the enemies, and retreated with inconsiderable loss *.

Froiss. l. 12. 5th, A Scottish knight was brought in prisoner. Having been strictly questioned, he acknowledged, that general orders had been issued for all men to hold themselves in readiness to march that evening, and to follow the banner of Douglas. The English concluded that the Scots had formed the plan of a night-attack: All preparations were made for opposing them; the army was drawn up in order of battle, great fires lighted, and strict guard kept.

Froiss. l. 22. 6th, On the morning, two Scottish trumpeters were brought in prisoners. They reported, that the Scottish army had decamped before midnight, and were already many miles on their march: And that they, the trumpeters, had been left by the Scottish commanders to convey this intelligence to the English. The English were unwilling to credit this strange and unwelcome report. Suspecting a stratagem, they continued in order of battle for several hours longer, and still hoped and looked for the appearance of the enemy; at length, some scouts having crossed the river, returned with certain intelligence that the Scottish camp was totally deserted.

Froiss. L. 22. In the Scottish camp there were found five hundred beeves, all slaughtered;

---

* Froissart says, that Douglas and his party 'en toa lui et sa compaignie, avant qu'ils ceslassent, plus de trois cens.' And ' perdit aucuns de ses gens à la retraite, mais, ce ne fot mie grandement;' vol. i. p. 20. 21.

slaughtered *; three hundred caldrons made of skins, and fixed upon stakes, in which there was meat ready for boiling, and a still greater quantity of meat prepared for roasting †; there were also found upwards of ten thousand old brogues made of leather, with the hair on. The Scots left behind them five English prisoners, all naked, and bound to trees. Some of them had their legs broken ‡.

7th, It having been resolved to lay aside all thoughts of pursuing the enemy, the English decamped, and lay that night at Stanhope ‖.

Fœd. L. 12.
Fœd. iv. 301.

8th,

---

* Froissart supposes that the Scots killed the beeves, lest they should fall alive into the hands of the English, as if it had been of any importance whether the Scots killed the cattle on one day, or left them to the English to be killed on the next. It is plain that they were killed, and a great quantity of meat prepared for dressing, that the soldiers might not suspect the intention of their commanders to retreat. Had the daily preparations for supplying the army been omitted, every man in the camp would have discovered the cause, and it would have been in the power of a single deserter to reveal it to the English.

† Froissart says, ' plus de mille *bastiers*,' which is translated by Barnes ' a thousand ' spits,' *bestier* imports a machine on which three or four spits might be hung, one above another.

‡ En y avoit aucuns qui avoyent les jambes toutes rompues. Si les delivreret et les ' differents aller,' *Froissart*, v. i p. 22. Tyrrel, T. iii p. 345. and Barnes, p. 16. erroneously suppose that the legs of all the prisoners were broken. It is difficult to account for this barbarity of the Scots. Had they meant to prevent the prisoners from making their escape, and from giving intelligence to the English, they would have led them along with the army, or they would have broken the legs of all of them. Perhaps they were wounded men. Froissart tells the story in an inaccurate manner; one might be led to suppose, that the English *let the men go* whose legs were broken.

‖ Edward III issued writs at Stanhope, 7th August, for assembling a parliament; *Fœdera*, T. iv. p. 301. He mentioned the escape of the Scots from Stanhope Park. This is an important date. We have seen that the King and council were at Durham 17th July, and here we see that the Scots had escaped before the 7th of August; between the two dates, there is an interval of twenty days, during which all the operations of the campaign must, of necessity, have occurred. And here it is that Froissart seems

Froiss. l. 11. 8th, Marched from Stanhope, and lay in the neighbourhood of an abbey two leagues from Durham. At this, and the former nights quarters, there was abundance of forage found for the horses, who, by long marches, and scanty sustenance, were so reduced that they could hardly crawl.

9th, Halted.

10th, Marched into Durham. Here they found their baggage which they had left in the fields on the 19th of July. The citizens of Durham had conveyed it into the town, and preserved it with great care. The army was quartered at Durham, and in the neighbourhood.

11th and 12th, Halted.

13th, Marched towards Yorke.

14th, Continued to march.

Froiss. l. 13.
Fœd. iv. 302. 15th, Arrived at Yorke *. The King thanked his barons for their good and loyal service, and dismissed the army.

No. III.

seems to have misunderstood his informer: He says, v. i. p. 21. ' Les Anglois se loge-
' rent là endroit contre eux, [at Stanhope Park,] et demourerent xviii jours tous pleins
' sur cette montaigne.' The only method that I can discover of accounting for this
is, that Froissart's informer told him the army had been engaged among the mountains
against the Scots for eighteen days; and this is precisely the space between the 19th
July, when they left their baggage, to their encampment at Stanhope, after the escape
of the Scots.

* The first instrument by the King that occurs in *Fœdera*, after his return from
the campaign, is dated at Yorke, 15th August. See T. iv. p. 302.

No. III.

OF THE GENEALOGY

OF THE

FAMILY OF SETON,

In the Fourteenth Century.

ANNALS Vol. II. pag. 148.

OUR genealogical writers have given a fair pedigree of the family of Seton in the fourteenth century.

Christopher Seton suffered death 1306.	=	Christian Bruce, sister of Robert I.
Alexander Seton slain at Kinghorn 1332.	=	Isobel, daughter of Duncan, 10th Earl of Fife.
Alexander Seton governour of Berwick, 1333, died 1337.	=	Christian Cheyne daughter of Cheyne of Straloch.

1. William slain at Berwick 1333.   2. Thomas slain at Berwick 1333.   3. Alexander, who carried on the line of the family, and was a commissioner to England in 1340.

This pedigree, however, will not stand the test of historical criticism.

That

That all possible indulgence may be shown to it, let it be supposed
that both Alexander the son, and Alexander the grandson of Christian
Bruce were married at fourteen, and that each of them had a son at
fifteen.

This is to hold circumstances for true, which are always exceedingly improbable, and which can scarcely ever happen in times of public disorder.

The first husband of Christian Bruce was Graitney Earl of Marr.
Their children were, Donald Earl of Marr, slain at Duplin in 1332,
and Helen, or Ellyne, through whom the earldom of Marr did, in after times, devolve on the family of Erskine. Graitney Earl of Marr
was alive in 1296.

Sir Robert Douglas says, that Graitney Earl of Marr died *about*
1300; but, of this assertion, he produces no evidence; and therefore
I lay no weight on it, although it would make considerably for the argument which I am to use. Indeed, I do not, at present, recollect any
mention of Graitney Earl of Marr after autumn 1296; and, therefore,
let it be supposed that he died in the end of that year.

We cannot suppose that Christian Bruce married her second husband Christopher Seton before 1297, or that she could have had a son
by him till about 1298.

This son Alexander [slain at Kingborn 1332] may have been married
at fourteen, to Isobel the daughter of Duncan, 10th Earl of Fyfe, *an.*
1312, and may have had a son, [Alexander governour of Berwick
1333,] *an.* 1313.

Alexander governour of Berwick may have been married at fourteen,
an. 1327, and may have had a son William, *an.* 1328, and a son Thomas, *an.* 1329, [both said to have been slain before the walls of Berwick 1333,] and also a son Alexander, *an.* 1330, [who carried on the
line of the family.]

All this is matter of figures; and the reader is entreated to attend to
the calculation, and to observe its consequences.

1. Alexander

See Annals of Scotland, I.
135. 138.

Peerage of Scotl. 460.

1. If Alexander Seton, the son of Chriſtian Bruce, married, in 1312, the daughter of Duncan, 10th Earl of Fife, when he himſelf was but fourteen, it follows that his wife was twenty-four at leaſt; for Duncan 10th Earl of Fife, her father, died in 1288.

Annals of Scot. i. 185.

2. As Alexander Seton, the grandſon of Chriſtian Bruce, could not have been born before 1313, and yet was governour of Berwick in 1333, he muſt have been intruſted with that government at the age of twenty-one. A very eminent perſon, having a numerous vaſſalage, might have obtained ſuch a command; but it is not probable that it would have been conferred on a private baron, at ſo early a time of life, when the preſervation of Berwick was the great object of the national councils.

3. As William, the eldeſt ſon of Alexander Seton, governour of Berwick, could not have been born ſooner than 1328, he muſt, if given as an hoſtage to Edward III. in 1333, have been put to death when he was a child of *five* or *ſix* years old.

4. As Thomas, the ſecond ſon of Alexander Seton, governour of Berwick, could not have been born ſooner than 1329, he muſt, if given as an hoſtage to Edward III. in 1333, have been put to death when he was a child of *four* or *five* years old.

5. As Alexander, the 3d ſon of Alexander Seton, governour of Berwick, could not have been born ſooner than 1330, it follows, that he was a commiſſioner to treat of peace with England in 1340, at the age of *ten*.

Thus the conſequences of this pedigree of the Setons, when viewed in the moſt favourable light, are inconſiſtent with all the probabilities of moral evidence *.

Some

* If the age of Chriſtian Bruce could be diſcovered, a collateral argument might thence ariſe. Let us inquire what may be done in that way. Robert Bruce, the Father

298   GENEALOGY OF THE

Some new hypothesis may, perhaps, be devised in order to prop
the old one: The moſt ſpecious would be, that Chriſtian Bruce might
have been divorced from Graitney Earl of Marr, and might, during
his lifetime, have married Chriſtopher Seton. This would have the
consequence

that of Chriſtian, could not have married the *Counteſs of Carrick* before 1271; for the Earl of Carrick, (either her father or her huſband,) died in the holy wars, A.D. 1270. As Iſobel the mother of Randolph was her eldeſt daughter, and as her ſon Robert Bruce was born 11th July 1274, it follows that Chriſtian Bruce could not have been born ſooner than 1273. If ſhe was born in 1273, ſhe was aged 53 in the year 1326. But we know, from Fordun, that, in 1326, ſhe was married for the third time to Sir Andrew Murray of Bothwell, *Lib.* xiii. c. 12. It is admitted that ſhe brought him two ſons, who were ſucceſſively Lords of Bothwell. Therefore, ſhe muſt have born the elder at the age of 54 and the younger at the age of 55. Now, this is exceedingly improbable; and, therefore, we may conclude, that, when Chriſtian Bruce was married for the third time in 1326, ſhe was conſiderably younger than 53, and conſequently, that ſhe was born ſeveral years after 1273. Let us ſee how calculations will anſwer on the hypotheſis, that, in 1326, at the age of 45, ſhe married Sir Andrew Murray; if ſo, ſhe was born in 1281, and, conſequently, was 15 at the ſuppoſed death of the Earl of Marr in 1296, and, as ſhe brought him two children, ſhe muſt have remained in wedlock for two years, and the muſt have been married in 1294, at the age of thirteen. If ſhe married Chriſtopher Seton in 1297, ſhe muſt have been a widow with two children, and have married a ſecond huſband at the age of ſixteen. According to this hypotheſis, it appears that the events of her life were ſtrangely crowded; but, if we ſuppoſe, with Douglas, that the Earl of Marr lived to about 1300, and that Chriſtian Bruce married Chriſtopher Seton in 1301, every thing will have a probable appearance.

Chriſtian Bruce Born	1281,	
Married Earl of Marr	1295,	at 14
Bare a ſon Donald Earl of Marr	1296,	ʼʼ 15
Bare a daughter Ellyne	1297,	at 16
A widow	1300,	at 19
Married Chriſtopher Seton	1301,	at 20
Bare a ſon Alexander	1302,	ʼʼ 21
A widow	1306,	ʼʼ 25
Married Sir Andrew Murray	1326,	ʼʼ 45
Bare a ſon	1327,	ʼʼ 46
Bare another ſon	1328,	ʼʼ 47

consequence of advancing the birth of her son and grandson some few years; and, by this means, would, in some measure, soften the deformity which appears on the face of the popular tale. The hypothesis, however, of a divorce, can gain no credit. For, 1*st*, The very tender age of the child who was heir of Marr in 1306, precludes the notion of such a divorce before 1296, in which year, I am willing to hold, that Graitney Earl of Marr died. 2*d*, Christian Bruce possessed the castle of Kildrummy, the chief seat of the family of Marr, in 1333, which she would not have done, had she been divorced from Earl Graimey.

Annals of Scot. li. 17.

The reader will now be led to inquire, Whether the received genealogy of the family of Seton is to be overturned without any thing more probable being substituted in its place? To reduce things into a state of scepticism is very different from what I hold to be the office of an historian; and they who ascribe this to me do me great wrong.

It has been shewn, that Alexander Seton, slain at Kingborn 1332, Alexander Seton, governour of Berwick in 1333, and Alexander Seton, a commissioner to treat with England in 1340, cannot all subsist together, as son, grandson, and great-grandson, of Christian Bruce. The question is, *which* shall we reject?

If Fordun intended to say, that Alexander Seton, slain at Kingborn 1332, was the father of Alexander Seton, governour of Berwick in 1333, and the grandfather of William and Thomas, slain at Berwick in 1333, it has been demonstrated that that story is absurd and impossible. For Alexander, the son of Christian Bruce, could not have been above 32 years of age, and, consequently, his grandson could not have been a soldier in the same year. We must either hold, that the son of Christian Bruce was not slain at Kingborn in 1332, or that the Alexander Seton, who had two sons slain at Berwick in 1333, was not the grandson of Christian Bruce; and, of course, we must hold, that all the genealogical writers who have supposed this pedigree have been in an error.

If we adhere to the first part of the story, and hold that Alexander Seton, the son of Chriftian Bruce, was flain at Kingborn in 1332, the tragical event of his grandfons, the young Setons, put to death at Berwick in 1333, is annihilated; and it muft be admitted to have been wholly a fable.

But, although by adhering to the firft part of Fordun's ftory, as underftood by later writers, we fhould be relieved for ever of the ftory of the cruelty of Edward III. at Berwick, yet I cannot lay hold on fuch evidence.

To me it feems probable, that Fordun has either committed a miftake as to the name of the perfon flain at Kingborn in 1332, or that the *Alexander Seton* mentioned by him was fome other perfon, of whofe parentage we have no knowledge.

And, inclining to be of this opinion, I alfo think, that the *Alexander Seton*, who was one of the perfons that addreffed the letter to the Pope in 1320, who is faid by Fordun to have been governour of Berwick in 1333, who was prefent at Balliol's parliament in Edinburgh 1333-4, and who was a commiffioner to England in 1340, was one and the fame perfon, the fon of Sir Chriftopher Seton and Chriftian Bruce; and thus the pedigree of the fon, grandfon, and great-grandfon, of Chriftian Bruce, will be curtailed, and the events which have been fuppofed applicable to *three* Alexander Setons, will be found to have relation to *one* and the fame perfon.

No. IV.

No. IV.

LIST OF THE SCOTTISH ARMY

AT THE

BATTLE OF HALIDON,

19th July 1333.

ANNALS, Vol. II. pag. 166.

ALTHOUGH the numbers of the Scottish army, at the battle of Halidon, are variously reported by historians, the evidence of W. Hemingford, or his continuator, a contemporary writer, and of H. de Knyghton, a writer in the succeeding age, ascertains their numbers with a greater degree of certainty than is generally required in historical facts.

W. Hemingford minutely records the numbers and arrangement of the Scottish army. He says, that, besides Earls and other Lords, or great barons, there were 55 knights, 1100 men at arms, and 13500 of the commons lightly armed, amounting in all to 14655 : But he is guilty of an unpardonable exaggeration when he adds, ' that the ' Scots covered the face of the earth like locusts.'

W. Heming. 275. 276.

He

LIST OF THE SCOTTISH ARMY

He thus describes the disposition of the Scottish army:

	Knights	Men at arms	Commons lightly armed
1st Body	15	300	2200
2d Body	11	300	3000
3d Body	17	300	4300
4th Body	12	200	4000
Total	55	1100	13500

Knght.1363. 1364. II. Knyghton concurs with Hemingford as to the division of the Scots into four bodies, as to the number and arrangement of *the knights* [*], and as to the number of *men at arms*, and of *commons lightly armed*, in the 1st and 4th bodies.

With respect to the 2d and 3d bodies, there is a diversity, arising merely from the inattention of the transcribers, or the publisher of Knyghton.

Thus the printed copy of Knyghton bears, ' in secunda acie Seneſ-
' callus Scotiae, &c. &c. cum trecentis viris bene armatis, et trecentis
' de communibus armatis.' Knyghton could not mean, that, in the main body, or center, there were no more than six hundred men.
' Trecentis,' i. e. iii. C. or 300, appears to be an error of the transcriber for iii. M. or 3000.

Again, the printed copy of Knyghton bears, ' in tertia acie, scilicet
' *le Rerewurde*, Comes de Carrick, Dominus Archibaldus Douglas, cum
' vexillo, &c. cum ccc armatis de communibus armatis.' Here the number of the commons is omitted; but, as in all the other particulars, Knyghton exactly agrees with Hemingford, we may well conjecture that the passage ought to be read thus: [' Cum ccc armatis, et iiii. m. &c.] de communibus armatis;' and thus there will be a perfect coincidence

---

[*] There is a very inconsiderable variation as to the number of the knights, but which deserves not to be mentioned; it shews, however, that the one historian did not copy from the other.

cidence between the two historians, as to the number and arrangement of the Scottish army, a coincidence fully justifying what has been asserted in the Annals, 'that the number of the Scots exceeded not '15000 *.'

It must not be dissembled, that Barnes has published a list of the Scottish army from a MS. at Cambridge, very different from the list in Hemingford and Knyghton. According to it, there were, besides the barons and knights whom those two historians mention, the numbers following: *Hist. Ed. III. 76.*

	New Knights.	Men at arms.	Commons.
1st Body	40	600	3000
2d Body	30	700	17000
3d Body	40	900	15000
4th Body	30	900	18400
Total	140	3100	53400

This makes in all 56640 men. The anonymous writer of this list was not satisfied with swelling the Scottish army to such an exorbitant amount: For he adds, that the Earl of March, keeper of the castle of Berwick, and Alexander Seton, captain of the town, brought 150 men at arms in aid of the Scots, and that the people of Berwick brought 400 men at arms, and 10800 infantry; and thus, according to him, the Scots mustered at Halidon no fewer than 67990 combatants.

These

* There is a passage in *Knyghton*, ap. Twisden, Vol. ii. p. 2563. corrupted beyond correction, and utterly unintelligible. ' Et fuerunt ibidem *occisi ad summam xxxvi. 'mill. hominum.* scilicet, Comites, Comes de Strathern, Comes de Sutherland, Comes ' de Lennox, Comes de Menteth, Comes de Athole; Baronetti, Dominus Walterus ' Stewart, Dominus Johannes de Graham, Dominus Humfridus de Boys, Dominus ' Johannes de Strivelin, Dominus Willielmus Tweedy. Numero M. et C. de communi. ' nibus non armatis, MDCCC. *Summa summarum occisorum Scotorum XL millia.*' Here the numbers of the slain are not only inconsistent with Knyghton's own account of the numbers of the army, but the particulars and the total are absolutely irreconcileable. This seems to be rather an interpolation, than an error in transcribing.

304 LIST OF THE SCOTTISH ARMY

These accounts are, in every respect, extravagant and incredible; and, being given by an anonymous writer, can never be placed in competition with the united testimonies of Hemingford and Knyghton.

See Abr. ii. 27.
Indeed, to suppose that, immediately after the carnage at Duplin, the Scots could assemble an army of near 70000 combatants, is greatly to over-rate the populousness and internal force of Scotland in that age. This is said, not to extenuate the disasters of the Scots, or invidiously to diminish the glory of the English arms, but from regard to historical truth.

In recording the names of the noble persons who fought for the Scottish cause at Halidon, I pay a just and pleasing tribute to patriotic, although unfortunate valour *.

FIRST

---

* Their names are to be found in Hemingford and Knyghton, but so miserably disfigured by the ignorance of transcribers, that some of them can only be traced by conjecture, while others cannot to be discovered at all. *Fordun*, L. xiii. c. 28. has given a very imperfect list, because, as he says, ' nomina per singulos recitare magis lacrimabile quam expediens est.'

AT THE BATTLE OF HALIDON. 305

FIRST BODY.

1. JOHN EARL OF MORAY, Commander
    2. James Frafer, killed
    3. Simon Frafer, killed
    4. Walter Stewart, killed
    5. Reginald de Chene
    6. Patrick de Graham
    7. John Grant
    8. John de Carlyle
    9. Patrick ———
                                                10.

(1) John Earl of Moray, fon of the renowned Randolph. He fucceeded his brother Thomas, flain at Gaftmore, which is vulgarly called *the battle of Duplin*. Hemingford and Knyghton concur in afferting that he was prefent at Halidon. Knyghton adds, that he was a very young man, 'adhuc juvenis.' Boece, and the later hiftorians, fuppofe, that he was detained from the army by indifpofition, and that one John de Moray commanded the firft divifion of the Scots. But of this there is no probability. As the Earl of Moray was a young man, it may be prefumed, that the two Frafers had the command of the firft divifion. They are mentioned by Hemingford as being fuperior in rank to the other perfons here mentioned.

(2) James Frifel, or Frafer. He and Simon Frafer, both flain at Halidon, are faid by *Fordun*, L. xiii. c. 28. to have been brothers. The received opinion is, that they were the fons of Sir Alexander Frafer, flain at Duplin, and the nephews of Robert I. by their mother Mary Bruce.

(3) Anceftor of the family of Lovat.

(4)

(5) His name appears in the letter to the Pope 1320.

(6) He is called *Patrick de Graham* by Hemingford; but Knyghton calls him *Patrick de Graham fourth*. This is corrupted: Perhaps it fhould be *fenior*. He is probably that Patricius de Graham who joined in the letter to the Pope 1320.

(7)
(8)
(9) *Berechere* H. *Carster* En. *Parker* MS. quoted by Barnes, p. 78.

306   LIST OF THE SCOTTISH ARMY

       10. Robert de Calderotes
       11. Patrick de Meldrum
       12. William Jardin
       13. Thomas Kirkpatrick, prisoner
       14. Gilbert Wysman
       15. Adam Gordon
       16. James ———
       17. Alan Grant
       18. Robert Boyd, prisoner

SECOND BODY.

1. ROBERT, STEWART OF SCOTLAND
    2. James Stewart, prisoner

                                       3.

(10)
(11) *Philip II.*
(12) *Gareyne*, Kn. Qu. Are not Garden, Cairn, and Jardin, all one and the same name?
(13) Knyghton has *Thomas Teher*, which may be *Thomas of Lochore*, who appears in the parliament 1315. In enumerating the prisoners, Knyghton mentions *Roger Kirkpatrick*.
(14)
(15)
(16) *Garnegath*, H. *Cranegransbe*, Kn. *Cremont*, MS. quoted by Barnes.
(17)
(18) Probably that Robert Boyd who adhered to Robert Bruce during his greatest calamities, and who was rewarded by that monarch with the estate of Kilmarnock, and other lands, which had belonged to the Balliol family. In MS. Barnes, *Brady*.

(1) As the Stewart of Scotland was then a youth just turned of sixteen, it cannot be supposed that the conduct of the second division, or center, was committed to him. It is probable that his uncle actually commanded.

(2) Sir James Stewart of Rosyth, brother of Walter Stewart of Scotland.

3. Malcolm Fleming
4. William Douglas, prisoner
5. David de Lindesay
6. Duncan Campbell
7. John Stewart, killed
8. Alan Stewart, killed
9. William Erskine
10. William Abernethy
11. William Morrice
12. Walter Fitz Gilbert
13. John de Kirketon, prisoner
14. William Morrice de ———

THIRD

(3) This name is strangely corrupted in Knyghton. 'Maclinus filius Andenfis.' *Maclinus* is *Malcolinus* or *Malcolm*. The rest of the name has been written *Flandrenfis*, i. e. *Fleming*, which the transcriber has mistaken for *Fil. Andrefis*.

(4) Rather *Archibald*, the natural son of the renowned Sir James Douglas. Knyghton calls him ' filius Jacobi Douglas ejus,' [i. e. ejusdem,] or ' James Douglas of Dou-' glas.' In *Scala Chronica*, he is erroneously numbered among the slain.

(5) Eldest son of David Lindsay of Crawfurd.

(6)

(7) Erroneously called James. It is said in Fordun, most absurdly, that James, John, and Alan Stewart, were brothers of Robert the Stewart of Scotland. This John Stewart is called *of Dalsin*. MS. Barnes, *Colden*.

(8) Called *Adam* by Knyghton. The person meant is Alan Stewart of Dreghorn, son of John Stewart of Bonkil, slain at Falkirk 1296. He was the ancestor of the Darnley family.

(9)

(10) William Abernethy Lord of Salton. His name appears in the letter to the Pope 1320.

(11)

(12) Of Cadiow, by grant from Robert Bruce; the ancestor of the Duke of Hamilton.

(13)

(14) Distinguished from the other Morrice by the title of Glawlton. Qu.

Qq 2

LIST OF THE SCOTTISH ARMY

THIRD BODY.

1. ARCHIBALD DOUGLAS LORD OF GALLOWAY, REGENT OF SCOTLAND, mortally wounded, and prisoner.
    2. Alexander Earl of Carrick, killed
    3. Alexander ———
    4. Malcolm Earl of Lenox, killed
    5. The banner of the Earl of Fyfe
    6. John Earl of Athole, killed
    7. Robert Lauder, junior

8.

(1) Archibald Douglas, vulgarly called *Tineman*, brother of the renowned Sir James Douglas. *Fordun*, L. xiii. c. 28. mentions him among the flain, *Knyghton* among the prisoners. It is probable that he was mortally wounded, and left on the field of battle.

(2) Alexander Bruce Earl of Carrick, a natural fon of Edward Bruce. Hemingford feems to suppose that he led the third body, and perhaps he did fo, but still under the command of the Regent.

(3) This perfon is called *Alexander Larneys* by Knyghton. He muſt have been of diſtinction; for he had a banner difplayed *cum vexillo*. It might be conjectured that Alexander Ramfay of Dalwolfy [now Dalhoufie] was the perfon here intended: But it feems, from the fequel in Knyghton, that Alexander Ramfay was in Berwick. Perhaps he efcaped into the town after the battle.

(4) Malcolm Earl of Lennox, an aged Lord, the companion in arms of Robert I.

(5) At that time Duncan Earl of Fyfe was a priſoner. It is not known who led his vaſſals.

(6) The earldom of Athole fell to the crown by the forfeiture of David de Strathbogie, [or Haſtings.] Robert I. beſtowed it on his nephew John Campbell of Moulin, fon of Sir Nigel Campbell. The Engliſh hiſtorians, not admitting the juſtice of the forfeiture, fay, 'fe clamavit Comitem de Athole.'

(7) In Knyghton, he is called *Robert le Wyther, filius*. Mention is afterwards made of *Robert de Londre, pater*. From a careful examination of the liſts in Knyghton, it appears that *Robert de Lauder* is here meant.

AT THE BATTLE OF HALIDON. 309

8. John de Strivelin, or Stirling, prisoner
9. William de Vypont
10. William de Linlithgow, prisoner
11. John de Lindsay
12. William de ———
13. Bernard Frisel
14. Alexander de Lindsay, killed
15. Alexander de Gray
16. William de Umfraville
17. Patrick de Polwarth
18. Michael de Wemyss, prisoner.
19. [Michael] Scot

20.

(8) This person is called by Knyghton *Joras de Skerlyngbong*, *Johannes de Sherlinghowe*, and *Johannes de Strivelin duo*, if so, there were, probably, two *John Stirlings*, one made prisoner; the other slain. See *Knyghton*.

(9) Knyghton says, *W. de Vesoun*. As I know no such person, and as *William de Vypont* occurs afterwards in the history of David II. I conjecture that he is the man here intended, and so it is in Barnes's MS.

(10) Knyghton says *W. de Lyngifton*; but, in enumerating the prisoners, he speaks of *William de Linlifeun*, [or Linlithgow.]

(11)

(12) Knyghton says, *William de Fryfleye*. If this does not mean Frisel or Frafer, I know not what to make of it.

(13)

(14) Alexander de Lindsay, the younger son of David Lindsay of Crawford. He married the daughter and sole heir of John Stirling of Glenesk.

(15) He is mentioned in *Scots Chronicle*; probably *Andrew*.

(16)

(17) Called By Knyghton *le Tiwuard*.

(18) Knyghton, in enumerating the commanders, says *David*; but, in enumerating the prisoners, *Michael*, which seems to be the true reading.

(19) Knyghton says *William Scot*; perhaps it should be M i c. Michael Scot of Murthockstone, now Murdiestoun, the ancestor of the Duke of Buccleugh.

LIST OF THE SCOTTISH ARMY

    20. William de Landales
    21. Roger Mortimer
    22. Thomas de Boys, killed
    23. William de Cambo

FOURTH BODY.

    1. Hugh Earl of Ross Commander, killed
    2. Kenneth Earl of Sutherland, killed
    3. Malife Earl of Strathern, killed.
    4. Walter de Kyrkeby
    5. John de Cambron
    6. Gilbert de Haye
    7.

(20) William de Land, in Knyghton.

(21) He was probably a stranger. Roger de Mortimer, or *de Mertuo Mari*, held lands of John Campbell Earl of Athole.

(22) Knyghton says, J. de Veys, which seems an error for *Bois* or *Boys*. Among the slain he mentions Humfridus de Boys, whom I take to be the same man.

(23)

(1) *Fordun*, L. xiii. c. 28. mentions the Earl of Rofs as commanding the attack on the flank of the English army.

(2) The *third* Earl of Sutherland, fo far as can be difcovered from record.

(3) Malife Earl of Strathern was one of the Scottish nobles who addressed the letter to the Pope in 1320. I observe, by the way, that, in the chartulary of Inchaffray, [Infula Missarum,] there are many particulars concerning the old Earls of Strathern which have escaped the observation of our genealogical writers.

(4)

(5) His name appears in the letter to the Pope 1320.

(6) Knyghton says *de Saye*, which is a name unknown in Scotland. It should probably be *de Haye*. Sir Robert Douglas quotes a MS. history of the family of Errol, in proof that the famous Gilbert de la Haye, Constable of Scotland, was killed at Hallidon; *Peerage*, p. 250. The manuscript histories of noble families in Scotland, are

                                                                       generally

7. David de Marre
8. Christian de Harde
9. ———
10. Oliver de St Clair.

It will be remembered, that the Scots dismounted, and attacked on foot. Knyghton mentions the names of the following persons who were not present in the battle. It is probable that age or infirmities prevented them from acting.

1. Alexander de Menzies.
2. William de Plendergast
3. Robert de Lauder, senior
4. Robert de Keith
5. Edward de Keith
6. Patrick de Brechin

Knyghton, generally of most uncertain authority. Had the Constable of Scotland been killed at Halidon, Fordun, or some one of the English historians, would have mentioned it. It is impossible that a knight in the fourth body, fighting without a banner, could have been the Constable. If, therefore, the person here meant was a *Gilbert de Hays*, he must have been one of that heroic name, altogether different from the Constable.

(7)
(8) *Cristinus de Harde*, in Knyghton. Qu. Whether *Airth?*
(9) Knyghton says, *Dom. filius de Brening*, which is unintelligible.
(10)
Historians agree, that Murdoch Earl of Menteth fell at Halidon; yet, by some accident, his name is omitted in the lists. Knyghton, however, enumerates him among the killed.

(1) He was made prisoner at Berwick; *Knyghton.*
(2) He is mentioned in *Scala Chronica.*
(3)
(4)
(5)
(6)

LIST OF THE SCOTTISH ARMY, &c.

Knyghton, in enumerating the slain and the prisoners, mentions several persons who are not in his list of commanders.

S L A I N.

1. Murdoch Earl of Menteth
2. J. de Graham
3. W. Tweedy

P R I S O N E R S.

4. William Keith
5. James Douglas
6. Alexander Fryfell
7. Robert le Warde

No. V.

(1) See above, p. 311.
(2) Probably the same person in the list who is called P. de Graham.
(3) W. Tedy, Knyghton.
(4) He performed the functions of Marshal of the army. He is mentioned in Scala Chronica.
(5)
(6)
(7)

No. V.

WHETHER EDWARD III. PUT TO DEATH

THE SON OF

Sir ALEXANDER SETON,

At BERWICK in 1333.

ANNALS Vol. II. pag. 168.

FORDUN relates, that the befieged in Berwick obtained a truce from Edward III. and became bound to deliver up the town, unlefs relieved within a time limited; that, for the faithful execution of this treaty, Thomas, the fon and heir of Alexander Seton governour of the town, was given as an hoftage; that, after the lapfe of the time limited, Edward required thofe in Berwick to furrender, and, on their refufal, hanged Thomas Seton on a gibbet before the gates, in fight of both his parents. *Ford. xiii. 17. ib.*

Boece, and his imitator, Buchanan, improve on the fimple narrative of Fordun, and relate, that Edward hanged, not only the hoftage, but alfo another fon of Alexander Seton, who was a prifoner of war.

This feems to have been added to heighten the horrors of the narrative; and it is not improbable that Boece, much converfant in antiquity, might have held it lawful, in certain circumftances, to kill an hoftage; and, therefore, that, to make the character of Edward compleat-

314   WHETHER EDWARD III. PUT TO DEATH

ly deteſtable, he repreſented him as a violator of the law of nations, by murdering a priſoner.

The heroic ſpeech uttered by the wife of the governour is now given up on all hands as a rhetorical fiction.

In none of the antient Engliſh hiſtorians, hitherto publiſhed, is there any mention made of this cruel incident; and hence the modern hiſtorians of that nation are generally inclined to conſider it as a tale abſolutely fabulous.

Tyrr. iii.379. Tyrrel, however, has drawn up a narrative from the chronicle of Lanercoſt, and the treatiſe called *Scala Chronica*, both in MS. which greatly favours the account given by Fordun. What he ſays, when diveſted of embarraſſed expreſſions, pleonaſms, and tautology, amounts to this: ' The beſieged obtained a truce for fifteen days, and became
' bound to ſurrender, if not relieved within that term ; for this there
' were given twelve hoſtages; and, among them, the ſon of Sir Alex-
' ander Seton the governour. After the lapſe of the term, Edward
' required the governour to ſurrender; but he refuſed. Then Edward,
' by advice of his council, commanded young Seton to be hanged in
' ſight of his father. This ſeverity ſo intimidated the other perſons,
' whoſe children were hoſtages, that they ſought and obtained a pro-
' longation of the truce for eight days more, under the condition of
' ſurrendering, if they were not relieved;' and ' that, the Scots having
' ineffectually attempted to relieve Berwick, a capitulation was con-
' cluded.'

The ſtory in Tyrrel is certainly incorrect; for we learn from an authentic inſtrument, *Foedera*, T. iv. p. 564.—568. that what is called the *ſecond truce*, was not for *eight* days, but for a ſhorter ſpace, from the 15th to the 19th of July.

To the ſtory, as related by Fordun, and in Tyrrel, there lies a capital objection, which, ſince the publication of *Foedera Angliae*, is obvious to every one, namely, ' That Alexander Seton is ſaid to have
' been governour of the town of Berwick in July 1333; whereas, it is
' certain,

'certain, from record, that Sir William Keith held that office, and, in
'the character of governour of the town of Berwick, entered into a
'negotiation with Edward III.'

Mr Ruddiman observes, that it might be anfwered, 'That, when
'Sir William Keith, the governour, obtained permiffion to go from
'Berwick, and lay the ftate of affairs before the regent, he left Sir
'Alexander Seton as his deputy.' Nw. ad Bu-
chanan, 419.

But this folution is altogether unfatisfactory. 1. Any one who per-
ufes Fordun with attention, muft perceive that he fuppofed Alexander
Seton to have been governour of the town of Berwick from the beginning of the fiege. 2. The paffport granted by Edward III. to Sir
William Keith, is dated 16th July, and therefore, if there were *two*
treaties, muft relate to the *fecond*. Now, if Sir William Keith appointed Alexander Seton to be deputy-governour in his own abfence,
this muft have happened after the fecond treaty was made, and, confequently, after the death of young Seton, who is faid to have been
put to death, becaufe the conditions of the firft treaty were violated;
and this feems effectually to confute the ftory, that at the death of
young Seton, his father was deputy-governour, in abfence of Sir William Keith.

Another attempt might be made to get free of this difficulty, and
it is by fuppofing, 'that, on occafion of the firft treaty, Sir William
'Keith obtained a paffport to go to the Scottifh army; that he left Se-
'ton as his deputy; that he returned in the interval between the death
'of young Seton and the fecond treaty; and that then he obtained a-
'nother paffport, which is on record, to go again to the Scottifh ar-
'my.' But this hypothefis is aukward and improbable, and is not
fupported by any evidence.

Hitherto the weight of the argument is againft the ftory related by
Fordun, and the prefumption feems to be for the general opinion of
the later Englifh hiftorians.

As to the MS. authorities of *the Chronicle of Lanercost*, I can say nothing, never having been able to discover in what library it is preserved.

With respect to *Scala Chronica*, I have been more fortunate, having obtained a copy of what it contains with respect to the siege of Berwick, on 1333 [a].

The reader will not be displeased to see the passage from *Scala Chronica*; it brings many curious circumstances to light, and may serve in a great measure to terminate the controversy concerning the death of young Seton.

' Le roy desirant les armys et honors, et soun counsail enprovauntz
' et coveitaunz les gueres, qy tost sez acorderent à cest conditioun, et
' le plus tost par desire à reconquer lors pris sur eaux, par queux ils le
' avoint perduz. Dez plus privé du counsail le Roy moverent ove
' Edward de Baillol. Qui en le second semayn de qaresme assigerent
' la vile de Berewyk par mere et terre; et procheynement devaunt la
' Pentecost, le Roy d'Englet. y veint meismes, et assaillerent la vile,
' mais ne la pristrent point; mais reaparaillerent meutz lors horduz
' pour reassailler la dit vile. En le mene temps ceaux dedenz la vile
' parlerent de condiciouns, que sils ne ussent rescous devaunt un certain
' jour, qe' ils renderoint la vile; et sur ceo baillerent hostages. Devaunt quel temps limitez tout le poair d'Escoce, un si graunt multitude dez genz qi a mervail, passerent l'eaw de Twede en un aube
' de jour a le Yarforde, et sez monstrerent devaunt Berewik del autre
' Twede devers Engleter au plain vieu du Roy et de son ost, et bouterent gentz et vitaillis dedenz la vile, et demourerent là tout le jour
' et la nuyt. Et lendemain à haut hour delogerent et moverent parmy
' la tere le Roy en Northumbreland, ardauntz et destruyauntz le
' pays

[a] The manuscript of *Scala Chronica* is in the library bequeathed to Corpus Christi college in Cambridge, by Archbishop Parker. The reverend Mr Nasmith, late fellow of that college, transcribed it for my use, with a ready politeness which enhanced the favour.

THE SON OF SIR ALEXANDER SETON.

' pays au plain vien del oſt as Engles. Ceſtes gentz departyz à la
' maner le counſail le Roy al aſſege demanderent la vile ſelonc lez con-
' diciouns, le terme paſſé de lours reſcous. Ceaux dedenz diſoint,
' qils eſtoint reſcous et dez gentz et des vitails. Si monſtrerent novelis
' gardeins de la vile et chevalers eynz boutés de lour oſt, dount Willm
' de Keth eſtoit un od autres. Fuſt avys au dit counſeil qe ils avoint
' perduz louz oſtages. Si firent pendre le fitz Alex. de Setoun gar-
' deyn de la vile. Ceſt oſtage mort à la maner, lez autres dedenz la
' vile par tendreſce de lours enfauntz q'eſtoient oſtages, renovelerent
' condicioun par aſſent dez chevalers einz boutes as queux eſtoit avys
' qe lour poair d'Eſcoce furmountoit le oſt le Roy d'Englet. Si pri-
' ſtrent tiel novel condicion qe devaunt lez xv. jours ils butroient ij
' centz homs darmis par force par ſek tere dedenz la vile entre l'oſt
' des Engles et la haut mere, ou qe ils lez combateront au playn.
' Willm. de Keth, Willam de Prendregeſt, et Alex Gray, chevalers qe-
' ſtoient einz boutez dedenz la vile avoient conduyt à paſſer parmy l'oſt
' devers lour gentz d'Eſcoce, od ceſt condicioun qe furent amenez par
' conduyt parmy Northumb. qi lour oſt d'Eſcoce troverent a Witton-
' Undrewod et les reamenerent à Berewik à performer lour reſcous,
' ou ils vindrent combattre, et ou ils furent deſcounfitz. Archebald de
' Douglas al hour gardein d'Eſcoce de par le Roy David de Brus fuſt
' là mort, lez Countis de Roſſce, Muret, de Meneteth, de Levenaux, et
' de Suthirland furent là mortz. Le Scigoour de Douglas Fitz James
' de Douglas qi moruſt en le frounter de Cernate ſur lez Sarazins, qavoit
' enpris ceſt ſaint veage od le quere Robert de Bruys lour Roys qi le-
' avoit deviſe en ſoun moriaund, et touz plain dez barouns dez che-
' valers et dez comunes furent illoeqs un tres graunt noumbre mortz.
' La vile ſe rendy ſur condiciouns taille. Le Count de la Marche
' qavoit le chaſtel de Berewik à garder, deveint Engles, qi n'avoit my
' graunt gree de nul coſte, qi en le mene temps fiſt afferrmer par ſuf-
' fraunce le Roy ſoun chaſtell de Dunbar, qi puis fiſt grant mal.'

That

That is, 'the King was eager to be at the head of armies, and to
' gain renown. His counsellors approved of war, and wished for it:
' And, therefore, they speedily agreed to the conditions proposed [by
' Balliol and his adherents.] And *this* the rather, because they fought,
' by the means of the Scots themselves, to recover what the Scots had
' taken from England. Some of the chief counsellors of the King
' went with the army of Edward Balliol; and, in the second week of
' Lent, they laid siege to the town of Berwick, by sea, as well as on
' the land-side. And shortly before Whitsuntide, the King of Eng-
' land came thither in person. They assaulted the town; but they
' did not master it. Then they busied themselves in repairing their
' hurdles for a new assault. At this time, the besieged entered into a
' treaty with the besiegers, and agreed to surrender the town, unless
' succoured before a certain day: And to that effect they gave hostages.
' Before the day thus limited, the whole power of Scotland, in astonish-
' ing numbers, crossed the river of Tweed one morning at day-break,
' at the Yareford, and shewed themselves before Berwick, on the south
' side of the river, towards England, in full view of the King, and his
' army. They conveyed some men and provisions into the town, and
' they remained on their ground all the day, and the night following;
' and next day, before noon, they removed into the territories of the
' King in Northumberland, burning and ravaging the country in full
' view of the English army. These men having thus departed, the
' King's counsellors required the town to be given up, as the term
' stipulated for their being succoured had now elapsed. The besieged
' made answer, that they had received succours both of men and of
' provisions; and they shewed that there were new governours in the
' town, and also knights, who had been sent from their army. *Sir*
' *William Keith* was one, and there were others besides. It was the
' opinion of the English council that the Scots had forfeited their
' hostages, and, therefore, they caused the son of Alexander Seton, go-
' vernour of the town, to be hanged. On his death, after this sort,
' the

THE SON OF SIR ALEXANDER SETON. 319

' the other people of the town, from affection for their children, who
' were also hostages, renewed the treaty of capitulation. The Scot-
' tish knights, who had found entrance into the town, advised them
' to this, being of opinion that their forces were superior to the army
' of the King of England. By the new conditions, it was agreed to
' surrender the place, unless, within fifteen days, the Scots should either
' throw 200 men at arms in a body into the town by dry land, be-
' tween the sea and the English army, or combat [and overcome] the
' English army in open field. William de Keith, William de Prende-
' gest, and Alexander Gray, all knights who had thrown themselves
' into the place, had a passport to go through the English camp to
' their countrymen in Northumberland. They found the Scottish
' forces at Witton Underwood, and brought them back to the relief
' of Berwick. The Scots fought, and were discomfited. Archibald
' Douglas, then Regent of Scotland for King David Bruce, was *there*
' slain, together with the Earls of Ross, Murray, Menteth, Lenox,
' and Sutherland. The Lord Douglas also fell. He was the son of
' James Douglas who perished on the frontiers of Granada, in battle
' against the Saracens. This James Douglas had undertaken that
' holy expedition with the heart of Robert Bruce King of Scots, in
' consequence of his dying request. There were slain, besides them,
' many barons and knights, and a great multitude of the common
' sort. The town surrendered according to treaty. The Earl of March,
' who held the castle, became English; a man lightly esteemed by all
' parties. At the same time, by permission of the English King, he
' fortified his own castle of Dunbar, which afterwards had fatal con-
' sequences.'

Such is the narrative in *Scala Chronica*, of which Leland has made Leland, *Col-*
this very brief extract : ' After that the hole Englifch hoste had faught *lect.* i. 534.
' with the Scottes, and had so great a victory, the toune of Berwick
' was given up to King Edward.'

The narrative of *Scala Chronica* appears, in general, to be authentic, although not altogether free from errors.

From

From it we discover the solution of that difficulty in the accounts given by the Scottish historians, which hitherto has been inexplicable; namely, 'how Sir Alexander Seton could have been *governour of the town of Berwick* in July 1333, while it appeared from record, that, 'at that very time, Sir William Keith was governour.'

We now learn, that Sir Alexander Seton had been originally governour, but that Sir William Keith, having found means to enter Berwick towards the end of the siege, assumed the command, with a view, no doubt, to favour the pretext of Berwick having received succours, according to the letter of the treaty.

Hence, also, we may discern why the English were so exceedingly minute in the *second treaty*, as to what should be held as *succours to Berwick*. It was to prevent any ambiguity like that which had arisen from the too general terms, in which, as it seems, the *first treaty* had been conceived.

Grotius de Jure belli et pacis, lib. 4. 14. The right of putting an hostage to death, when the conditions of the treaty, for which he was given in pledge, are not performed, has been examined by the writers on the law of nations, more diligent in collecting *precedents*, than in establishing *principles*. That parties contracting may agree to give some of their own number as hostages, to be put to death if the treaty is violated on their part, appears to be a proposition of more difficulty than is generally apprehended; but that they may agree to give their children as hostages, under such conditions, is repugnant to every notion of morality; and, therefore, I neither pretend to justify Sir Alexander Seton for exposing his child to death, nor Edward III. for killing him.

No VI.

No. VI.

LIST OF THE PERSONS OF DISTINCTION

IN THE

SCOTTISH ARMY KILLED OR MADE PRISONERS

AT THE

BATTLE OF DURHAM,

17th October 1346.

ANNALS, Vol. II. pag. 219.

KNYGHTON is the historian who has given the most ample list of the killed at the battle of Durham; yet it is, in various particulars, erroneous; and it has been strangely disfigured by the mistakes of transcribers. Knyghton has afforded the ground-work of the following list; and care has been taken to correct his errors, whenever they could be detected. This was the more necessary, because our writers seem to have despaired of being able to correct the list, and have left many names as erroneous as they found them. Thus, Abercrombie has *Humphrey de Dieu* and *Robert Multalent*, and, to conceal his ignorance, he affirms them to have been Frenchmen. He has also *David Banant* and *Nicholas Clopodulian*, names which he has not ventured

Martial Atchievements, ii. 95.

ventured to account for. Some additions have been procured from Fordun, although his list is not so full as that in Knyghton. These additions are marked, F.

It is impossible to give a correct list of all the prisoners of distinction taken at Durham; for it appears, that many persons privately took ransoms for the prisoners whom they had made, and suffered them to depart. This practice became so general, that it was prohibited under pain of death, [20th November, and 13th December 1346.]

Most of the prisoners of distinction, who had not escaped by means of this connivance, were ordered to be conveyed to the tower of London, [8th December 1346.] From that instrument, and from some other scattered notices, I have drawn up a list of prisoners, not so compleat, indeed, as might have been wished, yet more authentic and intelligible than any that has been hitherto exhibited.

KILLED.

1. John Randolph, Earl of Moray
2. Maurice Moray, Earl of Strathern
3. David de la Haye, Constable, F
4. Robert Keith, Marshall, F
5. Robert de Peebles, Chamberlain, F

6.

(1) The younger son of Randolph the Regent. With him the male line of that heroic family ended. He was succeeded in his honours and estate by his sister, the Countess of March, vulgarly termed *Black Agnes*.

(2) In right of his mother Mary. The English, in general, did not acknowledge his title. Knyghton mentions him again under the name of *Maurice de Murref*.

(3) Knyghton mentions his name, but without his title of office.

(4) Grandson of Sir Robert Keith, mentioned Vol. ii. p. 47.

(5) There is considerable uncertainty as to this name.

AT THE BATTLE OF DURHAM. 283

6. Thomas Charters, Chancellor, F
7. Humphry de Boys
8. John de Bonneville, F
9. Thomas Boyd
10. Andrew Buttergask, F
11. Roger Cameron
12. John de Crawfurd
13. William Frafer, F
14. David Fitz-Robert
15. William de Haliburton
16. William de la Haye
17. Gilbert de Inchmartin, E
18. Edward de Keith
19. Edmunde de Keith

20.

(6) De Carnuto. A name of great antiquity in Scotland. See *Crawfurd*, Officers of State, p. 19.

(7) Knyghton, and his copiſts, fay, *de Bloys*, probably *Boys*, the ſame with *Boyſe*, or *Boece*.

(8)

(9) This is a miſtake in Knyghton, unleſs there were two perſons of that name; for there was a *Thomas Boyd* among the priſoners.

(10) This family ſubſiſted until about the beginning of the 15th century, when the heireſs, *Margaret Buttergaſk of that Ilk*, made over her eſtate to the family of Gray.

(11)
(12)
(13) Of Cowie; anceſtor of Lord Salton.
(14) Probably ſome perſon who had not as yet aſſumed a ſurname.
(15) Fordun ſays *Walter*; but there is a *Walter de Haliburton* among the priſoners.
(16)
(17)
(18)
(19) According to Knyghton, the brother of Edward de Keith.

S ſ 2

LIST OF PERSONS KILLED, &c.

20. Reginald Kirkpatrick
21. David de Lindefay
22. John de Lindefay
23. Robert Maitland
24. ———— Maitland
25. Philip de Meldrum
26. John de la More
27. Adam Moygrave
28. William Moubray
29. William de Ramfay, the father
30. Michael Scot, F
31. John St Clair
32. Alexander Strachan
33. ———— Strachan
34. John Stewart

35.

*(20)
(21) Said by Fordun to have been 'the fon and heir of Lord David de Lindefay,' anceftor of the Earls of Crawfurd and Balcarras.
(22)
(23) Called *Matulant* by Knyghton. From whence Abercromble formed ' Matta-lent, a French knight.' Plainly *Matulant*, now *Maitland*, of Thirleftane, anceftor of the Earl of Lauderdale.
(24) The brother of Robert Maitland of Thirleftane.
(25) Called *de Mildren* by Knyghton.
(26)
(27)
(28) There was a *William Moubray* among the prifoners.
(29) A *William de Ramfay*, probably *the younger*, was among the prifoners.
(30) Of *Murtho Iftonī*, now *Murdiefton*, anceftor of the Duke of Buccleugh.
*(31) There was a *John St Clair* among the prifoners.
(32) Called *Stragy* by Knyghton.
(33) The brother of Alexander Strachan.
(34)

AT THE BATTLE OF DURHAM.

35. John Stewart
36. Alan Stewart
37. Adam de Whitfom

PRISONERS.

1. David II. King of Scots
2. Duncan Earl of Fife
3. John Graham, Earl of Menteth
4. Malcolm Fleming, Earl of Wigton
5. George Abernethy

6.

(35) I conjecture that Sir John Stewart of Dreghorn is meant, whose father Alan was killed at Halidon.

(36) The brother of John Stewart.

(37) Knyghton has *Adam de Nyften*, which is plainly an error in transcribing. Perhaps *de Dennifton* is the right name. Knyghton reckons *Patonus Heryng*, i. *Patricius Herm*, among the flain. It appears from *Fœdera* that he was a prifoner. Knyghton also reckons *the Earl of Sutherland* among the flain. Pardon, among the prifoners. It is certain that he was not killed; and, if he was made prifoner, he muft have been among thofe who were fuffered to efcape immediately after the battle.

(1) He received two wounds before he yielded himfelf a prifoner.

(2) He had fwo n fealty to Balliol. He was condemned to fuffer death as a traitor, but obtained mercy.

(3) In right of his wife *Mary*, according to the mode of thofe times; he was executed as a traitor. He had formerly fworn fealty to Edward III.

(4) He is called *Malcolm Fleming*, without any addition; *Fœdera*, T. v. p. 537. He had a grant of the earldom of Wigton in 1342. See *Crawfurd*, Peerage, p. 493. But the Englifh government did not acknowledge the right of David II. to confer titles of honour. It is probable that he made his efcape; for, in *Calendars of Antient Charters*, p. 203, there is this title, 'de capiendo Roberto Bertram, qui Malcolmum Fleming, Scotum, inimicum Regis, evadere permifit.'

(5) Of Salton, anceftor of Lord Salton.

326   LIST OF PERSONS KILLED, &c.

  6. David de Annand.
  7. William Baillie
  8. Thomas Boyd
  9. Andrew Campbell
  10. Gilbert de Carrick
  11. Robert Chisholm
  12. Nicholas Knockdolian
  13. Fergus de Crawfurd
  14. Roger de Crawfurd
  15. Bartholomew de Dermond
  16. John Douglas
  17. William Douglas, the elder
             18.

(6)
(7) Supposed to be Baillie of Lambistoun or Lambistoun, vulgarly Lamington; *Nisbet*, vol. ii. Appendix, p. 137. But see *Sir James Dalrymple*, p. 410.
(8) Probably of Kilmarnock. The son of that Boyd who was the faithful and fortunate companion of Robert Bruce.
(9) Of Loudoun. In right of his mother Susanna Crawfurd, heritable sheriff of Airshire, ancestor of the Earl of Loudoun.
(10) Ancestor of the Earl of Cassilis. His son assumed the name of Kennedy.
(11)
(12) Called *Clapdolian* by Knyghton, and by Abercrombie, *Clapdolian*, in Galloway, although the name has a German air.
(13)
(14)
(15) A German, as the record in *Foedera* bears. This is mentioned, because Abercrombie, vol. ii. p. 99. says, ' perhaps *Drummond*,' although he had perused *Foedera*.
(16) Probably the younger brother of William Douglas of Liddesdale, ancestor of the Earl of Morton.
(17) This person, I am confident, is William Douglas, the bastard brother of William Douglas of Liddesdale. There is no evidence that William Lord Douglas, son of Archibald, surnamed *Tineman*, and first Earl of that family, was made prisoner at Durham, or, indeed, that he was present at the battle. *Fordun*, L. xiv. c. 6. expressly
                              says,

18. Patrick de Dunbar
19. Adam de Fullarton
20. John Giffard
21. Laurence Gilibraad.
22. David Graham
23. Alexander Haliburton
24. John de Haliburton
25. Walter de Haliburton
26. Patrick Heron
27. William de Jardin
28. Roger de Kirkpatrick
29. Thomas de Lippes
30. William de Livingston

31.

says, that he did not come from France till after the battle. We learn from *Fœdera*, that he was at liberty while others were prisoners; and we do not learn from *Fœdera*, that he was ever a prisoner. To support an erroneous hypothesis of Boece, concerning William Lord Douglas, records have been misconstructed and misapplied.

(18)
(19)
(20)
(21)
(22) Of Monroſe; anceſtor of the Duke of Monroſe.
(23 24) *Douglas*, Peerage, p. 321 conjectures, not improbably, that they were the brothers of Walter de Haliburton. But he ought not to have referred to Fordun, v. ii. [L. xiv. c. 3.] in proof of this, for Fordun mentions them not.
(25) Predeceſſor of the Lords Haliburton of Dirleton.
(26)
(27)
(28) Made prisoner by Ralph de Haſtings. Haſtings died of his wounds. He bequeathed the body of Roger de Kirkpatrick to his joint legatees, Edmund Haſtings of Kynthorp, and John de Kirkeby; *Fœdera*, T. v. p. 515.
(29) Called, in *Calendars of Antient Charters*, *Chevalier*. If he was not a foreigner, I know not who he was.
(30)

328   LIST OF PERSONS KILLED, &c.

31. ——— Lorein
32. Duncan M'Donnel
33. Duncan M'Donnel
34. ——— de Makepath
35. John de Maxwell
36. Walter Moigne
37. David Moray
38. William de Moray
39. William More
40. William Moubray
41. Patrick de Polwarth
42. John de Preston
43. Alexander de Ramsay
44. Henry de Ramsay
45. Ness de Ramsay
46.

(31) Said in the record to have been the son of Eustace Lorein. This Eustace, called *Taffy* by *Fordun*, L. xiv. c. 5. was captain of Roxburgh under Douglas of Liddesdale, the governour.

(32) Not in the list in *Foedera*, T. v. p. 535. but mentioned as a prisoner, *Foedera*, T. v. p. 554.

(33) See *Foedera*, ib. the son of the former.

(34) Were it not for the article *de*, I should suppose that some person of the name of M Beth was here understood.

(35) Of Carlaverock, ancestor of the Earl of Nithsdale.

(36)
(37)
(38)
(39)
(40)
(41) Ancestor of the Earl of Marchmont.
(42) Supposed to have been the ancestor of Preston Lord Dingwall.
(43)
(44)
(45)

46. William de Ramfay
47. William de Salton
48. John St Clair
49. Alexander Steel
50. Alexander Stewart
51. John Stewart
52. John Stewart
53. John de Vallence
54. William de Vaux
55. Robert Wallace.

No. VII.

(46) Probably Sir William Ramfay of Collothy. He was at the battle of Poidiers in 1356, and was made prifoner there.

(47) Not in *Fœdera*, but mention is made of him, *Calendar of Antient Charters*, p. 199.

(48)
(49)
(50)
(51) Of Dalfwinton, as the record bears. Anceftor of the Earl of Galloway.
(52) A baftard, as the record bears.
(53)
(54)
(55)

No. VII.

KINGS.	MARRIAGES.	CHILDREN.
Robert born 11th July 1274; began to reign 27th March 1306.	1. Isabella, daughter of Donald Earl of Marre. 2. Elisabeth, daughter of Aymer de Burgh, Earl of Ulster. She died 26th October 1327. Buried at Dunfermline.	By his first wife. Marjory, married Walter the Stewart of Scotland 1315. Died about the end of the same year. By his second wife. David, born 5th March 1323-4. Margaret, married William Earl of Sutherland. Matildis, married Thomas Isaac. Elizabeth, married Sir William Oliphant of Gask, [but this is doubtful.]
David II. began to reign 7th June 1329.	1. Johanna, daughter of Edward II. King of England, 12th July 1328. She died, 1362. 2. Margaret, daughter of Sir John Logie, Knt. 1363. She survived her husband.	

DEATHS.	ENGLAND.	FRANCE.	POPES.
Robert I. died at Cardross 7th June 1329, in the 55th year of his age, and 24th year of his reign. Buried at Dunfermline. He had a natural son, Robert, slain at Duplin, 12th August 1332.	Edward I. 1272. Edward II. 1307. Edward III. 1326.	Philip le Bel, 1285. Lewis X. 1314. Philip le Long, 1316. Charles le Bel, 1322. Philip de Valois, 1328.	Benedict X. or XI. 1303. Clement V. 1305.
David II. died in the castle of Edinburgh, 22d February 1370-71, in the 47th year of his age, and the 42d year of his reign. Buried in the church of the abbey of Holy-rood.	Edward III. 1326.	Philip de Valois, 1328. John, 1350. Charles V. 1364.	John XXII. 1316. Benedict XI. or XII. 1334. Clement VI. 1342. Innocent VI. 1352. Urban V. 1362.

No. VIII.

CORRECTIONS

AND

ADDITIONS.

ANNALS, Vol. I.

WITH the assistance of my friends, I have been enabled to correct many errors in *the Annals of Scotland*, and to make considerable additions to the work. Much, however, remains to be corrected, and there is much to be added.

P. 1. note *. The authors of *the Critical Review*, and of *the London Review*, selected the account of M'Beth as a specimen of the nature and execution of this work. Hence it may be presumed, that any information concerning the real name of the Lady M'Beth of Shakespere, will be acceptable. In an instrument subjoined to *Crawfurd's Lives of Officers of State*, the wife of M'Beth is called ' *Gruach* filia *Bodhe*.'

P. 2. note †. For ' accompt' r. ' account.'

L 7.
P. 2. note ‡. Vary the note thus : ' In Aberdeenshire, two miles north-west of
' the village of Kincardin O'Neil, just by the parish-church of Lum-
' fanan, there is a valley where the vestiges of an antient fortress are
' still to be discerned, of an oblong figure, in length near an hundred
' yards, and twenty yards in breadth. A brook, which waters the
' valley,

'valley, appears to have been led round the fortrefs. As no remains,'
&c. The note as it ftands in the Annals, was communicated by a
correfpondent. There occurred in it an ungrammatical expreffion: The
error was pointed out in one of the periodical publications at London.
I wifh that the fame critic had pointed out the other errors in the Annals; for there are very many things difcernible by a reader, which
an author is apt to overlook.

For 'probably,' r. 'and probably.'   P. 4. note *. l. 12.
Del. the words, 'his errors,' &c.   P. 9. N. 1. l. 6.
For 'polititian, r. 'politician.'   P. 10. N. †. l. 1.
For 'fe,' r. 'the.'   P. 14. note, l. 14. 15.
For 'probably,' r. 'perhaps.'   P. 16. N. l. 7.
Add, 'at this day, the Solway, where it becomes navigable, is cal- P. 17. N. l. 8.
'led *the Wead*, or *the Scot-wead*.'
Del. the words after *giftas*, and add, 'in High Dutch, *Geifel*, teftis, P. 17. N. l. 13.
'fponfor; fidejuffor, obfes.'
Add, 'Doctor Percy, Dean of Carlifle, has favoured me with fome P. 14. N. *.
'obfervations on this fubject. They are curious, and will be accept-
'able to my readers.—The common ftory of the death of Malcolm III.
'*from being pierced in the eye*, begins to be difcredited, becaufe the
'old Scottifh hiftorians have connected it with a circumftance that was
'not true, namely, that it gave rife to the name of *Piercy*. William
'de Percy, who came over with the Conqueror, founded, before the
'death of Malcolm, the monaftery of Whitby in Yorkfhire, and had
'then the name *de Percy*, or *de Perci*, as appears from the charter of
'his foundation, and other public deeds, which Dugdale has printed
'at large in his *Monafticon*. So that there can be nothing more cer-
'tain than that the name of *Percy* was not taken up from the cir-
'cumftance of Malcolm's death; nor, indeed, had the Percy family
'the moft remote connection with Northumberland till after the reign
'of Edward I.' See *Dugdale*, Baronage, vol. i. v. *Percy*.

'On

'On the other hand, I am inclined to believe, that there is some
' truth in the account of the stratagem employed by the soldier that
' killed Malcolm; because I find it related by annalists who were most
' likely to know it, although their history has never yet been printed.
' This is the old Chronicle of Alnwick abbey, of which a transcript
' is preserved in the British Museum, among the Harleyan MSS.
' No. 692. (12.) fol. 195.
' It is thus intitled, *Cronica Monasterii de Alnwyke*, &c. and the
' transcript thus begins:
' *Incipit Genealogia Fundatorum et Advocatorum Abbatiae de Aln-*
' *wyke, primò scilicet de Ricardo Tisoune fundatore capellae sancti*
' *Wilfridi monialium de Gisings.*
' It begins with the conquest, gives the history of the foundation
' of Alnwick abbey by the family of *de Vescy*, barons of Alnwick,
' and presents a short summary of the history of those barons, and of
' some of the principal events relating to the abbey during their times:
' And, upon the extinction of the family of de Vescy, gives the his-
' tory of the first Percys who succeeded them, and ends with the ac-
' cession of King Richard II. to the throne.

' There are so many circumstances of local history and description
' scattered through the whole composition, that there is no doubt but
' that the annals were really composed within the monastery of Aln-
' wick. It indeed includes a history of the Abbots, and has all the
' marks of a genuine history compiled from short minutes, made at,
' or soon after, the time when most of the events happened. Now the
' history of Malcolm's death is related in the following very peculiar
' and circumstantial manner.

' Speaking of the second Lord, Eustace de Vescy, son of William,
' the Annalists say, *confirmavit omnia bona patris et avi nobis collata:*
' *Et insuper dedit nobis quandam rure porcionem, quae dicitur* Quarel-
' flat, *pro illa terra super quam fundavit capellam Sancti Leonardi, pro*
                                                                ' Malcolmi

' *Malcolmi Regis Scotiae anima, sponsâ scilicet sanctae Margaretae Re-*
' *ginae Scotorum, qui ibidem occisus est, cum filio suo primogenito*
' *Edwardo, anno Dom. 1093, anno scilicet Regis Willielmi Rufi, filii*
' *bastardi, 7mo. Ista sancta Margareta obiit eodem anno, quo et vir*
' *suus.*

' *Hoc autem anno ecclesia nova Dunelmensis incepta est, episcopo Wil-*
' *lielmo, et Malcolmo Rege Scotiae, et Turgone Priore ponentibus primos*
' *lapides in fundamento. Huic autem Eustathio filio Willielmi de Vescy*
' *dedit Willielmus Rex Margaretam, filiam Willielmi Regis Scotiae, filii*
' *Malcolmi, in uxorem, ex illegitimo tamen thoro progenitam, cum baro-*
' *nia de* Sprouftoun, *pro fundatione capellae sancti Leonardi, quam prae-*
' *dictus Eustathius fundaverat pro anima Malcolmi Regis Scotiae, ibidem*
' *letaliter vulnerati juxta quendam fontem; eidem fonti nomen suum*
' *relinquens usque in perpetuum, unde fons iste vocatur Anglico Ydio-*
' *mate,* Malcolm's well. *Iste Malcolmus Rex fuit vulneratus ab Ha-*
' *mundo tunc constabulario praedicti Eustathii de Vescy, cum quadam*
' *lancea, eidem lanceae claves castelli de Alnwyck ad cautelam super-*
' *imponendo, quasi eidem Regi Scotiae Malcolmo castellum cum omnibus*
' *inhabitantis,* [sic MS.] *subjiciens. Hoc facto, rediit idem* Hamundus
' *concito gressu, sanus, illaesus, et incolumis, transiens vadum aquae im-*
' *meabilis, et supra modum tunc inundantis, voluntate divinâ, nomen suum*
' *eidem vado relinquens, unde vadus ille, ubi transiit, dicitur Anglico*
' *Ydiomate,* Hamundeford, *ab illo die et deinceps.*'

' Here it is obfervable, that the annalift makes no mention of the *eye*
' as the vulnerable part; *that* was a pofterior invention, and probably
' fuggefted to compleat the etymology of *Piercye*. With regard to the
' ford, that would ceafe, together with the name, when the bridge was
' built over the Alne; and as to *Malcolm's well*, the ground (near
' which ftood a crofs, the reliques of which are extant to this day, and
' called *Malcolm's crofs*,) hath undergone fuch changes, principally by
' finking coal-pits, a long time ago near the crofs, that both the well

' and

'and its name have been lost out of memory. But, about a stone's
throw below the cross, still oozes a little streamlet of water, which
proves that a well might have been supplied thereabouts with plenty
of water.

'The name of the soldier here was *Hamond*; but if his commander
was *Moubray*, that will account for the confusion and misnomers of
the Scottish historians. Though he held the place of Constable of
Vescy's castle, yet Moubray may have commanded at that time in
Northumberland; and Hamond's exploit would naturally enough be
attributed to him by distant relators of the transaction.—

'I am not yet satisfied as to the authenticity of this relation. The
silence of the Saxon Chronicle is a strong circumstance against it, and
the silence of S. Dunelm. [or Turgot] is a still stronger.

'The passage relating to Malcolm III. in the annals of Alnwick
abbey, is more modern than it appears to be at the first inspection.
It was written after the marriage of Eustace de Vescy and the natural
daughter of William King of Scots. Now, that marriage did not
take place till 1193. *Chr. Melros*, p. 179. a compleat century after
the death of Malcolm III.; besides, there is reason to suppose, from the
narrative, that that marriage was not a recent event when the annals
were drawn up, and that William was not then the reigning King of
Scotland. Now William died in 1212. A Northumbrian author, who
could suppose that William the Lion was the son of Malcolm Can-
more, must have lived in a later age. He says that King William
gave Margaret the daughter of William King of Scotland in marriage
to Eustace de Vescy. This passage detracts from the antiquity of the
Annalist. By *King William*, he certainly meant *William Rufus*. Now,
it is impossible that any one who lived near the times of Eustace de
Vescy and his wife Margaret, could have supposed that William Rufus was their contemporary. The Annalist speaks of Margaret Queen

'of

‘ of Scotland as *a faint*. But it is not probable that she obtained that
‘ title before the year 1250, that is, 157 after the death of Mal-
‘ colm III. See *Fordun*, L. r. c. 3.

‘ In the Saxon Chronicle it is afferted, that Morel of Bamburgh, the
‘ fteward of Moubray, flew Malcolm III. And furely the author of
‘ that chronicle had better opportunities of information than the Anna-
‘ lift of Alnwick abbey, who wrote at leaft 100 or 150 years after the
‘ event. If the Saxon Chronicle is to be credited, the whole fabric of
‘ the ftory in the annals of Alnwick abbey falls to the ground. I ad-
‘ mit the probability of the place called *Malcolm's crofs* being the place
‘ at which Malcolm III. was flain; for fuch memorials were frequently
‘ erected on the fpot where any eminent perfons loft their lives. But,
‘ for the reafons affigned, I ftill doubt as to the origin of the name of
‘ *Hammond's ford*. Perhaps, in all this, I am too fceptical; but one na-
‘ turally wifhes to difbelieve a tale of infamous treachery.’

Del. ‘ a ftrange picture of that age;' not fo much from my own P. 39. L. 16.
judgement, as in deference to the opinion of a correfpondent.

For ‘ inveterate,’ r. ‘ eftablifhed.’ P. 50. L. 14.
For ‘ St Andrew's,’ r. ‘ St Andrews.’ P. 50. L. 15.
For ‘ I imagine,’ r. ‘ I formerly imagined.’ P. 78. N. L. 4.

After ‘ contemptuous fenfe,' add, ‘ *Caterans* is from *Ceatherne*, a P. 78. N. l. 8.
‘ general term derived from *Cath*, battle. It properly fignifies *men*
‘ *fit for fervice, but of a rank inferior to that of the nobility*. But, how-
‘ ever plaufible this conjecture may appear, I prefer the opinion of
‘ thofe who obferve, that the people of *Lorn* are here underftood. In
‘ the Gaelic language, they are ftill called *Labhern*, [pronounced *La-*
‘ *vern*.] This word, extended by a Latin termination, might natu-
‘ rally enough have produced *Lavernanus, Lavernani*.’

Del. ‘ I prefume that he placed no confidence in them.’ P. 78. N. L. 10.
‘ I have been cenfured for this note, and I have been ferioufly told, P. 81. N. †.
‘ that there are many reafons which juftify Hector Boece for afcribing
‘ the

338   CORRECTIONS

'the victory to the Scots. Hector Boece wrote about four hundred
'years after the battle of Cutton moor, and Aldred lived at the court
'of David I. *Which* of the two authorities ought to preponderate?'

P. 83. L. 11.   For 'By,' r. 'of.'
P. 96. N. *.   Del. this note, it appears to be erroneous.
P. 96. N. †.   For 'In the Anglo-Saxon language, &c.' r. 'in the Anglo-Saxon
l. 4.   'language, *faer, fere,* means *dry, withered, waste*.'
P. 96. N. ‡.   For 'Salisbury or Selisbury,' r. '*Saerisbury, Serisbury, Salisbury,* is
l. 12.   'the *dry,* or *waste habitation.*'
P. 97. N. *.   After 'Lefmahagow,' add, '[or Ecclefia Machati.]' And, at the
l. 4.   end of the note, 'the common people sometimes preserve the true
                'pronunciation of names, but generally they disfigure them. Thus,
                '*Les, Cleish, Eagles,* are vulgar corruptions of *Ecclefia.*'
P. 107. N. §.   Add, 'It appears that the inhabitants of Moray again rebelled in
                'the year 1171; *Selden*, titles of honour, Part ii. c. 7. §. 2. So that
                'the policy of Malcolm had not the consequences expected from it.'
P. 108. N. ‡.   Add, 'The word *Somerled*,' says a correspondent learned in the
                Gaelic language, 'is formed by a double translation and corruption
                'from *Samuel,* which the Caledonians express by *Somberle,* from
                'which the Latins formed *Somerledus,* rendered by our modern cri-
                'tics *Somerled.* [It seems that the error of our modern critics consists
                'in writing *Somerled* instead of *Somberle.*]'

The same correspondent adds a curious and instructive note. '*Gil-*
'*lecalm,*' says he, 'is the same with *Malcolm,* in general; *Gille* and
'*Mael,* pronounced *Gil* and *Mil* nearly, denote *servant*. Originally,
'and uncompoundedly, they are not synonymous, as the former
'means *servus,* and the latter *calvus.* So that this last, in the for-
'mation of proper names, seems to imply *consecrated by tonsure.* [But
'if hair was anciently a sign of freedom, why might not *bald,* or
'*shaved,* imply *servant*?] *Gilchrist* is *servus Christi*; *Gilespie,* or
'*Gilescop,* is *servus Episcopi*; *Giltride,* is *servus Brigidae*; and *Gil-*
                                                                    '*patria*

'*patric* is *servus Patricii*; *Gilcolumb*, *Gilcolumb*, and *Gillscolam*, all
' mean *servus Columbae*. Again, *Malcolumb*, or *Melcolumb*, according
' as the orthography, or the pronunciation, is followed, is also *servus*
' *Columbae*; *Mal*, or *Milmaire*, is *servus Mariae*; and *Mildomaich* is
' *servus Domini*, which last is generally used in speaking of infants
' before baptism. These, and all such, were first assumed as Christian
' names; though many of them became afterwards family names,
' with the usual patronymic of *Mac* prefixed. Thus, *Mac-gil-bbride*
' is *natus servo Brigidae*; *Mac-gil-eandreas* is *natus servo Andreae*;
' and *Mac-gil-ion*, or *Mac-gil-eoin*, contracted into *Macleon*, is *natus*
' *servo Johannis*. Such modest names the first Caledonian converts
' seem to have used before they grew bold enough to assume the
' sacred names of *John*, *Andrew*, *Mary*, *Bridget*, &c. unqualified.'

For ' 28th,' r. ' 9th.'   P. 109. L. 14.
For ' agreeable,' r. ' agreeably.'.   P. 110. L. 5.
Add, ' 1171. In this year there was an insurrection of the inhabi- P. 112. L. 9.
' tants of Moray.' Add on the margin, ' *Selden*, Titles of Honour,
' ii. c. 7. §. 2.'
For ' to make,' r. ' to send.'   P. 113. L. ult.
For ' assisted.' r. ' was present.'   P. 120. L. 11.
For ' at any rate,' r. ' besides.'   P. 120. L. 18.
For ' the forgers of England, and the forgers of all England.' r. P. 121. N. 1.
' the forgers of Yorke and of Canterbury.—The original expression
' was sufficiently intelligible to those who understand the distinction
' between *England* and *all England*; but, as some of my readers do
' not, I thought it better to change the expression, than to explain it
' by a commentary.'

For ' these names are probably in *Ch. Melros*,' r. ' these names, P. 121. N. 2.
' probably corrupted, are in *Ch. Melros*.'

After ' Durham,' add, ' proud of new authority.'   P. 125. L. 1.
For ' communication,' r. ' excommunication.'   P. 125. L. 13.
After ' impartiality,' add, ' he was succeeded by his son Richard, P. 131. L. 7.
' surnamed *Coeur de Lion*.'

340   CORRECTIONS.

P. 135. N.°.   Del. the note, and say, 'Lord Lyttelton, Vol. I. p. 401.—411. has
'a differtation on the value of money, from the conqueft to the death
'of Henry II. He fays, " From the beginning of the reign of Wil-
" liam I. till after the death of Henry II. the Englifh pound muft
" be underftood to mean a pound weight of filver, containing three
" times the quantity of filver contained in our prefent pound Ster-
" ling; the fhilling and penny weighing alfo three times as much as
" ours.—The common mark in thofe days was two thirds of a pound
" of filver, that is, twice the value of our prefent pound Sterling.—
" The proportion that the value of filver then bore to the common
" value of it at prefent, has been eftimated differently by authors who
" have treated the fubject; fome thinking that it ought to be reckon-
" ed at twenty, fome at fifteen or fixteen, and fome at ten times the
" prefent rate. To form fome conjecture *which* of thefe computa-
" tions is neareft the truth, or rather to fhow that they are all much
" too high, I fhall tranfcribe a few paffages from the contemporary
" authors," &c. The inference which his Lordfhip draws from the
examples quoted, is, ' that the value of filver, from the conqueft to
' the death of Henry II. ought to be reckoned at *five* times the pre-
' fent rate.'

Thus, when, in that period, we read of a *pound* and a *mark*, we
muft figure to ourfelves fomething which, for the common purpofes
of life, was equal to *fifteen pounds*, and *ten pounds*, Sterling, of our
own times. I do not pretend to fay that Lord Lyttelton's calculation
is precifely exact.

P. 154. L. 14.   Add this note. ' I have been told, that *I doubt here, but give no*
' *reafons for my doubts; that I am determined to doubt,* &c. But, in-
' deed, I made no queftion as to the poffibility of the adventures faid
' to have befallen the Earl of Huntington. I only faid, that *the evi-*
' *dence was fomewhat fufpicious;* and any one who is as well ac-
' quainted with Hector Boece as I am, will fufpect all wares from that
' magazine.'

                                                                    Add,

AND ADDITIONS. 341

Add, 'A copy of this very rare and curious book is in the library P. 134. N. ª.
'of Richard Gough, Efq; finall 4to, 151 leaves, *imprimé à Paris, par
'la Veufve feu Jehan Trepperel, demourant en la rue neufve noftre
'Dame a l'enfeigne de l'efcu de France.* The title runs thus: *S'en-
'fuyt le livre des trois filz de Roys, c'eft affavoir, de France, d' An-
'gleterre, et d'Efcoffe, lefquels en leur jeuneffe pour la foi Chretienne
'eurent de glorirufes victoires fur les Turcs, au fervice du Roi de Ce-
'cille, lequel fut faict apres ung des lecteurs de l'empire.* This book
'is altogether fabulous. J. Major fuppofes *the Earl of Huntington* to
'be one of its heroes, becaufe it treats *of a David, fon of the King of
'Scots.* That name, however, has been employed at random; for it is
'faid in the romance, that David, on the death of his father, became
'King of Scotland; and, under that title, diftinguifhed himfelf in a
'tourneament at Vienna.

'The note concerning the names of Caithnefs and Sutherland ought P. 137. N. †.
'to be omitted; for I am pofitively affured that it is altogether erro-
'neous.'

For 'St Bartholomew's day,' r. 24th Auguft.' P. 136. L. 6.
'The derivation of the word *Perth* ought to be omitted. I have P. 138. N. ª.
'been favoured with different interpretations of the word. Not know-
'ing *which* to choofe, I judge it beft to omit them all.'

After l. ii. add, '1214.' P. 139. L li.
For '5th,' r. '10th.' P. 142. L 4.

Add, 'I am informed by one correfpondent, that *Kinank Macabi* is P. 142. N. †.
'*Cranachmahoet*, which implies, in the Gaelic language, *the chief of
'a diftrict:* By another correfpondent, that *Kenauk* is the man's
'name, *Macabs* his furname. Sutherland is termed in the Gaelic
'language *Cad or Cabs.* Hence the Earl of Sutherland is termed
'*Morar Chat,* that is, *the Lord of Sutherland. Kenauk Ma-
'cabs* might have been a Sutherland man who joined *Makentagart.*
'But a third correfpondent fays, the word, though corrupted and
'difigured, is ftill very intelligible to every Caledonian ear. It is
'*Caineoch-*

CORRECTIONS

' Caineach-mac-Eacbain, that is, Kenneth son of Hector. Both Cain-
' each, and Earbain, mean ductor equitum, or rector equorum, with
' this difference, that the former is Archippus, and the latter Hippar-
' chus. Further, he remarks, that the Clan Eachuin still subsists, and
' that M'Kenzie of Carloch is the head of it.—Makentagar is certain-
' ly Mac-in-tsagaird, or the son of the priest. Sagard is priest; in the
' genitive, Sagaird, or of a priest;—in-tsagaird is of the priest; in
' which last, the radical letter s is mute, and the servile t pronounced
' in its room.

' It is said, that, before the local surname of Ross was assumed, the
' clan Ross had the surname of Mackintagaird, because their ancestor
' was the son of a priest. Such surnames were not uncommon before
' the introduction of clerical celibacy into Scotland. Thus we have
' M'Nab, that is, the son of the abbot; and M'Pherson, that is, the son
' of the parson; and M'Vicar, that is, the son of the vicar.'

P. 143. N. °.   For ' calendar,' r. ' calendars.'
L 2.
P. 151. N. °.   Add, ' One learned person conjectures that her name was Doruag-
' beal, or fair hands. But another says, that the name on the seal is
' the only intelligible one, implying filia or virgo magna, candida.'

P. 152. L 3.   Add this note at Gilrodh. ' Properly Gilruadh, that is, the red-
' haired lad. And hence the modern corrupted name of Gilderoy.'

P. 152. N. °.   Instead of ' So that the name,' &c. say, ' the word Thomas is placed
' here, by an error of transcribers, instead of Comes. As to M'Kinta-
' gart, or M'Kintagaird, see p. 142.'

P. 172. L 14.   For, ' had married, as it would seem,' r. ' appears to have married.
' Whenever the erroneous expression, it would seem, occurs, it ought
' to be changed into it appears, or it seems, or it is probable.'

P. 177. L 11.   For ' Lewis,' r. ' Lewes.'
P. 183. L 24.   For ' for that, r. ' because.'
P. 309. N. °.   Add, ' I have collected a pedigree of Robert de Pinkeny from dif-
' ferent passages in Dugdale, Baronage, Vol. ii. p. 556. 769. John
' de Lindesay, called, 6. Hen. III. the kinsman of Alexander II. King

' of

AND ADDITIONS.   343

' of Scots, married Marjory, supposed to have been the daughter of
' Henry Prince of Scotland. John de Lindesay had two sons, David
' and Gerard, who died without issue, and a daughter, and heiress,
' Alicia, married to Henry de Pinkeny, grandfather of Robert de Pin-
' keny, the competitor. This will be better understood by a genea-
' logical tree.

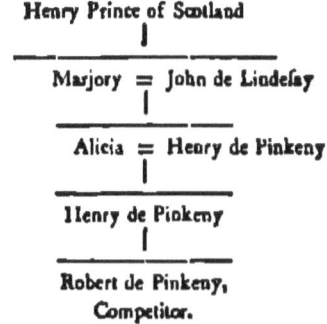

' In this pedigree there are several things doubtful; and, particu-
' larly, the existence of *a Marjory*, daughter of Prince Henry.'
 For ' it would seem,' r. ' it is probable.' P. 229. N. †.
 At ' Lamelay,' add note, ' *P. Langtoft* has Lanercost and Hexham P. 235. L. 22.
' instead of Lamelay, Vol. ii. P. 273.'
 Vary the note thus : ' In this carnage 4000 men perished, according P. 236. N. †.
' to *Langtoft*, Vol. ii. p. 272. although his translator says 40000.
' 7500 perished according to Fordun,' &c.
 Add, ' it was this renunciation which made Langtoft exclaim, P. 237. N. °.
' Vol. ii. p. 265. " Scotland, whine not I se be tonken to helle
" ground." ' This *old English* is intelligible enough.'
 Add on the margin, ' *Hemingford*, i. 96. *Langtoft*, ii. 277. P. 238. L 8.
 For ' never,' r. ' and never.' P. 241. L 7.
                 For

CORRECTIONS

P. 241. l. 9.   For 'at,' r. 'and at.'

P. 242. l. 4.   Add on the margin, 'Langtoft, ii. 282.'

P. 243. l. 5.   Add on the margin, Langtoft, ii. 297.'

P. 246. N. °.   After 'book,' add, ' for it is characteristical.'

P. 251. l. 7.   At 'ford,' add note, ' probably the ford of Maner, at which place 'there was an advanced post in the days of the Romans.'

P. 251. N. °.   Add, ' it is the general tradition of the country, that, in those times, ' the bridge was about a mile higher up the river than the present ' bridge is.'

P. 253. N. °.   Add, ' Dugdale, Baronage, Vol. ii. p. 555. says, that Robert de ' Ros of Werke, a great Northumbrian baron, joined himself to Wal- ' lace, and aided him in wasting the north of England.'

P. 257. N. °. l. 2.   For 'idea,' r. 'fancy.'

P. 258. l. 13.   Add on the margin 'Langtoft, ii. 305.'

P. 258. N. °. l. 1.   Del. ' is the only historian who,' and add at the end of the note, ' much to the same purpose, Langtoft, Vol. ii. p. 305. speaks,—ther ' formast courey ther bakkis togidere sette, ther speres poynt over ' poynt, so fare and so thikke, and fast togidere joynt, to se it was fer- ' like. Als a castelle thei stode that were walled with stone, thei wende ' no man of blode thorgh tham suld haf gone.'

P. 259. note, l. 11.   For ' if you can,' r. ' gif you cun.'

P. 259. note, l. 19.   For 'can,' r. ' cun.' Add to note, ' Langtoft, Vol. ii. p. 305. as ' translated by Brunne, reports the words thus : *To the renge ere ye* ' *broubt, bop now if ye wille.* But he does not seem to have under- ' stood the import of the words.'

P. 263. l. 5.   Add on the margin, ' Hemingford, i. 165.'

P. 264. N. †.   Add, 'I have seen the title of a public instrument which runs thus: " *Acte contenant les responses faites par pierre Flotte seigneur de Revel* " *Commis par le Roy [de France] pour traitter et conferer avec les Am-* " *bassadeurs Anglois, touchant l'execution du traité de treve, et repara-* " *tion des infractions d'icelle. Simon de Melcun l'arbitre nommé par le* " *Roy offrit au Roy d'Angleterre de delivrer tous les prisonniers Anglois,*

AND ADDITIONS.

" *en rendont par lui le Roy d'Escoffe et son fils, et les Escoffois detenus en*
" *Angleterre et ailleurs, ou les mettant en la garde d'un prelat Francois,*
" *qui les gardera soubs le nom du Pape pendant que le Pape jugera de*
" *leur differend.*" 'The original, if extant, might serve to explain
' several circumstances respecting this treaty; particularly, that Ed-
' ward Balliol was in captivity, together with his father; and that the
' Pope proposed himself as umpire between Edward I. and his diso-
' bedient vassal.'

At the top, for ' 1298.' r. ' 1299.' P. 165. 64.

Add on the margin, '*Langtoft*, ii. 308.' P. 166. l. 8.

Add on the margin, '*Langtoft*, ii. 310.' And after ' Annandale,' P. 166. l. 12.
add note, '*Langtoft*, Vol. ii. p. 310. says, that Edward's army *a
' povere hamlete toke, the castle Karekeverock.*'

Add '*Langtoft*, vol. ii. p. 311. seems to blame Edward I. for ha- P. 165. N. 3.
' ving consented to this truce. He describes a character in the fol-
' lowing terms: " The antient Britons," says he, " forsook that man
" who was a dissembler, lived at ease, lay long in bed, gave himself to
" surfeiting at night, solaced himself in lechery, put confidence in
" traitors, and shewed mercy to his enemies, [assisance of feloun, of
" enemy haf pité;] who was unreasonably obstinate, and avoided the
" counsels of wise men; who was greedy, avaritious, and churlish."
' Under this satyrical disguise, Langtoft intended to libel Edward I.'

After ' guarding them,' add, '*Langtoft*, vol. i. p. 318. says, that P. 173. N. 1.
' the son of Segrave was made prisoner, together with his brother l. 3.
' uterin, [his brother of bedde,] sixteen knights, and thirty men,
' whom he terms *serjeants*. He says, that Sir Thomas Nevil was
' slain.' At the end of the note, add, ' it appears that *Rulph, the*
' *Cofferer*, was an ecclesiastic, and that the Scots would not receive him
' to quarter; *Langtoft*, vol. ii. p. 319.'

Add on the margin, *Langtoft*, ii. 321. P. 175. l. 11.

Add, ' The Espringal threw large darts, [called *muschettae*,] some- P. 179. N. ".
' times, instead of feathers, winged with brass. *Espringal,* balista va-
' lidior

'lidior quâ telum emittitur; *muschetta*, telum quod baliftâ validiori
' emittitur; *Du Cange*. This note is taken from Grose's antiquities.
' Pref. p. 11.—*Langtoft*, vol. ii. p. 326. mentions also an engine used
' at this siege, called a *ludgare*, or *lurdure*. This is plainly a cor-
' ruption of *loup de guerre*, *lupus belli*, *warwolf*.'

P. 180. l. 6.   After l. 6. place ' 1305.'

P. 180. N. *.   Add, ' according to *Langtoft*, vol. ii. p. 326. there were in the castle,.
' beside Sir William Oliphant the governour, Sir William of Duplin,
' and twenty more gentlemen.'

P. 181. at top.   From p. 281. the year ought to be ' 1305,' not ' 1304.'

P. 181. l. 8.   For ' his mangled,' r. ' and his mangled.'

P. 182. N. 1.   For ' committed,' r. ' apprehended and committed.' And at the end
l. 1.   of the note add, ' My apology for Menteth has been received with
' wonderful disapprobation by many readers; for it contradicts vulgar
' traditions, and that most respectable authority, *Blind Harry*. A corre-
' spondent has pointed out a passage, which, as he imagines, ought,
' to silence all scepticism concerning the treason of *Stewart*, [com-
' monly called *Menteth*.] It is the conclusion of *Blair, Relationes*,
' quoted in Nicolson, *Scottish Historical Library*, p. 88. and which is
' to be found at the end of the modern edition of *Blind Harry*. With-
' out inquiring into the age and authenticity of the fragments called
' *Relationes A. Blair*, I answer, that the passage referred to is obvi-
' ously a memorandum interpolated by some patriotic and passionate
' transcriber.

' They who condemn Sir John Menteth, ought to condemn him
' for having acknowledged the government of Edward I. and for ha-
' ving accepted an office of trust under him, not for having discharged
' the duties of that office.—There is a curious passage in *Langtoft*,
' vol. ii. p. 329. which, in modern language, runs thus. *Sir John
' of Menteth pursued Wallace so closely, that he took him unawares
' one night while he was in company with his mistress. This hap-
' pened through the treason of* Jack Short, *the servant of Wallace.
' Wallace,

'Wallace, it is said, had slain the brother of Jack Short, who, on that
'account, was the more inclined to do him that ill office.'

'This note is erroneous as to the word *Urquhart*; the true name P. 185. N. 9.
'in the record is *de Monbaud*, or *de Monte Alto*, now pronounced l. penult.
'*Mowat*.'

For 'had formed no plan, nor concerted,' r. 'had not concerted,' P. 194. l. 18.
&c.

After '*pure blood*,' add note, 'From this passage it has been con- P. 199. l. 3.
'cluded, that the author of *the Annals of Scotland* is excessively credu-
'lous. He must still remain under that imputation; for he cannot
'submit to acknowledge, that he does not believe that a fountain near
'Kilwinning ran blood for eight days and eight nights without in-
'termission.'

Add, 'A correspondent has favoured me with the following note:— P. 304. N. 1.
'*Gilmory*, a servant of the Virgin Mary, probably so called in honour l. 6.
'of her, as the gift was made on the day of the annunciation. His
'former name has been *Gil-andeus*, that is, *the southern lad*; pro-
'bably an English prisoner.'

'This passage has afforded a pretext for much senseless ribbaldry P. 313. l. pen
'in news-papers; and, therefore, I incline to vary it thus: "For, when
'"once the meaning of a word is ascertained, inquiries into its etymo-
'"logy are rather curious than useful."

For '*Annandale*,' r. '*Nithidale*.' This alteration is adapted to mo- P. 339. l. 3.
'dern geography, which has circumscribed *Annandale* within narrow
'bounds.'

Del. from 'one' to 'language,' and add, '*Manelet* is a Gaelic word. P. 339. N. 9.
'In the Welsh, Cornish, and Armoric dialects, *melyn*, or *melen*, is yel-
'low, and, in the Irish, *lus* is a plant. Thus, *melenlus* is *the yellow
'plant*, and *menelus* is the same word transposed, as *Alan*, in the
'Armoric dialect, is transposed to *Anil* in the Irish. See *Lhuyd*, Ar-
'chaeologia, p. 7. and at the words *fluvus* and *planta*, p. 207. 289.
'and *Luteus*, p. 294.

P. 348. L. 12. 'For 'Misereenrdia,' r. 'misericordia.'
P. 350. L. 12. Add on the margin, 'Langtoft, ii. 278.' And add this note, 'Langtoft gives a very distinct account of the prisoners. He says, *to the toure of London the thre Erles were sent*; but he speaks not of the execution of the Earl of Menteth; and it is not probable that he would have omitted it, if he had ever heard the story. Langtoft, a passionate historian, would have rejoiced at the execution of a Scottish rebel; for he thus speaks, vol. ii. p. 279. *God gyve, at the parliament, the Scottis be alle schent and hanyed bi the hals.* The whole passage is curious, and deserves to be perused. He afterwards says, p. 304. that Edward released the prisoners; and, particularly, *the Earl of Menteth.*'
P. 356. L. 19. 'Leave out the passage concerning Sir G. S. and the M. of R. I still consider that passage as an apt illustration of my subject; but it has been strangely misunderstood by some readers, and construed into a censure of the persons alluded to; a censure which, surely, I never intended.'
P. 359. L. 13. Del. from 'Besides' to 'Northumberland.'
Tables. At JOHN BALLIOL, add, 'He married *Isabella*, the daughter of John de Warren, Earl of Surrey.'
At EDWARD BALLIOL, add, 'died childless, 1363.'

No. LX.

No. IX.

CORRECTIONS

AND

ADDITIONS.

ANNALS, Vol. II.

ADD, 'A learned friend has supplied me with some farther il- P. 4. N. †.
'lustrations of this dark subject. He observes, that one of the
'most solemn vows of knights, was what is termed *the vow of the*
'*Peacock*. This bird was accounted noble. It was, in a particular
'manner, the food of the amorous and the valiant, if we can believe
'what is said in the old romances of France; *St. Palaye*, Memoires
'sur l'ancienne Chevalerie, T. i. p. 185. and its plumage served as
'the proper ornaments of the crowns of the *Troubadours*, or *Proven-*
'*çal poets*, who consecrated their compositions to the charms of gal-
'lantry, and the acts of valour.

'When the hour of making the vow was come, the peacock,
'roasted and decked out in its most beautiful feathers, made its ap-
'pearance. It was placed on a bason of gold or silver, and supported
'by ladies, who, magnificently dressed, carried it about to the knights
'assembled for the ceremony. To each knight they presented it
'with'

350   CORRECTIONS

' with formality; and the vow he had to make, which was some pro-
' mise of gallantry or prowess, was pronounced over it.
  ' Other birds beside the peacock were beheld with respect, and ho-
' noured as noble. Of this sort was the pheasant; *St. Palaye*, T. i.
' p. 186. Vows and engagements, accordingly, were made, and
' addressed to the pheasant. A vow of this sort, of which the express
' purpose was to declare war against the infidels, was conceived in
' these words: *Je voue à Dieu mon Createur* tout premierement et à
' la glorieuse Vierge sa mere, et apres aux dames *et au faisan*, &c. *ib.*
' T. i. p. 191.—This serves to prove, that vows were made to *Pea-*
' *cocks* and *Pheasants*; and that, by analogy, they might have been
' made to *swans* likewise. But the origin of a custom seemingly so
' profane and ridiculous still remains unknown.

P. 7. l. 23.   For * put †.
P. 8. l. 13.   After ' all,' add ' persons.'
P. 12. N. *. For ' learned,' r. ' learnt.'
l. 1.
P. 24. L. 18. Add on the margin ' *Boece*, Aberdon. Episcop. Vitae, 6. a.' and to
  the text, ' it was, probably, about this time that the citizens of Aber-
' deen, and other partizans of Bruce, stormed the castle of Aberdeen,
' flew the English garrison, and razed the fortifications. The Eng-
' lish, in the neighbourhood, marched against Aberdeen. While they
' were on their march, the loyal citizens encountered and overthrew
' them. All the prisoners taken in this conflict were put to death.—
  Add note. † This story is related by Boece, *Aberdonensium Episcopo-*
' *rum vitae*, fol. 6. a. b. He says, " *Placuit victoribus quos captos ha-*
" *bebant ad terrorem extra oppidum furcâ suspendere: Sed vetuere Ca-*
" *nonici, utque ut caesorum corpora ad posticum templi Divi Nicolai terrâ*
" *conderentur—obtinuerunt,* ubi eorum ossa cum titulis in rei monumen-
" tum adhuc cernuntur." The canons of Aberdeen endeavoured to save the
' lives of prisoners, whose chief offence was, that they had Edward I.
' for their Sovereign. Amidst the loud calls for bloody *reprysals*, the
' voice of religion and humanity was not heard. The Canons, how-
                                          ' ever,

'ever, obtained a place of sepulture for the slaughtered prisoners; per-
'haps not honourable, yet still in confecrated ground.—The excellence
'of their charity must be estimated by the notions of the age in which
'they lived.—

'Boece relates, that, in his days, the bones of the Englishmen, with
'inscriptions in memory of their death, were still to be seen.—I pur-
'posely omit some singular traditions concerning the slaughter of
'the English prisoners, because they are not sufficiently authenticated.

'But there is one circumstance which I must not omit. In 1580,
'James VI. revoked a grant of a fishing in the mouth of the river of
'Don, which had been made to George Auchinleck of Balmanno.
'In this revocation, a grant by Robert I. to the borough of Aberdeen,
'is thus recited: That, whereas, *his Highness progenitor, King Ro-
'bert of good memory, who rests with God, sometime being within the
'said burgh, perceiving the barrenness and sterility of the country
'where the said burgh is situated, and the great Honesty thereof, to-
'gether with the fervent love shewn by them to his Highness, and his
'progenitors, then, and at all times of before; considering also their
'bauld manheid in the recovering and destroying of the strong castel big-
'get and maintained there by the Englishmen, sometime for daunting
'and suppressing of the town and country, upon these respects, doth the
'said burgh, and comonty thereof, of his bountifull liberality and
'clemency, with certain commodities, liberties, and immunities, for the
'aid and support of the same; and, namely, with an piece of ground
'called the Stocket, adjacent to the burgh, and the salmon fishings of
'the same burgh upon the waters of Dee and Don, for yearly payment
'to his Grace, and his successors, of 320 merks usual money of this
'realme, in name of feu-farm.' &c.

'One would naturally suppose, that the substance, at least, of this
'preamble, was to be found in the grant by Robert Bruce to the
'borough of Aberdeen.

'Robert

" Robert Bruce granted to the borough of Aberdeen, *curam et custo-*
" *diam totius forrestae de* Stokett *salvis nobis viridi et venatione tan-*
" *tùm,* [Dundee 24th October, 8th year of his reign.]

" The same King made a grant to the borough of Aberdeen of *the*
" *Stocket* in property. Its tenor is,—Robertus, Dei gratia, Rex Sco-
" torum, omnibus probis hominibus totius terrae suae, salutem: Sciatis,
" nos, de consilio et ordinatione proborum regni nostri, concessisse, et
" *ad feodofirmam* assedasse, ac praesenti cartâ nostrâ confirmâsse burgen-
" sibus nostris, et communitati burgi nostri de Aberdene, burgum
" nostrum de Aberdene praedictum, et forrestam nostram *del Stocket,*
" cum pertinentiis. Tenend. et habend. praedictis burgensibus et com-
" munitati, eorum haeredibus et successoribus, in perpetuum, de nobis,
" et haeredibus nostris, in feodo et haereditariè, et in libero burgagio,
" per omnes rectas metas et divisas suas, cum molendinis, aquis, pis-
" cariis—————custumis, toloneis, curiis, ponderibus, mensuris, et
" cum omnibus aliis libertatibus, commoditatibus, aisiamentis, consue-
" tudinibus, et justis pertinentiis suis, ad assedationem dictorum burgi
" et forrestae de jure et consuetudine spectantibus, vel spectare valenti-
" bus, in futurum: Reddendo inde nobis annuatim, et haeredibus nostris,
" dicti burgum, eorum haeredes et successores, ut supra dictum est,
" *ducentas et tresdecem libras sex solid.'* et *octo denar.* Sterling,
" [L. 213 : 6 : 8 Sterl] tent. in cameram nostram, ad duos anni ter-
" minos, videlicet, medietatem ad fest. Pentecostes, et aliam medie-
" tatem ad fest. Sancti Martini in hyeme; pro omni alio servicio, ex-
" actione, consuetudine, seu demanda; volumus etiam et concedimus,
" quod dicti burgum nostrum haeredes et successores eorundem, li-
" berè, et sine impedimento quocunque, in campis, moris, et aliis qui-
" buscunque locis dictae forestae, extra boscum *del Stocket* praedicto
" burgo de Aberdene, proximè adjacentem, possint omnimodam cultu-
" ram facere, mansiones et aedificia constituere, focalia fodere, ac alias
" quascunque commoditates exercere, pacificè et ordinariè prout melius
" viderint expedire ; salvo tantùm nobis et haeredibus nostris viridi
" [one

AND ADDITIONS. 353

' one word illegible,] arborum in praedicto bosco, et venatione simili-
' ter, si in eadem foresta casualiter inveniatur. Concessimus etiam
' eidem burgo nostro, burgensibus et communitati, ejusdem haeredi-
' bus, et successoribus suis, quod nullus justiciarius forestae, aut aliquis
' alius regni nostri, cujuscunque conditionis fuerit, sive status, super
' custodia praesentis concessionis, et infeodationis jure, vel super defect.
' [some words illegible,] aut contradictionem habeant, nisi tantum
' Camerarius noster, qui pro tempore fuerit, ita tamen quod quisque
' ex hujusmodi defectibus, aut si destructor viridis, aut venationis, in
' dicta foresta legaliter convictus fuerit, poenam hujusmodi criminis
' suppotet in ipsa persona, et nullis aliis, principali tamen concessio-
' ne et infeodatione nostra in suo robore [firmiter] et perpetuò perma-
' nente. In cujus rei testimonium praesentibus sigillum nostrum prae-
' cipimus apponi. Testibus Willelmo, et Willelmo, Sancti Andreae
' et Dunkeldae episcopis, Bernardo Abbate de Aberbrothock, Cancel-
' lario nostro; [Thoma] Ranulphi, Comite Moraev, et Domino Vallis
' Anandiae, et Manniae; Roberto de Keith, Marescallo nostro; Gil-
' berto de Haya, Constabulario nostro; Alexandro Fraser, Camerario
' nostro, militibus. Apud Berwicum super Twed, decimo die Decem-
' bris, anno regni nostri quarto decimo. [*Archives borough of Aber-
' deen.*] In this grant, although abundantly verbose, there is no men-
' tion of the circumstances which the preamble of the revocation by
' James VI. recites.'

Read, ' A person nowise distinguished either for rank or for mili- P. 15 N. l.
' tary prowess.' L. 2.

For, ' but intelligence,' &c. r. ' but timely intelligence of his mo- P. 25. L. 3.
' tions was received.'

For, ' is adjacent,' r. ' lies next.' P. 25. N. 1.
For ' letters,' r. ' despatches.' L. 5.
 P. 29. L. 14.
Add, ' The clergy of Scotland, assembled in a provincial council, P. 30, L. 7.
' issued a declaration to all the faithful, bearing, that the Scottish na-
VOL. II.   Y y   ' tion,

CORRECTIONS

'tion, seeing the kingdom betrayed and enslaved, had assumed Robert
'Bruce for their Sovereign; and that the clergy had willingly done
'homage to him in that character,' [at Dundee, 24th February.] Add
on the margin, ' *Anderson*, Independency, Appen. No. 12.'

P. 50. N. †. L 2.	For ' Forth,' r. ' the Forth.'
P. 51. L 13.	For ' encountering,' r. ' to encounter.'
P. 52 l. 8.	For ' learned,' r. ' learnt.'
P. 52. N. *. L. 7.	For ' Stewart,' r. ' Steward.'
P. 54. l. 8.	For ' was,' r. ' is.'
P. 56. l. 7.	For ' Scots,' r. ' Scottish.'
P. 57. l. 15.	For * put †.
P. 58. N. †.	Add, ' His name was probably *Peter Luband*. In *Roll. Rob.* I. ' No. 63—64. there are grants of the lands of Garmilton and Elwynf- ' ton, " quae fuerunt quondam *Petr. Luband*, militis, in curia nostra " de proditione erga nostram regiam dignitatem nuper convicti.'
P. 52. N. last.	For † put ‡.
P. 60. l. 14.	For ' to have rejected ' r. to reject.'
P. 63. N. *. L 1. & l 7.	For ' where,' r. ' in which.'
P. 64. l. 8.	For ' stranger,' r. ' a stranger.'
P. 65. l. 10.	Del. ' irretrievably.'
P. 68. l. 21.	For ' move on,' r. ' march.'
P. 69. l. 8.	For ' rod,' r. ' rode.'
P. 70. l. 6.	For ' Liffy,' r. ' the Liffy.'
P. 71. l. 16.	For ' learned,' r. ' learnt.'
P. 74. L 1.	This passage is erroneously pointed. r. " Sinclair shall be my " Bishop. Under the appellation of *the King's Bishop*."
P. 75. L 14.	For ' messenger,' r. ' messengers.'
P. 80. N, last.	For † put ‡.
P. 81. N. †.	For ' learned.' r. ' learnt.'
L 1. P. 83. l. 11.	For ' administring, &c.' r. ' of taking upon himself the admi- ' nistration of government.'

For

AND ADDITIONS. 355

For 'prohibites,' r. 'prohibited.'   P. 85. L. 8.

After 'Damory,' add an inverted comma.   P. 91. N. 1. l. 2.

At 'John de Logie,' add note, 'From a charter granted by Robert   P. 96. l. 4.
'Bruce to the Black Friars at Perth, there is some reason to suspect,
'that John de Logie forfeited at an earlier period. That charter is
'dated 2d Feb. anno regni nostri quarto decimo, and mentions the te-
'nement of Logy, *quod fuit quondam Johannis de Logy, militis, et
'quod forisfecit*. This charter is in the archives of the borough of
'Perth. As Bruce ascended the throne on the 27th March 1306, *the
'2d day of February, in the 14th year of his reign*, seems to be 2d
'February 13.9-20.'

Add, 'Randolph, ambassador from the King of Scots, concluded   P. 116. l. 17.
'an alliance, offensive and defensive, with France, [at Corbeil, April.]
'And on the margin, *Leibnitz*, Cod. Jur. Gent. i. 116.'

For 'on the morn,' r. 'next morning.'   P. 120. l. 13.

Del. from 'But 3. to David and Thomas.' For, although I have   P. 151. N.
seen it most confidently asserted that Thomas Hay was a commis-   l. 22.
sioner to England in 1753, I cannot discover evidence of that fact.

For 'excursions,' r. 'incursions.'   P. 159. l. 16.

For 'and Sir William Keith,' r. 'and Sir Alexander Seton; and   P. 163. l. 8.
afterwards, Sir William Keith.'

For 'man,' r. 'mean.'   P. 173. l. 6.

For '21st,' r. '20th.'   P. 135. l. 3.

Add, 'There is a curious passage concerning the Portuguese at   P. 177. N. †.
'Goa, in the travels of a zealous Roman catholic, *de la Boulaye le
'Gouz*, c. 25. p. 204 " Les Portugais—ayment extrememeut Sainct
" Anthoine de Lisboa, ils lui tont une particuliere devotion lors qu'il
" ne fait point de pluye ; ils prennent sa statue, l'attachent par les
" pieds, la trempent dans des puys la teste la premiere, et apres l'avoir
" bien mouillée et trempé plusieurs fois, ils la retirent par la corde
" qu'elle

" qu'elle a attachée aux pieds, et font la mefme à celle de la Vierge
" Marie. Comme je m' eſtonnois de cette ceremonie extraordinaire,
" j'en demandai la raifon au l'ere Gardien des Capuches de Damaon,
" lequel me dift, que Sainct Anthoine vouloit eſtre ainfi traitté, et avoit
" operé par ce moyen une infinite de miracles, et la Sainte Vierge,
" laquelle fit retrouver l'enfant d'une pauvre femme, qui alla dans
" l'eglife apres l'avoir perdu, et prenant le petit Jefus d'entre les bras
" de noſtre Dame, lui diſt, *ſi tu ne me rends mon fils, je ne te rendrai pas*
" *le tien* ; et à quelque tems de là, l'enfant revint à la maifon fain et
" fauve. Une autre fois, un frere portier d'une ordre de Francifcains
" perdit per mefgarde les clefs du couvent, et ne ſçachant où ils les
" avoit eſgaré: a, alla dans l'eglife et lia la ſtatuë de St. Anthoine de
" Lifbon par les pieds, la trempa dans un puys où il l'avoit defrendue
" la teſte la premiere, la retira, et elle apporta les clefs penduës mira-
" culeufement à fon col ; ce qui eſt digne d'admiration, et non d'imita-
" tion."

That is, 'The Portuguefe are extremely fond of St Anthony of
' Lifbon ; they pray to him, in particular, whenever a drought hap-
' pens. They take his image, fix a rope to its feet, and fink it head-
' long into a well. Having thoroughly and often wet it, and foaked
' it, they draw it out again ; and they do the like to the ſtatue of the
' Virgin Mary. Surprized at this extraordinary ceremony, I applied
' to the guardian of the Capuchins at Damaon to learn its reafon ; he
' told me, that St Anthony chofe to be treated fo ; and that, in this
' way, he had wrought an infinity of miracles ; that the bleſſed Vir-
' gin made a child to be found again which a poor woman had loft :
' The manner was this ; the woman having loſt her child, came into
' the church, and taking the infant Jefus out of the arms of our Lady,
' faid to her, *Unlefs thou giveſt me back my fon, I will not give thee*
' *back thine* : Some time after, her child came home fafe and found.—
' On another occafion, a friar, porter of a convent of Francifcans, ha-
' ving

'ving carelessly mislaid his keys, and not knowing where he had put
'them, went into the church, took the statue of St Antbony of Lisbon,
'immersed it headlong in a well, and drew it out again. Then the
'statue brought back the keys, hung miraculously about its neck.
'This is worthy of admiration; yet the conduct of the friar ought
'not to be imitated.'

CHRONOLOGICAL ABRIDGEMENT.

A. D.			Page
1306.	March 27.	ROBERT I. was crowned at Scone	1
	29.	He was again crowned by Isabella de Fife, Countess of Buchan, officiating for the heir of M'Duff	2
		Edward I. prepared to revenge the death of Comyn, and to quell the insurrection in Scotland, but sickened at Carlisle.	3—5
	June 19.	Robert Bruce came before Perth; was attacked and defeated at Methven, by Aymer de Vallence Earl of Pembroke	5—6
	August 11.	Bruce was defeated by the Lord of Lorn, at Dalry	7
		He eluded the pursuit of his enemies, and escaped to Rachrin, on the northern coast of Ireland	7
		Edward I. inflicted various punishments on the partizans of Bruce	8—17
	October 23.	James, the Stewart of Scotland, did homage to Edward I. at Lanercost, near Carlisle	17
	Feb. —	Bruce and his adherents were excommunicated by the cardinal legate at Carlisle	17
		Bruce passed over from Rachrin to Arran, and from thence to Turnberry in Carrick, surprised the English in their cantonments; but was obliged, by superior numbers, to take shelter among the hills	17—19

Thomas

CHRONOLOGICAL, &c.   359

A. D.			Page
1306.	Feb. 9.	Thomas and Alexander, the brothers of Bruce, landed in Galloway, were defeated by Duncan M'Dowal, made prisoners and executed.	19
	March 19.	Sir James Douglas surprized the English, at Douglas castle, and put them to the sword	20
1307.		Bruce defeated the Earl of Pembroke at Lowdoun-hill	20
		After having made a vain attempt on the castle of Air, Bruce was again obliged to take shelter among the hills	21
		The English burnt the monastery of Paisley	21
	July 7.	Edward I. died on his march against the Scots, at Burg on Sande in Cumberland	21
	August 26.	Edward II having entered Scotland, impowered the Earl of Pembroke to receive the Scots to mercy, under certain exceptions	22
		Edward II. ingloriously returned into England	22
	Sep. 13.	He appointed the Earl of Richmond guardian of Scotland in the room of Pembroke	23
		Bruce invaded Galloway. Was put to flight by the guardian, and retired into the north	23
	Dec. 25.	The Earl of Buchan attacked Bruce, and was discomfited	23
1308.	May 22.	The Earl of Buchan, and Moubray, an English commander, totally routed by Bruce, at Inverury	24
		Sir David de Brechin, and other Scotsmen, abandoned the English	24
		About this time, according to common report, the citizens of Aberdeen, and other partizans of Bruce, stormed the castle of Aberdeen, slew the English garrison, razed the fortifications, and defeated the English, who endeavoured to regain that castle	24
	June 29.	Edward Bruce invaded Galloway, overthrew the enemies of Scotland, expelled the English, and subdued the country	24—25
		Sir James Douglas surprised and made prisoners Alexander Stewart of Boukill and Thomas Randolph, the King's nephew.	

Randolph

			Page
A. D.		Randolph having spoken petulantly to the King, was committed to close custody	25
1308.	July 16.	James the Steward of Scotland died	30
	August 13.	Bruce invaded Lorn, defeated the troops of Lorn at Crethinben, and made himself master of that country	26
	11.	William de Lambyrton, Bishop of St Andrews, having been received into favour with the English, undertook to publish the sentence of excommunication against Bruce and his adherents	27
		Edward II. made frequent changes in the office of guardian of Scotland	28
		Philip King of France endeavoured to promote a reconciliation between Edward II. and Bruce	28
		Edward, through the mediation of the King of France, consented to a truce with the Scots; but he presently charged them as guilty of violating the truce, and he summoned his barons to march against them	29
	August 2.	Edward complained to the King of France of the duplicity of de Varennes his ambassador, who had sent despatches openly to the *Earl of Carrick*, and secretly to *the King of Scots*.	29
		The King of France, by other ambassadors, solicited a truce for Scotland. Edward consented to negotiate at the request of the King of France, as his father-in-law, and friend, but not as an ally of Scotland	29
	Nov. 14.		
	Dec. 3.	Bruce besieged the castle of Rutherglen. It was relieved by the young Earl of Gloucester	30
	Feb. 16.	The negotiations with Scotland were renewed. The Bishop of St Andrews was one of the commissioners on the part of England. A truce was concluded; but the Scots disregarded it	30
	14.	The Scottish clergy issued a declaration, importing, that they, together with the rest of the nation, had assumed Robert Bruce for their sovereign	30

Edward

ABRIDGEMENT. 361

A.D.			Page
1310.		Edward II. made preparations for invading Scotland.—The English barons, difgufted at his government, repaired flowly to the royal flandard - - - -	30
	Sept.	He invaded Scotland; penetrated by Selkirk and Biggar to Renfrew, and then retired to Berwick, while Bruce remained on the defenfive - - - -	31
	Dec. 9.	Edward II. iffued a proclamation, prohibiting his fubjects, under pain of forfeiture, from fupplying the Scots with military flores	32
		Bruce projected an invafion of the Ifle of Man, but was prevented by the vigilance of the Englifh - -	32
1311.		William Binnok, a poor peafant, won the caftle of Linlithgow from the Englifh by ftratagem - - -	32
	July 14.	Edward II. again purpofing to invade Scotland, ordered a rendezvous of his forces at Rokefburgh - -	34
		Bruce invaded England, and ravaged the country about Durham - - - -	34
	Jan. 8.	Bruce took Perth by efcalade - -	34
	26.	Edward II. empowered the Earl of Athole, and others, to conclude a truce with the Scots - - -	36
	Feb. 8.	He endeavoured, by conferring favours, to fecure the fidelity of fuch of the Scots as had hitherto remained in his intereft	36
1312.		Bruce invaded England, burnt great part of Durham, and threatened to befiege Berwick. Edward II. fixed his refidence at Berwick - - - - -	36
		Bruce took the caftles of Butel, Dumfries, and Dalfwinton, and many others - - - -	36
	March 6 & 7.	Douglas furprifed the caftle of Rokefburgh - -	37
	14.	Randolph, guided by one William Frank, furprifed the caftle of Edinburgh - - -	38
1313.		The Earl of Athole revolted to the Scots - -	38

VOL. II.   Z z   Through

A.D.			Page
1313.	May 17.	Through the mediation of France, conferences for a truce with Scotland were renewed - - - -	39
	25.	The Scots ravaged Cumberland - - -	39
	June 11.	Bruce subdued the Isle of Man - - -	39
	July —	Edward II. attempted to assemble forces for resisting the Scots, but was thwarted by the Earl of Lancaster, and other discontented barons - - - -	39
	Nov. 28.	Such of the Scots as continued in the English interest sent a deputation to Edward II. representing their distresses, and imploring aid. Edward dismissed the deputies with many fair promises - - - - -	40
		Edward Bruce, brother of the King of Scots, took the castles of Rutherglen and Dundee, and besieged the castle of Stirling. Philip de Moubray agreed to surrender it, unless relieved on the 24th June 1314 - - - -	40
		Bruce ratified this singular capitulation - -	40
1314.	March 26.	Edward II. made great preparations for the relief of the castle of Stirling. He invited many Irish chiefs to his aid; and he summoned his English subjects in Ireland to join the army under the command of the Earl of Ulster -	40
	May 27.	He ordered a great army to be assembled for the succour of the castle of Stirling - - - -	41
		Bruce assembled his army at Torwood, between Falkirk and Stirling; and he chose the ground on which he was to combat the English - - - -	42
	June 23.	Edward II. with his army, came in sight of the Scots, who were posted between Stirling and the stream called Bannockburn.— There were skirmishes, this day, in which the Scots had the advantage.—Bruce slew Henry de Bohun in single combat	45
	24.	The two nations fought.—The English were totally routed.—Edward II. fled sixty miles without halting. The Earl of March threw

A.D.		Page
1314.	threw open the gates of his castle of Dunbar to Edward; and conveyed him by sea into England	45—49
	The castle of Stirling surrendered according to treaty.—Moubray, the governour, entered into the service of Scotland	51
	The castle of Bothwell was besieged. The Earl of Hereford, who had taken refuge *there* after the rout at Bannockburn, capitulated	53
	Edward Bruce, and Douglas, wasted Northumberland, laid the bishoprick of Durham under contribution, penetrated to Richmond in Yorkshire, burnt Appleby, &c. and returned home loaded with plunder	53
August	Edward II. summoned a parliament at Yorke, in order to concert measures for the public security	54
10.	He appointed the Earl of Pembroke, late Guardian of Scotland, to be Guardian of the country between the Tweed and the Trent	54
Sep. 18.	Bruce having made overtures for peace, Edward II. appointed	
October 17.	commissioners to treat with the Scots	54
	The Scots again invaded England, and levied contributions	54
	John Balliol died, leaving his son Edward heir to his fatal pretensions	55
1315.	The Scots invaded England, penetrated into the bishoprick of Durham, and plundered Hartlepool	55
April 26.	The succession to the crown of Scotland was settled in parliament at Air	55—59
July	Bruce besieged Carlisle, but was repulsed. The Scots also failed in an attempt to surprise Berwick	55
	Walter, the Stewart of Scotland, married Marjory, daughter of the King of Scots	60
	The Irish of Ulster implored the aid of Bruce against the English, and offered to acknowledge his brother Edward for their Sovereign. Bruce accepted their offers	60

Z z 2   Edward.

A. D.			Page
1315	May 15.	Edward Bruce landed at Carrickfergus, in the north of Ireland, with 6000 men - - - -	60
		Aided by his new subjects, he wasted the possessions of the English settlers - - - -	61
	June 29.	The Scots stormed, plundered, and burnt Dundalk -	61
		They burnt Atherdee, and other places - -	61
		Richard de Burgh, Earl of Ulster, assembled forces to oppose Edward Bruce - - -	61
	July 22.	Edmond Butler, Justiciary of Ireland, having gathered together the forces of Leinster, offered to assist the Earl of Ulster; but the Earl scornfully rejected his assistance -	62
	Sep. 10.	The Earl of Ulster was surprised and defeated by the Scots at Coyners - - - -	62
	15.	Randolph went into Scotland for reinforcements -	62
	Dec. 6.	Edward Bruce besieged the castle of Carrickfergus.—Raised the siege.—Randolph brought over a reinforcement of 500 men.— The Scots penetrated into Kildare - - 62—63	
	Jan. 26.	The Scots defeated the English under the command of Butler the Justiciary, near Arscoll in Kildare -	63
	Feb. 14.	Edward Bruce was compelled, by want of provisions, to retreat towards Ulster - - -	63
		Roger Lord Mortimer endeavoured to cut off his retreat. The troops of Mortimer were dispersed by the Scots, at Kenlis in Meath - - -	63
	March	Edward Bruce acted as Sovereign in Ulster. Randolph went again into Scotland for fresh reinforcements -	64
		In the course of this year Bruce subdued the western isles	64
	2.	Marjory, daughter of Bruce, and wife of Walter, the Stewart of Scotland, brought forth a son, *Robert*, and soon after died	65
1316.	April 11.	Edward Bruce resumed the siege of the castle of Carrickfergus.	

Lord

A. D.		Page
1316.	Lord Mandeville entered the castle with succours, sallied out and surprised the Scots. While pursuing his advantage he was slain, and the troops of the sally were cut to pieces	65—66
May 2.	Edward Bruce was crowned King of Ireland -	66
31.	The garrison of the castle of Carrickfergus agreed to surrender; unless relieved within a certain day; that term having elapsed, they desired the Scots to send a detachment to take possession. They seized the detachment, and perished in maintaining the castle - - -	67
	Bruce, having committed the charge of his kingdom to the Stewart and Douglas, conducted a reinforcement to his brother	67
	The garrison of the castle of Carrickfergus, after having endured the extremities of famine, surrendered -	67
October 15.	The English appeared in Ulster, and defeated a part of the Scottish army - - -	68
Feb. 16.	Bruce and his brother, by forced marches, entered the province of Leinster, and approached to Dublin.—The inhabitants of Dublin made preparations for defending their city -	68—69
Feb. 23.—28. March 12.	The Scots, after having remained some days in the neighbourhood of Dublin, marched to Callen in Kilkenny, and continued their progress to Limerick - -	70
1317. March 31.	The English assembled their whole forces in the neighbourhood of Kilkenny - -	71
April 7.	Roger Lord Mortimer arrived from England in the character of deputy. He ordered that no attempt should be made against the Scots until he joined the army - -	72
May	Meanwhile the Scots, having eluded the enemy, retreated leisurely into Ulster - - -	72
	During the absence of Bruce, the English made several unsuccessful attempts against Scotland. The Earl of Arundel invaded the forest of Jedburgh; Douglas drew him into an ambush,	

and

A. D.			Page
1317.		and defeated his troops. Edward de Cailaud invaded Teviotdale. Douglas routed his troops and flew him. Robert Neville fallied out from Berwick against Douglas, was defeated and flain. - - -	72—73
		The English invaded Scotland by fea, landed near Inverkeithing, and routed the Earl of Fyfe, and others, who oppofed their landing. William Sinclair, Bifhop of Dunkeld, rallied the fugitives, attacked the English, and drove them back to their fhips - - -	73—74
		Pope John XXII. defpatched two cardinals into Britain to proclaim a papal truce for two years between the English and Scots; and he conferred on the cardinals a difcretionary power of excommunicating Bruce, and whomever elfe they thought fit	74
	Sep.	The cardinals fent meffengers to Bruce. He refufed to receive letters not addreffed to *the King of Scots*, and difmiffed the meffengers with a mild, but refolute anfwer -	74—75
	Dec. 30.	The cardinals fent Adam Newton, a Minorite friar, to proclaim the papal truce in Scotland. The King of Scots turned him back to Berwick unheard. The friar, in his return, was waylaid, ftript, and robbed of all his parchments, letters, and inftructions - - -	76
1318.	March 28.	Randolph and Douglas, conducted by one Spalding, a malecontent citizen of Berwick, furprifed the town of Berwick. The garrifon of the caftle fallied out to regain the town; but was repulfed, chiefly by the valour of Sir William Keith of Galfton	77—79
		Bruce attacked and won the caftle of Berwick. He committed the defence of the town and the caftle to the Stewart -	79
		The Scots invaded Northumberland; and took the caftles of Werk, Harbottle, and Mitford - -	79
	May	They again invaded England, penetrated into Yorkfhire, burnt Northallerton, Burrough-bridge, Scarborough, and Skipton in Craven, and exacted contributions from Rippon -	79

ABRIDGEMENT. 367

A. D.			Page
1318.	June 18.	The Pope commanded Bruce, and his adherents, to be excommunicated for their contempt of the papal truce -	80
	June 8. and 10.	Edward II. summoned his forces to assemble at Yorke for defence of the country - -	80
	Sept.	A parliament, held at London, appointed an army to be raised, the quotas of soldiers being furnished by the different cities and towns. This army was assembled; but, on account of party-animosities among the soldiers, was immediately disbanded	80—81
	Oct. 5.	Edward Bruce, contrary to the opinion of all his officers, fought the English under Lord Bermingham, at Fagher near Dundalk His army was totally defeated and dispersed, and himself slain	81
	Dec.	The death of Marjory, the King's daughter, and of Edward, his brother, made new arrangements necessary as to the regal succession. They were accordingly settled in parliament at Scone	82—83
		Many wise and salutary laws were enacted in that parliament	84—86
		About the same time, the two cardinals, who resided in England, pronounced the sentence of excommunication against Bruce, and his adherents.—From Scotland messengers were sent to solicit the repeal, and from England, the confirmation of this sentence	87
		The Pope having been informed, by the English King, of a correspondence by letters between Avignon and Scotland, imprisoned the Scots who were within his territories, and the persons who had corresponded with Scotland -	87
1319.		Robert Count of Flanders refused to prohibit trade with Scotland, ' because Flanders was the common country of all men, and ' prohibitions as to trade would ruin his people' -	87
	April 14.	Edward II. obtained leave from the Pope to treat with certain concealed traitors in Scotland - -	87—88
	July 20. 24.	Edward II. resolved to regain Berwick. He requested the prayers of the clergy, together with a great loan, and ordered his forces to assemble at Newcastle upon Tyne -	88

The

A.D.			Page
1319	Sep. 7.	The English drew lines of countervallation round Berwick, affaulted the town, and were repulfed	88
	13.	They made a general affault, and were again repulfed. The Stewart diftinguifhed himfelf by his courage and conduct in defence of Berwick	88—90
	20.	Fifteen thoufand Scots, under Randolph and Douglas, entered England by the weft-marches, wafted Yorkefhire, and fought and overcame the Archbifhop of Yorke, and his followers, at Mitton near Burrough-bridge	91
		The northern barons, whofe eftates were moft expofed to the inroads of the Scots, forced Edward II. to raife the fiege of Berwick. Edward in vain attempted to cut off the retreat of the Scots	91
		Commiffioners were appointed for negotiating a treaty between the two nations	92
	Nov. 17.	The Pope interpofed, and ordered the general fentence of excommunication to be publifhed againft Bruce, and his adherents, and alfo the antient fentence againft Bruce for the flaughter of Comyn	92
	Dec. 31.	A truce, until Chriftmas 1321, was concluded between the two nations	92
1320.	April 6.	In a parliament held at Aberbrothock, the barons, freeholders, and whole community of Scotland, drew up a letter to the Pope, afferting their independency, and juftifying their caufe	93—95
		William de Soulis, and other perfons of quality, confpired againft Bruce. The Countefs of Strathern revealed the confpiracy	96
	Auguft	The confpirators were tried in a parliament at Scone. Some of them were condemned and executed.—Soulis, and the Countefs of Strathern, were imprifoned for life	96
	July 11.	The Pope addreffed a Bull to Edward II. recommending peace with Scotland	97

Bruce

A B R I D G E M E N T.   369

| | | | Page |

A. D.			
1310.		Bruce, by his ambassadors, applied to the Pope for a repeal of the sentence of excommunication. The Pope questioned the power of the ambassadors, but allowed Bruce again to apply	98
	Sep. 15.	Edward II. appointed commissioners for treating of peace with Scotland	98
	Nov. 17.	Edward II. appointed commissioners for receiving into favour all the Scots who might be desirous of reconciliation with England;	
	Dec. 11.	and granted an indemnity, with few exceptions	98—99
1311.	May 14.	Edward II. stopt certain letters sent by the Pope to Bruce, because they contained expressions which it was not held safe to communicate to the Scots	99
	Dec. 7.	The Earl of Lancaster entertained a treasonable correspondence with the Scots	99—100
		The Scots invaded Northumberland, and the Bishoprick of Durham	100
	Feb.	The Earls of Lancaster and Hereford rose in arms against their Sovereign	100
	March 16.	They were defeated near Borough-bridge by Sir Andrew Hartcla. Hereford was slain. Lancaster yielded himself up	101
	22.	The Earl of Lancaster was tried, found guilty, and beheaded	101
1322.	March 25.	Sir Andrew Hartcla was made Earl of Carlisle, and had a pension of 1000 marks yearly	101
		Edward II. informed the Pope that he had suppressed the rebellion, and was preparing to invade Scotland; and he declared that he would no longer listen to any proposals for a truce	101—102
		Meanwhile the Scots invaded England, penetrated into Lancashire, and spoiled the country without opposition	102
	August	Edward II. having requested the Pope to enforce the sentence of excommunication against the Scots, invaded Scotland	102
		Bruce ordered the whole cattle and flocks to be driven off from the Merse and Lothian, and fixed his camp at Cardrofs, on the north side of the Frith of Forth	102

Vol. II.   A a a   Edward

A. D.			Page
1322.		Edward II. advanced to Edinburgh, but was obliged to retreat for want of provisions. His soldiers plundered the abbeys of Holy-rood and Melros, and burnt Dryburgh. It was computed that one half of the English army died in this campaign	103
	Sept. 15.	Edward II. appointed Andrew Hartcla guardian of the west marches, and the Earl of Athole of the east -	104
		The Scots besieged Norham. They surprised Edward II. at Biland in Yorkshire, stormed his camp, and defeated his army	104
		The Scots wasted Yorkshire, and continued their incursions to Beverly in the East-riding - -	106
	Feb. 1.	Andrew Hartcla having engaged in a treasonable correspondence with the Scots, was arrested as a traitor -	106
	5.	Edmund Earl of Kent, brother of the English King, was appointed sole guardian of the marches -	106
	27.	Commissioners were appointed for the trial of Hartcla -	107
	March 2.	Hartcla was condemned to be degraded, and to suffer as a traitor. This sentence was immediately executed -	107
	21.	Edward II. agreed to a cessation of arms ' with the men of Scot-' land.' But Bruce would not, until he was treated as ' a prin-' cipal party' - -	108—109
1323.	March 30.	Edward II. demanded the opinion of his counsellors, as to the expediency of a truce. Henry de Beaumont refusing to give any opinion, was removed from the council board -	109
	30.	The treaty of truce, to endure until 12th June 1336, was concluded, at Thorpe near Yorke - -	109
	June 7.	Bruce, under the style of *King of Scotland*, ratified the treaty at Berwick, with the consent of his bishops, Earls, and barons	110
		Meanwhile, Edward II. requested the Pope to publish the sentence of excommunication against Bruce and his adherents, but the Pope would not - -	110

Bruce

A. D			Page
1323.		Bruce sent Randolph to the papal court, who prevailed with the Pope to bestow the title of *King* on Bruce	111—113
	Jan. 13.	The Pope, reflecting that his concessions were too ample, apologized to the English King	112—113
	March 5.	A son was born to Bruce at Dumfermline—named *David*	114
1324.	April 1.	Edward II. remonstrated against the concessions which the Pope had made to Randolph, the Scottish ambassador	114
	July 9.	Edward II. required Edward, the son of John Balliol, to come to his court	115
	Nov. 8.	Commissioners appointed for a treaty of peace between the two nations	115
		The Scots prayed to be reconciled to the church. Edward II. prevailed on the Pope to reject their prayer, until restitution of Berwick should be made. But the Scots rather chose to remain excommunicated than to restore Berwick	116
1326.		The parliament, held at Cambuskenneth, took an oath for the performance of fealty and homage to *David*, the King's son, and his issue, whom failing, to *Robert Stewart*	116
		Andrew Moray of Bothwell, married *Christian*, sister of the King of Scots, and widow of Sir Christopher Seton	116
	April	Randolph, ambassador from Scotland, concluded an alliance, offensive and defensive, with France, at Corbeil	126
	9.	Walter Stewart, the King's son-in-law, died	116
	Jan. 14.	Edward II. resigned his crown to Edward III. a youth of 15	116
	March 4. 8.	Edward III. renewed the negotiations for peace with Scotland, and ratified the truce	116
	April 5.	Having received intelligence that the Scots had resolved to infringe the truce, he summoned his barons to meet him in arms at Newcastle, but without discontinuing the negotiations for peace	117

A.D.			Page
1326.	May 18.	He contracted with John de Beaumont, brother of the Count of Hainault, for a body of heavy-armed cavalry -	117
	July 11.	He invited Edward Balliol from France -	117
	15.	He fortified Yorke - -	117
	June 15.	Meanwhile, Randolph and Douglas invaded England by the west marches, with an army of 20,000, chiefly horsemen -	118
	July 13.	Edward III. with an army of 50,000, came to Durham, in order to oppose the invaders - -	118
	August 1.	The English army came in view of the Scots -	119
	4.	Douglas surprised the English camp at Stanhope-park, and assaulted the King's tent. On being repulsed, he made good his retreat - - -	120
	6.	The Scots, when their retreat appeared to be cut off, disengaged themselves by a skilful movement, and retired without loss!	122
	15.	Edward III. having marched to Yorke, disbanded his army	122
		Bruce besieged the castle of Norham. Randolph and Douglas made an unsuccessful attempt on the castle of Alnwick	125
	October 9.	Henry de Percy, and others, were appointed plenipotentiaries for concluding a peace with Scotland. The treaty, however, was	
	Nov. 23.	managed by Mortimer for the English, and Douglas for the Scots - - -	126
	October 26.	Elizabeth, the consort of the King of Scots, died	126.
	Dec. 10.	The commissioners for the treaty met at Newcastle, and drew up articles of pacification. Edward II. summoned a parliament to meet at Yorke for deliberating on the articles	126
	Jan. 15.	Meanwhile, a short truce was concluded with Scotland	126
	March 1.	In the parliament at Yorke Edward II. consented, ' That Scotland ' should remain unto Robert King of Scots, and his heirs and ' successors, free, and divided from England, without any sub- ' jection or right of service' -	127

In

A.D.			Page
1328.	April	In a parliament at Northampton, peace was concluded with Scotland	127—131
	July 18.	In confequence of an article in the treaty of Northampton, David Prince of Scotland, married Johanna the daughter of Edward II. at Berwick	131
1329.	June 7.	Robert Bruce, the reſtorer of the Scottiſh monarchy, died at Cardroſs, and was ſucceeded by his only ſon *David* II.	131
		In confequence of the act of fettlement 1318, Randolph affumed the character of Regent.	133
1330.	June	Douglas had promiſed to convey the heart of Bruce to the Holy Land: He ſet out on this expedition: Having heard that Alphonſus, King of Leon and Caſtile, waged war with the Moors in Granada, he refolved to fight the infidels in his progreſs to Jeruſalem.	134
	Aug. 25.	Douglas, incautiouſly purſuing the enemy, was ſlain, near Teva, on the frontiers of Andaluſia	135—136
1331.	Nov. 24.	David II. and his confort Johanna, were anointed and crowned at Scone	137
		Edward Balliol began to revive his pretenſions to the crown of Scotland	137
		Mortimer, the great miniſter in England, having been difgraced, and executed, Edward III. required the Scottiſh regency, in terms of the treaty of Northampton, to reſtore the eſtates of Henry de Beaumont, and Thomas Lord Wake, who had been enemies of Mortimer. The Regent, diſtruſting the ſincerity of the Engliſh in the performance of the other articles of the treaty of Northampton, delayed the performance of the article as to Beaumont and Wake	141
		Balliol and the difinherited barons, under the guidance of Henry de Beaumont, refolved to invade Scotland with an army of 400 men at arms, and 3000 infantry, which they had aſſembled	142

Edward

A.D.			Page
1332.	March 24.	Edward III. would not permit them to march into Scotland and issued a specious proclamation enforcing observance of the treaty of Northampton - -	142
		Balliol and his followers, without any obstacle, embarked at Ravenshere in Holderness -	142
		Randolph had assembled an army and marched to Colbrandspath, on the frontier of East Lothian; but hearing of the embarkation, he marched northwards -	144
	July 10.	He expired on his march, at Muffelburgh -	146
	Aug. 1.	The Scottish parliament, at Perth, elected Donald Earl of Marre to the office of Regent. - -	147
	9.	Edward III. impowered Henry de Percy to punish all his subjects who should presume to array themselves in contempt of his proclamation of the 24th March, and also impowered Percy to arm for repelling an imaginary invasion of the Scots	148
	July 31.	Balliol appeared in the Frith of Forth -	148
		He landed near Burntisland, in Fife, and routed the Earl of Fife, who, with troops hastily gathered together, opposed the landing - - -	148
	Aug. 11.	Balliol encamped near Fort-Teviot, with the river Earn in front	148
		The Earl of Marre, with a numerous army, encamped at Duplin, on the opposite bank of the river. The Earl of March, with another army, approached, and quartered at Auchterarder, eight miles to the west of Fort-Teviot -	149
	12.	Balliol, being thus in imminent jeopardy, crossed the river by night, surprised and totally defeated the Scots. The Earl of Marre, and many other persons of distinction, were slain -	149
		The Earl of Fife having been made prisoner, submitted to the victors - - -	152
	23.	Balliol took possession of Perth, and hastily fortified it.	153

The

A.D.		Page
1331.	The Earl of March's troops hurried on to affault Perth; but, inftead of affaulting, blockaded it - -	154
	John Crabbe, a Fleming, in the fervice of Scotland, came with a fleet of ten fhips to the mouth of the river Tay. He took a fhip belonging to Henry de Beaumont. He was foon after defeated, in a general engagement, and his whole fleet was burnt	
August 14.		154
	The Earl of March abandoned the blockade of Perth, and ordered his troops to difperfe - -	154
Sept. 14.	Edward Balliol was crowned at Scone; Duncan Earl of Fife and William Sinclair Bifhop of Dunkeld affifted at the folemnity	155
	He repaired to the fouth of Scotland, intrufting the cuftody of Perth to the Earl of Fife - -	155
Oct. 7.	James and Simon Frafers, and Robert Keith, furprifed Perth, and razed its fortifications. The Englifh faid that the Earl of Fife, the governour, betrayed the town. ' -	155
	The Scots who remained faithful, conferred the office of Regent on Sir Andrew Moray of Bothwell - . -	156
	Edward III. having been counfelled by his parliament to draw near the Scottifh frontiers, repaired to Yorke -	156
Nov. 23.	Balliol, at Rokefburgh, made a folemn furrender of the liberties of Scotland to the Englifh King; became bound to put Berwick, and its appurtenances, into his hands; offered to marry the Princefs Johanna, and to provide for the maintenance of her infant hufband, David II. and alfo to ferve the Englifh King in all his wars, excepting in England, Wales, and Ireland 156—157	
	He renounced even this exception, on Edward III. becoming bound to maintain him in the poffeffion of Scotland -	157
Oct. 26.	Edward III. without mentioning the revolution in Scotland, requefted the Pope to prefer Robert de Ayleflon to the fee of St Andrews, becaufe he was well affected to England, and ' the ' plighted fidelity of the Scots was frail' -	157

Edward.

A.D.			Page
1331.	Dec. 15.	Edward III. in addressing the Pope, on another occasion, was silent as to Balliol's submission - -	158
	14.	Just about the same time, he appointed plenipotentiaries to treat with the ambassadors from the Regent and the barons of Scotland - -	158
		Many of the Scottish royalists submitted to the conqueror. The Earl of March, and Archibald Douglas, obtained a truce until the 2d of February - -	158
	16.	John Randolph, now become Earl of Moray, Archibald Douglas, the youngest brother of the renowned Douglas, together with Simon Fraser, surprised Balliol at Annan. Henry, his brother, was slain ; himself, almost naked, escaped into England	158
	Feb. 12.	Balliol, now an exile, appointed commissioners to swear to the performance of his promises to the English King -	159
	March 23.	The Scots having made incursions into the English borders, Edward III. proclaimed that *they* had violated the treaty of Northampton - -	159
	9.	Balliol, having been joined by many English barons, returned to Scotland, took and burnt the castle of Oxnam in Teviotdale, fixed his quarters near Rokesburgh, and prepared to besiege Berwick - - -	160
		Archibald Douglas, with 3000 men, invaded Cumberland, and wasted the district of Gillesland - -	160
		Sir Anthony de Lucy made an inroad into Scotland, defeated and made prisoner William Douglas, called *the Knight of Liddesdale*, near Lochmaben - -	161
1333.	March 28.	Edward III. commanded the knight of Liddesdale to be put in irons - - -	161
		Sir Andrew Moray, the Regent, attacked Balliol's troops at the bridge of Rokesburgh. While attempting to rescue Ralph Golding, who had advanced too far, he was made prisoner	161

Archibald

A.D.		Page
1333.	Archibald Douglas was acknowledged as Regent by the Scots	162
March 30.	Edward III. ordered an army to rendezvous at Newcastle	162
May 7.	He rejected the solicitations of the King of France in behalf of the Scots; and declared, that he was resolved to chastise their outrages	162
10.	He ordered the Isle of Man to be seized in his name; and, soon after, he made it over to William de Montague	163
	Edward III. and Balliol, laid siege to Berwick	163
	The besieged, although successful in burning great part of the enemies fleet, were reduced to extremities	164
July 11.	The Regent appeared with an army in the neighbourhood; attempted to relieve Berwick, but in vain; marched into Northumberland, and made an unsuccessful attack on Bamburgh castle, where Philippa, the consort of Edward III. resided	164
	During a general assault, Berwick was set on fire, and great part of it burnt. The inhabitants insisted to capitulate. It was agreed that the town and castle should be surrendered, unless relieved on the 19th of July	164
19.	The Regent returned out of Northumberland, attacked the English at Halidon, and was totally defeated. He was made prisoner, and died of his wounds. The Earls of Lenox, Rofs, Sutherland, Menteth, Carrick, and Athole, [Campbell], with many other persons of distinction, were slain	165—167
	Berwick surrendered to the English	167
16.	Edward III. granted his protection to the Earl of March, who had commanded in Berwick, and appointed him to an important office	168
	The castles of Dunbarton, Lochleven, Urquhart, and Kildrummy, with a strong hold in Lochdoun, were the only places in Scotland which remained in possession of the partizans of David II.	168

A.D.			Page
1333.		Malcolm Fleming conveyed David II. and his confort, from Dunbarton into France - - -	168
	Oct.	Balliol held his first parliament -	169
		Edward III. fummoned Balliol to his parliament; but Balliol excufed himfelf, by reafon of the unfettled ftate of Scotland	169
	Feb. 10.	Balliol held a parliament at Edinburgh	169
	12.	In that parliament, the treaty between Balliol, and his liege-lord, was ratified - - -	169
1334	June 12.	Balliol furrendered great part of the Scottifh dominions, to be annexed for ever to England; at Newcaftle upon Tyne	171
	June 15. and 21.	Edward III. appointed officers of juftice in his new dominions	172
	18.	Balliol did homage to Edward III. for the whole kingdom of Scotland, and the ifles adjacent; at Newcaftle upon Tyne	172
	June 18.	The private eftates of Balliol happening to have been *comprehended* under the general words of Balliol's ceffion, Edward III. declared them *excluded*, ' becaufe he had too much reverence ' for God, juftice, and good faith, to mean that the ceffion ' fhould be prejudicial to private rights.' -	173
	Auguft	A quarrel arofe among *the difinherited*, or *claimants*, who had fupported the caufe of Balliol. Alexander de Moubray claimed an inheritance as heir-male of his brother John de Moubray. Henry de Beaumont, Earl of Buchan, and David de Strathbolgie, or Haftings, Earl of Athole, efpoufed the caufe of the heirs-general. Perceiving that they were not heard, they left the court in difguft. Balliol difmiffed Moubray, and courted his oppofers - -	173
		Sir Andrew Moray of Bothwell having been releafed from captivity, affembled the furviving friends of Scotland. Alexander de Moubray joined him; and Geffrey de Moubray, governour of Rokefburgh, revolted to the Scots -	174

Richard

ABRIDGEMENT. 379

A.D.		Page
1334	Richard Talbot, an eminent person among *the disinherited Lords*, endeavoured to pass into England from the north. He was intercepted, defeated, and made prisoner, by Sir William Keith of Galston	174
	The Regent and Sir Andrew Moray, with Moubray, besieged Henry de Beaumont in his castle of Dundarg; and, on his capitulating, allowed him to depart into England	174
	The Stewart, who had lain concealed in Bute, took arms, won the castle of Denoon in Argyleshire, and made himself master of Bute, and the territory of Renfrew	175
	Godfrey de Ross, the English governour of Airshire, submitted to the Stewart	175
	The Earl of Moray had escaped into France after the battle of Halidon: He now returned. The Scots acknowledged him and the Stewart as joint Regents	175
	The Earl of Moray suddenly invaded the territories of [Hastings] Earl of Athole, cut off all supplies, and compelled him to surrender. Athole went over to the Scots	176
	Balliol again fled to England for protection	176
Nov. 14.	Edward III. marched into Scotland to quell the insurgents	176
Dec.	Balliol, with a detached body, wasted Avondale, and the neighbouring country	176
25.	He royally celebrated Christmas at the castle of Renfrew; distributing lands and offices among his guests.—His chief favourite was William Bullock, an ecclesiastic	177
	Edward III. led the rest of his army into the Lothiens, and ruled at pleasure	177
	Patrick Earl of March renounced his fealty to Edward III.	177
1335.	John de Strivelin [or Stirling] besieged Alan de Vipont in the castle of Lochleven	178

B b b 2   While

A.D.			Page
1335.	June 19.	While he was celebrating the festival of St Margaret at Dunfermline, the Scots surprised and destroyed his works	178
		John de Strivelin passionately vowed, never to desist from his enterprise, until he had overthrown the castle, and put the garrison to the sword: Yet he raised the siege -	178
	April	The Stewart, and the Earl of Moray, Regents, held a parliament at Dairsy, [near Coupar in Fife.] The members, distracted by party-animosities, separated without concerting any general plan of defence - - -	179
	July 11.	France had offered her mediation; but the English parliament rejected all terms of peace; and Edward III. again invaded Scotland, and marched, with Balliol, towards Perth -	179
	30.	Count Guy of Namur landed at Berwick with a body of foreign auxiliaries, and advanced to Edinburgh. He was encountered, and vanquished, at *the Borough Muir*. He and his troops were allowed to depart, on their promise not to serve again in the Scottish wars - -	180—181
		The Earl of Moray, Regent, while he returned from escorting Count Guy, was set upon, and made prisoner, by William de Pressen, warden of Jedburgh - -	181
	August 18.	The Moubrays, and others, pretending to have powers from the Earl of Athole and the Stewart, concluded a treaty with Edward III. at Perth - - -	183
	24.	Edward III. granted a pardon to the Earl of Athole, restored him to his English estates, and appointed him Lieutenant in Scotland	184
		Athole, invested with new authority, punished the partisans of the cause which he had deserted. He besieged the castle of Kildrummy. Sir Andrew Moray and the Earl of March having collected 1100 men, surprised Athole in the forest of Kilblain. Athole, abandoned by his troops, was slain -	185

Balliol

A. D.			Page
1335.	Dec. 12.	Balliol concluded a treaty with John, Lord of the Isles, on very disadvantageous terms - -	187
		Edward III. made grants of his new acquisitions to his principal Lords - - -	187
	Jan. 27.	After having lent L. 300 to Balliol, he settled a daily pension on him of five marks, to be enjoyed during pleasure -	188
		Sir Andrew Moray assembled a parliament at Dunfermline, and was acknowledged by that assembly as regent -	188
	March 8.	A short truce had been granted to the Scots, through the mediation of the ambassadors from the Pope and the King of France, and had been renewed from time to time; nevertheless, the Scots still kept the field. Edward III. renewed the truce, on condition that the Scots should desist from the blockade of the castles of Coupar and Lochindorp, and not besiege any other fortresses - - -	190
1336.	April 7.	Edward III. appointed the Earl of Lancaster to the command of the troops in Scotland - -	190
	10.	He vested him with full powers of pardoning the Scots	190
	May 4.	He authorised Lancaster, and others in commission with him, to conclude a short truce with Scotland -	190
	August.	Edward III. came unexpectedly to Perth, marched into the north, raised the siege of Lochindorp, wasted Moray, and penetrated to Inverness. The Scots avoided encountering him	191
		Meanwhile Thomas Rosheme, a foreigner in the service of England, landed with a body of troops at Dunoter. The citizens of Aberdeen attacked him, and were worsted; but Rosheme fell in the action. Edward, on his return from the north, burnt Aberdeen - - -	191
		Edward III. endeavoured to secure Scotland by a chain of fortresses; and left his brother, John Earl of Cornwall, to command in Scotland - - -	191—192

The

A.D.			Page
1336.	October.	The Earl of Cornwall died at Perth	192
	October.	Sir Andrew Moray, the Regent, besieged the castle of Stirling; but was obliged to abandon the enterprise.	193
		Sir Andrew Moray won the castles of Dunoter, Lauriestoo, and Kincleven, and thus broke the chain of the English fortresses	193
		The Knight of Liddesdale attacked Lord Berkeley near Blackburn, but was discomfited, and hardly escaped	193
		The Scots hired some gallies, at Genoa, to act against the English; but the Genoese regency burnt them	193
		A naval armament, fitted out by the partizans of David II. took many English ships near the Isle of Wight, and plundered Guernsey and Jersey	194
	Feb. 18.	Sir Andrew Moray cast down the tower of Falkland, won the castle of Leuchars, and, after a siege of three weeks, took the castle of St Andrews	194
1337.	March.	The castle of Bothwell surrendered to the Scots	195
		Sir Andrew Moray invaded Cumberland, and wasted the country in the neighbourhood of Carlisle. He besieged the castle of Edinburgh. The English came to its relief; they fought the Scots at Crichton in Mid-Lothian; the Scots kept the field; but their commander, the Knight of Liddesdale, was dangerously wounded; Sir Andrew Moray raised the siege	195
		Henry de Beaumont, in the north, revenged the death of Athole, his son-in-law, by slaying the Scots who had been at the battle of Kilblain, whenever they fell into his hands	196
		A great famine in Scotland: Many persons died of want, and many emigrated	196
	August	The wives and children of the Scottish barons who had fought an asylum in Flanders, embarked in two ships to return home, under the guidance of John de Lindesay Bishop of Glasgow; John de Ros,	

A. D.		Page
1337.	Ros, the English admiral, took them: The Bishop of Glasgow was mortally wounded, and many persons of distinction slain	197
October 7.	Edward III. publicly asserted his claim to France. -	197
—7. 15.	Meanwhile the Scots were amused with negotiations for peace	198
15.	Edward III. empowered the Earls of Arundel and Salisbury to receive the Scots to pardon and favour -	198
Jan. 18.	The Earl of Salisbury besieged the castle of Dunbar, which was bravely defended by the Countess of March, daughter of Randolph - - -	198—200
1338. June 10.	Alexander Ramsay having brought succours into the castle of Dunbar, made a successful sally. The English abandoned the siege, and consented to a cessation of arms -	201
	Alexander Ramsay, with a company of resolute young men, lurked in the caves of Hawthornden, infested the country, and even made inroads into the English borders. He encountered Robert Manners at Preston, near Werk-castle, made him prisoner, and totally defeated his forces - -	202
	The Knight of Liddesdale expelled the English from Teviotdale	202
	Sir Andrew Moray, Regent of Scotland, died; Robert The Stewart succeeded him in the office of Regent -	202
	The Regent made preparations for besieging Perth, and despatched the Knight of Liddesdale into France to implore aid for the Scots - - -	203
August 4.	Edward III. required Balliol to commit Perth to the care of Thomas Ughtred - - -	203
	Balliol obeyed, and went to reside in England -	204
1339.	The Stewart came before Perth. The Knight of Liddesdale returned with French auxiliaries -	204
	William Bullock, bribed by the Stewart, yielded up the castle of Coupar, and swore fealty to David II. -	205

The

A. D.			Page
1339.		The Stewart, assisted by the counsels of Bullock, besieged Perth. The Earl of Ross, by the artifice of a mine, drained the fossé.	
	August 17.	Ughtred capitulated - -	205
		The Stewart rewarded, and dismissed the French auxiliaries	205
		The Stewart besieged and took the castle of Stirling, where Thomas Rokesby commanded - - -	205
		The Stewart made a progress through Scotland for the administration of justice - - -	206
	Sep. 26.	Edward III. entered the French territories -	206
		The armies of England and France, after having been in sight for some days, mutually withdrew, at Viron-fosse, in the Cambresis	206
		David II. it is said, was in the French army -	206
1340.		Edward III. having unsuccessfully besieged Tournay, made a truce	
	Sep. 25.	with France; in that truce the Scots were comprehended	206
		The Scots, commanded by the Earls of March and Sutherland, made an inroad into England: They were repulsed by Thomas de Gray - - -	206
1341.	April 17.	The castle of Edinburgh was surprised by a stratagem of William Bullock - - -	207
	May 4.	David II. and his consort Johanna, landed from France, at Inverbervie, in Kincardineshire - -	207
1342.	March 30.	Alexander Ramsay of Dalwolsy took the castle of Roxburgh by escalade - - -	208
		David II. rewarded him with the office of sheriff of Teviotdale, which the Knight of Liddesdale enjoyed -	208
	June 20.	While Ramsay held his courts in the chapel of Hawick, the Knight of Liddesdale assaulted and wounded him, and carried him prisoner to the castle of Hermitage.—Ramsay was starved to death - - -	209
		William Bullock, accused of treasonable practices, was thrust into the castle of Lochindorp, where he expired through cold and hunger - -	209

The

A.D.		Page
1340.	The Knight of Liddesdale, through the intercession of the Stewart, was pardoned, restored to his office, and made keeper of Rokesburgh castle - - -	210
	During this year, the Scots infested England by frequent inroads: 1. The Earl of Moray burnt Penreth. The King served as a volunteer under him. 2. The King erected the royal standard, invaded Northumberland, received a check from Robert Ogle, and retired ingloriously. 3. A third inroad was repressed by Balliol, lieutenant to the north of Trent -	210
	The Scots besieged the castle of Lochmaben in Annandale, where Walter Selby commanded. Selby, aided by John Kirkeby, Bishop of Carlisle, and Thomas de Lucy, repulsed the Scots	211
Feb. 10.	Edward III. made proclamation, that he had consented to a truce with France, and her allies, until Michaelmas 1346. Military operations were every where suspended -	211
1343. August 18.	Edward III. began to make attempts on the fidelity of the Knight of Liddesdale - - - -	212
1344. August 25.	The Scots, weary of the truce, made inroads on the marches: Balliol, with the forces of the north of England, was appointed to oppose them - -	213
1345. March 15.	Edward III. charged Philip King of France, with having aided the Scots, contrary to the conditions of the truce -	213
1346. April 24.	He declared that the King of France had violated the truce, and he commanded hostilities to be re-commenced -	213
	David II. instigated by France, undertook to invade England. His army rendezvoused at Perth. The Earl of Ross assassinated Raynold of the Isles, in a monastery, and, abandoning the King's host, led back his followers to their mountains -	213
	David II. stormed the castle of Lidel, and beheaded Walter Selby the governour, who had alternately plundered and defended England - - -	213

Vol. II.   C c c   The

		Page
A. D. 1346.	The Knight of Liddesdale advised the King of Scots to abandon his enterprise against England; but his barons urged him on	214
	David II. marched through Northumberland, and wasted the bishoprick of Durham, not even sparing the patrimony of St Cuthbert - - -	214
October 16.	He pitched his camp at Bear Park, within view of Durham, while Edward III. lay before Calais with his best troops -	214
	William le Zouche Archbishop of Yorke, with the northern barons, prepared to oppose the Scots -	214—215
	The Knight of Liddesdale, being on a foraging party, encountered the English forces, and was defeated at Ferry of the hill	215
17.	The Scots and the English fought at Nevils cross, near Durham; the Scots were utterly discomfited; David II. was wounded and made prisoner; and many of the Scottish nobility were slain	216—219
20.	The English regency appointed commissioners to pardon the Scots and receive their fealty - -	220
Nov. 20.	Some of the English having connived at the escape of their prisoners; this was prohibited, under pain of death -	219
Jan. 2.	The King of Scots was imprisoned in the Tower of London	220
20.	John Copland, who took him, and Robert de Bertram who took the Knight of Liddesdale, were amply rewarded	220
	The English entered Scotland, took the castles of Rokesburgh and Hermitage, and advanced their posts to the neighbourhood of the low country of the Lothians - -	220
	Balliol, who then resided in Galloway, having been joined by some English troops, wasted the Lothians, Clydesdale, Cuningham, and Niddesdale - -	221
	The Stewart was elected to the office of Regent, in absence of the King - - - -	221

William

A.D.			Page
1346.		William Lord Douglas, having returned from France, expelled the English from Douglasdale, the forest of Etrick, and Teviotdale	221
		John de Graham, Earl of Menteth, and Duncan Earl of Fyfe, prisoners at Durham, were convicted of treason. Edward III. together with the warrant for trying them, transmitted to their judges a schedule containing the sentence of condemnation. Sentence was executed against the Earl of Menteth, but not against the Earl of Fyfe.	221—222
1347.	Aug. 4.	Edward III. won Calais, after a tedious siege	222
	Sep. 28.	He concluded a truce with France, to endure, by various prorogations, until the 1st of April 1354. Scotland was comprehended in the truce	222
1348.	April 16.	Negotiations were commenced for procuring the liberty of the King of Scots	222
	October 10.	Queen Johanna obtained permission to visit her husband the King of Scots, after he had been in captivity for two years	222
1349.		The great pestilence reached Scotland	222
1350.		John St Michel and his accomplices assassinated Sir David Berkley at Aberdeen. The Knight of Liddesdale, it is said, hired the murderers, in revenge of the death of his brother Sir John Douglas, assassinated by Berkley	223
	Aug. 23.	Philip King of France died; succeeded by his son *John*	223
	March 5.	A treaty was carried on for releasing the King of Scots, and for establishing peace. Balliol in vain protested against this treaty: He was, however, admitted to the conferences	223
1351.	Sept. 4.	The King of Scots obtained a temporary enlargement from prison, on giving hostages	223
1352.		The English engaged in certain dark negotiations with the King of Scots and Lord Douglas	224
		The negotiations proved unsuccessful, and the King of Scots was remanded to prison	225

Ccc2 The

A. D.			Page
1352.	July 17.	The Knight of Liddesdale, while a prisoner, entered into articles of agreement with Edward III. inconsistent with his duty as a Subject of Scotland, [at London] -	225—227
1353.		Duncan M'Dowal, a powerful chief in Galloway, was induced by Lord Douglas to acknowledge the sovereignty of the King	
	Aug. 18.	of Scots. Edward III. ordered his estates to be seized, and his goods confiscated - -	227—228
		The treaty was renewed for the release of the King of Scots. David II. was permitted to assist at the conferences at Newcastle; but nothing was determined. The Scots, it is said, suspected their King - -	228
	Aug.	The Knight of Liddesdale was assassinated at Galvord, in Etrick forest, by his kinsman Lord Douglas, in revenge, it is said, for the murder of Ramsay and Berkley -	228
	July 13.	The treaty for the ransom of David II. was finished at Newcastle. The ransom was 90,000 marks, in yearly payments of 10,000 marks. A truce concluded for nine years, in which all the allies of England, and especially Balliol, were comprehended. Twenty young men of quality were given by the Scots as hostages - -	229
	Nov. 12.	The treaty was ratified by commissioners from Scotland	230
	Dec. 5.	And by Edward III. and the Prince of Wales -	230
		Edward III. about this time, negotiated with Balliol, as well as with David Bruce - -	230
	Oct. 8.	Edward III. secured the possession of Hermitage castle, by a treaty with the widow of the Knight of Liddesdale -	230
	March 12.	The Scottish government debased the coin. Edward III. issued a proclamation forbidding its currency. This proclamation sets forth, 'that the antient money of Scotland was wont to be of 'the same weight and alloy as the Sterling money of Eng-'land' - -	231

The

A. D.			Page
1355.	April	The King of France, in order to procure a breach of the truce, sent Eugene de Garencieres to Scotland with a body of troops, and a confiderable fum of money. The Scots agreed to break the truce, and to invade England -	232
		The Earl of March, who had affifted at the treaty with England, was active in forwarding the negotiations with France	232
	August	Taking a pretext from an incurfion of Northumbrian borderers into his eftates, he ordered Sir William Ramfay of Dalwolfy to pillage the town of Norham. Sir Thomas Gray, the keeper of Norham caftle, fallied out, was drawn into an ambufh by Ramfay, and, after a courageous refiftance, was made prifoner, with moft of his followers, at Nifbet in the Merfe -	233
	Nov.	Thomas Earl of Angus furprifed the town of Berwick from the fea, while the Earl of March, and the French auxiliaries, affaulted it on the land-fide. The town was pillaged -	233
		The Regent came to Berwick, and made provifion for its defence. He fent the French auxiliaries home -	234
	Jan. 13.	Edward III. expeditioufly marched againft Berwick. The garrifon obtained favourable terms of capitulation -	234
	20.	Balliol made an abfolute furrender to Edward III. of all his private eftates in Scotland, [at Rokefburgh] -	234
		And, on the fame day, he furrendered his kingdom and crown to Edward III. - -	234—235
		Edward III. became bound to pay 5000 marks to Balliol, and to fecure him in an annuity of 2000 pounds Sterling, [at Bamburgh] - -	236
		Edward III. after having remained at Rokefburgh for fome days, in hopes of the fubmiffion of the Scottifh barons, marched into Scotland, defolated the country, and then retreated, not without confiderable lofs - -	236—237

He

A. D.			Page
1355.	March 15.	He issued a proclamation, declaring his resolution to maintain the antient laws and usages of Scotland	238
1356.		After Edward's retreat, the Scots expelled his partizans from the west marches. Roger de Kirkpatrick stormed the castles of Dalswinton and Carlaverock, and reduced Nithsdale. John Stewart, the eldest son of the Regent, reduced Annandale, and Lord Douglas Interior Galloway	238
	March 15.	Edward III. appointed the Earl of Northampton, Warden of the marches, and others, commissioners for treating of a peace with Scotland	239
	April 17.	Lord Douglas became bound to the Warden not to molest the English, as long as they abstained from hostilities against his estates, and those of the Earl of March	239
	Sept. 19.	Battle of Poictiers. The French were defeated, and their King made a prisoner. There was great carnage of the Scots who had crowded to the French standard. Lord Douglas, although wounded, escaped. Archibald Douglas, although made prisoner, escaped unknown	240
	Jan. 17.	In a parliament at Perth, the Scots appointed the Bishop of St Andrews, and others, commissioners to treat for the ransom of the King, and for peace	241
	March 13.	A truce for two years was concluded between Edward III. and the French King, (at Bourdeaux)	241
1357.	May 6.	The Scots, negotiating for themselves, concluded a truce with England for six months	241
	June 14.	Sir James Lindesay assassinated, under trust, Roger de Kirkpatrick at Carlaverock castle. He was seized, tried, and executed	242
		Notwithstanding the truce, certain Scotsmen sent out three vessels to cruise against England. They were forced into Yarmouth by a tempest, together with the ships which they meant to seize, and were confiscated	242

David

A. D.			Page
1357.	August.	David II. was conveyed to Berwick, where the conferences for peace were held - - -	242
		The English demanded a ransom of one hundred thousand marks for the King of Scots - - -	242
	Sept. 26.	In a parliament held at Edinburgh, the Scots consented to the demands of the English, and took every method for rendering their consent effectual - - -	243
	Oct. 3.	The treaty was at length concluded at Berwick. The ransom was 100,000 marks, in ten equal yearly payments. Many hostages of distinguished rank were to be given. A truce, until payment of the ransom, was stipulated - 244—245	
	3.	The King of Scots, the nobility, and the boroughs, ratified the treaty - - -	245
	4.	The Bishops also ratified it - -	245
	Nov. 6.	David II. having been released, held a parliament at Scone, laid the treaty before the three estates, obtained their approbation, and then ratified the treaty anew - -	245
1358.	June 21.	The Scottish bishops had engaged to subject the ecclesiastical revenues in payment of the ransom; but the Pope peremptorily refused to ratify their engagement -	245
	July 14.	David II. obtained permission from Edward III. to visit England	245
		The Pope granted a tenth of the ecclesiastical revenues in Scotland for three years, towards payment of the ransom, under condition that nothing more should be exacted from the Scottish clergy on that account - - -	246
1359.	June 19.	Sir Robert Erskine and Norman Lesley, ambassadors from Scotland, entered into a negotiation with France. It was agreed, that, on Easter-day 1360, the French should pay fifty thousand marks Sterling to the Scots, and that the Scots should renew the war with England. A ratification of the former alliance between France and Scotland was also stipulated, [at the Louvre] 246—248	

A.D.			Page
1360.	May 8.	The first step that the French took after a treaty so solemn on their part, and so hazardous to Scotland, was to conclude a treaty of peace with the English, [at Bretigny near Chartres.]. By it the King of France renounced every alliance with Scotland, and the King of England, every alliance with the people of Flanders	248
	Oct. 24.	But both Kings protested, that such renunciations should only take place, in the event of the articles of peace being reciprocally fulfilled - - - -	248
	Aug. 20.	Meanwhile negotiations for a final peace between England and Scotland were commenced - -	248
		Catharine Mortimer, a favourite concubine of David II. was murdered. Thomas Stewart Earl of Angus, suspected of having been privy to the murder, was imprisoned in the castle of Dunbarton - - -	249
1361.		The plague broke out in Scotland. It was computed that one third of the people perished in this general calamity. The Earl of Angus died of it; as also some of the hostages in England	249
		David II. retired to the north of Scotland to avoid the infection. Some differences arose between him and the Earl of Marre. The King besieged and took his castle of Kildrummy; but he soon received him into favour again - -	249
1362.		Johanna, the consort of David II. died childless -	250
1363.		In a parliament held at Scone, David II. proposed to the three estates, that, in the event of his dying without issue, they should chuse for their King Lionel Duke of Clarence, son of Edward III. The three estates unanimously rejected the proposition.	250—251
		Many of the Scottish nobility now formed associations for their mutual support. The Stewart, in particular, with his own sons, and with the Earls of March and Douglas -	251
		The malecontents took up arms, and committed many outrages. The King also armed. The malecontents submitted, and a general	

A. D.			Page
1363.		general amnesty was proclaimed, on condition that the barons should renounce their associations, become bound to abstain from such confederacies, and renew their oath of fealty	252
	May 14.	The Stewart, in particular, renounced his associations, under the penalty of forfeiting all title to the crown of Scotland, &c.	253
		David II. again repaired to London, and involved himself in secret negotiations with England	253
	Nov. 13.	The two Kings were present at a conference, in which a plan was formed for settling the crown of Scotland on the King of England for the time being, in default of David II. and his issue male	253—259
		David II. married Margaret Logie, a woman of singular beauty	259
	Feb.	David II. visited England, under pretence of performing his devotions at the shrine of the Virgin at Walsingham	260
1364.	April 8.	John King of France died at London. Succeeded by his son *Charles*	260
1365.	June 12. and 20.	A treaty was concluded which settled the arrears of the ransom, and the penalties for delay of payment, at 100,000 marks Sterling, to be paid in moities of 6000 marks yearly. But the parties seem to have restricted the sum to 80,000 marks. [*Note.*] The truce was prolonged until 2d February 1370-1.	261
1367.		Committees of parliament, with parliamentary powers were introduced, under the pretence of general conveniency	261
1369.	July 20.	The truce between the two nations was prolonged for the farther space of fourteen years; and, it was agreed, that the residue of the ransom-money should be cleared by annual payments of 4000 marks	262
	Feb. 18.	In a parliament, at Scone, some wise laws were enacted	262—263
		David II. yielding to the suggestions of his consort, imprisoned the Stewart and his three sons, John, Robert, and Alexander	263

D d d David II.

A.D.		Page
1370.	David II. applied to the Scottish Bishops to be divorced from Margaret Logie. They pronounced sentence of divorce; but she appealed to the Pope, and repaired in person to Avignon to prosecute her appeal. The cause was never determined	264
	On the disgrace of Margaret Logie, the Stewart and his sons were set at liberty	265
Feb. 22.	David II. died in the castle of Edinburgh. And was succeeded by his nephew ROBERT, The Stewart of Scotland	265—266

MISCELLANEOUS OCCURRENCES.

1306.	A daily allowance of sixpence was made for the Bishop of St Andrews, while a prisoner in England, of three pence for his serving man, of three halfpence for his foot-boy, and three halfpence for his chaplain	267
	Elisabeth, the consort of Robert Bruce, while a prisoner in England, had a foot-boy to make her bed	267
1308.	John Duns Scotus, called *Doctor Subtilis*, died, a person excessively admired by his contemporaries, as a teacher of philosophy and theology	268
1310.	So great famine in Scotland, that many persons fed on horse flesh	269
	One Harding asserted, that his coat armorial had been usurped by one Seintlowe. The question was decided by single combat, in presence of the King of Scots. Seintlowe having been vanquished, acknowledged the right of Harding. [Qu. as to the truth of this incident?]	269
1314.	Five shillings the value of a cow, and six shillings and eight pence the value of an ox	270
1327.	Fire-arms first employed by the English in their wars with Scotland	270

The

A.D.		Page
1329.	The manner of living of the Scots during their military expeditions, described by Froissart	270
	Theft was so frequent, that husbandmen housed their plough-shares every night. Randolph, Regent, in the minority of David II. ordered, that all ploughshares should be left in the fields; and, if stolen, that the county should refund their value. The iron-work of a plough was estimated at two shillings	270
1335.	From a grant by Edward III. of the estate of Edrington, in the Merse, it appears, that, antiently, *salmon fishings and mills* were *extended*	271—272
	By an article of the alliance between Balliol and the Lord of the Isles, it was provided, that the Lord of the Isles should have right to stand godfather to any heir of Balliol's body	272
1336.	Alan of Winton forcibly carried off the heiress of Seton. This produced a feud in Lothian. 'An hundred ploughs were laid 'aside from their labour,' says Fordun	272
	Henry de Lancaster, commander of the English at Berwick, courteously invited the Knight of Liddesdale, and his friends, to partake of the diversion of a tournament. In the course of the sports, the Knight of Liddesdale was wounded, and two Scottish gentlemen and three English were killed	272—273
1339.	A great famine in Scotland; the poorer sort fed on grass; and many were found dead in the fields	273
1340.	The Scots employed cannon at the siege of the castle of Stirling	273
1345.	Ten marks Sterling settled as a stipend on the vicar of Aberdeen	274
1346.	A person pretending himself to be Alexander Bruce Earl of Carrik, slain at Halidon in 1333, appeared in Scotland, and deceived the vulgar. He was convicted as an impostor, and hanged; yet his story still obtained credit	274
1347.	Edward Balliol, and others, engaged to serve the King of England. The daily pay of Balliol was sixteen shillings; of the chief commanders,	

A. D.		Page
	manders, eight shillings; of a banneret, four shillings; of a knight, two shillings; of an esquire, one shilling; of an archer on horseback, four pence. Twenty eight days were reckoned to the month, and ninety days to the quarter -	274
1349.	David II. while a prisoner, appeared at a tournament with the badge of *a white rose* - - -	275
1350.	The great pestilence, which had desolated the continent, reached Scotland - - -	275
	A perpetual annuity of eight marks Sterling, secured on land, was purchased for one hundred and twenty marks -	275
1354.	Wallace and Prudholm, whom Heron had charged as guilty of horse-stealing, offered to justify themselves by single combat. Heron obtained permission from Edward III. to send two champions into Scotland to prove his charge -	275
1355.	After the action at Nisbet, a Frenchman in the service of Scotland, purchased some English prisoners, and privately slew them, in revenge for the death of his father, whom the English had slain in France - - -	276
	Edward III. having permitted Balliol to hunt in the forest of Inglewood, an indemnity was granted to all men who had hunted in his company - -	276
1356.	A like indemnity was granted as to fishing: It mentioned the species and the size of the fish caught -	276
1358.	A great inundation happened in Lothian. A nun of the convent at Haddington, is reported to have stayed the waters by threatening to throw the statue of the Virgin Mary into the river	276—277
1361.	The pestilence again in Scotland - -	277
1362.	One hundred shillings provided to the vicar of Cloveth and Kildrummy, in Aberdeenshire -	277
1370.	Andrew Demster of Caraldston became bound that he and his heirs should furnish a person to administer justice in the courts of the abbey	

ABRIDGEMENT. 397

Page

abbay of Aberbrothock The salary twenty shillings, to be paid out of the issues of the courts - - 277

APPENDIX.

No. I. Of the manner of the death of Marjory daughter of Robert I. 278—284
No. II. Journal of the campaign of Edward III. 1327 285—294
No. III. Of the genealogy of the family of Seton in the fourteenth century - - - 295—300
No. IV. List of the Scottish commanders at the battle of Halidon, [19th July 1333] - - 301—312
No. V. Whether Edward III. put to death the Son of Sir Alexander Seton? - - - 313—320
No. VI. List of the Scottish commanders killed or made prisoners at the battle of Durham [17th October 1346] - 321—329
No. VII Tables of Kings - - - 330.
No. VIII Corrections and additions Vol. I. - - 332—348
No. IX. Corrections and additions Vol. II. - - 349—357

FINIS.

www.ingramcontent.com/pod-product-compliance
Lightning Source LLC
Chambersburg PA
CBHW030430300426
44112CB00009B/931